D0982582

Essays on the Foundations
of Aristotelian Political Science

Essays on the Foundations of Aristotelian Political Science

EDITED BY

Carnes Lord and David K. O'Connor

CONTRIBUTORS:
Richard Bodéüs · Carnes Lord · W. R. Newell
Josiah Ober · David K. O'Connor · Stephen G. Salkever
Abram N. Shulsky · Barry S. Strauss

UNIVERSITY OF CALIFORNIA PRESS
Berkeley   Los Angeles   Oxford

University of California Press
Berkeley and Los Angeles, California
University of California Press, Ltd.
Oxford, England
© 1991 by
The Regents of the University of California

Library of Congress Cataloging-in-Publication Data
Essays on the foundations of Aristotelian political science / edited
  by Carnes Lord and David K. O'Connor; contributors, Richard Bodéüs . . . [et al.].
    p.   cm.
  ISBN 0-520-06711-8
  1. Aristotle—Contributions in political science.   2. Aristotle—
Contributions in social sciences.   I. Lord, Carnes.   II. Bodéüs,
Richard.
JC71.A7E87   1990
320'.01—dc20   90-37112
                                                                          CIP

Printed in the United States of America

1   2   3   4   5   6   7   8   9

CONTENTS

ACKNOWLEDGMENTS

To a greater extent than many collections of essays, this one represents a collective endeavor. While the contributors do not necessarily endorse particular views of the other contributors or of the editors, most share an appreciation of the need for and the possibility of a rethinking of the fundamental bases of Aristotelian political or practical science.

This volume owes much to the steady encouragement of Richard Holway and Mary Lamprech of the University of California Press. The editors would also like to thank Marian Shotwell for her fine work as manuscript editor.

INTRODUCTION

Carnes Lord

When one stands back from the immense and exceptionally competent scholarly literature on Aristotle and tries to attain some perspective on the historical significance of this remarkable thinker and his relevance to contemporary problems, one is struck by the extent to which academic habits and the residues of various modern intellectual orthodoxies continue to work against a full appreciation of Aristotle's achievement. This is true above all in the area of the human sciences. On the one hand, Aristotle writes in a language and a cultural idiom sufficiently remote from the present to license treatment of his writings as mere objects of historical study. On the other hand, many of these writings remain timeless to a degree that encourages their use as guides to understanding fundamental features of the human condition. The result is, unfortunately, that Aristotle tends to be approached today at once too historically and not historically enough—too historically in the sense that Aristotle tends to be viewed through the lenses of a historicist hermeneutic that takes him to be fundamentally of his time and place; not historically enough because the uncanny contemporaneity of many Aristotelian texts often seduces modern readers into losing sight of broader contexts that establish or illuminate their meaning. That these tendencies do not check one another will be readily appreciated by those who have experienced the compartmentalization and parochialism of much academic study today.

Aristotle's extant writings in the human sciences encompass the *Poetics* and the *Rhetoric* as well as the *Politics* and the various ethical and historical treatises that have come down under his name. In all of these areas, Aristotle's work is original and fundamental in the sense that it virtually constituted fields of philosophic or scientific study that had not previously existed. Precisely because Aristotle was the first to give recognizable shape to a curriculum of academic study in all areas of human knowledge, however, it is easy to take for granted basic aspects of his writings in the human sciences that are in fact extremely problematic. Contemporary scholars (and other readers) tend to make the following assumptions when approaching an Aristotelian treatise: that it corresponds to a discrete and autonomous field of study, that it is addressed exclusively to students or scholars, and that its single purpose is to advance the bounds of knowledge or of science in a theoretical sense. Whatever the merits of these assumptions for the study of Aristotle's writings on physics, metaphysics, or biology, there is good reason for caution in applying them to the study of his treatises in the human sciences. Indeed, what makes the human sciences so distinctive for Aristotle is precisely that they are something other than purely theoretical in character. The human sciences are preeminently "practical" (*praktikai*) sciences whose express purpose is not simply to increase knowledge but rather to benefit human life or human action (*praxis*).[1]

The extent to which Aristotle's notion of a "practical" science of man has been ignored in recent Anglo-American scholarship and philosophy is, in fact, striking testimony to the strength of academic conventions. In Germany, the distinctively "practical" orientation of Aristotle's ethical and political writings has received considerable emphasis in interpretations of Aristotle and the Aristotelian tradition in modern times.[2] What is more, the Aristotelian approach has served as a critical point of reference in the fundamental challenges to positivist and historicist orthodoxies in philosophy and the social sciences that have been offered over the last several decades by such diverse figures as Wilhelm Hennis, Jürgen

1. Aristotle occasionally distinguishes "practical" from "productive" (*poiētikai*) sciences, and it is commonly assumed that rhetoric and poetics belong in the latter category. In his *Rhetoric*, however, Aristotle is at pains to underline the subordinate status of rhetoric relative to political science. The term "human sciences" (an imperfect English substitute for *Geisteswissenschaften*) is used here solely as a term of convenience; the expression is not Aristotelian—although Aristotle does once refer to his study of ethics and politics as "the philosophy that concerns the human things" (*Eth. Nic.* 1181b15). It is not intended to prejudice the question of the extent to which Aristotelian practical science is grounded in theoretical or natural science, on which see particularly S. R. L. Clark, *Aristotle's Man: Speculations on Aristotelian Anthropology* (Oxford, 1975).
2. See J. Ritter, *Naturrecht bei Aristoteles* (Stuttgart, 1961); O. Höffe, *Praktische Philosophie: Das Modell des Aristoteles* (Munich and Salzburg, 1971); G. Bien, *Die Grundlegung der politischen Philosophie bei Aristoteles* (Freiburg and Munich, 1973); M. Riedel, *Metaphysik und Metapolitik: Studien zu Aristoteles und zur politischen Sprache der neuzeitlichen Philosophie* (Frankfurt, 1975). See also W. Kullmann, "Aristoteles' Staatslehre aus heutiger Sicht," *Gymnasium* 90 (1983): 456–77.

Habermas, and Hans-Georg Gadamer.[3] In the United States, only Leo
Strauss has undertaken a similarly comprehensive critique of the assumptions and methods of contemporary social science from an Aristotelian perspective.[4]

This is by no means to say that interest in Aristotle as a source of insight into contemporary issues is otherwise lacking in the Anglo-American orbit. In the field of political philosophy, Eric Voegelin and Hannah
Arendt have also sought to rehabilitate an Aristotelian or broadly classical understanding of the *polis* and political life.[5] There has been a strong
revival of Aristotelian ideas in recent years within Anglo-American
moral philosophy, the most powerful expression of which is Alasdair
MacIntyre's *After Virtue*.[6] And figures such as Charles Taylor and Amar-
tya Sen have sympathetically explored the relevance of the Aristotelian
perspective to aspects of contemporary social science.

Yet much of this literature is only of limited help in coming to grips
with the totality of Aristotle's achievement in the human sciences. The
main limitation of the approach characteristic of Anglo-American moral
philosophy, as well as the interpretive scholarship influenced by it, is that
it tends to treat the Aristotelian ethical writings as an essentially self-con-
tained system and does not take account of the extent to which ethics for
Aristotle is formally and substantively but one part of a comprehensive
science of politics. Moreover, students of moral philosophy and political
theory alike have generally paid scant attention to the hermeneutic problems created by the practical intention of Aristotle's work in political science, and to the cultural and historical context this science presupposes.

Some brief remarks may be added on the current state of historical
and philological study of Aristotle's work. The authority of Werner Jaeger's well-known theory of Aristotle's intellectual development has stead-
ily eroded, yet no new approach to textual and interpretive problems has

3. W. Hennis, *Politik und praktische Philosophie: Eine Studie zur Rekonstruktion der politischen
Wissenschaft* (Neuwied, 1963); J. Habermas, *Theorie und Praxis* (Frankfurt, 1971) (*Theory and
Practice* [Boston, 1974], 41–81); H.-G. Gadamer, *Wahrheit und Methode* (Tübingen, 1960)
(*Truth and Method* [New York, 1975], 278–89). The wider German debate is documented in
M. Riedel, ed., *Rehabilitierung der praktischen Philosophie*, 2 vols. (Freiburg, 1972).

4. L. Strauss, "An Epilogue," in *Essays on the Scientific Study of Politics*, ed. H. J. Storing
(New York, 1962), 307–27; id., *The City and Man* (Chicago, 1964), 13–49. Consider the
remarks of Gadamer, *Truth and Method*, 489–91.

5. E. Voegelin, *Plato and Aristotle* (Baton Rouge, 1957); H. Arendt, *The Human Condition*
(Chicago, 1958). See also R. Beiner, *Political Judgment* (Chicago, 1983).

6. A. MacIntyre, *After Virtue: A Study in Moral Theory* (Notre Dame, 1981). See also, for
example, A. O. Rorty, ed., *Essays on Aristotle's* Ethics (Berkeley, 1980); D. Charles, *Aristotle's
Philosophy of Action* (London, 1984); B. Williams, *Ethics and the Limits of Philosophy* (Cambridge, 1985); and M. C. Nussbaum, *The Fragility of Goodness* (New York, 1985).

emerged, and much work°on the *Politics* in particular remains tied to this self-validating and sterile scholasticism.[7] Attempts to harness statistical analysis in the service of traditional philological approaches to the ethical treatises have not proven especially persuasive, although some stimulating work has been done in recent years on this perennial tangle of problems.[8] In history, largely as a result of scholarly frustration over the puzzles of his *Constitution of Athens,* Aristotle's stock is not very high, in spite of recent demonstrations of appreciation by some distinguished scholars of the superiority of Aristotle's understanding of class conflict in ancient Greece to that of much modern historical scholarship;[9] and the *Politics* remains relatively underutilized as a tool of historical analysis. In literary studies, the *Poetics* no longer enjoys the canonical position nor generates the scholarly attention it once did.[10] This is not to deny that work of considerable competence continues to be produced in all these areas. It is rather to suggest that there has been a dramatic loss of interest in larger questions concerning the nature of the Aristotelian project and its connections with the realities of the classical world.

Probably the greatest weakness in virtually all current work on Aristotle's practical writings is a lack of attention to the fundamental issue of interpretation. That the very real problems relating to the composition and transmission of the Aristotelian corpus have long overshadowed other hermeneutic questions is certainly not surprising, but the effect has been an unjustifiable neglect of what is arguably a more basic matter—the question of the literary character and purpose of Aristotle's extant writings. In the case of Aristotle's practical or political writings, the question of purpose takes on acute importance for the reason just sug-

7. See, for example, J. P. Dolezal, *Aristoteles und die Demokratie* (Frankfurt, 1974); E. Schütrumpf, *Die Analyse der* Polis *durch Aristoteles,* Studien zur antiken Philosophie 10 (Amsterdam, 1980). For a sceptical discussion of the Jaeger thesis in relation to the *Politics,* see C. Lord, *The* Politics *of Aristotle* (Chicago, 1984), 8–17; for the broader philological issues underlying the interpretation of Aristotle's extant writings, see id., "On the Early History of the Aristotelian Corpus," *American Journal of Philology* 107 (1986): 137–61. A noteworthy contribution to improved understanding of the intention and architecture of the ethical and political writings is R. Bodéüs, *Le philosophe et la cité: Recherches sur les rapports entre morale et politique dans la pensée d'Aristote* (Paris, 1982); see the critical appreciation of P. Vander Waerdt, "The Political Intention of Aristotle's Moral Philosophy," *Ancient Philosophy* 5 (1985): 77–89.

8. See especially A. Kenny, *The Aristotelian Ethics* (Oxford, 1978), with the review of J. M. Cooper, *Nous* 15 (1981): 381–92.

9. G. E. M. de Ste. Croix, *The Class Struggle in the Ancient Greek World from the Archaic Age to the Arab Conquests* (Ithaca, N.Y., 1981); M. I. Finley, *Politics in the Ancient World* (Cambridge, 1983), 1–23.

10. Though several studies in this area have appeared very recently: C. Lord, *Education and Culture in the Political Thought of Aristotle* (Ithaca, N.Y., and London, 1982); R. Janko, *Aristotle on Comedy* (London, 1984); S. Halliwell, *Aristotle's* Poetics (London, 1986).

gested. If, or to the extent that, an Aristotelian treatise is not simply intended to convey a theoretical analysis but to have a certain practical effect, it becomes necessary to pay careful attention to rhetorical and dialectical elements in Aristotle's argument and to consider the nature of his audience. Yet even when the importance of Aristotle's programmatic statements concerning the distinctive character of practical science is acknowledged by scholars, this acknowledgment tends to have little operational significance for the interpretive effort.

The question of the operational meaning of practical science in Aristotle should be situated in the context of the broader debate that has taken place in recent years over the proper approach to interpreting the classic works of political philosophy. In a series of articles and in a recent book on the origins of modern political thought, Quentin Skinner has raised far-reaching questions concerning the nature of the issues addressed by political philosophers, the relationship of political philosophy to subphilosophic political thought and opinion, and the resulting implications for the methodology of interpretation.[11] Skinner's approach denies the existence of genuinely trans-historical questions and emphasizes the necessity of interpreting the major texts of the tradition of political philosophy in the context of the political language and ideas of their time. Whatever the merits of Skinner's fundamentally historicist argument in other instances, it is difficult to dispute the value of his reminder of the importance of the historical and cultural context in the case of an author like Aristotle, who declares that his works serve a practical intention and makes no difficulties about borrowing the language and argumentation of the contemporary political arena.[12]

At the same time, however, there would seem to be little reason to give up the effort to understand Aristotle's practical writings as active participants in a trans-historical debate. The task of interpretation is not exhausted by the attempt to understand a thinker's response to the pressing political issues of his day.[13] The exigencies of literary presenta-

11. See especially Q. Skinner, "The Limits of Historical Explanations," *Philosophy* 4 (1966): 199–215; id., "Meaning and Understanding in the History of Ideas," *History and Theory* 8 (1969): 3–53; id., "Some Problems in the Analysis of Political Thought and Action," *Political Theory* 2 (1974): 277–303; id., "Hermeneutics and the Role of History," *New Literary History* 7 (1975): 209–32; and id., *The Foundations of Modern Political Thought,* 2 vols. (Cambridge, 1978), especially vol. 1, x–xiv.

12. Also worth emphasizing in view of its continuing neglect by interpreters is the question of Aristotle's relationship to political figures and movements of his time. I have attempted to make the case that Aristotle's links to Philip of Macedon were closer than is generally assumed (*The* Politics *of Aristotle,* 2–8).

13. Valuable in this regard is the detailed response to Skinner by N. Tarcov, "Quentin Skinner's Method and Machiavelli's *Prince,*" *Ethics* 92 (1982): 692–709; and id., "Political Thought in Early Modern Europe," *Journal of Modern History* 54 (1982): 56–65. See more

tion may compel an author to forego a systematic exposition of matters of only theoretical interest for his contemporaries, but this does not mean that such matters were not of interest to him; the assumption that he could not have performed such analysis for his own purposes is unsupportable and merely dogmatic. Accordingly, it is entirely legitimate to pose questions to texts of Aristotle or thinkers of similar rank from the standpoint of a later historical period. In fact, it can be argued that a comprehensive understanding of Aristotelian practical science *requires* an understanding not only of Aristotle's own positions, but of his probable attitude toward positions—ancient or modern—that represent a fundamental alternative to his own.

Actually, Aristotelian practical science must be accounted of unique interest in this connection. Aristotle's practical writings offer what is very probably the clearest and most illuminating point of contact between ancient and modern modes of moral and political thought across a wide range of issues. This is not entirely accidental. Although the nature and extent of the break between classical and early modern political philosophy remain controversial, a good case can be made that much of what is distinctively modern in modern political thought emerged by way of a self-conscious rejection of the method and substance of moral and political philosophy as practiced by Aristotle.[14] Yet it is not only in the sphere of moral and political philosophy that Aristotle's teaching has continuing relevance. In their detailed concern with contemporary political and social realities, Aristotle's practical writings—the *Politics* above all, of course—may be justly considered a forerunner of the empirical social science of our own day. Indeed, Aristotle should be viewed historically not only as a preeminent moral and political philosopher, but as the founder of the social sciences.

Considering Aristotle in this broader context can be extraordinarily illuminating for the light it casts on the basic assumptions of the tradition of early modern political philosophy as well as of contemporary social science. At the same time, as suggested above, the context serves to illuminate Aristotle himself, allowing us to penetrate more effectively to the not always explicit assumptions that underpin Aristotelian practical science. Indeed, if Aristotelian social or political science is a *practical* science, it can be argued that such an approach is essential in order to disentangle the theoretical, and for that reason unarticulated, premises underlying Aristotle's enterprise as a whole.

---

generally J. Tully, ed., *Meaning and Context: Quentin Skinner and His Critics* (Princeton, 1988).

14. See especially L. Strauss, *The Political Philosophy of Hobbes: Its Basis and Genesis* (Chicago, 1952).

The present volume seeks—in, admittedly, a provisional and partial fashion—to rectify the methodological and substantive weaknesses in current approaches to Aristotle's practical science. Though focusing largely on topics that center on the *Politics*, its scope extends to the entire corpus of Aristotle's ethical and political writings. Most importantly, it eschews textual commentary as such in order to raise larger questions concerning the foundations of Aristotelian political science in its various aspects.

The expression "political science" has been chosen as the least misleading of the alternatives available to describe Aristotelian practical science or philosophy. It is intended to reproduce the term *politikē*, an ambiguous expression that Aristotle appears to use generally of the teaching of his ethical and political treatises ("political expertise" is the translation perhaps most appropriate to its vagueness). "Political science" seems preferable to "political philosophy" insofar as it suggests a greater intimacy with political practice (which is not to deny that much that currently passes under the former term is in key respects more remote from practice than much traditional political philosophy is). The expression also seems preferable to "social science" insofar as the overarching framework of Aristotelian practical science is emphatically a political one.

The essays collected in this volume are organized in three groups. Part 1 is intended to provide a broad framework for understanding what is distinctive in Aristotle's approach to social science generally. The essays in Part 2 undertake to survey Aristotle's teaching across a range of what would today be independent disciplines within social science, apart from political science in the narrow sense of the term. In Part 3, some key themes in Aristotle's ethical and political writings are analyzed.

In Part 1, Stephen G. Salkever offers a general analysis of the implicit methodology of Aristotelian social or political science with reference to the contemporary debate between hermeneutic and empiricist approaches to social scientific inquiry. He argues that Aristotle declines or transcends this debate in the sense that he is able to do justice to the existence of both universality and uniqueness in human things, as well as to the demand for a social science that is genuinely practical in that it provides nonarbitrary normative guidance for political life.

Part 2 includes studies of Aristotle's approach to the areas of human behavior that today fall under the jurisdiction of the disciplines of anthropology, economics, and sociology. In the first paper of this group, I attempt to reconstruct Aristotle's views concerning human nature, prepolitical society, and the development of the state. Beginning with an examination of Aristotle's dictum that man is a political animal, I emphasize the extent to which the *polis* is not a natural or necessary result of human social evolution for Aristotle, and establish connections between

Aristotle's position and modern political anthropology. I try to show that the evolutionary account of Book 1 of the *Politics* needs to be qualified or corrected on the basis of scattered passages elsewhere in Aristotle's works. Relying especially on the important discussion of ethnology in *Politics* 7, I call attention to the centrality of the psychological phenomenon of "spiritedness" (*thymos*) for understanding Aristotle's view of the character and development of the *polis* and political rule. I further suggest that Aristotle's approach represents a highly plausible alternative to modern anthropological and sociological interpretations of primitive society and the origins of the state that treat kinship and religion as the key mechanisms of social evolution.

Next, Abram N. Shulsky examines the relationship between economics and politics in Aristotle's thought and attempts to show that Aristotle's approach to economic phenomena, while radically different from that of the modern discipline of economics, is nevertheless deserving of greater respect than it is usually accorded. He makes the argument that the "natural economics" developed in the first book of the *Politics* must be understood as part of Aristotle's rhetorical strategy for defending the naturalness of the city against sophistic conventionalism and cannot be taken as his last word. He suggests in particular that Aristotle's understanding of the problematic character of slavery as a social institution leads him to a more favorable evaluation of the alternative of the modern commercial republic (represented in the account of Carthage in Book 2) than is generally recognized.

Josiah Ober investigates Aristotle's understanding of the nature and political role of social class and status and of economic and social differentiation generally. He concludes that Aristotle's view is more nuanced than is sometimes realized. While giving full recognition to the political importance of the struggle of rich and poor in most Greek cities, he argues, Aristotle finally has more in common with Max Weber than with Marx in that he acknowledges the autonomous role of political or ideological factors in the creation of social groups and the management of class conflict.

The final group of essays addresses a number of topics bearing on Aristotle's understanding of virtue, the city and the constitutional order or regime, democracy, and the nature of political rule.

David K. O'Connor treats the question of Aristotle's view of the human motives that give rise to justice and injustice. He contends—contrary to the approach characteristic of contemporary moral philosophy (and of interpretations of Aristotle reflecting that approach)—that Aristotle does not see injustice as rooted in human selfishness as such. Rather it is a consequence of the soul's misorientation relative to concrete goods (wealth and honors). Thus justice and injustice are really the political or interpersonal symptom of virtue or vice understood as the orientation of the individual soul toward happiness.

Stephen G. Salkever discusses the fundamental issue of the relationship between the city and the household or family and between men and women, with reference to the views of Plato as well as of Aristotle. He holds that the use of classical moral and political theory by recent thinkers such as Hannah Arendt and Jürgen Habermas to support a more participatory approach to citizenship and political life should be considered in connection with the question of gender difference and the civic role of women and that contrary to what is generally assumed, both Plato and Aristotle had significant reservations about a type of politics in which virtue is identified with courage or manliness and women are excluded from the public sphere.

W. R. Newell takes issue with contemporary participatory or communitarian interpretations of Aristotle from a different vantage point. He analyzes Aristotle's treatment of monarchy, the one best man, and "superlative virtue" in order to focus attention on Aristotle's reservations about the egalitarianism of the city and his understanding of the potentialities— both good and bad—of absolute rule. For Aristotle, he argues, political life is a complex mixture of the self-government of political communities and the prudent skill of monarchlike statesmen or legislators.

Barry S. Strauss addresses the question of Aristotle's relationship to democratic Athens. He contends that Aristotle's characterization of Athenian democracy as the "extreme" and most dangerous form of popular rule appears to exaggerate the historical reality of fourth-century Athens. He suggests that at least part of the reason for this may have had to do with Aristotle's sensitivity to the rhetorical requirements of his immediate audience.

Finally, Richard Bodéüs discusses Aristotle's approach to legislation, stressing the importance of ensuring the stability and durability of regimes and therefore of laws, institutions, and education that, while diverging from the best possible, are best suited to preserving the character of specific regimes. He thus shows how the *Politics* as a whole, in spite of its apparently "utopian" emphasis on the model of a city that is likely to remain out of reach for most actual societies, nevertheless retains a highly practical approach to reconciling the requirements of the possible and the desirable in political life.

There is much else that might have been included in a volume of this sort. The survey of the social sciences in Part 2 could profitably have included a treatment of Aristotle's political psychology analyzing the implicit or explicit psychological theory of the ethical and political works (and the neglected discussion of human passions and characters in the second book of the *Rhetoric*) as well as its relationship to Aristotle's writings on biology and theoretical psychology. Attention could have been given to Aristotle's treatment of "friendship" (*philia*) in the ethical writings and its overall role in his political thought. Or a study might have been included of Aristotle's view of war and international relations generally. In any event, it is to be hoped that the essays assembled here will provide a stimulus to further work on these and other topics, as well as lending plausibility to the claims advanced here concerning the intrinsic interest and the continuing vitality of Aristotelian political science.

ONE

Aristotle's Social Science

Stephen G. Salkever

The purpose of this essay is to defend the claim that Aristotle's approach to social science is different from and superior to the two principal approaches characteristic of our time, empiricist and interpretive social science. My defense is not of the specific results of Aristotle's analysis; my claim, in fact, is that the great merit of Aristotle's approach (I avoid the term "method" here for reasons that will become clear) is that it yields, when practiced well, results that are both interesting and open to further discussion. The *Politics* and the *Ethics,* the primary texts to be considered, are not repositories of immutable truths calling for belief or rejection any more than they are oblique reflections of popular Greek opinion. Instead we find in them a discourse made up of arguable judgments of four major kinds: (1) descriptions of general facts or phenomena, the kind of thing that might be referred to as empirical assertions, as, for example, the claims that most human beings consider that any amount of virtue is enough but seek without limit to amass quantities of wealth or possessions or powers or reputation and that the place of deliberation is less powerful in women's lives than in men's;[1] (2) propositions about the efficient causal relationship of several phenomena or variables, which are hypothetical propositions, such as the claim that large cities tend to be freer of internal conflict than small cities;[2] (3) teleological proposi-

---

Translations throughout are my own, though greatly aided by the translations of the *Nicomachean Ethics* by M. Ostwald (Indianapolis, 1962) and T. Irwin (Indianapolis, 1985) and of the *Politics* by H. Rackham (Cambridge, Mass., 1959) and C. Lord (Chicago, 1984).

1. *Pol.* 1323a36–38, 1260a12–13. The claim that democrats tend to identify freedom with unlimited power (1310a31–32) or that in barbarian cultures women are treated as slaves (1252b5–6) might also be cited.

2. *Pol.* 1296a9–10. Another such proposition is that equalizing property will not result in a decrease in some classes of crime (1267a2–17).

tions about the place or function of various activities in the lives of human beings, such as the claim that security and friendship are necessary, but not constitutive, conditions of political life;[3] and finally (4) evaluative judgments, both general and particular, such as the political life is better than the life of war and conquest, and the Spartan culture rests on a mistaken conception of human virtue.[4]

To summarize then, the Aristotelian approach to social science that I propose to defend characteristically weaves together four separate kinds of questions in a particular order: on the basis of descriptions of observed phenomena, propositions of two distinct kinds, hypothetical and teleological, are set out; on the basis of these propositions, action-orienting evaluative conclusions are drawn about institutions, policies, and ways of life. By comparison, an initial contrast with modern social science would suggest that Aristotle's approach is more inclusive than either the empiricist (which culminates in a system of hypothetical propositions) or the interpretive (which culminates in teleological propositions relative to the particular context under study, more or less "from the native's point of view").[5] This much could well be granted by empiricists and interpretive social scientists, who would then go on to challenge Aristotle's procedures by pointing out—quite correctly—that his four types of discussion do not occur in a metaphysical vacuum but presuppose a particular theory of human nature and of nature simply. In order to defend Aristotle's social science, I will have to explain just what that background theory is and how it allows Aristotle to do two things that I believe to be of the greatest value for any social science: to reach conclusions of the sort that can inform practical discussion and to do so in a nondogmatic language that invites further discussion and revision. My claim will be that the conception of human nature on which Aristotle's social science rests is both more plausible in itself and more likely to result in an adequate social science, one that is both practical and open, than either of the contemporary alternatives.

Before taking this up, however, I need to explain briefly why I am treating Aristotle as any kind of social scientist at all, rather than as a political philosopher or theorist. Aristotle's own name for what he is doing is *politikē*, or "the science of the *polis*." *Politikē* does seem to be the equivalent of modern social science with respect to the subject matter it

3. *Pol.* 1280b8–1281a3. Or one could cite the proposition that the activities of leisure are more determinative of the quality of a human life than are the activities of occupation and war (1333a30–1333b5).

4. *Pol.* 1333b5–1334a10.

5. C. Geertz, "From the Native's Point of View: On the Nature of Anthropological Understanding," in *Interpretive Social Science: A Reader*, ed. P. Rabinow and W. M. Sullivan (Berkeley, 1979), 225–42.

embraces; Aristotle uses the term throughout the *Politics* and the *Ethics* to refer to the consideration of topics we would today assign to political science, anthropology, sociology, psychology, economics, and history. This substantive equivalence is my primary reason for rendering *politikē* as "social science." The objection may be raised, however, that Aristotle's approach is at odds with the current implications of the term "science." Part of my argument will be an attempt to show that *politikē*, for Aristotle, was indeed a science, and even a kind of natural science. The surface plausibility of this reading is indicated by the way Aristotle uses the word. While *politikē* most frequently in both Plato and Aristotle stands by itself as a noun, its ordinary meaning flows from its adjectival function; it modifies nouns like *technē* ("skill or craft"), *epistēmē* ("science"), and *philosophia.*[6] The question, for Aristotle, seems not to be whether social science is possible, but rather just what kind of a science *politikē* is.

The "social" in "social science" poses a more difficult problem. As Carnes Lord remarks in the introduction to this volume, "the overarching framework of Aristotelian practical science is emphatically a political one."[7] It is surely true that for Aristotle the *polis* is the most important human community or form of relationship, rather than just one among many. But it also is true that his definition of politics and his account of its importance do not simply reproduce standard Greek views on the subject. Briefly, politics according to Aristotle is a kind of human interaction marked by two structural and one functional characteristic. The interaction is structured by *nomoi* ("laws," "customs") rather than by unstructured individual choice; decisions are made according to some procedure for ruling and being ruled in turn, rather than, say, by force, chance, or wisdom; and decisions are motivated by the desire to improve the lives of all the citizens. The reasons for defining politics in this way will be taken up later; here it should be noted that Aristotle is fully aware that Greeks generally use the term *polis* to refer to communities that do not exhibit these features, and further that genuine (in Aristotle's sense) *poleis* are extremely rare. A large part of Aristotle's *politikē*, then, is devoted to explaining why politics is so unusual and how other kinds of interactions (e.g., families, armies, friendships, markets) approximate or distort the looks of Aristotle's sense of politics. Thus the focus of attention is not on the kinds of interactions we call political (as is the case with our "political science"), but on a wide range of human associations and failures to associate, on the advantages and dangers of human relationships of many kinds.

6. For its use as a modifier of *technē*, see *Pol.* 1288b10–1289a25; of *epistēmē, Eth. Nic.* 1094a24–29; of *philosophia, Pol.* 1282b23.
7. See the Introduction, p. 7.

Before returning to the details of Aristotle's views concerning the place of politics in his account of human affairs in general, more needs to be said about why we might want to consult Aristotle in the first place. Why, in other words, is it desirable to look for a third alternative to the claims of empiricist and interpretive social science?

EMPIRICISM AND INTERPRETATION

The genealogy and general structure of the debate between the proponents of empiricism and interpretation in contemporary social science is too well known to call for extended comment here. The central issue—the question of whether there is an essential difference between methods appropriate to natural science and the methods of the human or social sciences—is one that has a history of several centuries. The empiricist position holds that there is no serious methodological difference and that all science aims at explanations that take the form of propositions connecting separate events or dimensions of variance in a hypothetical way. These propositions, when sufficiently general and sufficiently tested, can be treated as general or covering laws that serve to explain particular events. As far as method and logic are concerned, there is no difference between establishing connections among force, mass, and acceleration and establishing connections among social class, ethnic identification, and political behavior. The purpose of social scientific inquiry understood in this way is the prediction and control of behavioral events; moral quandaries no doubt arise, but this is at least equally true of the natural sciences. For an empiricist there is no strong connection between explanation and evaluation, between giving accurate explanations and deciding how to act in a given situation. As W. G. Runciman observes:

> The difference of subject-matter imposes difference of technique, as it does between one science and another on both sides of the frontier between nature and culture. But this does not impose a requirement on social scientists either to adopt different criteria of validity or to disclaim a capacity to achieve it at all. It is true that there is a difference in the level at which theoretical grounding is to be sought. But again, it is a difference which can be paralleled within the natural sciences as well as between the natural and the social; and it is still a difference within a common mode of reasoning.[8]

It must be remembered, however, that this "common mode of reasoning" of which Runciman speaks has a very definite pedigree and rests—at least historically—on a distinctly uncommon view of the world, to be

8. W. G. Runciman, *The Methodology of Social Theory* (Cambridge, 1983), 221.

explained by scientific reasoning. This is the world of Cartesian *res extensa,* within which, according to Thomas Kuhn,

> most physical scientists assumed that the universe was composed of microscopic corpuscles and that all natural phenomena could be explained in terms of corpuscular shape, size, motion, and interaction. That nest of commitments proved to be both metaphysical and methodological. As metaphysical, it told scientists what sort of entities the universe did and did not contain: there was only shaped matter in motion. As methodological, it told them what ultimate laws and fundamental explanations must be like: laws must specify corpuscular motion and interaction, and explanation must reduce any given natural phenomenon to corpuscular action under these laws.[9]

Two features of this program call for comment. First, scientific reasoning thus understood explains natural phenomena by treating them as wholes in need of being reduced to the lawful motion of their smallest parts: real science is in part the search for the smallest element. Scientific sophistication involves unwillingness to treat apparent wholes—such as plants and animals—as if they were real wholes. Thus modern science privileges physics over biology,[10] or rather it implies that the best biology and the best social science will resemble mathematical physics as closely as the awkwardly large and protean quality of their data permit. The second aspect of the project that is relevant here is that historically it takes its bearings from a rejection of Aristotelian physics. This was in many ways a clear gain; overcoming Aristotle's mistakes about the immobility of the earth, circular inertia, and especially his distinction between sublunary (changeable) and celestial (unchanging) matter made extraordinary scientific progress possible.[11] On the other hand, it is not so easy to justify the rejection of another part of the Aristotelian worldview—the idea that living organisms and species were in some respects individuals, wholes that could not be reduced without loss of meaning to an interaction of their elements.[12] What results is the rejection of all teleological

---

9. T. S. Kuhn, *The Structure of Scientific Revolutions,* 2d ed. (Chicago, 1970), 41.

10. See E. Mayr, *The Growth of Biological Thought: Diversity, Evolution, and Inheritance* (Cambridge, Mass., 1982), chap. 2.

11. B. Cohen, *The Birth of a New Physics* (New York, 1985).

12. Mayr's point about the distorting character of reduction in biology is worth noting. He remarks, "One can translate these qualitative aspects into quantitative ones, but one loses thereby the real significance of the respective biological phenomena, exactly as if one would describe a painting of Rembrandt in terms of the wave lengths of the prevailing color reflected by each square millimeter of the painting" (*Growth of Biological Thought,* 54). As Mayr says, the case for reductionism in modern biology has been immeasurably strengthened by the widespread acceptance of the false view that the only possible alternative to reductionism was vitalism.

explanation as unscientific, methodologically inappropriate. This rules
out talk about the relationship between particular traits or behaviors and
the way of life of an organism, except insofar as these teleological propositions can be restated as predictive hypotheses. Thus, for example, the
teleological hypothesis that the function of politics is to make economic
exchange easier would be replaced by the prediction that politics results
in easier economic exchange. But the two propositions are not equivalent: the latter is only a claim about the consequences of politics, while
the former, the teleological hypothesis, makes the additional evaluative
claim that politics is a good thing for human beings *because* it leads to
certain economic consequences. In other words, the teleological analysis
includes the predictive but adds to it a claim about the relationship of
particular phenomena to the whole (in this case, the life of the species) of
which they are a part. For modern, anti-Aristotelian, science, on the other
hand, there are no universals save universally valid laws. As Thomas
Hobbes notes, there is "nothing in the world Universall but Names; for
the things named, are every one of them Individuall and Singular."[13]

This rejection of the nonconventional reality of all wholes is historically linked with the rejection of other and manifestly false Aristotelian
claims about the world—special ethereal matter and so on—but the
modern premise seems much less well grounded in observational necessity. Many biologists would now argue that the reductionist aspect of the
modern scientific program was a mistake and that teleological (or teleo-
nomic) analysis is a central part of scientific inquiry, given the reality of
organisms and perhaps of species as more than simply a collection of ele-
mentary parts.[14] Be that as it may, the first challenge to the extension of
modern empiricist science into the study of human affairs came not
from biologists but from those contesting the view that human beings
could be studied in the same way that natural phenomena can be. Sharing the empiricist view that animals are in no essential way different
from machines, critics of a unified natural and social science argued that
there was a fundamental difference between human beings and "merely"
natural beings. Rousseau is one of the first to adopt this position. As he
expressed it, "nature commands every animal, and the beast obeys. Man
feels the same impetus, but he realizes that he is free to acquiesce or resist; and it is above all in the consciousness of this freedom that the spiri-

13. T. Hobbes, *Leviathan*, chap. 4, par. b.

14. See Mayr, *Growth of Biological Thought*, 21–82; and N. Eldredge, *Time Frames: The
Rethinking of Darwinian Evolution and the Theory of Punctuated Equilibrium* (New York, 1985),
98–218. For an account of a parallel development in social science and moral philosophy—the rejection of Aristotelian practical wisdom and casuistry and the triumph of the
"tyranny of principles"—see A. R. Jonsen and S. Toulmin, *The Abuse of Casuistry: A History
of Moral Reasoning* (Berkeley, 1988).

tuality of the soul is shown." [15] This assertion of the essential uniqueness of human beings shares with empiricism—against Aristotle—the questionable view that animals are essentially machines. It differs from empiricism in its claim that human action is so different from animal-mechanical behavior as to require an entirely different form of explanation. As elaborated in the nineteenth century, this sense of difference is expressed in terms of concepts like historicity and the historical sense, categories that draw their vitality from the belief that human beings indirectly constitute themselves, create their own significance, through social action. [16]

The twentieth-century heir to the romantic reaction against the Enlightenment ideal of a unified science is interpretive social science. Instead of being, in effect, "laws-and-causes social physics," to use Clifford Geertz's phrase, the study of human affairs should aim at emulating the process of construing a text; societies are to be "read" rather than "predicted." [17] While it would be an exaggeration to say that this method requires a deep empathy or perfect identification with the culture being studied, it is surely very different from the business of providing causal explanations by reference to universal hypothetical laws. It does, however, equally aim at explanation, though teleological rather than predictive, insofar as it attempts both to describe "particular symbolic forms (a ritual gesture, an hieratic statue) as defined expressions," and to place "such forms within the whole structure of meaning of which they are a part and in terms of which they get their definition." [18] But if this is teleology, the limits of its explanatory power are strictly local: the aim is to explain the society in its own terms, given the principle that "societies, like lives, contain their own interpretations." [19]

Interpretation, however, cannot be simply passive, allowing societies or "natives" to speak for themselves. If cultures are texts, then they are texts of a special kind. For Geertz, "doing ethnography is like trying to read (in the sense of 'construct a reading of') a manuscript—foreign, faded, full of ellipses, incoherencies . . . but written not in conven-

15. J.-J. Rousseau, *Discourse on the Origin of Inequality*, trans. J. R. Masters and R. D. Masters (New York, 1964), 114.

16. On the centrality of "historicity" in the development of interpretive social science, see H.-G. Gadamer, "The Problem of Historical Consciousness," in *Interpretive Social Science*, ed. Rabinow and Sullivan, 103–62.

17. C. Geertz, *Local Knowledge* (New York, 1983), 3. Nietzsche provides the link between Diltheyan historical romanticism and the more recent claims for the primacy of interpretation without any historical ground. See *Beyond Good and Evil*, part 1, par. 22.

18. C. Geertz, *Negara: The Theater State in Nineteenth-Century Bali* (Princeton, 1980), 103.

19. C. Geertz, "Deep Play: Notes on the Balinese Cockfight," in *Interpretive Social Science*, ed. Rabinow and Sullivan, 223; see generally 181–224.

tionalized graphs of sound but in transient examples of shaped behavior."[20] For the interpretive social scientist, the meaning of an action is internal to the social context, but it is assumed to be hidden from the view of the actors themselves. Geertz's interpreter does not aim at establishing universal laws, but he seems at least as sure as any physicist (or economist) that his data are not capable of supplying an adequate self-interpretation:

> The ethnographer does not, and in my opinion, largely cannot, perceive what his informants perceive. What he perceives—and that uncertainly enough—is what they perceive 'with,' or 'by means of,' or 'through' or whatever word one may choose. In the country of the blind, who are not as unobservant as they appear, the one-eyed is not king but spectator.[21]

Just as the physicist ferrets out the laws of the interaction of matter, the interpreter unmasks the hidden categories that inform perception and action; each supplies by science the coherence their data otherwise but mutely display. Indeed, for Geertz, the "study of culture [is] a positive science like any other," no matter what the metaphor of social textuality may suggest.[22] Empiricists aim at universal laws, interpreters at "local knowledge," but both understand their activity as fundamentally disinterested; evaluations are to be avoided in the analysis, and few if any evaluative conclusions can be drawn from the analysis. The function of social science relative to everyday political life thus appears as archival rather than action-orienting, on either account.[23] This situation is characterized by Hans-Georg Gadamer as a "false objectification," falsely treating the subjects of analysis as fundamentally different from the analyst.[24] In interpretive social science, this is achieved by treating the "human"—that attribute shared by analyst and subject—as a property of minimal significance.

The problem with this orientation is that it means that social science can never function as a means of self-criticism, as a way of arriving at conclusions concerning how to change or maintain our lives. To serve this goal, social science must try to do more than "seek and acknowledge the immanent coherence contained within the meaning-claim of the other." What is required in addition is in Gadamer's words, "a readiness to recognize the other as potentially right and let him or it prevail against

20. C. Geertz, *The Interpretation of Cultures* (New York, 1973), 10.

21. Geertz, "From the Native's Point of View," in *Interpretive Social Science*, ed. Rabinow and Sullivan, 228.

22. Geertz, *Interpretation of Cultures,* 362.

23. Ibid., 230–31.

24. H.-G. Gadamer, *Truth and Method* (New York, 1975), 280. Gadamer's criticism of Dilthey seems to apply fully to Geertz.

me."[25] Thus the moral danger posed by cultural relativism is that it leads its adherents not into anarchy—they are a generally civilized lot—but to smugness.[26]

It is his interest in a future- or action-oriented approach to human affairs that leads Gadamer to suggest that Aristotle can supply a language for inquiry that is superior to that of the contemporary adversaries, whether empirical or interpretive.[27] To this it may be added that Aristotle also differs from both varieties of current social science in being open to the possible influence of biological reflection in the study of human affairs. In this way, Aristotle's account of human action rejects both the empiricist assumption that animals are machines (or that nature as such is mechanical) and the romantic dichotomy between the human and the natural.[28]

I believe that an Aristotelian social science begins with a sense of nature, or biological inheritance, as neither determinative of human action nor irrelevant to it, but rather as a potentiating source of problems to be solved and of capacities and inclinations to be shaped. In presenting the Aristotelian possibility, I will consider first his conception of human action and convention and then discuss his notion of the kind of social science that can provide the most adequate account of these actions and conventions.

ARISTOTLE AND *PRAXIS*

Both of Aristotle's great works of social science, the *Nicomachean Ethics* and the *Politics,* begin with observations concerning the intentional character of human conduct: "We see that . . . everyone does everything for the sake of some apparent good"; "Every art . . . and similarly every *praxis* and choice seems to aim at some good."[29] This serves to distinguish human actions from several other classes of events in nature: those that serve a purpose in the life of the organism but are not intentional, like blinks of the eye and the motion of the heart, and those that serve no

25. Gadamer, "The Problem of Historical Consciousness," in *Interpretive Social Science,* ed. Rabinow and Sullivan, 108.

26. C. Geertz, "Anti-Anti Relativism," *American Anthropologist* 86 (1984): 263–78.

27. Gadamer, *Truth and Method,* 278–89.

28. Gadamer appears to deny this, maintaining: "Aristotle sees ethos as differing from physis in that it is a sphere in which the laws of nature do not operate, yet not a sphere of lawlessness, but of human institutions and human attitudes that can be changed and have the quality of rules only to a limited degree" (*Truth and Method,* 279). My argument is that Aristotle's natural science does not aim at the discovery of natural laws and that he is thus able to overcome the reduction/transcendence dilemma.

29. *Pol.* 1252a1–4; *Eth. Nic.* 1094a1–2.

purpose, like eye color.[30] Human actions are intentional in the sense that they are voluntary (*hekōn*). A motion is not identified as voluntary by any prior events (such as internal processes of reasoning or willing) that may have led up to the motion. "Both 'voluntary' and 'involuntary' must be said when the action occurs. An action is voluntary when the source [*archē*] of the motion of the bodily parts is the agent."[31] Voluntary actions are distinguished from other events or kinds of motion by the presence in the agent of the power to act or not at the moment of action. But this power is not the privileged preserve of any uniquely human or transcendent faculty. Other animals are as capable of voluntary action as are human beings, because this internal source of motion is neither reason nor will, but desire (*orexis*), which is common to all animals.[32] Desires are always directed toward some object of desire (some apparent good), and this is an object of sensation or imagination (*phantasia*), a power that is also common to all animals.[33] Thus intentional or voluntary motion can be understood as an interaction of an apparent good, the agent's perception of that good, and the agent's desire for the good in question. Nonetheless, it makes sense to call desire the source or efficient cause of action, because neither the object nor the perception of the object can cause motion in the absence of desire.[34]

Yet it is also possible for Aristotle to say, in response to Democritus' claim for the universality of external efficient cause (a claim shared by modern science), that *all* animals move by choice (*prohairesis*) or intellection (*noēsis*).[35] The reason for the apparent ambiguity here is Aristotle's view that reason and desire are not separate entities but interacting "parts" or aspects of soul (*psychē*). Soul itself, moreover, is not a thing separate from body, but is "a beginning [*archē*] of animal life."[36] That is, to speak of soul, for Aristotle, is to consider the manner in which living things are self-moving and thus distinct from inanimate existence; "of natural things, some have life and some not; we say 'life' where there is nurture, growth, and decay owing to the thing itself."[37] The Aristotelian soul is not separate from the body, but body and soul are properties that

30. *Part. An.* 657a31–b3; *Mot. An.* 703b5–6; *Gen. An.* 778a32ff.; cf. 778b11ff.
31. *Eth. Nic.* 1110a14–17.
32. *De An.* 433a32–33. This seemingly different account of the origin of voluntary motion is given in *Metaphysics* 1072a29–30: "We desire [an object] because it seems [good], rather than it seems because we desire; for thinking [*noēsis*] is the *archē*." These passages can be reconciled if we bear in mind that "desire" and "opinion" are both abstractions; when it comes to action, they are both aspects of a single process, a process that is common to all animals.
33. *Mot. An.* 700b15–18.   34. *De An.* 433a15–b1.   35. Ibid. 406b24–25.
36. Ibid. 402a6–7, 408b25–27. Plants are also living things insofar as they are capable of taking in food from the environment (413a25–28).
37. *De An.* 412a13–15.

exist relative to one another as aspects of the individual animal whose being they define; that is to say that my body is to my soul as the potential of an individual is to its actuality or function.[38] This conception of soul as the definitive activity of a creature is nicely captured in Aristotle's analogy, "If the eye were an animal, sight would be its soul."[39]

Just as soul is not a unique and supernatural immaterial substance for Aristotle, it is also not a peculiarly human property. Even if some kinds of activities, such as deliberation, belong primarily to humans, it is interesting to note that Aristotle explicitly rejects the view that soul and mind (*nous*) are the same. In fact, he attributes such a view to the atomist Democritus and says that it follows from the false relativistic belief that truth and opinion are one and the same.[40]

Thus human actions are not distinct from the motions of animals by virtue of their intentionality or spirituality. Still, there is a distinction to be made. In the *Ethics*, Aristotle says that he wants to reserve the term *praxis* as a characterization of human conduct alone. "There are three things in the soul," he observes, "that are decisive concerning actions and truths: perception, thought, and desire. Of these, perception is in no way the source [*archē*] of *praxis;* for beasts have perception but no share in *praxis*."[41] This is not to say that praxis is *caused* (in the sense of efficient causality) by mind and not desire, since *praxis* is a kind of motion, and "thought by itself moves nothing," at least insofar as actions are concerned.[42] The problem is as follows: the subject of *politikē* is *ta prakta*, matters concerning practice. *Praxis* is uniquely human, but it is not attributable to the existence of any uniquely creative or volitional faculty in human beings,[43] nor can it be said to follow simply from the fact that human beings are capable of thinking in ways that other animals are not.

38. Ibid. 412a15–21. For Aristotle, "the soul is just the functional organization of the entire living body" (M. C. Nussbaum, "Shame, Separateness, and Political Unity: Aristotle's Criticism of Plato," in *Essays on Aristotle's* Ethics, ed. A. O. Rorty [Berkeley, 1980], 415; see generally 395–435). This is another instance of the way Aristotle avoids an unfortunate Cartesian dualism. See also K. V. Wilkes, *Physicalism* (Atlantic Highlands, N.J., 1978), 114–37. Because "soul" in current usage implies the separation of body and soul, it might be best to avoid translating Aristotle's *psychē* altogether.

39. *De An.* 412b18–19.

40. Ibid. 404a27–31. The problem with Democritus' view is that it cannot account for our experience of making errors. This is fundamentally the same criticism that Socrates makes of Protagoras' *anthrōpos metron* in the *Theaetetus.* This would be the core of the Platonic-Aristotelian critique of the prevailing relativisms of modern social science, whether individual (the economist's "consumer sovereignty") or communal (the anthropologist's "cultural relativism").

41. *Eth. Nic.* 1139a17–20.

42. Ibid. 1139a35–36.

43. Here Aristotle parts company decisively with any hermeneutic or interpretive social science.

If *praxis* is peculiarly human, it must be as a result of a certain kind of desire.

There can be no desire without imagination, that is, an imagined object of desire, an apparent good.[44] No objects are good or desirable in themselves (and so Aristotle criticizes the Platonic form of the good in the first book of the *Ethics*), but only relative to the animal desiring them: the same object or way of life may be desirable or good for cats, but not for horses.[45] Animals are defined, for Aristotle, by the kind of activity or way of life that is peculiar to them when they are functioning at their best, their *ergon* or *energeia*.[46] Another way of saying this is that a healthy animal is one whose parts or elements are arranged according to the *logos* that defines the animal in question.[47] The *ergon* of an animal is determined by its *logos* or, in other words, by its soul and is identical with the goal or *telos* it pursues.[48] Things that seem good to an animal, and are thereby desired by it, may or may not actually be good for that animal; the souls of animals are frequently mistaken, so that a certain kind of attractive food may serve either to support or to baffle the way of life of its consumer.[49] In general, though, an animal's pleasures are determined by its *ergon;* most dogs, spiders, and mules take pleasure in the sorts of things that all members of their species accurately desire.[50] Human beings, however, are different. "Among humans there is no small difference in pleasures, for the same things that give enjoyment to some and pain to others are painful and hateful to some and sweet and dear to others."[51] With other animals, pleasures and apparent goods, the starting points of desire, vary mostly by species; with humans, they vary from individual to individual and are the major source of human inequality.

Thus human *praxis* differs in the first instance from other kinds of voluntary motion in its problematic quality and its variability. Aristotle

44. *De An.* 433b29.

45. While critical of Plato's essentialism here, Aristotle at the same time clearly rejects a nominalist interpretation of the term "good." "Good" is for him an equivocal term whose instances may be related to one another by being derived from one core meaning, by pointing to the same thing, or by analogy (*Eth. Nic.* 1096b26–29). John Burnet, *The Ethics of Aristotle* (London, 1900), 29n., suggests that the last proposal (analogy) represents Aristotle's own view. But on the basis of *Metaphysics* 1075a18–23, it seems that "good" is a *pros hen* equivocal. At any rate, Aristotle's opposition to Plato is not nominalist or conventionalist, and so cannot provide grist for the interpretivist mill.

46. *Eth. Nic.* 1176a3–5.

47. *Part. An.* 639b15–16.

48. *Metaph.* 1050a22: "For the *ergon* is the *telos*, and the *energeia* the *ergon*."

49. *De An.* 427b1–2, 433a26–27.

50. *Eth. Nic.* 1176a5. What we call learning and Aristotle calls *ēthos* or habit plays a relatively small role in establishing the preference schedules of nonhuman animals.

51. *Eth. Nic.* 1176a10–12.

states this difference in the following way in the *Politics:* "Other animals live primarily by nature [*physis*], and some in a lesser way by habits [*ethos*], but human beings alone live also by reason [*logos*] because he alone has *logos*."[52] The health (in a sense, the actuality or *energeia*) of nonhuman animals is largely determined by their inherited specific potentiality (*dynamis*) or, as we would now say, their genotype. This is much less the case with human beings, for whom biological inheritance is much less powerful in determining their way of life than is the case for any other species, whether of beasts or gods. To a greater extent than other animals, we desire things as the result of habituation (or "acculturation" or learning) rather than as a direct consequence of biologically inherited responses. As a result, there will be important differences between the goals, and hence the lives, of members of different societies or cultures.

Furthermore, humans can live and desire in a thoughtful way—in a way involving a deliberate choice of goals—whereas other animals cannot.[53] It is at this point that the famous definition of humans as the animals who have *logos*, who have the potential to live by reasoned speech, comes into play. But this is not at all simply to praise human beings, since this capacity for choice (*prohairesis*) is in no way transcendent or divine and since the consequence of having such a capacity is that individuals among us can turn out to be either the best or the worst of animals.[54] It is, rather, to identify a basic problem at the center of human affairs. Our goals as individuals, the shape of our lives, are not set for us by our biologically inherited natures or capacities; still, since we are natural beings defined by a certain definite *telos* or goal, our conception of the good for us as individual human beings can either be correct or mistaken; we can organize our particular capacities and problems relatively well or not. Therefore, our actions and the customs and thoughts that inform them (that is, our ways of life) can be read and judged as a series of attempts to answer the question, What is the human good?

The judgment that human beings are the rational animals signifies the claim that the structure of our lives is provided by desires that are informed by thought as well as by sensation. But the capacity for thinking well does not actualize itself; rather, it comes into being as the result of the development over time of certain habits over which we initially have no control. As a result, Aristotle should not be understood to claim that human lives are spontaneously, or even usually, happy or flourish-

52. *Pol.* 1332b3–5.
53. Ibid. 1280a35. For an excellent Aristotelian discussion of the differences between *prohairesis* or choice and mere voluntary action, see R. Sokolowski, *Moral Action: A Phenomenological Study* (Bloomington, Ind., 1985), 11–21.
54. *Pol.* 1253a32–34.

ing. Instead, his position is that our lives are uniquely controversial answers to the question of how beings like us should live. It is this controversy that provides the central problem for, and the *raison d'être* of, the social scientist.

BEING A KIND OF ANIMAL

In addition to being rational animals, human beings are also said to be the most political animals. But the latter assertion is quite ambiguous, since Aristotle also identifies us as "dualizers," beings whose way of life—unlike that of social insects—is both political and scattered, and perhaps even solitary.[55] This ambiguity is expressed as follows in Book 1 of the *Politics:* "By nature there is an impulse [*hormē*] in all humans toward such a community [the *polis*], but the first person to establish one was the cause of the greatest good things."[56] The problem is that our biological inheritance includes a number of impulses, not all of them compatible with one another. We also desire our preservation, and this may set us at odds with one another. The point is that there is no single impulse or structure of drives that controls human life. One of the central natural facts about us is that we generally care for one another, or exhibit some aspects of *philia* or friendship, the impulse "to wish for someone else what one thinks to be good, for that person's sake and not for one's own."[57] With this complex of social and asocial impulses, it would appear that if humanity were to be defined by its strongest spontaneous social drives alone, then we should be called familial, rather than political, animals. As we are told in Book 7 of the *Nicomachean Ethics,* "friendship between male and female seems to be especially by nature, for the human being is by nature a familial [or pairing], rather than a political animal, inasmuch as the household [*oikos*] is earlier and more necessary than the *polis*."[58] We have a natural (in the sense of biologically inherited) impulse to live together, but "the purpose of politics is not to make living to-

55. *Hist. An.* 487b. On the concept of "dualizing," see C. Lord, "Aristotle's Anthropology," 55–56, in this volume.

56. *Pol.* 1253a29–31.

57. *Rh.* 1380b35–1381a1.

58. *Eth. Nic.* 1162a16–19. With regard to the phrase "more necessary," "necessity" for Aristotle is equivocal since "cause" is equivocal. Necessity may refer either to efficient-material causality or to final-formal causality, or it may be used as the antithesis of "natural." Four meanings of "necessity" are given in *Metaphysics* 1015a20–b6. Three types of necessity are distinguished in the first book of *Parts of Animals* (639b21–640a9, 642a32–b4): simple necessity, characteristic of eternal things; teleological or hypothetical necessity, characteristic of natural things and of the products of art; and elemental necessity, characteristic of the parts of natural things (earth, air, fire, water).

gether [*syzēn*] possible, but to make living well [*eu zēn*] possible."⁵⁹ What does this mean? To answer this, it is necessary to consider the second and more important sense in which human beings are political animals.

Aristotle's argument for the proposition that human beings are uniquely political animals is stated in extremely compact form in Book 1 of the *Politics*.⁶⁰ This concision has led to two important misconceptions of the meaning of "political animal" for Aristotle, and it will be useful to consider them before offering my own reading of the passage. The first of these is that in saying we are political animals Aristotle is endorsing the Greek ideal of civic virtue and the superiority of the political life to all others. This is, for example, the view of J. G. A. Pocock, who speaks of "the ancient ideal of *homo politicus* (the *zōon politikon* of Aristotle), who affirms his being and his virtue by the medium of political action."⁶¹ This position suggests that Aristotle is defending the intrinsic value of political life to those who would see it as having only instrumental value (such as Plato or the Sophists,⁶² or, prospectively, Hobbes and Locke). But this reading runs afoul of Aristotle's apparent derogation of the political life to a rank below the theoretical life in the concluding books of both the *Politics* and the *Nicomachean Ethics*. As a result, the politics-as-intrinsic-good reading is forced either to ignore these quite prominent passages or to interpret them as a residue of generally overcome Platonism.⁶³

The other position I want to contest centers on the claim at *Politics* 1253a29–30 that all humans have an impulse (*hormē*) toward political community. If this is the case, some ask, then why don't human beings seek political life as avidly as beavers build dams or Hobbesian individuals pursue their constant endeavor for power after power? Bernard Williams presents this view in its characteristically critical form:

> In Aristotle's teleological universe, every human being (or at least every nondefective male who is not a natural slave) has a kind of inner nisus toward a life of at least civic virtue, and Aristotle does not say enough about how this is frustrated by poor upbringing, to make it clear exactly how, after that upbringing, it is still in this man's real interest to be other than he is.⁶⁴

59. *Pol.* 1280b39–1281a4.
60. Ibid. 1253a7–38.
61. J. G. A. Pocock, *The Machiavellian Moment* (Princeton, 1975), 550. Pocock's view relies on Hannah Arendt, who is the modern founder of this reading of Aristotle.
62. M. C. Nussbaum, *The Fragility of Goodness* (Cambridge, 1986), 345–53.
63. Ibid. 373–77.
64. B. Williams, *Ethics and the Limits of Philosophy* (Cambridge, Mass., 1985), 44. This reading suggests the kind of criticism of Aristotle's "metaphysical biology" made by A. MacIntyre, *After Virtue: A Study in Moral Theory* (Notre Dame, 1981).

The politics-as-spontaneous-drive view leads to the conclusion that Aristotle is hopelessly caught in a contradiction between his biological claim about the human political drive and his ethical and political claims that people do not usually or spontaneously act well.

I want to argue, against both these views, that Aristotle's understanding of the place of politics in human life has an integrity and interest of its own, one that seems to me to be both relatively unusual and plausible. The appeal of the other two views is, however, quite clear. The politics-as-intrinsic-good view allows some modern readers to find in Aristotle a powerful ally against the liberal individualism they oppose, while the politics-as-spontaneous-drive reading permits others to identify Aristotle as a familiar sort of biological student of human affairs—perhaps the biologist of the *polis* in the sense that Freud is called the biologist of the mind. The two interpretations differ most profoundly in their view of the theoretical basis of Aristotle's social science. The intrinsic-good view tends to see Aristotle as making an autonomous ethical argument, and not applying to political issues concepts developed in his biology.[65] The spontaneous-drive view holds that Aristotle is in fact a biological determinist. My contention is that Aristotle's social science is indeed biological, but that it is in no sense determinist—as, indeed, Aristotle's biology is not determinist. For Aristotle, humans inherit a variety of inclinations biologically—toward politics, but also toward living as we please, toward sexual partnership, toward imitation, among others. None of these genetic potentialities should be seen simply as conduct-determining drives; instead, they are potentiating inclinations that can be reinforced or inhibited by any number of experiences as we grow and encounter the world. This is true of animals other than ourselves. What is uniquely human is that our potentialities are many and varied and by no means always compatible or consistent with one another. This lack of strict biological definition is both a strength and a problem for us. Thus for Aristotle, as I will try to demonstrate here, politics—a way of living relative to laws and customs (*nomoi*) and involving both ruling others and being ruled by them—is neither an ethical ideal nor an overwhelming biological drive, neither an end in itself nor an inevitability. It is, instead, the best reasonably possible way of organizing that variety of inclinations and needs that comprise the human biological inheritance, a way that has not arisen either spontaneously from or in opposition to our biologi-

65. Nussbaum's discussion of this view in *The Fragility of Goodness* claims that, for Aristotle, the basic truth about ethical matters is to be sought in "shared human beliefs" (349) or "deeper appearances" (321) rather than in his biological conception of human nature. This would seem to have the questionable advantage of reconciling Aristotle to MacIntyre, in language recalling a similar move to embrace contextualism by J. Rawls, "Justice as Fairness: Political Not Metaphysical," *Philosophy and Public Affairs* 14 (1985): 223–51.

cal inheritance, but an activity that has developed as the unintended consequence of our attempts to live securely.

Before trying to present the argument about political animals in *Politics* 1253a7–38, I will provide a translation of what I take to be the key
portions of that passage, leaving as many of the important terms as possible untranslated. "The reason why human beings are political animals
more than the bee or any other herding animal is clear. For nature, as we
assert, does nothing in vain, and human beings alone among animals
possess *logos*." Other animals have a voice, and so can make significant
sounds indicative of pleasure and pain to one another, but *logos* is more
than this. "*Logos* makes plain the *sympheron* and the *blaberon* [interest and
its opposite] and *therefore* [my emphasis] the just and the unjust. For this
is unique to human beings as compared with other animals, that they
alone have a perception [*aisthēsis*] of good and bad, just and unjust, and
other things, and it is a community [*koinōnia*] in these things that makes
an *oikos* and a *polis*. And by nature a *polis* is prior to both the *oikos* and the
individual." Human beings are unique in having the capacity to perceive
what is best for them ("living well") and to order their lives according to
that perception. Justice is such an ordering and is, like politics, neither
desirable nor natural in itself but only as a way in which "living well" or
simply "our interest" (*to sympheron*) can be brought into being. Differing
conceptions of justice are not to be treated as expressing commitment to
a moral realm separate from self-interest, but as different judgments
about our long-term interests. Polities, the organized communities that
assert different views of justice, are neither good nor bad as a whole;
rather, they are to be treated as expressing judgments about what our
lives require that can be evaluated as correct or mistaken.[66]

Aristotle's claim that our ability to speak reasonably is the human
need that explains and justifies the political order is not easy to grasp.
The difficulty is caused by the fact that his sense of the function or place
of human speech in human life differs radically from conceptions that
are familiar to us. In particular, Aristotle holds neither that speech is for
the sake of communicating information from one person to another
(else it would be the same as "voice") nor that it serves the purpose of
expressing or constituting an identity, building up a human world along-
side the world of nature. The place of speech in human life is that *logos*
makes it possible for us to discover, through argument, conjectures, or
narratives, the kinds of goals in terms of which we can most sensibly or-

66. W. Ambler, "Aristotle's Understanding of the Naturalness of the City," *Review of
Politics* 47 (1985): 163–85, makes a strong case for treating the first book of the *Politics* as
both asserting and calling into question the naturalness of the polity. Part of his argument
is the claim that the *polis* springs more from the "sense (*aisthēsis*) of the good, bad, just, and
unjust, than from his ability to explain them in speech" (172).

ganize our lives. Errors can of course be made in the process of discovery; as a result, Aristotelian speech is criticizable in a way in which world- or identity-constituting speech is not. Our deliberative conclusions about goals are also always uncertain. Nevertheless, some such conclusions are needed if we are not to drift from moment to moment, because they are uniquely not available to us as an immediate consequence of our biological inheritance.

But these reasoned conclusions about our interests do not spring forth spontaneously or by necessity, even though without them we are incapable of becoming flourishing human beings. The capacity of reasonable speech is a potentiality that may or may not be developed; human beings are capable, to a unique degree, of living badly as well as living well. Of no other animal could this be said: "it is sweet for most to live without order [*ataktōs*] rather than moderately."[67] Laws and conventions of human construction are necessary to help bring us to an awareness of what is best for us, "for when he has reached his *telos* the human being is the best of animals, but when apart from *nomos* ["law," "convention," "custom"] and justice, the worst."[68] The sense in which we are political animals can now be formulated in this way: human beings are uniquely capable of, *and uniquely in need of,* a reasonable perception of their interest in order to live well, and such a perception (and therefore such a life) is somehow dependent upon the presence of *nomoi*. This statement marks off the tasks of the social scientist, marks a special quality of that science, but requires clarification at three major points. We need to ask, What does "living well" mean? What does it mean to say that this is an object of rational perception? In what way is political life a condition for living well, however defined?

The first of these three questions is taken up in the first book of the *Nicomachean Ethics*, where it is suggested that we live well (or are virtuous—exhibit human *aretē*) insofar as our lives are ordered by the specifically human *telos*, or goal. But strangely enough to our ears, this goal is expressed not in terms of some transcendent ideal or universal rule of obligation, but as a mean,[69] which in turn is defined as an appropriate *logos* or proportion of opposing tendencies. This mean, which indicates the substance or content of human well-being, is said by Aristotle to be a *hexis*. *Hexis* is a word that turns out to be quite difficult to render in English. It is a key term in Aristotle's social science, and that science becomes inaccessible to us when *hexis* is translated as "characteristic" or

67. *Pol.* 1319b31–32.

68. Ibid. 1253a31–33.

69. See S. R. L. Clark, *Aristotle's Man: Speculations on Aristotelian Anthropology* (Oxford, 1975), 84–97. The human good is similarly figured as a mean in several of the later Platonic dialogues: *Statesman* 283e–284c; *Philebus* 66a.

"habit" or "trained ability." Perhaps the best way to get at the sense of the term is by example. If I say, "Mary is courageous," or "Mary is a coward," I am describing Mary's *hexis*, making a statement about those relatively stable qualities—desires, feelings, thoughts—that define Mary as an individual. Relative to her biological inheritance, Mary's *hexis* is an actuality or actualization of a particular potentiality; relative to her actions, it is a sort of potentiality.[70] One's *hexis* is of course subject to change over time, but it represents those qualities in a person that are relatively firm and definite at any given moment, those qualities that identify a person as more, or at any rate other, than a bundle of unrealized potentials. The closest English word to *hexis* in this context might be "personality," if by that word we understand those qualities that define a person and distinguish him or her from others. Thus, to live well for Aristotle is to have (or "be") a good personality, and the primary task of the social scientist is to determine as far as possible what such a personality looks like or what sorts of personalities are better than others, in the sense of being better blends or mixtures of those elements (drives and capacities) from which all humans are constituted.

But interpreting *hexis* as "personality" involves real distortion, insofar as "personality" ordinarily refers only to human beings, and so conceals the way in which reference to *hexis* introduces Aristotle's technical language of potentiality and actuality into the discussion of human action (prior to Aristotle, the term was employed in something like his sense by Plato and by the medical writers).[71] For this reason, Terence Irwin's "state" might be the single best translation.[72] At any rate, in the *Categories, hexis* is defined generally as a certain quality (*poion*) "by virtue of which things are what they are."[73] Thus all natural things, insofar as they are composed of elements that are organized in a certain way, can be said to exhibit a *hexis* (or at any rate a *diathesis*, which is simply a less stable, less permanent *hexis*). The term has the function of drawing attention to the way in which individuals are ordered wholes, rather than heaps of elements. Thus health and sickness are said to be *hexeis* of bodies,[74] and stating the *hexis* of a substance is simply another way of describing the actuality (*energeia*) of that substance.[75]

70. Thus it is called a "first actuality" in *De Anima* 417a21–b16.
71. Some Platonic instances are *Theaetetus* 153b and 197b and *Sophist* 247a.
72. T. Irwin, trans., Aristotle, *Nicomachean Ethics*, 426–27. The term *hexis* is used less frequently in the *Politics*, but at 1265a35 Aristotle speaks of *hexeis hairetai* ("choiceworthy dispositions," in Lord's translation) and at 1334b19 he uses the word to refer to actualizations of different parts of the soul.
73. *Cat.* 8b25–9a13.
74. A blending of hot and cold expressed as a body temperature of 98.6°F indicates a healthy *hexis* as far as the nonvoluntary health of human beings is concerned.
75. *Metaph.* 1022b4–14.

The introduction of the potentiality-actuality distinction for Aristotle's social science indicates that at least some of the key terms of this science are not as radically distinct from the categories of the other sciences of natural things as modern interpretive social science might suggest. Our *psychē* is analogous to our body in that it can be either well or badly ordered. More precisely, we need to recall here that soul and body are attributes of individuals, rather than separate entities. As Martha Nussbaum says, "the soul is just the functional organization of the entire living body."[76] Each individual has a certain actuality (soul) and potentiality (body) proper to it, and the soul is simply a higher level of organization than the body for that individual, where "higher" refers to nearness to those activities that specifically define the individual as who or what it is. One way to speak of illness in all animals, human beings included, is to say that it is an unnatural condition in which our body rules our soul, when the battle to stay alive effaces the possibility of living well.[77]

Just as the healthy involuntary motions of the body can be identified by reference to a healthy (or normal) physical condition,[78] so healthy voluntary actions are defined relative to a good or healthy personality. Of course, Aristotle is aware that both the elements and the correct blend or proportion are much more difficult to grasp in the realm of action than in that of bodily health,[79] but he can at least begin by asserting that if virtue or excellence is a *hexis*, then good actions are those that are performed by good (*spoudaioi* or *phronimoi*) human beings. Actions cannot be called good or bad by reference to some universally applicable moral rule, like the greatest happiness principle or the categorical imperative. Aristotle and the various schools of modern psychiatry might disagree radically concerning the specific character of a healthy personality, but they are in fundamental agreement that the basis for any understanding of human affairs must be a perception of what constitutes a well-ordered person, just as the practice of medicine must begin with a perception of what constitutes a healthy somatic condition.

POLITICAL RESOLUTIONS AND HUMAN PROBLEMS

We live well insofar as we perceive what living well is, and act according to that perception. This is also true of physical well-being, but with one important difference: human beings do not always or for the most part

76. See note 38 above.
77. *Pol.* 1254a39–b4.
78. See C. Boorse, "Health as a Theoretical Concept," *Philosophy of Science* 44 (1977): 542–73.
79. *Eth. Nic.* 1137a13–14.

spontaneously perceive their interest in becoming good persons or personalities. Our actions and the desires that initiate them can only become informed by a perception of the good human life as a result in the first instance of learning or socialization that is shaped by the laws and customs of our culture.[80] Good human beings act on the basis of rational choice, but in order to reach the possibility of rational conduct we require a very long period of habituation, of a sort of aesthetic education demanded by the relative thinness of our biological inheritance relative to our specific virtue, "for all art [*technē*] and education wish to supply what is lacking in nature."[81] Every culture can thus be seen as implying a solution to the question of the best life, or at any rate the question of the best life under the circumstances. This implicit solution is in fact the meaning or significance of cultural and political organization, even though the most efficient cause or most powerful motivation for the establishment of politics is not the desire to live well but rather the desire to live or to live together. As Aristotle remarks, "the *polis* comes into being for the sake of living, but *is* for the sake of living well."[82] The curious fact about human life is that we have a profound biological need for an institution that will shape our desires into healthy patterns, but at the same time we have a relatively weak natural inclination (or *hormē*) for institutions of that sort. Such political inclinations as we do inherit need to be supplemented by our much stronger social inclinations toward institutions that provide security or company rather than *paideia*. Thus it is not surprising that most existing cultures are not well designed for the purpose that justifies them and are instead promiscuous or random heaps of *ad hoc* custom and legislation.[83] Such a city is a *polis* in name only (as a corpse is a human body in name only) and may in fact be nothing more than a concealed form of despotism, the rule of the master over slaves.

Still, we cannot do without political life, without the process of habituation through customs and the practice in ruling and being ruled that are the necessary supports for human rationality. Since we cannot ever become virtuous by our own individual efforts, the shaping or habituating influence of law and custom is a necessary condition for the development of virtuous or flourishing personalities; it is biologically impossible

---

80. I am using "culture" here as an equivalent of Aristotle's *politeia*. The *politeia* is the form or order (*taxis*) of a given *polis* (*Pol.* 1274b38–39, 1276b5–10). A *polis* is its particular *politeia* (as a particular game is baseball), and when the *politeia* changes, the *polis* changes, even if people, buildings, and so on remain the same. The best discussion of the meaning of *politeia* is found in L. Strauss, *Natural Right and History* (Chicago, 1953), 135–38. Given present English usage, I think "culture" approximates *politeia* more closely than "regime," but since neither term evokes *politeia* with perfect accuracy, I will use them interchangeably in the text.

81. *Pol.* 1337a1–3.   82. Ibid. 1253b29–30.   83. Ibid. 1324b5–6.

for us to hope to skip over culture or to replace it with a set of rational principles. Thus music education, which trains us to be pleased by and, whenever we can, to emulate the right kind of exemplary characters or personalities, is the most significant, though not the most pressing, part of political life.[84] But this process of socialization is sufficient only to the extent that the conventions that inform it are in turn informed by a true conception of the human good *and* by a solid grasp of local circumstances. Just as a personality or a way of life may be based on a mistaken perception of what it means to live well, so may a *polis* or culture. Thus there may be a difference between a good human being without qualification and a good citizen of a particular city.[85] In spite of these problems, we need politics, and thus the social scientist's task is not that of fashioning an alternative institution. But because of the ever-imperfect character of political life, it is equally not sufficient simply to interpret the internal significance of the conventions of existing cities; rather, the business of the social scientist is to criticize and offer guidance to these cities in the light of an adequate conception of human flourishing or psychic health, a notion that is surely *contra* the goals of interpretive social science.

But this task of criticizing and reforming cultures is not so easy. It is a difficult and problematic project in part because of the sense discussed above in which politics is an unintended consequence of activity with other ends in view[86] and partly because of the unique importance of individuality and circumstance in human affairs, a fact that cannot be grasped by a social science that proceeds on the basis of strict empiricist assumptions. This essential variability of solutions to the problems posed by human affairs, which results in the peculiar difficulty and imprecision of social science understood as Aristotelian cultural criticism, has two causes: human diversity and the multifunctional character of political organization. The fact of diversity does not simply mean that some hu-

84. Ibid. 1337a11–12.
85. Ibid. 1276b16ff.
86. It is important to distinguish Aristotle's view from the interpretive conception of human beings as "incomplete animals." As can be seen in the following excerpt from Geertz, *Interpretation of Cultures*, 218, such a position derives largely, though perhaps unconsciously, from nineteenth-century German philosophy:

> The tool-making, laughing, or lying animal, man, is also the incomplete—or more accurately, self-completing—animal. The agent of his own realization, he creates out of his general capacity for the construction of symbolic models the specific capabilities that define him. Or—to return at last to our subject—it is through the construction of ideologies, schematic images of social order, that man makes himself for better or worse a political animal.

For Aristotle—as opposed to Geertz and Hegel—*all* animals are the agents of their own realization, and human beings are political animals prior to any human activity. Politics is one of our specific natural potentials, not the royal road out of nature.

mans are in various ways better and worse than others (which is also true for many other species), but refers to the way in which human individuals differ from one another with respect to inherited potentiality (which may fairly be called genetic differences) much more than do individuals of any other natural species or kind. Humans, unlike members of any other species, can be beasts or gods and much else in between. Individuals are each at their best when their elements constitute a mean, but since psychic capacity for action varies at least as much as somatic aptitude for good health, a good personality must be a mean relative to each individual's capacities and circumstances.[87]

The problems caused by the multifunctionality of political life are even more complex, and more interesting for social science. The essential or definitive purpose of politics—its reason for being—is the development of flourishing or virtuous persons. But this defining activity—living well—depends upon the simultaneous presence of two other activities. Before it is possible for individuals to live well, it is necessary for us both to live and to live together—*eu zēn* is the goal, but this presupposes *zēn* and *syzēn*.[88] Both survival or stability and political integration (a low level of *stasis*, or civil disorder) are only necessary conditions, but they are very necessary. Moreover, the relationship between necessary and constitutive conditions of political well-being cannot be viewed as a temporal sequence; so long as we remain the animals that we are, we will not live forever, and we will continue to inherit both sociable and unsociable impulses.[89]

Political organization and authority are not fully justified unless the laws and customs (*nomoi*) of that organization are reasonable means toward the development of healthy personalities; but that organization cannot continue to exist unless those same *nomoi* are also reasonable ways of providing for the stability and integration of the *polis*. Individuals lead a single life within a single *polis*, but this life is inevitably an ordering of several different, and sometimes conflicting, needs. Now, if those *nomoi* that were best suited to achieving the constitutive aim of politics (virtuous persons) were also in every case those most appropriate for achieving its simultaneous necessary conditions (peace and integration), then social science could in principle provide precise answers to questions concerning the sorts of *nomoi* that could best serve the ends of

87. *Eth. Nic.* 1106b36–1107a1.

88. *Pol.* 1280b30–35.

89. There is no standard Aristotelian formula for expressing this distinction between necessary and constitutive causes or conditions. One clear formulation of the distinction is presented as that between *sunaition* (co-cause or accessory) and *aition* (cause as such) in *De Anima* 416a12–15: heat is the *sunaition* of growth, while soul is the *aition*. Plato uses the same terms for the same distinction in *Statesman* 281d–e.

the *polis*. Unfortunately, the antecedent of this hypothesis is usually not the case; at the heart of the problem of human affairs sits a tension that does not admit of precise theoretical resolution.[90]

This tension emerges in the discussion of who should be admitted to citizenship in the *polis* in Book 3 of the *Politics*. Citizens, for Aristotle, are those who actively engage in the deliberations of public life, not simply those whose rights are to be protected by public authority.[91] Given this, the question of the appropriate requirements for citizenship seems at first to pose no serious problem for the theorist. Since the constitutive purpose of politics is virtue, only those who are capable of becoming virtuous should be admitted to citizenship, and so those who spend their lives in labor and commerce cannot be admitted without distorting the purposes of the political order. This is so even though labor and commerce (and military pursuits) are conditions necessary for the existence of the *polis*—"for this is true, that not all those without whom the *polis* would not be should be made citizens."[92]

This is all quite straightforward, but only a few pages farther along we are told that the problem of citizenship has not in fact been resolved. "There is an *aporia* ["perplexity" or "puzzle"] concerning who must be sovereign [*to kyrion*] in the city."[93] If the sole business of politics were education in virtue, there would be no *aporia* concerning who should rule; the only reasonable claim to citizenship would be made by those who were most virtuous themselves and most capable of recognizing and encouraging excellence in others. But since the *polis* must also provide stability (not to mention civic harmony), it is also reasonable for property holders and, indeed, all free persons to claim the honor of citizenship,

90. Leo Strauss presents this tension in these terms: "The political problem consists in reconciling the requirement for wisdom with the requirement for consent" (*Natural Right and History*, 141). For an interesting, quite Aristotelian account of contemporary American political and judicial deliberation in these terms, see A. T. Kronman, "Alexander Bickel's Philosophy of Prudence," *Yale Law Journal* 94 (1985): 1567–1616.

91. Citizenship means participating or sharing (*metechein*) in public offices and decisions (*Pol.* 1275a23–24) and not simply being entitled to protection against unjust acts (1280b11–13).

92. *Pol.* 1278a2–3. The argument may be stated as follows: (*a*) *poleis* will be well governed only to the extent that citizens (governors) have or are virtuous *hexeis;* otherwise, the resources of the *polis* are likely to be used for the wrong purposes; (*b*) leisure is needed for the development of a virtuous *hexis*, and hence for the development of the capacity to act politically; it is not sufficient, but someone whose life by chance or choice is devoted to work or commerce cannot be a good citizen; (*c*) such unleisurely ways of life are, however, absolutely necessary for the survival of the *polis*—even as they tend to distort political justice; hence, (*d*) some lives (or careers) that are necessary for *poleis* should as far as possible be excluded from active citizenship if the *polis* is not to be twisted by the pressing claims of private or economic interest.

93. *Pol.* 1281a11.

"for free people and possessors of taxable property are necessary, since there could be no *polis* composed entirely of the poor, just as there could be none composed of slaves."[94] There is thus no unequivocal theoretical solution to the central question of who should govern (barring the extremely unlikely limiting case of the appearance of a thoroughly godlike human).[95] A determination will have to be made in each case concerning how far to modify the claims of excellence against the subordinate, though indispensable, requirements of stability and integration. The final judgment in each case as to how the balance must be struck will be the work of the wise citizen (the *phronimos*), who has a solid grasp of the possibilities and dangers of local conditions, and not of the social scientists (although there is no reason why a social scientist might not also happen to be a *phronimos* in a given case). General theory based on considerations of human nature is not at all dangerous or irrelevant to political life (as interpretive social science characteristically claims), since it alone can provide a clear statement of the problems that politics must solve; but an adequate social scientific theory reveals its own limitations in showing that the problems it brings to light do not admit of precise theoretical solutions.[96]

The tension produced by the multifunctionality of political order becomes even more evident in Books 4–6 of the *Politics*, as the discussion shifts from the question of what constitutes the best political order simply to the question of the sources of stability and internal tranquility in *poleis*. In outline, the problem is this: leisure is a necessary condition for education in virtues and for political *praxis* generally, but an absence of leisure appears to be an equally necessary condition for the development of that internal stability without which a *polis* cannot exist. Thus in Book 4 Aristotle develops the argument that the most stable (and the least unjust) cultures are those in which leisure and hence genuinely deliberative political activity are at a relatively low level, such as those *poleis* in which farmers and small property holders are the preponderant power.[97] In an argument not unlike Madison's praise of the extended

94. Ibid. 1283a17–19.

95. *Pol.* 1332b24. If such a person does appear, the only reasonable conclusion is that politics—*nomoi* and the rotation in office—will no longer be necessary for the development of virtue (1284b30–34). Even then, Aristotle suggests that it would be safer to allow the laws of the *polis* to rule, since "passion perverts even the best when they are ruling" (1287a31–32). But the possibility itself is so unlikely as to be negligible; even ordinarily virtuous people are a small minority (1302a1–2).

96. Plato takes up the question of the relationship of the subject matter of different sciences and their relative precision in several dialogues. His conclusion appears to be compatible with Aristotle's: the precision of any science is relative to the intelligibility of the mean that defines that science; see *Statesman* 283d–284d; *Philebus* 55e–56e.

97. *Pol.* 1292b25–29 and 1295a25–31.

commercial republic in *Federalist* 10, Aristotle contends that people who have to work for a living will be the least ambitious, the least likely to oppress one another, and the most likely to live together in friendship.[98] But as soon as we recall that the constitutive goal of politics is not friendship (or integration) but virtue, we are forced to conclude that the hardworking heroes of Book 4 cannot be citizens in the best-ordered city. This recollection occurs in Book 7, where Aristotle remarks that "in the most finely ordered *polis* . . . it is necessary that the citizens live neither a worker's nor a businessman's life . . . nor should they be farmers (since leisure is necessary both for the development of *aretē* and for political *praxis*)."[99]

The conclusions of Books 3 and 7 do not contradict those of Book 4; rather, they point to that tension uniquely characteristic of the subject matter of social science, the political order within which human excellence can be formed. The definitive purpose of that order is to shape our perception of our interest (or of what is good for us) so that we may, as expressed in the Aristotelian formula, live well (*eu zēn*). But this project cannot occur unless several important preconditions are satisfied simultaneously, necessary conditions that are summarized by the formulaic terms "living" (*zēn*) and "living together" (*syzēn*). Those *nomoi* best suited to achieving and maintaining the necessary conditions of political life are often not those best suited to developing virtue in those who live and die within their light. This does not mean that politics is an inherently absurd or paradoxical or tragic activity. It does, however, mean that solutions to political problems—or problems about human lives as such—will always (so long as our nature is what it is) be somehow perplexed and imprecise in a way that distinguishes political questions from all others. What will be the character and limits of that scientific or theoretical inquiry that addresses these questions, if indeed such inquiry is possible?

First of all, it is an extremely difficult inquiry. If social science were simply a matter of interpreting the *nomoi* of a particular *polis*, it would not be difficult, "because it is not hard to have understanding concerning those things which the *nomoi* say." But since the purpose of political inquiry is not merely interpretive understanding—not adding to the archives of human political narratives—but evaluation and criticism of cultures in the light of the possibility of better *nomoi*, it is not so easy. *Nomoi* always seem just to those who love them as their own, but in reality they may or may not be just. As Aristotle points out, "these things [the things which the laws say] are not just things, except contingently [*kata sym-*

98. Ibid. 1295a25ff.; see also 1318b6–17.
99. Ibid. 1328b37–1329a2.

bebēkos]." Thus "knowing how just things are done and how they are distributed is a greater work than knowing the healthy things."[100] Moreover, hard as it is to determine what a just ordering is, it is even more difficult to persuade people to be just when they have the power to act unjustly—social science must always contend with a rhetorical problem.[101] Nevertheless, difficult and imprecise as the conclusions of social science must be, they are not for that reason indeterminate or arbitrary; although it is not possible to say what the best *nomoi* are in a way that abstracts from the circumstances (possibilities and limits) of each particular culture or *polis*, it is still the case that there is one way of ordering human affairs that will be best for each (as opposed to every) *polis*.[102] This element of determinacy arises from the fact that it is possible to understand what the natural functions of political activity are and to evaluate existing polities in terms of their success or failure in performing these functions. "Human beings combine for the sake of some interest [*sympheron*], to provide some of the things necessary for life. And the political community seems to be for the sake of interest . . . and this is what lawgivers aim at, and they say that the just is the common interest [*to koinēi sympheron*] not with respect to a part of life, but concerning life as a whole."[103] Political activity is neither a self-generating end in itself nor an association for the protection of individual rights; its constitutive function is the development of virtuous personalities or ways of life,[104] and social science can criticize and guide this activity although it can never replace it. One can say that social science is, in a sense, continuous with political activity in that it too addresses the basic question, How should we order our lives? But it addresses it from a more universal perspective—that of the human species good or goods as such, rather than from the necessarily parochial and culturally specific perspective of us political people—the perspective of what is currently good for ourselves and our polity. Thus from an Aristotelian point of view social science cannot simply be an orderly reconstruction of the perspective of the citizen (as it is for Geertz) nor can it replace that perspective with a perfectly adequate general theory (as in the Hobbesian dream of empiricist social

100. *Eth. Nic.* 1137a10–14.

101. *Pol.* 1318b1–5.

102. *Eth. Nic.* 1135a5. This passage has received several readings. I adopt the one defended by J. J. Mulhern, "*Mia Monon Pantachou Kata Physin Hē Aristē*," *Phronesis* 17 (1972): 260–68. As Strauss, *Natural Right and History*, 159, argues, for Aristotle, natural right or law resides ultimately in particular decisions, and not in universal rules or principles. Gadamer states the consequences of this: "The idea of natural law has, for Aristotle, only a critical function. No dogmatic use can be made of it, i.e., we cannot invest particular laws with the dignity and inviolability of natural law" (*Truth and Method*, 285).

103. *Eth. Nic.* 1160a9–23.

104. *Pol.* 1280b6–12.

science). The goal of this social science is the improvement of local political discussion, rather than the formulation of universal laws or the spinning of narratives based on what the natives think.

THE TASKS AND LIMITS OF THE SOCIAL SCIENTIST

What, then, are the appropriate questions for the social scientist to address? At the beginning of Book 4 of the *Politics,* Aristotle lists four problems that an adequate social science must address. First, the scientist must have a theoretical understanding (*theōrēsthai*) of the best regime (or ordering of the *polis*), given the most favorable circumstances with respect to the necessary conditions of stability and integration and individual potentiality. In this category fall the discussions of the theorists of the best regimes found in Book 2 and Aristotle's own suggestions about the institutions of the best possible city in Book 7. Aristotle characteristically prefaces such discussions by saying that he is about to consider how politics should be organized under conditions that are "according to a prayer" (*kat' euchēn*).[105] Such conditions, which seem to be those in which security and civic friendship can be taken for granted, are objects of prayer not in the sense that they are impossible, but rather because their actual occurrence is a matter of chance, rather than a result of conscious planning.[106] Aristotle's best regime in Book 7 is not an unfounded dream, insofar as it rests on an adequate human psychology and in particular on a true conception of what constitutes the most desirable life for a human being.[107] But these institutions cannot be a plan or blueprint for legislators or reformers, since the conditions they presuppose can come about only by the remotest of chances.

The second task described in Book 4 is that of knowing what sort of culture will be best under less than optimal or providential conditions, when we cannot take stability and integration, the necessary conditions of political activity, for granted. Aristotle's answer for his Greek world is provided in the discussion of the middle-class polity and of farming democracy in Book 4. Third, the social scientist must be able to say how any culture or regime, no matter how imperfect, can be made more stable and coherent. This forms the subject matter of Book 5 of the *Politics,* with its lengthy and painstaking discussion of how democracies, oligarchies, and even tyrannies can reduce internal conflict. This section of the *Politics* contains the greatest density of predictive explanations of the kind familiar to empiricist social science, but even here the discussion is in-

105. Ibid. 1260a29, 1288b23, 1295a29, 1325b36.
106. Ibid. 1331b22.
107. Ibid. 1323a13–15.

formed by the evaluative hypothesis that any regime can be made less unjust by being made more stable, even though a stable regime is not necessarily a good or just political ordering. Finally, the social scientist must know the techniques for bringing existing regimes closer to the best, and so must understand the ways and uses of reforms and persuasion. Aristotle is particularly insistent that these four tasks are part of a single science, rather than that they represent different ways of considering human affairs. This insistence is repeated at the end of the *Nicomachean Ethics,* where it is argued that the social scientist must understand both the purpose or function of political life—*eu zēn*—and the ways in which different cultures implicitly carry out that function.

But what kind of a science is this? Are there any other sciences that can serve as paradigms for social scientific inquiry? Clearly, mathematical physics cannot serve as such a paradigm, since there is too much variance from case to case to permit all cultures to be treated as instances to be subsumed under a set of precise general laws (although many lawlike generalizations about political life are both possible and highly informative). Nor can we look to procedures of literary analysis for guidance; social science must indeed "read" the meaning of regimes or cultures, but it cannot take the coherence of their *nomoi* for granted nor assume that every relatively coherent *polis* (such as Sparta) is for that reason, or simply because it understands itself as such, a good *polis.* Yet social science is not *sui generis;* Aristotle has continual recourse to one other science in his discussions of what constitutes an adequate social science and in his arguments about the relation of that science to other kinds of thought. This is the science of medicine.[108] In the first instance, the physician, like the social scientist, must have experience of particular individuals, as well as general causal knowledge.[109] Like medicine (or physical training), an adequate social science requires both an experience of cases and general theory; neither element can satisfactorily replace or be reduced to the other. But why is this true of social science? And why, if it is true, is Aristotle compelled to rely so heavily on medical analogies to illustrate correct social scientific procedure, rather than arguing more directly? I think the best way of approaching these questions is by considering the four characteristics that Aristotle claims (in the first two books of the *Nicomachean Ethics*) distinguish social science from other sciences: the relative imprecision of social science, its dependence on the

---

108. G. E. R. Lloyd, "The Role of Medical and Biological Analogies in Aristotle's Ethics," *Phronesis* 13 (1968): 68–83; and W. Jaeger, "Aristotle's Use of Medicine as Model of Method in His Ethics," *Journal of Hellenic Studies* 77 (1957): 54–61, collect and discuss the relevant citations. Clark's analysis (*Aristotle's Man*, 84–97) is especially provocative.

109. *Metaph.* 981a12–29.

proper upbringing or habituation of the practitioner, its dependence on his or her maturity, and the fact that social science (unlike other sciences and unlike Aristotle's most frequent characterizations of political activity itself) is not an end in itself, but is an inquiry undertaken for the sake of acting and living well.

The truth or falsehood of all these methodological contentions depends on the nature of the subject matter that defines the project of the social scientist: human conventions and cultures understood and evaluated as attempts to solve the problem that is unique to human beings, the problem of how to live well under a particular set of circumstances. Given the nature of its subject, social science is bound by certain restrictions (imprecision and instrumentality) and dependent upon certain external presuppositions (the good upbringing and maturity of the social scientist).

In Book 1 of the *Ethics,* Aristotle states that the precision of any art or science depends on its underlying subject matter and that social science is particularly imprecise. "The noble and just things, which *politikē* studies," he says, "have so much variation and irregularity that they seem to be by *nomos* alone and not by *physis.*"[110] In Book 2 he amplifies this point, comparing social science to medicine, as follows: "In matters concerning *praxis* and the things that are in our interest [*ta sympheronta*], there is nothing fixed, just as in matters of health."[111] The good social scientist must know two different kinds of things, both of which can be known, but neither of which (because of the differences among individuals and cultures) can be known precisely. The first sort of thing to be known is the human good, which is the *telos* or function of both individual and *polis.*[112] This can be expressed variously as flourishing (*eudaimonia*) or as that which is in our interest (*to sympheron*) or as excellence or virtue (*aretē*). The human good can be known in general[113]—it is a deliberative life, the kind of *hexis* or personality called the mean—but it cannot be known precisely for each individual, given the diversity of biologically and culturally inherited problems we each must solve simultaneously. The second kind of thing to be known (which is logically dependent on the first) are the just things—that is, those laws and customs that tend to promote the human good. Now those *nomoi* that might be just in one place—say, Athens—might not necessarily be just in another—say, the United States. Nevertheless, for each place there will be one set of *nomoi*

110. *Eth. Nic.* 1094b14–16.   111. Ibid. 1104a3–5.   112. Ibid. 1094b6–7.
113. Social science is imprecise relative to some other sciences, but it is nevertheless determinate. That is, while its subject matter cannot be precisely defined, it does admit of definition in outline: the human good has limits or boundaries and is hence definable. See *Eth. Nic.* 1106b30.

that are most just relative to human interest and to the peculiar circumstances of that place and time. In the discussion of justice in Book 5 of the *Ethics*, Aristotle responds to the doubt he earlier raised about whether justice can be said to be by nature (whether *nomoi* can be criticized and evaluated in terms of some determinate natural standard) in the following way: "Among us, some things are by nature even though they are changeable."[114] Social *science* is possible, but its most important findings cannot be presented and transmitted as a set of fixed and precise rules and precepts, as can those of sciences like mathematics and, to some degree, medicine.[115]

The requirement that a good upbringing is a necessary (though not sufficient) condition for the development of a competent social scientist is likely to strike us as hopelessly prescientific. But Aristotle is not claiming that only members of the upper class can be good social scientists. The argument is that in order to get a preliminary grasp of the central concept of social science, the human good, it is necessary to have been habituated or socialized in such a way that we are inclined to perceive that there is a human good that is somehow different from our own spontaneous pleasures and pains. This is simply another way of stating the claim that human beings are biologically or genotypically unique in not spontaneously perceiving their own good, their interest in a well-organized life. So in Book 1 of the *Ethics* Aristotle says, "Thus it is necessary to have been brought up nobly in order to understand sufficiently the noble things, the just things, and the political things as a whole."[116] The indispensable starting point of social science is a sense of the difference between a life (*bios*) or personality (*hexis*) that is flourishing and one that is not. Since, as we have seen, the human good or human interest is so composite and varied that knowledge of it cannot be transmitted by a set of precise theoretical precepts, it cannot be perceived at all except by an observer whose experience and *hexis* are relatively healthy. If poorly brought up, the observer will either have no coherent sense of the human good or be led to misperceive that good by a certain unsoundness of *hexis*.[117] This is not a problem for those sciences that are sufficiently simple to allow teaching by precept, such as arithmetic and geometry. The secondary element of social science, predictive knowledge of what sorts of *nomoi* are likely to produce what sorts of consequences, can to a

114. *Eth. Nic.* 1134b29–30.
115. Ibid. 1104a7–9; *Pol.* 1287a33–35.
116. *Eth. Nic.* 1104a7–9. Irwin's translation of the passage is a good commentary: "This is why we need to have been brought up in fine habits, if we are to be adequate students of what is fine and just, and of political questions generally."
117. *Eth. Nic.* 1181b9–11.

certain extent be transmitted by precepts or textbooks.[118] But such text-books (or empirical studies) cannot be adequately employed unless those who study them have (or are) a good *hexis*, since without this basis they are incapable of making the relevant critical determinations. As Aristotle puts it, "those who go through such things without [the appropriate] *hexis* cannot judge them nobly."[119]

In Book 1 of the *Nicomachean Ethics* (1095a2–13), Aristotle presents two related reasons for thinking that youths (*hoi neoi*) are not prepared to study social science: lack of experience and the tendency to be guided by passive emotion (*pathos*) rather than by active *logos*. Aristotle explains, "For this reason a youth is not a suitable student of social science, for he is inexperienced in the actions [*apeiros praxeōn*] of life, and the arguments [*logoi*] are drawn from and concern actions. . . . And it makes no difference whether he is young in age or in habits, for his defect is not a matter of time but comes from living according to emotion [*to kata pathos zēn*] and pursuing everything in this way." In order to have a preliminary teleological understanding of human *praxis* as an attempt to solve the human problem of how to live well or according to our interest under particular circumstances—as opposed to, say, *praxis* as a way of maximizing pleasures or as reproductive strategy—experience is required. This experience cannot be replaced by a textbook discussion of the nature of *praxis*, such as is provided by Book 1 of the *Ethics* and Book 7 of the *Politics*.[120] Furthermore, it is an experience of a complex sort, since it cannot be had by those who interpret their own and others' doings through the lenses of passion or emotion. This experience of the human interest, and of the consequent distinction between living and living well, is something that occurs only through the generalizing operations of *logos* (recall *Politics* 1.1253a14–15), rather than through the senses. If we are incapable of seeing our actions and those of others as subject to criticism and justification, viewing them instead in the context of our passionate likes and dislikes, we will be constitutionally (in other words, because of our *hexis*) incapable of forming an idea of human interest based on our experience of humans *qua* humans, rather than as friends or enemies, good guys or bad guys, which from an Aristotelian point of view is the typically immature way of interpreting the human world.

Thus our experience of the human good or interest is an experience

118. This was the purpose of the Aristotelian collection of regimes or "constitutions," of which the *Constitution of the Athenians*, delineating the movement from moderate to extreme democracy in Athens, survives.

119. *Eth. Nic.* 1181b9–11.

120. For a critical discussion of the attempt by modern empirical social science to escape the maturity requirement, see R. N. Bellah, "The Ethical Aims of Social Inquiry," in *Social Science as Moral Inquiry*, ed. N. Haan et al. (New York, 1983), 360–81.

of the possible existence of a fact or a thing, rather than an experience of a relationship.[121] This possible existence is the starting point or *archē* of social science and as such is not something that can be demonstrated or derived from prior principles of that science or from any other science. Aristotle's psychology can never *prove* either that there is a human interest (or a final cause that defines human being) or that the substance of this interest is a deliberative life supported by a variety of moral virtues. What it can do is seek to make our understanding of this interest more precise and secure by setting forth the human capacities and problems that might render such a conception of the human good intelligible.

The human good is thus both a phenomenon and also not immediately visible to the senses, but it is important to note here that it is by no means the only fact that has these characteristics in the Aristotelian universe and that, as a result, maturity and experience are *not* uniquely required of social scientists. That the world of sensible substance is organized into natural kinds (human, horse, and so on) is a fact like that,[122] as is the fact that the same thing cannot both be and not be at the same time.[123] So it makes sense for Aristotle to say that since the *archai* of first philosophy and natural science, like those of social science, come from experience, the young cannot become philosophers or natural scientists, although they can be first-class mathematicians or geometers "because the principles of mathematics come from abstraction, but the principles [*archai*] of the others [natural science, social science, and first philosophy or metaphysics] come from experience."[124]

Thus maturity, like a good upbringing, is a necessary condition for social science, but it is of course not sufficient; else social *science* would be otiose. Nor is the experience of the human good in any way mystical or

121. At *Metaph.* 1051b22ff., Aristotle distinguishes between taking hold of a substance or entity and asserting a relationship to be the case. Aristotle's conception of experience (*empeiria*) is different from the notion of sensation. To have an experience of a thing means to have many connected memories of the same thing. Thus humans are more capable of experiencing things than beasts, though all animals are capable of sensation. See *Metaph.* 980b28–981a3.

122. *Ph.* 193a1–6. For Aristotle, as for Newton and Darwin, there is no such thing as an active universal *physis*, except as a metaphor. This requires argument, however, especially in the light of Aristotle's occasional personification of nature as a craftsman in the statement that "nature makes nothing in vain" (e.g., *Pol.* 1256b21). A good case against ascribing universal teleology to the Aristotelian conception of nature is made by M. C. Nussbaum, *Aristotle's* De Motu Animalium: *Text with Translation, Commentary, and Interpretive Essays* (Princeton, 1978), 95–99.

123. *Metaph.* 1011a8–13. This same book contains Aristotle's best joke, concerning the problems of talking to people who insist on demonstrations of the indemonstrable (1106a11–15).

124. *Eth. Nic.* 1142a12–19.

ineffable; the point, however, is that before the human good can be expressed in theoretical terms (such as Aristotle's theory of the *psyche* and his account of *praxis* in terms of *orexis* and *prohairesis*) it must be known in some pretheoretical and relatively inarticulate way. Since theory presupposes this preunderstanding, it cannot establish its own starting point in precise theoretical terms. This is the second aspect of the rhetorical problem, which is inseparable from social science understood in an Aristotelian way (the first being the problem of political rhetoric, of how to intervene in political debate): in order to persuade or remind us of the existence of human interest as a fact, Aristotle has continual recourse to medical analogies, suggesting that just as we all acknowledge the health of the body to be a fact, so we should acknowledge something like "health" to exist concerning human life as a whole.[125] Of course, these analogies prove or demonstrate nothing to someone who is not already disposed to grant the contention that human flourishing or interest exists independently of subjective preferences, but then no such proof is possible—any more than one can prove the law of the excluded middle or that natures exist. Rather, these analogies are metaphoric attempts to render the project of social science plausible by suggesting that social science is to the invisible health of the person as a whole what medicine is to the relatively visible health of our relatively visible bodies. If the subject matter of social science were clearer and less disputed, we could dispense with such analogies; but as Aristotle says after one such comparison, "it is necessary to use visible witnesses for invisible things."[126]

The medical analogy also serves to indicate a secondary sense in

125. This is much like Socrates' analogical argument for the existence of human *arete* at the end of *Republic* 1.

126. *Eth. Nic.* 1104a13–14. Aristotle's position concerning the role of metaphor in philosophy is complex. See L. Arnhart, *Aristotle on Practical Reasoning* (De Kalb, Ill., 1981), 172–76. Aristotle is sometimes critical of metaphoric speech, as in his discussion of the Platonic notion of participation. Yet he says that analogical metaphors are naturally pleasing as ways of helping us learn about something through seeing its resemblance to something else that is more clearly known to us (*Rh.* 1410b). As Arnhart remarks, this movement may plausibly be said to be, for Aristotle, "the underlying structure of all human reasoning" (175). See also Gadamer, *Truth and Method*, 388–89. At any rate, it would be difficult to imagine Aristotle doing without several of his key analogical metaphors: the physician for the social scientist, nature as creative god for self-sustaining natures in his natural science, language for being in first philosophy, the eye for the soul in *De Anima*, the doctor doctoring himself for nature causing itself in *Physics*. By contrast, empiricist social science aims at being perfectly nonmetaphorical, perhaps in the Hobbesian way, in which "metaphors and senseless and ambiguous words are like *ignes fatui;* and reasoning upon them is wandering amongst innumerable absurdities" (*Leviathan*, chap. 5). At the other extreme, a fully interpretive social science might view metaphor as a way of building a human world separate from natural actuality, without any reference to independent reality.

which experience is a necessary component of social science. Just as the point of medical science is to cure particular individuals,[127] so the point of social science is to offer criticism of and guidance for particular regimes and cultures, or perhaps more directly to improve the quality of our conversation about our local political life. Some general theoretical grasp of what constitutes health or what constitutes a good *polis* may well be one of the necessary conditions for an adequate pursuit of these goals; however, experience of the particular patient or culture is still required in addition to theory, because the variance among human individuals prevents particular persons or groups of persons from being treated as instances of general laws, as the empiricist model requires. This notion of the unique variability that pertains to human things does not, as we have seen, rest on any romantic notion of individual or cultural creativity; rather, it is perfectly explicable, as far as social science is concerned, in terms of human diversity, the complexity of human need, and the consequent natural multifunctionality of political order.

Perhaps the best-known of Aristotle's statements about the nature of social science, and the one that is frequently cited as evidence of his affinity with the interpretive approach, is his claim that the purpose of studying *politikē* is not the acquisition of scientific theory, but the development of virtue or excellence; in his own words, "the present study is not for the sake of theory, as are the others (for we are not inquiring in order to see what virtue is, but in order to become good individuals, since otherwise there would be no profit in it)."[128] But why would there be "no profit" in a theory of human interest and virtue independently of the consequences of that theory for virtuous *praxis*? It surely cannot be due to any supposed superiority or priority of *praxis* to *theōria;* that much is clear from the surprisingly strong defense of the theoretical or contemplative life that is present in both Book 10 of the *Ethics* and Book 7 of the *Politics*.[129] Then why is it the case that the science of human affairs, unlike other sciences, cannot be considered an end in itself?

The first Aristotelian thought that supports this conclusion about the unique instrumentality of social science is his judgment, strongly at odds with the interpretivist identification of humanity and transcendence, that human beings are not the best things in the cosmos; consequently, social science is not the appropriate field for reflection concerning the primary instance of being. "It would be strange," Aristotle remarks, "if someone thought that social science [*politikē*] or practical wisdom

127. *Metaph.* 981a12–29.
128. *Eth. Nic.* 1103b26–29.
129. Ibid. 1177a12ff.; *Pol.* 1337a27–30.

[*phronēsis*] were the most serious [*spoudaiōtate*] [forms of knowledge], since human beings are not the best of the things in the cosmos." [130] It thus appears that the serious theorist or scientist will not be concerned with human affairs but will look instead to the unchanging entities that in some sense inform all the rest. But strangely enough, it appears that the study of beasts, who are farther from the divine things than are humans, *is* an end in itself; Aristotle does not say that we should study the parts and lives of animals for the sake of improving agriculture or pharmacology. In the introduction to his *Parts of Animals,* he concedes that animals are indeed very far from the unchanging things, but he adds this in defense of natural philosophy: "Nevertheless, for theory, the nature that fashions animals provides immeasurable pleasures for those who are able to distinguish causes and are philosophers by nature." [131]

Theoretical activity is the constitutive cause of its own being, a self-justifying *telos,* insofar as it provides access to the structure of things, to the articulation of final-formal and efficient-material causality. But human affairs are not a good field of inquiry for such theoretical activity because of their implicit and natural variability and complexity and the resulting way in which the actualization of human potentiality is uniquely problematic. Human affairs are thus peculiarly resistant to the theoretical project and to that desire for understanding that the first sentence of the *Metaphysics* tells us is ours by nature (in other words, by biological inheritance), though not on the romantic ground of a profound separation between humanity and nature.

Thus social science is set apart from the other sciences in that it is not a self-sufficient theoretical activity. Its function is that of an instrumental condition of practical wisdom (*phronēsis*), the excellence at deliberating about particular choices that Aristotle sees as the way to the best of goods for human beings among the practical things. [132] Theorizing about the human things is perhaps best placed as an aspect of practical wisdom, as an inclination toward the universal that can clarify deliberation about our particular lives both by enriching our political vocabulary and by suggesting possible alternatives to political life as such. Aristotle himself

130. *Eth. Nic.* 1141a20–22. The word *spoudaios* is a difficult and interesting one; it can mean "eager" or simply "excellent," as well as "serious." As Irwin (Aristotle, *Nicomachean Ethics,* 400), notes: "Aristotle regularly uses the term as the adjective corresponding to 'virtue', and hence as equivalent to 'good'." But that sense of the term is clearly different from its meaning in the famous definition of tragedy as the imitation of a *spoudaia praxis* in *Poetics* 1449b24.

131. *Part. An.* 645a7–11.

132. *Eth. Nic.* 1141b13–14. The practical things (*ta prakta*) here may or may not include theory; theorizing is universal and practice not, but for human beings theorizing is surely, for Aristotle, a *praxis;* see *Pol.* 1325b21.

provides only one very compressed statement about the relationship between *phronēsis* and *politikē;* he says that they are the same *hexis* but that their essence or being (*to einai autais*) is not the same.[133] The deliberative *hexis*, like nearly everything human, is composite; its primary and constitutive element, *phronēsis*, looks squarely at the particular context at hand, while social science, its complement, looks beyond for the sake of a more adequate particular choice.

The other scientific activity that is similar to social science in this respect is, of course, medicine.[134] The critical judgments of the social scientist vary from case to case just as the judgments of the physician vary from patient to patient, in a way in which the judgments of the natural scientist do not vary from frog to frog or the metaphysician's judgments from unmoved mover to unmoved mover. And yet while social science is in this way analogous to medicine, it is by no means identical with it. The best *hexis* under the circumstances and the *nomoi* that are most likely to encourage and maintain it are the psychic and political analogies of the best somatic *diathesis* and consequent medical treatment. They are analogous for Aristotle in that they both can be expressed as a mean, a certain optimal ordering of the elements of the thing being ordered, whether that thing is a person or simply a body (a subordinate aspect of a person). But the mean that social science has in view is much more difficult to discern than the medical mean, and it is even more subject to case-by-case variation. While we may say that social science as Aristotle understands it is a sort of psychiatry, it by no means follows that psychiatry understood in this way is simply a specialized branch of medicine.[135]

Aristotelian social science is novel in our time in the sense that it cannot be identified with either of the two contemporary approaches to understanding human affairs. But my reconstruction of that social sci-

---

133. *Eth. Nic.* 1141b23–24.

134. Ibid. 1104a9; *Metaph.* 981a18–20.

135. Plato's discussion of *politikē* in the *Gorgias* and the *Laws* also makes systematic use of the medical analogy, but with rather different results. In the *Gorgias* (464b), *politikē* is said to be to the soul what gymnastic and medicine are to the body, namely, the true arts (*technai*) concerned with each. These are contrasted with the sham arts, like sophistry and cosmetics, the difference being that the sham arts are not based on causal understanding but on mere experience (*empeiria*). Hence philosophy is identical with *politikē*, and Socrates is the only true practitioner of the art of politics (521d). Similarly, in the *Laws*, good laws are distinguished from bad via an analogy of two types of medicine: that practiced by the slavish doctors whose skill is based on *empeiria* alone, on slaves, and that practiced by free doctors, who study nature as do the philosophers, on free people. All existing legislation is said to be comparable to slavish (empirical) medicine (720b–723a and 857c). Among other differences, Plato's use of the analogy downgrades *empeiria* for the sake of showing the unity of the sciences in philosophy, while Aristotle is attempting to indicate the *difference* between *politikē* and philosophy by showing the resemblance of the former to medicine.

ence introduces no exotic new program of social inquiry. Rather, what I think is most valuable about the Aristotelian approach is that it can give us a new way of thinking about human affairs, a way that permits a conversation among various forms of inquiry by freeing social science from its present pervasive concern with the supposed dichotomy between nature and uniqueness and between science and practical discourse. Human beings are both natural and unique, and only the broadest social science, one that is profoundly uneasy about the current academic divisions between moral philosophy, political theory, and the particular social sciences, can continue to understand the ways in which this is so.

While Aristotelian social science yields no rules of method, it is just as surely not a blanket endorsement of everything that claims to be social science. The structure of the Aristotelian approach is a set of questions that define the task of the social scientist. These questions have to do with how, given our specific nature and the various environmental circumstances we confront, particular communities can best solve the three great problems that as simultaneous problems are unique to the experience of human being: living, living together, and living well. Such a social science may improve political activity, but not by restating or formalizing it. The questions it poses are indeed the same as those raised by prescientific political life. But such a social science may well suggest very different answers to those questions, or perhaps a different attitude about their significance. Recalling Aristotle's remarks about the rank of human beings in the overall scheme of things, we might conclude that the best work of social science would be the development of clearer-headed and less vehemently serious citizens.

TWO

Aristotle's Anthropology

Carnes Lord

Two developments in contemporary social science point to the need for a reconsideration of classical theories of human nature, prepolitical society, and the origins of the state. Sociobiology has reopened the question of the political relevance of man's biological inheritance, thereby suggesting the possible superiority of political teachings based on the classical notion of nature or natural right to modern political idealism in its various forms.[1] At the same time, the growing field of political anthropology has brought into sharp relief the historical inaccuracy of the "state of nature" theories underpinning much of modern political philosophy, while at the same time challenging the assumptions that have governed discussions of primitive social evolution in this century.[2] What one is entitled to call the rediscovery of the political by contemporary anthropologists invites comparison with the approach characteristic of classical political philosophy. Such a comparison seems especially appropriate in the light of recent treatments of the origin and character of the classical *polis* and classical politics that in important respects support the analysis of those phenomena by the classical political philosophers as against prevailing trends in modern historiography and historical sociology.[3]

1. See, for example, R. D. Masters, "The Value—and Limits—of Sociobiology: Toward a Revival of Natural Right"; and A. Somit, "Human Nature as the Central Issue in Political Philosophy," in *Sociobiology and Human Politics*, ed. E. White (Lexington, Mass., 1981), 135–80.

2. See particularly E. R. Service, *Origins of the State and Civilization* (New York, 1975); R. Cohen and E. R. Service, eds., *Origins of the State: The Anthropology of Political Evolution* (Philadelphia, 1978); G. Balandier, *Political Anthropology*, trans. A. M. Sheridan Smith (New York, 1970); and S. L. Seaton and H. J. M. Claessen, eds., *Political Anthropology: The State of the Art* (The Hague, 1979).

3. See particularly M. I. Finley, "The Ancient City: From Fustel de Coulanges to Max Weber and Beyond," in *Economy and Society in Ancient Greece* (Harmondsworth, England,

For a number of reasons, Aristotle is the natural beginning point for such an investigation. Unlike Plato's treatments of the origins of man and political society, which appear principally in mythological contexts, Aristotle's remarks on this subject, scattered and brief though they are, seem to reflect a relatively straightforward scientific or historical approach. In general, Aristotle's attitude toward man's beginnings betrays no sign of that idealization of the primitive that is common in classical literature and that is present to some extent even in the Platonic accounts.[4] Moreover, as demonstrated in his work in the sciences of biology and zoology, Aristotle was particularly sensitive to the processes of growth and development as well as to physiological influences on human behavior; and Aristotle's *Politics* virtually begins with an account of the development of the *polis* from prepolitical associations. But most importantly, Aristotle's notion of man as a political animal remains a fundamental point of reference for understanding the specific character of classical political philosophy taken as a whole.

The chief obstacle to an inquiry of this sort is the lack of an extended or thematic treatment of man's origins and early condition in any of Aristotle's extant writings. It is usually supposed that this situation is not accidental; a serious interest on Aristotle's part in the origins and development of human society is assumed to have been precluded by his teleological understanding of nature. If, or to the extent that, the *polis* is for Aristotle a necessary manifestation of man's political nature, the question of its origins would seem to be essentially uninteresting from a theoretical point of view.

Yet it is far from clear that such an assumption is warranted. Appeal may be made in the first instance to the example of the fourteenth-century historian and philosopher Ibn Khaldûn, who shows that it is entirely possible to construct an anthropology or historical sociology that accords fundamentally with Aristotelian principles.[5] In the second place, the absence of a scientific anthropology in Aristotle's extant ethical and political writings must be understood in connection with the expressed

1981), 3–23; id., *Politics in the Ancient World* (Cambridge, 1983); and C. Meier, *Die Entstehung des Politischen bei den Griechen* (Frankfurt, 1980).

4. A. O. Lovejoy and G. Boas, *Primitivism and Related Ideas in Antiquity* (New York, 1965), 169–91 and passim.

5. Although several of its key concepts have no counterpart in Aristotle, Ibn Khaldûn's *Muqaddima* reveals a fidelity to Aristotelian terminology and concepts that is particularly remarkable given the unavailability of the *Politics* within the medieval Muslim world; see the account of M. Mahdi, *Ibn Khaldûn's Philosophy of History* (Chicago, 1957). The point is worth stressing, as it is customary among anthropologists (see, for example, Service, *Origins of State and Civilization*, 22–24) to dismiss Aristotle's thought as "theistic," "antievolutionary," or "antiscientific," while extolling Ibn Khaldûn as a founder of their discipline.

intention of these writings. According to Aristotle, the ethical and political treatises have as their primary purpose the improvement of human action or practice; only secondarily (if at all) are they concerned to elaborate a comprehensive and theoretically satisfying account of the phenomena with which they deal.[6] There is little reason to believe that Aristotle viewed man's remote past as a source of edification. But this is by no means to say that he regarded it as wholly irrelevant for understanding the fundamental character of politics and political society. It is well to remember that Aristotle himself grew up on the periphery of the Greek world, in a society in many ways quite unlike the society of the classical *polis*, and in close contact with peoples even less removed from simple barbarism. So far from taking for granted the naturalness or inevitability of the *polis* as a form of social organization, Aristotle may plausibly be credited with a lively sense of the fragility of the *polis* and the strength of the alternatives to it.

It is fruitless, then, to argue from the silence of the extant writings that Aristotle was unable or unwilling to elaborate a scientific anthropology. But one should also keep in mind the distinct possibility that the relevant issues received much more extensive treatment in Aristotelian works that are now lost. A definite interest in primitive society and its development is apparent in the fragmentary remains of the writings of several of Aristotle's students (Theophrastus and Dicaearchus), and a case can be made, as will be seen, that Aristotelian language and ideas had an important influence on the well-known account of primitive society in the sixth book of Polybius' *Histories*. This suggests that there may have been thematic treatment of these questions in one or more of the no longer extant Aristotelian dialogues.

The inquiry proposed here is further embarrassed at the outset by the necessity of questioning the value of the one passage in which Aristotle most directly and extensively addresses the question of the development of political society. Aristotle's discussion, in the second chapter of Book 1 of the *Politics*, of the growth of the *polis* from the household and the village is generally accepted as the foundation of any analysis of Aristotle's scientific understanding of man's beginnings, although the difficulties, omissions, and imprecisions of this account are also very generally remarked. If the *Politics* is essentially a practical, rather than a theoretical, work, however, it is necessary to raise the question of the practical intention underlying what might appear to be a purely theoretical discussion. In fact, it is not difficult to see that the argument of the opening chapters of Book 1 is meant to serve an overarching rhetorical purpose that dominates Book 1 as a whole—justification of the naturalness of the compo-

6. See the Introduction, pp. 4–6.

nent parts of the city, and thereby of the city itself. The naturalness of
the city stood in need of justification because a powerful current of contemporary philosophic and intellectual opinion denied it. Contemporary
"conventionalism" held that the city is fundamentally unnatural because
there is no natural common good binding superiors and inferiors, rulers
and ruled, or because justice as the city understands it is purely conventional.[7] Such a view entailed practical consequences that Aristotle certainly considered pernicious—above all, the emancipation of political
ambition from the restraints of civic solidarity and customary virtue.[8] At
all events, it is certainly the case that Book 1 is silent about a number of
considerations that are of critical importance for understanding Aristotle's overall view of the nature of man and political society. Chief
among them, as will be seen shortly, is the phenomenon of "spiritedness"
(thymos), which is central to Aristotle's analysis of civic solidarity and political rule. Book 1 is best viewed not as a comprehensive account of the
genesis of the polis, but rather as a prolegomenon to a practical science of
politics, its principal purpose being to counter the most powerful theoretical misconceptions standing in the way of a proper appreciation of
the character of rule and participation in political life. Close interpretation of the argument of Book 1 in the light of its intention confirms that
Aristotle's view of the natural character of the polis and its component
parts is more complex and problematic than is generally recognized.[9]

It should go without saying that "anthropology" did not in any sense
constitute a distinct discipline or unified field of study for either Aristotle or his contemporaries. Even today, the boundaries of the science of
anthropology are somewhat elastic, particularly as regards its relationship to historical sociology. In order to avoid misunderstanding, use of
the term here will be limited to describing Aristotle's views concerning
primitive or prepolitical society and human nature insofar as it contributes to an understanding of the evolution of society and the polis. A case

7. According to Aristotle, "all the ancients" considered law and nature as opposites and
denied that justice is something fine or noble by nature (Soph. El. 173a7–18); cf. Pl. Laws
889e–90a.

8. The political consequences of philosophic conventionalism are vividly portrayed by
Plato (Rep. 358b–62c; Grg. 482c–86d; Prt. 337c–e). For the distinction between philo-
sophic and political or vulgar conventionalism, see L. Strauss, Natural Right and History
(Chicago, 1953), 114–15.

9. A number of recent studies have exposed the inadequacy of conventional approaches to Politics 1; see particularly W. J. Booth, "Politics and the Household: A Commentary on Aristotle's Politics Book One," History of Political Thought 2 (1981): 203–26;
W. R. Brown, "Aristotle's Art of Acquisition and the Conquest of Nature," Interpretation 10
(1982): 159–95; and W. H. Ambler, "Aristotle on Acquisition," Canadian Journal of Political
Science 17 (1984): 487–502. See also A. N. Shulsky, "The 'Infrastructure' of Aristotle's Politics: Aristotle on Economics and Politics," in this volume.

can certainly be made for considering these views in the context of Aristotle's biological and metaphysical writings.[10] A fully adequate treatment of the subject would have to give detailed consideration to Aristotle's views on a number of related issues, many of them equally complex and controversial. Especially relevant are topics such as the nature and origins of justice, friendship or solidarity (*philia*), the origins and evolution of the household, economic activity and the arts (*technai*), and the relationship between men and women. All of these issues can be dealt with here only in passing.[11] This discussion will be devoted principally to elucidating Aristotle's understanding of the nature of politics or the political and its role in the evolution of human society, and to indicating its significance for assessing Aristotle's position in the history of political philosophy and the potential relevance of his teaching to problems of contemporary social science.

In spite of its fundamental character, Aristotle's assertion that man is by nature a political animal remains enigmatic and exposed to misinterpretation.[12] Contrary to a common view, Aristotle does not mean that all or most men should or do engage continuously in politics. A healthy democracy is precisely one in which the bulk of the population has little time or inclination for politics, and the "practical" or "political" way of life characteristically pursued by elites is not unambiguously preferable to a way of life devoted to the leisured pursuit of culture or philosophy.[13] Nor does Aristotle mean to deny that men require socialization in order to become functioning members of a particular type of regime or of political society generally; he admits and even emphasizes that the city is a disparate multitude that must be "made one and common" through "education."[14] The meaning is rather that man is a being constituted by nature so as to be capable of, and find fulfillment in, living in a certain kind of society. Yet uncertainty persists on two critical points. It is not

10. As has been attempted recently by S. R. L. Clark, *Aristotle's Man: Speculations on Aristotelian Anthropology* (Oxford, 1975).

11. Several of these topics are treated in detail elsewhere in this volume; see especially S. G. Salkever, "Women, Soldiers, Citizens: Plato and Aristotle on the Politics of Virility."

12. One scholar (R. Brandt, "Untersuchungen zur politischen Philosophie des Aristoteles," *Hermes* 102 [1974]: 191–200) has recently gone so far as to assert that *Politics* 1253a1–39 serves no function within the *Politics* as a whole and could be omitted without damage to the argument.

13. *Pol.* 1318b6–27, 1324a5–1325b32; for a discussion of the latter passage, see C. Lord, *Education and Culture in the Political Thought of Aristotle* (Ithaca, N.Y., and London, 1982), 180–202.

14. *Pol.* 1263b36–37; cf. 1310a12–18. Consider Somit, "Human Nature in Political Philosophy," in *Sociobiology and Human Politics*, ed. White, 170; and R. E. Dawson and K. Prewitt, *Political Socialization* (Boston, 1969), 6–7, 37.

clear to what degree (if any) the fulfillment of man's "political" potential is to be conceived as a natural or organic process, and it is not clear precisely what sorts of societies provide the conditions necessary for the fulfillment of this potential.

It is frequently asserted or assumed that the term "political" as used by Aristotle, in this context or more generally, can only refer to the *polis* as a distinct sort of political society. Yet this is by no means evident. In the key passage in Book 1 of the *Politics*, Aristotle says: "He who is without a city [*apolis*] through nature or by chance is either a mean sort or superior to man; he is 'without clan, without law, without hearth,' like the person reproved by Homer; for one who is such by nature has by this fact a desire for war, as if he were an isolated piece in a game of chess."[15] It seems relatively clear that Aristotle is here thinking not of the *polis* in its distinctive sense, but of organized political or social life generally; the alternative is not a different sort of society but isolated individuals in a virtual state of war with the rest of mankind, as in Thomas Hobbes's hypothetical state of nature. Furthermore, a broad or inclusive usage of the term "political" is to be found in Aristotle's biological writings; and such a usage is arguably the rule elsewhere in the ethical and political works.[16]

In two passages of the *Nicomachean Ethics*, Aristotle appeals to the notion of man as a political animal in a similar spirit to show that man cannot live happily as an isolated individual.[17] In another passage in the same work, he uses the phrase more restrictively, remarking that "man is by nature more of a pairing than a political animal, inasmuch as the household is prior and more necessary than the city, and procreation a more common thing among animals."[18] Yet even here it is not self-evident that Aristotle is thinking of the *polis* specifically as the only alternative to the subpolitical family or household. Aristotle evidently recognizes the existence of several types of organized societies other than the *polis*—the "village" (*kōmē*), which develops out of the household and appears capable of existing independently of the *polis*,[19] and the "tribe" or "nation" (*ethnos*), which can take the form either of an agglomeration of

15. *Pol.* 1253a2–7. All translations of the *Politics* are from C. Lord, *The* Politics *of Aristotle* (Chicago, 1984).

16. See R. G. Mulgan, "Aristotle's Doctrine That Man Is a Political Animal," *Hermes* 102 (1974): 438–45; W. Kullmann, "Der Mensch als politisches Lebewesen bei Aristoteles," *Hermes* 108 (1980): 419–43.

17. *Eth. Nic.* 1097b8–12, 1169b17–19.

18. Ibid. 1162a16–19; cf. *Eth. Eud.* 1242a21–26.

19. *Pol.* 1252b15–22. The *kōmē* is more properly a country district or canton (Lat. *pagus*), consisting of a number of small settlements linked by intermarriage. See note 50 below.

autonomous villages or of a fully developed monarchic state.[20] While lacking in political rulership or even in rulership altogether, these societies nevertheless appear to qualify as political communities in a weak sense of that term.

In an important yet very generally neglected passage in his *History of Animals*, Aristotle provides a brief account of the relation between man and the other animals. This passage at once sheds light on Aristotle's usage of the term "political" and suggests a basis for reconciling his apparently divergent statements concerning the relative naturalness of the city and the household. According to this account, all animals are either "solitary" (*monadika*) or "gregarious" (*agelaia*), and all gregarious animals are either "political" or "scattered" (*sporadika*). "Political" animals are those that "have a single and common work [*ergon*] for all," and include bees, wasps, ants, and cranes, in addition to man. Aristotle also indicates, however, that man is not simply a "political" animal: rather, man "dualizes" (*epamphoterizei*)—a technical term used by Aristotle to designate any ambiguity of zoological characteristics—as between a "political" and a "scattered" way of life.[21]

At the beginning of the *Politics*, Aristotle indicates that in ancient times men were "scattered" (*sporades*) after the manner of Homer's Cyclopes—that is, as it seems, they lived in autonomous family units with no law other than paternal command and no political relationships of

20. *Pol.* 1252b19–20, 1261a22–30, 1276a27–30, 1285b29–33, 1324b9–22, 1327b20–36. Wolfgang Weissleder, "Aristotle's Concept of Political Structure and the State," in *Origins of the State*, ed. Cohen and Service, 188, reveals a basic misunderstanding of Aristotle's view of the *polis* when he treats it as a "segmentary" state based on the consensual delegation of power by its component households. Aristotle evidently distinguished the *polis* as an aggregation of elements "differing in kind" (i.e., economically and socially diversified) from the federal states that had recently emerged among tribally organized Greeks such as the Arcadians (*Pol.* 1261a22–30), and *a fortiori* from the acephalous tribe (of which the basic unit in any event was the village rather than the household). There is of course no word in classical Greek corresponding to the modern "state." I use this term in a minimalist sense of societies in which a centralized authority is the ultimate arbiter in legal disputes (consider *Pol.* 1253a37–39) and exercises a monopoly of legitimate force. Given the peculiarities of the classical city, it is a mistake to equate "state" in this sense with the existence of "bureaucracy" (thus Service, *Origins of State and Civilization*, 9–10; cf. Finley, *Politics in the Ancient World*, 1–23).

21. *Hist. An.* 487b33–488a13. There seems little doubt that *kai tōn monadikōn* in a2 should be bracketed. It is not clear whether the text should be construed to mean that man "dualizes" between gregarious and solitary or between political and scattered; but the latter would seem by far the more plausible alternative in view of Aristotle's statements elsewhere concerning man's "pairing" nature and his tendency to seek to live with others. On the notion of "dualizing," see A. L. Peck, Aristotle, *Historia Animalium*, vol. 1 (Cambridge, Mass., 1965), lxxiii–lxxv.

any kind.[22] It seems legitimate to infer that the "scattered" mode of life
alluded to in the *History of Animals* is to be identified (at least in the case
of man) with the society of the household, and therefore that the "political" component of human nature is to be linked with any sort of organized society extending beyond the household—with those social relationships created by cooperation in a "common work" that cannot be
accomplished or accomplished well within the household.

That this indeed represents the primary sense of Aristotle's notion of
man as a political animal seems to be confirmed by the only other passage in the *Politics* in which it occurs, the discussion in Book 3 of the end
of the *polis*.[23] After recalling the earlier passage, Aristotle goes on to explain that men "strive to live together even when they have no need of
assistance from one another, though it is also the case that the common
advantage brings them together, to the extent that it falls to each to live
finely. It is this above all, then, which is the end for all both in common
and separately; but they also join together, and maintain the political
partnership, for the sake of living itself." The notion of man as a political
animal is here clearly connected with a generalized human social impulse rather than with the human goal of living well or finely, which is
fully realized only in the *polis* as distinct from other forms of organized
society, or with the biological and material needs that form the basis of
the society of the household. It is of particular interest that Aristotle
speaks here of a kind of "political partnership" that exists for the sake of
mere life rather than the good life and yet at the same time seems to
reflect a natural impulse rather than a calculation of common advantage
(which is here associated rather with the *polis* as the embodiment of the
good life).

Let us turn, then, to the second question posed earlier—the question
of the degree to which human social evolution is to be conceived as a
natural or organic process. Much has been made of Aristotle's alleged
penchant for biological analogies, and it seems to be widely believed that
the evolutionary process sketched in *Politics* 1 has to be understood as
more or less strictly analogous to an organic growth.[24] If so, this would

22. *Pol.* 1252b22–24; Hom. *Od.* 9.112–15.
23. *Pol.* 1278b15–30.
24. So, for example, E. Barker, *The Political Thought of Plato and Aristotle* (1906; reprint,
New York, 1959), 264–81. Kullmann goes so far as to wonder whether an evolutionary
development as such is not incompatible with the biological analogy, and men should not
rather be imagined as establishing cities immediately after a cataclysm; he concludes: "Nur
soviel wird man behaupten dürfen, dass für Aristoteles sub specie aeternitatis der Mensch
nur als ein konstant, d.h. von Natur aus, politisches biologisches Wesen vorstellbar ist"
("Der Mensch als politisches Lebewesen," 442–43).

provide an interesting point of contact between Aristotle and contemporary sociobiology. While Aristotle's perspective is obviously not that of modern evolutionary theory, he nevertheless recognizes the importance of the instincts of reproduction and self-preservation, and he seems to acknowledge the influence of the natural environment in determining man's way of life.[25]

The fact is, however, that Aristotle is too certain of the naturalness of human rationality and the freedom deriving from it to commit himself to any version of biological determinism.[26] To return to the crucial passage in the first book of the *Politics*, Aristotle observes that "man is much more a political animal than any kind of bee or any gregarious animal" because man alone has speech or reason (*logos*), and "speech serves to reveal the advantageous and the harmful, and hence also the just and the unjust. For it is peculiar to man as compared to the other animals that he alone has a perception of good and bad and just and unjust . . . ; and partnership in these things is what makes a household and a city."[27] Human society of any kind stands, then, on a radically different footing from animal society. In particular, man is *more* political than the political animals—*in spite of* the fact that he "dualizes" between the family and political society—precisely because or insofar as the bond of community is reinforced by thought—that is, by calculation of what is good or advantageous.

It is because he holds this view that Aristotle can make the apparently paradoxical assertion that "there is in everyone by nature an impulse [*hormē*]" toward the political partnership, "yet the one who first constituted it is responsible for the greatest of goods"; for, he continues, "just as man is the best of the animals when completed, when separated from law and adjudication [*dikē*] he is the worst of all. For injustice is harshest when it is furnished with arms; and man is born naturally possessing arms for prudence and virtue which are nevertheless very susceptible to being used for their opposites. This is why, without virtue, he is the most unholy and the most savage, and the worst with regard to sex and food."[28] Man's possession of the power of reason creates or reflects a lati-

25. Consider particularly *Pol.* 1256a19–38.
26. For an appreciation of this point, see in particular G. Bien, *Die Grundlegung der politischen Philosophie bei Aristoteles* (Freiburg and Munich, 1973), 199–207, and Clark, *Aristotle's Man*, 140–42. Aristotle's account of the development of tragedy in the fourth chapter of the *Poetics* is frequently cited as a conspicuous example of Aristotle's tendency to view human constructs in organic terms; but a close reading of this passage will not sustain such an interpretation (see C. Lord, "Aristotle's History of Poetry," *TAPA* 104 [1974]: 195–229).
27. *Pol.* 1256a19–38.
28. Ibid. 1253a29–39.

tude or indeterminacy in his behavior that is unique among the animals.[29] Virtue is a function of habituation rather than nature, and in its absence man is prey to a peculiar kind of savagery: man alone is capable of incest and cannibalism—of violating even the most sacred or natural prohibitions. It is not altogether accidental, then, that the cannibalistic Cyclopes are presented by Aristotle as the paradigm of the earliest human society.[30]

More generally, the combination in man's nature of reason and passions that are uniquely and powerfully informed by reason would appear to create inherent tensions between individual human beings and the societies to which they belong. Man alone is capable of experiencing passions such as ambition, envy, or pride. These passions are essentially social and rational in that they presuppose a consciousness of human relationships, yet at the same time they separate men from their fellows and lead to actions that can be highly destructive of social bonds. At the extreme, such passions can lead to the destruction of the city itself or the perversion of its essential purposes through the criminal rule of the tyrant.[31] Yet not even those raised and habituated to virtue are immune to the effects of the passions that Aristotle, following Plato, associates with the "spirited" part of the human soul. "Spiritedness [*thymos*] perverts rulers and the best men," Aristotle warns; and even "great-souled men" (*hoi megalopsychoi*)—the exemplars of virtue according to Aristotle's ethical teaching—are capable of reacting "savagely" when they feel that an injustice has been done them.[32]

Of critical importance for understanding Aristotle's overall position is a passage in Book 7 of the *Politics*. Aristotle there distinguishes between three fundamentally different types of peoples or societies:

29. Aristotle seems to go out of his way to call attention to this indeterminacy by the way he refers to man's ability to "live pleasantly" by combining several different modes of subsistence; "need" or the natural environment only "partly compel[s]" (*synanankazai*) man's manner of life (*Pol.* 1256b2–4, 6–7). It is further reflected in human omnivorousness as well as in more specifically biological characteristics, on which see Clark, *Aristotle's Man*, 14–27.

30. Consider *Eth. Nic.* 1103a17–b25, 1148b15–1149a20. On the question of cannibalism, see, for example, Hdt. 4.106; Diod. Sic. 1.14.1; Pl. *Laws* 680b, 701c, 766a, 782b and *Epin.* 974e–76c; cf. T. L. Pangle, *The Laws of Plato* (New York, 1980), 423–29. For a provocative discussion in the context of modern anthropology, see M. Harris, *Cannibals and Kings: The Origins of Cultures* (New York, 1977).

31. "The greatest injustices are committed out of excess, not because of the necessary things—no one becomes a tyrant in order to get in out of the cold" (*Pol.* 1267a12–13). Aristotle follows Greek tradition in associating tyranny with *hybris*—the arrogant assertion of one's superiority over other men in defiance of conventional restraints; consider particularly *Pol.* 1311a22–b34.

32. *Pol.* 1287a30–31, 1328a8–12.

The nations in cold locations, particularly in Europe, are filled with spiritedness [*thymos*], but relatively lacking in discursive thought [*dianoia*] and art [*technē*]; hence they remain freer, but lack political governance [*apoliteuta*] and are incapable of ruling their neighbors. Those in Asia, on the other hand, have souls endowed with discursive thought and art, but are lacking in spiritedness; hence they remain ruled and enslaved. But the stock of the Greeks shares in both—just as it holds the middle in terms of location. For it is both spirited and endowed with discursive thought, and hence both remains free and governs itself in the best manner and at the same time is capable of ruling all, should it obtain a single regime. The peoples [*ethnē*] of Greece also display the same difference in relation to one another. Some have a nature that is one-sided, while others are well blended in relation to both of these capacities. It is evident, therefore, that those who are to be readily guided to virtue by the legislator should be both endowed with discursive thought and spirited in their nature. For as to what some assert should be present in guardians, to be friendly toward familiar persons but savage toward those who are unknown, it is spiritedness that creates friendliness [*to philētikon*]; for this is the capacity of soul by which we feel friendship. . . . What is ruling and what is free [*to archon kai to eleutheron*] in everyone stem from this capacity: spiritedness is a thing expert at ruling and indomitable [*archikon kai aēttēton*].[33]

This passage is of interest in the first instance because of the light it sheds on the relationship between impulse and reason as determinants of political behavior. As indicated earlier, Aristotle locates the roots of human sociality in a natural human impulse to live together regardless of any calculation of advantage. Here he makes clear that the impulse in question is "friendliness" or solidarity and that the source of this impulse is the spirited part of the human soul. At the same time, he suggests that reason or calculation is essential for the cooperation of human beings in common endeavors of some degree of complexity—political governance and the military organization necessary for conquering and dominating other peoples.

The passage is of interest in the second place because it provides critical clues to Aristotle's understanding of the nature of man's social impulse and the passion or complex of passions underlying it. Adapting and extending the discussion of the spirited part of the soul in Plato's *Republic*, Aristotle indicates that spiritedness is the source both of the human impulse to rule and of the human impulse to resist rule in the interests of freedom or human dignity; it underlies man's aggressiveness as well as his resistance to the aggression of others. Spiritedness is, then, the root of political society in a double sense. On the one hand, it is the source of the bond of solidarity that unites men in groups larger than

33. Ibid. 1327b23–1328a7.

the household and causes them to seek to defend and preserve such groups. On the other hand, it provides the fundamental impetus for rule or domination both within the group and relative to outsiders—an impetus that appears to be of central importance for understanding the development of large and complex political structures.

Finally, the passage under consideration is of interest because it indicates that the factors responsible for the development of political society do not in Aristotle's view operate universally or in uniform fashion. Evidently, spiritedness is by no means universally present or operative in individual human beings or in particular peoples. Climate and other physical factors appear to account for the differences to which Aristotle alludes. In the cold regions to the north of Greece, men are spirited and warlike, and hence able to resist political domination; in the warm areas to the east and south, on the other hand, men are lacking in spiritedness, and hence tend to be ruled by other peoples (in large empires such as Persia) or by kings exercising despotic power.[34] When Aristotle distinguishes between societies or peoples that are apt for monarchic rule and those that are apt for political rule,[35] he would seem to have in mind in the first instance these differences in the distribution of spiritedness. Aristotle makes clear that the *polis* is, if not simply a Greek phenomenon, at any rate a political form that flourishes only among certain peoples and under certain conditions. The *polis* can exist only among peoples who are endowed both with spiritedness and with the intelligence or capacity for discursive thought that makes possible both differentiated economic activity[36] and the complex organizational structures required for political governance and the effective conduct of war.

It is only in a distinctly qualified sense, then, that Aristotle can be said to hold that man is by nature a political animal. In any event, it should be clear that biological analogies are inappropriate and misleading in attempts to understand Aristotle's view of the evolution of societies. Aristotle suggests that political society, while indeed reflecting a natural impulse, comes into being through a discontinuous act, and one that evidently does not occur always and everywhere. Political society for Aristotle is not a natural given, but a problem to be explained. And this is even truer in the case of the *polis* as a specific type of political society, with its evident lack of universality and its deviation from the monarchic model of household governance.

34. Cf. *Pol.* 1285a16–22. Aristotle also appears to attribute spirited characteristics to particular peoples; consider especially 1269b23–27, 1324b5–22.

35. *Pol.* 1287b36–1288a19.

36. Compare *Pol.* 1327b23–25 with 1261a22–29; cf. 1328b2–23.

How precisely does Aristotle envision the development from the earliest human condition to organized society and the *polis?* Aristotle evidently rejects the idea—later associated with the Epicurean tradition—that men once lived as solitary and mutually hostile individuals.[37] Yet the picture he suggests of the original family is not a particularly attractive one. Apart from the imputation of cannibalism, it seems not unlikely that Aristotle regarded the relationship between man and woman in the original family as approaching that of master and slave, as in the case of the "barbarians" of his own time.[38] That the family so understood could have been economically self-sufficient seems questionable; Aristotle indicates that poor households lack slaves, but it is difficult to imagine that slavery can have existed as an institution at a time when men lived in isolated homesteads. Nor does Aristotle appear to regard the family as sufficient for the task of socialization or moral training. In an important passage in the *Nicomachean Ethics,* Aristotle justifies the existence of law supported by force with the remark that "a father's command lacks strength and the element of compulsion," while noting that it is only among the Spartans and similar peoples that the legislator takes thought for the upbringing of the young, whereas elsewhere "each lives as he likes, presiding Cyclops-style over his children and wife."[39] In what sense, or to what extent, can the family so understood be considered a natural or independently viable stage in human development?

It will be well at this point to consider more directly the possible clues to Aristotle's thinking on prepolitical society available to us in the extended discussions of this subject in Plato's *Laws* and in Polybius' history.[40] The former discussion was of course known to Aristotle, and there is every reason to suppose it was in his mind as he composed the *Politics.* The latter is part of a larger account that the author explicitly states is derived from "Plato and certain other philosophers," and is similar to, but clearly not wholly dependent on, the discussion in the *Laws.* Its sources are uncertain; they are generally assumed to be Academic or Stoic, though a case has also been made for the influence of a sophistic-atomistic tradition deriving from Democritus. While the issue cannot be

37. The radicalness of Epicurean assumptions as to the murderous inclinations of early man and the extent to which Epicurean views of the origins of society resemble those of Hobbes do not seem generally recognized. The fullest account is the report of Hermarchus' *Letters on Empedocles* given by Porphyry (*Abst.* 1.7–12). See generally V. Goldschmidt, *La doctrine d'Épicure et le droit* (Paris, 1977).
38. *Pol.* 1252b5–9; cf. 1268b38–42, where Aristotle suggests that the Greeks originally used "barbaric" customs—in particular, the purchase of women. Cf. Thuc. 1.6.
39. *Eth. Nic.* 1180a14–29.
40. Pl. *Laws* 677a–83a; Polyb. 6.5–7.

adequately treated here, it would seem that at least as strong a case could be made for Peripatetic influence, given the affinities of Polybius' account with what may be discerned of Aristotle's own position as well as the evidence of interest in such questions on the part of several of his students.[41]

Common to the accounts of Plato and Polybius are the following elements: a cataclysm destroys organized society and knowledge of the arts and sciences; the survivors are scattered and without rule or law; as they become more numerous they begin to live in herds under a single leader; the idea of justice develops and laws are created; kings arise and found cities.

Of particular interest, to begin with, is the relative de-emphasis of the role of the family or household by both Plato and Polybius. For Plato, the earliest social condition, consisting of men "scattered in single households or clans [*genē*]" and obeying the eldest "like a flock of birds," is already a "kind of political regime"; he calls this regime "rule of the powerful" (*dynasteia*)—a term used generally to designate a narrow oligarchy based on personal rule rather than law.[42] Polybius does not even mention the household but presents men as gathering initially in "groups" or "aggregates" (*systemata*),[43] remarking that it is likely that those of the same species would "herd together" on account of their "natural weakness."[44]

In attempting to come to grips with the argument of the first book of the *Politics*, it is important not to be misled either by biological analogies or by characteristically modern notions of evolution as a gradual process. Although his view of man's origins is nowhere clearly presented, it would appear that Aristotle too assumed that the world has no beginning but is subject to recurrent cataclysms that result in the destruction of society and the loss of all scientific and technical knowledge.[45] If this is the case, however, it would seem that the existence of autonomous families or households is for Aristotle not so much the natural and universal beginning point of social evolution as an accidental result of natural catastrophes. That early men lived in a "scattered" fashion is only partially a

41. On the sources of Polybius, see T. Cole, *Democritus and the Sources of Greek Anthropology*, Philological Monographs 25 (Cleveland, 1967), 80–96, 107–30. For the larger framework of Cole's approach, see E. A. Havelock, *The Liberal Temper in Greek Politics* (New Haven, 1957), together with the incisive critique of L. Strauss, *Liberalism Ancient and Modern* (New York, 1968), 26–64. Of the later Peripatetic material, the most significant was undoubtedly Dicaearchus' anthropological treatise *Life of Greece (Bios Hellados)*, frags. 47–66 Wehrli; Theophrastus also seems to have made some relevant contributions.

42. Pl. *Laws* 680a, d.

43. Polyb. 6.5.7; cf. *Eth. Nic.* 1168b32. See Cole, *Democritus*, 118, n. 29.

44. Polyb. 6.5.10.

45. *Pol.* 1269a4–8; *Metaph.* 1074b10–13. Cf. Clark, *Aristotle's Man*, 135–38.

function of man's nature as a "pairing" animal; it reflects also—and more fundamentally—the operation of external necessity.

In the account of the first book of the *Politics*, Aristotle indicates no reason for the transformation of the household into the village apart from a natural increase in persons tied by kinship; nor does he explain how monarchic rule of the village develops from patriarchal rule of the household. Clearly, economic considerations are important; the household may be "constituted by nature for the needs of daily life," as Aristotle says, but it is by no means clear that it is fully adequate to satisfy those needs. Aristotle almost certainly pictured the earliest men as hunter-gatherers or herdsmen.[46] It would seem to be the precariousness of these forms of subsistence that gives rise to piracy or brigandage (*lēsteia*) as a way of life and to war (including the hunting of human beings for slaves—or food) as a "natural" mode of acquisition, although Aristotle also seems anxious to argue that nature provides men with what is necessary for their sustenance.[47] At all events, it is a plausible assumption that man's original condition is for Aristotle if not a state of war, then a state of penury and insecurity, and that the "nondaily needs" that motivate the expansion of the household into the village are principally the need for cooperation in the production of food on a reliable basis (namely, agriculture) and the need for cooperation in meeting external threats.

As just indicated, however, it is not clear that such explanations are necessary in order to account for the supercession of the household by larger social structures, given Aristotle's understanding of the naturalness of man's social impulse. Indeed, it seems probable that Aristotle regarded the "Cyclopic" family alluded to at the beginning of the *Politics* as a deviation rather than a norm—as an essentially degraded or bestial condition. To recall Aristotle's well-known formulation, a person unwilling or unable to participate in organized society must be "either a beast or a god."[48] The norm—the primitive social condition that is most according to nature—would seem rather to be the "village," the "clan" (to use Plato's expression), or the "group" (in the terminology of Polybius).

Unfortunately, Aristotle has very little to say about the nature of the "village" (*kōmē*). He stresses its basis in kinship in order to explain its de-

46. Compare *Pol.* 1256a31–40 with the evolutionary process described by Dicaearchus, frags. 48–49 Wehrli, and Pl. *Laws* 678e–79a.

47. *Pol.* 1256a36–b22. According to Theophrastus (*On Piety*, frags. 2, 4 and 13 Pötscher), man was driven to cannibalism when it proved impossible to subsist on grass, his original food. On the prevalence of *lēsteia* in early Greece, see Thuc. 1.5.

48. *Pol.* 1253a27–29. On human bestiality, see *Eth. Nic.* 1145a15–33, 1148b15–1149a20.

velopment from the household, and indicates that, like the household, it is governed by the eldest as a kind of king.[49] This suggests that Aristotle understands both political rule and social solidarity as being rooted ultimately in the family or kinship relationships. In his account of friendship or solidarity (*philia*) in the *Nicomachean Ethics*, however, Aristotle draws a basic distinction between two types of solidarity, "solidarity based on kinship" (*syngenikē philia*) and "solidarity based on comradeship" (*hetairikē philia*), and indicates that the latter encompasses relations between fellow members of a tribe (*phylē*) as well as fellow citizens as such. That solidarity so understood could have its origin in the primitive village or group is eminently plausible.[50]

Also of relevance in this connection is Aristotle's view of the origin of the idea of justice and of the practice of adjudication. Aristotle concludes his discussion of the development of the *polis* in the first book of the *Politics* with the following remark: "The virtue of justice is a thing belonging to the city. For adjudication is an arrangement of the political partnership; and adjudication is judgment as to what is just."[51] In the discussion of justice in the *Nicomachean Ethics*, Aristotle confirms the identification of justice in the proper sense of the term with the city as distinct from the household. Only an analogy of justice is possible in relationships based on marriage or kinship, where the distinction between one's own good and the good of others is attenuated or nonexistent; justice in the proper sense exists only among equals whose relations are regulated by law. Yet Aristotle also suggests that there may be a kind of justice "in a simple sense" (*to haplōs dikaion*) that obtains among persons who are independent of one another and not subject to law; he calls justice of this sort

49. *Pol.* 1252b15–22.

50. *Eth. Nic.* 1161b12–23; cf. *Rh.* 1381b34. The *kōmē* should almost certainly be understood as a country district or canton (Lat. *pagus*) with a number of small settlements, rather than as a "village" in the sense of a proto-urban commercial center. Although fourth-century Attic usage seems to have distinguished *dēmos* as a country district from *kōmē* as a town quarter (Isoc. 7.46), Aristotle elsewhere (*Poet.* 1448a35–38) appears to endorse the claim that *kōmē* was a term used by the Dorians in an equivalent sense to designate "outlying districts" (*hai perioikidai*); that it was generally understood as an older institution than the classical *polis* appears from Thuc. 1.5, 10; Xen. *Hell.* 5.2.7. In anthropological terms, the *kōmē* would seem to be what is sometimes called a "commune," a cohesive social and territorial entity consisting of a number of "basic lineages" (*genē*, or "clans") held together by the requirements of exogamy and, not unusually, by a variety of associations not based on kinship. See particularly R. M. Bradfield, *A Natural History of Associations: A Study in the Meaning of Community*, Vol. 1 (London, 1973), 1–5, 151–89.

51. *Pol.* 1253a37–39; *hē de dikaiosynē politikon˙ hē gar dikē politikēs koinōnias taxis estin, hē de dikaiosynē tou dikaiou krisis*. This highly compressed statement has generally been misunderstood; *taxis* ("arrangement") means here "institution" or "practice," and *dikē* refers to the practice of adjudication rather than to "right" in an abstract sense.

"reciprocity" (*to antipeponthos*). It is justice of this sort that governs economic exchange as well as retaliation for injuries received or return of benefits, in circumstances where settled law is not available.[52] Justice so understood appears to reflect both a conscious calculation of advantage and an instinctive understanding of the requirements of social solidarity. Thus, as Aristotle remarks in the *Rhetoric*, there are "unwritten" rules of justice governing "gratitude to a benefactor, return of benefit to a benefactor, being ready to come to the assistance of friends, and similar things."[53] It makes sense to assume that Aristotle recognizes justice in this sense as a factor essential to the cohesion of prepolitical society.

Some insight into Aristotle's assumptions about the nature of prepolitical society may perhaps be derived from the treatment provided by Polybius. According to Polybius, "common upbringing and familiarity" (*syntrophia kai synētheia*) in the group gives rise to the first "conception" (*ennoia*) of the noble and just.[54] Because man is the only animal with the ability to think and calculate, men are offended when they see children who do not show gratitude toward or defend their parents, since they calculate that the same may happen to them; and a similar thing occurs in the case of persons who injure those who had come to their assistance in dangers. By the same token, those who defend their fellows in dangers are rewarded with marks of goodwill and preference. In this way, the conception of duty, justice, or nobility arises, stimulated by what is useful or advantageous (*to sympheron*) for the group. Originally, the group is "led and dominated" by the individual who is preeminent in both "sturdiness of body and daring of soul." When the leader is supportive of these notions of justice and comes to be considered by the others as one "skilled at distributing [*dianemētikos*] to each what accords with his merit," then he is no longer feared but rather esteemed for his judgment, and his rule is defended by common consent even when he becomes old. In this way, the "one-man rule" (*monarchia*) that characterizes the earliest society is gradually and insensibly transformed into "kingship" (*basileia*), as reason takes the place of "spiritedness [*thymos*] and strength" as the source of the leader's authority.[55]

52. *Eth. Nic.* 1132b21–1133a5.
53. *Rh.* 1374a18–25. This notion of reciprocity as a basic or crude form of justice essentially corresponds to the definition of justice as "helping friends and hurting enemies" that is discussed in Plato's *Republic* (331d–36a) and ascribed to Socrates in the *Clitophon* (410a–b).
54. Cf. *Eth. Nic.* 1161b33–36, 1177a15.
55. Polyb. 6.6.1–12.

It is important to be clear as to what distinguishes this account from ancient conventionalist theories and their modern counterparts.[56] Polybius appears to share with the Epicureans the view that justice involves a rational calculation of personal advantage, and political society grows out of the securing of justice so understood more than out of an instinctive social impulse. For the Epicureans, however, man has no instinctive social impulse. In the account of Lucretius, "friendship" (*amicities*) extending beyond the family is indistinguishable from agreement to abstain from mutual injury;[57] in the more elaborate account of Hermarchus, the earliest men had to be persuaded to refrain from killing one another by appeal to their mutual interest in self-preservation, and law and political society developed solely from a rational calculation of this advantage.[58] For Polybius, on the other hand, the earliest social groups seem to coalesce without benefit of rational calculation or agreement, and primarily for the sake of protection against wild animals rather than other men.[59] At the same time, "common upbringing and familiarity" serve to develop group solidarity based on an active expectation of mutual assistance rather than a passive abstention from harm. Friendship or solidarity is the precondition for justice and law rather than a by-product of it.

There are many points of contact between the account of Polybius and Aristotle. While he connects man's "political" nature with a social impulse that is independent of advantage, Aristotle admits and even stresses the weakness or lack of self-sufficiency of mankind under primitive conditions and the role of the useful or advantageous (*to sympheron*) as a motive for political evolution.[60] Nor does Aristotle draw a sharp distinction between utility and justice: speech or reason, we are told in the *Politics,* "serves to reveal the advantageous and the harmful, *and thus also the just and the unjust.*"[61] As noted above, Aristotle appears to regard justice in prepolitical society as deriving from a calculation of reciprocity in benefit and harm. At the same time, both Aristotle and Polybius seem to understand the city and justice as grounded ultimately not in some kind of contractual obligation but rather in the social solidarity of prepolitical society, a solidarity deriving not simply from a calculation

56. It is particularly instructive to compare Machiavelli's account of prehistory (*Discourses on Livy* 1.2) with the account of Polybius, its ostensible source; the differences are well analyzed by H. C. Mansfield, Jr., *Machiavelli's New Modes and Orders: A Study of the 'Discourses on Livy'* (Ithaca, N.Y., and London, 1979), 35–37.

57. Lucr. 5.1011–27.

58. Hermarchus *Letters on Empedocles,* apud Porph. *Abst.* 1.10–11. Cf. Cole, *Democritus,* 71–75.

59. Polyb. 6.6.8.   60. See particularly *Eth. Nic.* 1160a9–30.

61. *Pol.* 1253a14–15.

of reciprocity but from a common perception of the moral or noble (*to kalon*).[62] There is one feature of Polybius' account that is directly reminiscent of Aristotle's discussion of solidarity. Although it would not seem specifically required by his argument, Polybius carefully distinguishes between the cases of ingratitude toward parents and ingratitude toward friends or neighbors.[63] Aristotle distinguishes similarly, as has been seen, between "solidarity based on kinship" and "solidarity based on comradeship."

Finally, some remarks are in order concerning the question of the evolution of political rule in Aristotle and Polybius. In agreement with the usage of Plato in the *Laws*, both Aristotle and Polybius use the term *dynasteia* to refer to rulership in a prepolitical context. For Aristotle, a "dynasty" is not simply a narrow oligarchy based on personal rule and resort to violence, but a form of rule fundamentally incompatible with the organized society of the *polis*. This is particularly clear in his account of the political arrangements of the Cretans.[64] It appears that the aristocrats who monopolized the most powerful offices could be expelled from them by force or withdraw voluntarily, thereby suspending the operation of central political authority; this, Aristotle says, is "characteristic not of political but of dynastic rule." And indeed, he continues, it is habitual with the Cretans "to have followings among the people and their friends, create personal factions [*monarchiai*], and engage in factional conflict and fighting against one another," thus causing the virtual dissolution of the "political partnership." It is particularly noteworthy that Aristotle uses the term *monarchia* to refer to the groups formed and dominated by the Cretan dynasts.

Nothing in Aristotle's treatment of the phenomenon of "dynastic" rule suggests that the basis of such rule is kinship or rule of the eldest. Accordingly, one is forced to raise the question whether the account of the origins of political rule in the first book of the *Politics* can be considered adequate in this respect. Polybius suggests quite a different origin of rulership in the earliest society. In his account, the leader of the first groups is distinguished not by age but by bodily strength as well as "daring of soul" or "spiritedness." Though the argument is not stated explicitly, it would seem to be this quality of soul that accounts for the ease with which the leader is transformed from one who dominates through strength and fear into one who rules through an understanding

62. Consider *Pol.* 1253a15–18: "For it is peculiar to man as compared to the other animals that he alone has a perception of good and bad and just and unjust and other things of this sort; and partnership in these things is what makes a household and a city."

63. Polyb. 6.6.2–6.

64. *Pol.* 1272b1–15.

of justice and its fair administration; for spiritedness is intimately bound up with the political passion for honor and recognition. The very fact that Polybius makes conspicuous use of the term *thymos* in this context is suggestive of a Platonic-Aristotelian source; and the argument supplies a dynamic factor in the development of primitive rulership that is missing in the account of *Politics* 1. It may be added that this sort of "charismatic" leadership in fact closely approximates contemporary anthropological descriptions of the primitive forms of rule observable in "band" or "segmentary" societies.[65]

Also paralleling Polybius is Aristotle's treatment of the origins and character of early kingship in the third book of the *Politics*.[66] According to this account,

> because the first kings had been benefactors of the multitude in connection with the arts or war or by bringing them together [in a city] or providing them land, these came to be kings over willing persons, and their descendants took over from them. They had authority regarding leadership in war and those sacrifices that did not require priests; in addition to this, they were judges in legal cases.

For Aristotle as for Polybius, the foundation of cities is a *result*—not the cause—of the establishment of kingship. Aristotle seems to go farther than Polybius, however, in suggesting that early kingship is not a form of political rule either in the sense of being a regime of the *polis* or in the sense of exercising true state authority. Early kingship, or what Aristotle calls "kingship of the heroic age," so far from being an absolutist rule modeled on paternal government of the household, is rather for him a limited form of leadership based on consent of the ruled and lacking the critical power of compulsion ("authority in matters of life and death") except in the course of military operations.[67] Aristotle's sketch of the king whose functions are essentially restricted to military leadership, adjudication of certain kinds of disputes, and certain religious duties in fact strikingly resembles the picture anthropologists have constructed of chieftainship in prestate societies.[68]

It may be helpful at this point to make some broader observations concerning the character of Aristotle's "anthropology" and its relationship to modern political philosophy as well as to contemporary anthropology. To the extent that modern social-contract theorists acknowledge a subpolitical or prepolitical source of human sociality, they find it in

65. See Service, *Origins of State and Civilization,* 47–70.
66. *Pol.* 1285b6–11.
67. Ibid. 1285a7–14, b4–5, 20–23.
68. See Service, *Origins of State and Civilization,* 71–102.

man's reproductive instinct and in the institution of the family.[69] Contemporary anthropologists, while generally rejecting the radical individualism posited by these theorists, have nevertheless tended to look to the family and to kinship relationships generally as the critical element in the constitution and evolution of primitive societies. If the analysis offered here is correct, Aristotle's approach was substantially different. For Aristotle, man's political nature seems to have a foundation that is independent of the family and kinship. In addition to his characterization of human beings as "dualizers" and in harmony with that characterization, Aristotle distinguishes between "solidarity based on kinship" and "solidarity based on comradeship." If anything may be concluded from the account of Polybius as to Aristotle's position, it seems clear that for Aristotle both sorts of relationship are of significance in developing man's notions of justice and nobility.

What is the origin or foundation of "solidarity of comradeship" in primitive society? The suggestion may be hazarded that Aristotle understood male comradeship, as manifested originally in cooperation in hunting and war, as the distinctive expression of man's "political" nature and as a critical causal factor in the evolution of political society. While admittedly hypothetical, this interpretation makes good sense in the context of Aristotle's appreciation of the importance of military organization in the evolution of the *polis* itself,[70] his understanding of the distinctive character of the Spartan regime, and his own prescriptions for the social organization of the best regime. Sparta lay before Aristotle as a striking example of a society oriented strongly toward war and based on communal social institutions that excluded women and fostered homosexuality among men.[71] In his own best regime, Aristotle tries to avoid the disadvantages of the Spartan system but relies on similar institutional arrangements—communal eating societies and age classes—to promote solidarity and minimize class stratification within the citizen body.[72]

It is characteristic of modern political philosophy that it ignores the (public or private) institutions or associations that mediate the relationship between the individual and the state and constitute the primary focus of social or civic activity for most persons at most times.[73] In a simi-

69. Consider, for example, John Locke, *Two Treatises on Government*, II, chap. 8, secs. 105, 110; David Hume, *Treatise of Human Nature*, bk. 3, chap. 2, sec. 2.
70. *Pol.* 1297b16–28, 1321a5–26.
71. Ibid. 1269a29–1271b19; consider especially 1269b13–37.
72. *Pol.* 1330a3–8, 1332b36–1333a11.
73. Noteworthy exceptions are Bodin, Althusius, and Hegel. For an illuminating account, see A. Black, *Guilds and Civil Society in European Political Thought from the Twelfth Century to the Present* (Ithaca, N.Y., 1984).

lar way, the role of nonkinship institutions and associations in primitive and other societies has been systematically neglected by modern anthropologists. In recent years, however, there has been a growing awareness among anthropologists of the importance of such phenomena and the need to achieve a better understanding of them. Of particular interest is the important political function evidently performed by male associations in at least some prestate societies.[74]

The idea that war and conquest are the key to understanding the historical development of socially stratified societies and the state, most fully developed in the nineteenth century in the historical sociology of Herbert Spencer, has reappeared in recent anthropological discussions of the formation of primary states.[75] The weakness of such theories lies in the fact that they tend to assume what needs explanation—namely, the existence of organized human groups capable of engaging in sustained combat for the sake of a common objective.[76] Because he does not begin from a position of radical individualism, Aristotle is able to account for the importance of war in social existence without understanding it as the factor that explains the major discontinuities in social evolution. For him, war is a by-product or epiphenomenon of politics. As we have seen, the effective conduct of war and the domination of other societies are possible only for those peoples who combine a spirited temper with the intelligence and organizing ability required for political governance.

For similar reasons, Aristotle's approach differs fundamentally from theories of Marxist inspiration that trace the origins of political rule and the state to the unequal development of private ownership and the rise of class structures. In agreement with what in fact appears the most plausible interpretation of the contemporary anthropological evidence, Aristotle presents differentiated ownership of land as an effect, rather than the cause, of early kingship.[77] This is by no means to deny the importance for Aristotle of economic factors and of differences in wealth in shaping political conflict and the nature of political regimes. In Aris-

74. The classic account is H. Schürtz, *Altersklassen und Männerbunde* (Berlin, 1902). See more recently, for example, P. Bohannen, *Social Anthropology* (New York, 1963), 144–63; Bradfield, *History of Associations,* vol. 2, 442–93; and (particularly for the political importance of age classes in prestate societies) B. Bernardi, *Age Class Systems,* trans. D. I. Kertzer (Cambridge, 1985).

75. See especially R. L. Carneiro, "Political Expansion as an Expression of the Principle of Competitive Exclusion," in *Origins of the State,* ed. Cohen and Service, 205–23; and H. S. Lewis, "Warfare and the Origins of the State: Another Formulation," in *The Study of the State,* ed. H. J. M. Claessen and P. Skalník (The Hague, 1981), 200–221.

76. Cf. Service, *Origins of State and Civilization,* 37–44.

77. *Pol.* 1285b6–11; compare Polybius' remark (6.10) concerning the role of the monarch in "distribution." Cf. Service, *Origins of State and Civilization,* 266–308.

totle's view, however, disputes over property are in the last analysis only
manifestations of more deeply rooted differences in the way men understand justice and seek recognition within the political community. In
particular, Aristotle would certainly consider intolerably reductionist
any effort to explain the phenomenon of political rule by material factors alone. For Aristotle, men are motivated in their political behavior
at least as much by a desire for honor as by a desire for wealth; and
the dynamics of political rule become incomprehensible if the psychological realities summarized in the term "spiritedness" are forgotten or
underestimated.[78]

Of particular relevance in this connection is the question of the origins and development of the classical *polis*. In the early modern period,
those writing under the influence of Machiavelli and the political philosophy of classical liberalism tended to stress the warlike origins and outlook of the ancient republics (often in contrast with the peaceful orientation of modern commercial republics such as England). The more recent
tendency, reflecting the influence of Fustel de Coulanges' classic study of
the ancient city,[79] has been to emphasize the role of religion and kinship
organization in the evolution of the *polis* from its tribal antecedents. In
the last few years, however, this approach has been sharply questioned,
and the "political" character of the *polis* has been reasserted against those
attempting to understand its social institutions as survivals of primitive
kinship organizations. In particular, it has been persuasively argued that
the phratries ("brotherhoods") of the Greek city most probably origi-
nated as mutual aid societies based on residence rather than as exten-
sions of kinship groups and that the same may have been true of aristocratic "clans" (*genē*) and "clubs" (*hetairiai*).[80] It seems clear in any event

78. While the question of Aristotle's relationship to contemporary economic anthropology cannot be discussed here, it may be noted that there is an important congruence between Aristotle's approach to economic phenomena and recent theories of the "embeddedness" of primitive economies in social and political relationships. See in particular K.
Polanyi, "Aristotle Discovers the Economy," in *Trade and Market in the Early Empires*, ed. K.
Polanyi, G. Arensberg, and H. W. Pearson (Glencoe, Ill., 1957), 64–94; M. I. Finley, "Aristotle and Economic Analysis," *Past and Present* 47 (1970): 3–25; and S. C. Humphreys, *Anthropology and the Greeks* (London, 1978), 31–75, 136–74. As regards the role of spiritedness in primitive society and its relationship to the economic order, compare Polybius'
comments concerning the leader who is "reputed by his subjects to be skilled at distributing
to each what accords with his merit" with the phenomenon of "bigmanism" in band societies such as those of the Solomon Islands (see, for example, Harris, *Cannibals and Kings*,
69–82).
79. N. D. Fustel de Coulanges, *La cité antique* (Paris, 1864). See Finley, "The Ancient
City," in *Economy and Society*, 3–23.
80. D. Roussel, *Tribu et cité*, Annales littéraires de l'Université de Besançon (Paris, 1970).

that such structures were decisively shaped, if not actually created, by the *polis* or in response to the requirements of the *polis* from the earliest times, as indeed was the household.[81] Such a view would seem quite in harmony with the position of Aristotle, who gives little ground for supposing that kinship relationships—or religion—played a significant role in the development of the *polis*.[82]

If anthropologists tend to assume that human nature is almost completely malleable and hence that culture is the decisive variable in man's development, sociobiologists tend to view that development as the outcome of the interaction of man's material and reproductive requirements with his environment. Aristotle's approach is wholly different. While admitting that human rationality is the source of a certain indeterminacy or malleability in human nature, Aristotle assumes that there are fundamental regularities in human behavior that are in some sense materially conditioned. At the same time, the regularities he recognizes cannot be understood in terms of material or reproductive requirements in a narrow sense. As discussed earlier, Aristotle holds that the human soul uniquely combines reason with "spiritedness"—a certain complex or type of passion that is distinctively human in that it is essentially concerned with the relationship of man to society. The strength of reason or spiritedness in individuals and peoples differs in accordance with material conditions of various kinds. However, it is not material circumstances as such but rather the interaction between reason and spiritedness in a people that fundamentally determines the pace and character of the development of political structures.

The character and implications of the complex phenomenon comprehended by Plato and Aristotle under the term *thymos* cannot be ade-

81. Max Weber's remarks on the rise of the city as a "confraternity" remain pertinent; see G. Roth and C. Wittich, eds., *Economy and Society*, vol. 2 (Berkeley and London, 1978), 1241–46. Compare also E. Meyer, *Elemente der Anthropologie*, Geschichte des Altertums I.1 (1894; reprint, Stuttgart, 1953), 5–19 (both Meyer and Weber were evidently influenced on this question by Schürtz, *Altersklassen und Männerbunde*). In a recent general analysis of the family and its relation to society, Claude Lévi-Strauss emphasizes the universality of the nuclear family, while at the same time arguing that the family cannot be reduced to its natural base or that "no family could exist if there were not first a society," that society generally "mistrusts the family and contests its right to exist as a separate entity," and that societies where family bonds are extremely weak (the example given is the Nayar of the Malibar coast of India, whose way of life strikingly resembles classical Sparta) "represent an extreme form of a tendency that is far more frequent in human societies than is generally believed" (*The View From Afar*, trans. J. Neugroschel and P. Hoss [New York, 1985], 39–62). See also W. K. Lacey, *The Family in Classical Greece* (Ithaca, N.Y., 1968), 51–83.

82. There is an interesting contrast in this connection between Aristotle's position and that of Ibn Khaldûn, who sees religion as an important component of "solidarity" (ʿaṣabiyya) and at the same time fails to recognize the *polis* as a distinct type of political society (see Mahdi, *Ibn Khaldûn's Philosophy*, 204–16, 261–70).

quately discussed here.[83] Clearly, however, it is of central importance for understanding Aristotle's view of the nature of the *polis* and the character and origins of political rule, providing, as it does, a critical link between man's biological and psychological nature and the structures of human society. Indeed, it is one of the features of classical political philosophy generally that most distinguishes it both from modern political philosophy and from contemporary social science. Unfortunately, the absence of a thematic discussion of it in the surviving works of Plato and Aristotle has caused its significance to be missed or underestimated.

Perhaps the principal objection to the foregoing argument will be that it unreasonably discounts the plain words of the single passage in which Aristotle coherently addresses anthropological issues, while seeking to reconstruct Aristotle's position from a combination of scattered and possibly casual statements and the evidence of other authors—notably Polybius—whose relationship to Aristotle is arguable at best. A full answer to this objection would require a comprehensive analysis of Book 1 of the *Politics* and its place within the work as a whole. It must suffice to refer to what was said earlier regarding the practical intention of the *Politics* and to reiterate that what seems to be a misleading emphasis on the household as the *fons et origo* of the *polis* can be readily explained as reflecting a double rhetorical intention on Aristotle's part. Aristotle is concerned in the first place to establish the naturalness of the *polis* and of political rule against the theoretical challenge posed by Greek conventionalism. In the second place, Aristotle is concerned not to reinforce—and may be argued to have an interest in combating actively—prevailing Greek conceptions of the role of war, manly virtue, and male association in political life.[84] For both of these reasons, it seems more than doubtful that Aristotle would have wished to elaborate his theoretical anthropology fully, whether in the *Politics* or elsewhere. This is unfortunate, since it would appear that Aristotle's theoretical approach has a richness that is lacking in the subsequent tradition of political philosophy, and at the same time is in many respects surprisingly close to plausible contemporary interpretations of man's political evolution.

83. An appreciation of its role in Aristotle may be found in L. Berns, "Spiritedness in Ethics and Politics: A Study in Aristotelian Psychology," *Interpretation* 12 (1984): 335–48. See also P. A. Vander Waerdt, "The Peripatetic Interpretation of Plato's Tripartite Psychology," *Greek, Roman and Byzantine Studies* 26 (1985): 283–302.

84. See S. G. Salkever, "Women, Soldiers, Citizens: Plato and Aristotle on the Politics of Virility," in this volume.

THREE

The "Infrastructure" of Aristotle's *Politics:* Aristotle on Economics and Politics

Abram N. Shulsky

INTRODUCTION

Greek political men, who lived under popular government, recognized no other force that could sustain them than that of virtue. Those of today speak to us only of manufacturing, commerce, finance, riches and even luxury.[1]

This observation of Montesquieu encapsulates a common view of Aristotle's political thought, and of ancient Greek political philosophy in general. According to that view Aristotle and other Greek philosophers did not, in the course of philosophizing about politics and about the best political order, take seriously the economic underpinnings or "infrastructure" of the society with which they were dealing. A consequence of this view, as Karl Polanyi notes, is that Aristotle's "economics" has in our day fallen into "contempt." Polanyi finds this somewhat paradoxical:

Very few thinkers have been listened to on a greater diversity of subjects over so many centuries as [Aristotle]. Yet on a matter to which he devoted a signal effort and which happens also to be reckoned among the issues vital to our own generation, the economy, his teachings are judged inadequate by the leading spirits of the time to the point of irrelevance.[2]

One can identify several types of reactions to Aristotle's writings on economics. One view holds that since Aristotle lived before the era of the market, he could not have understood very much about economics; the

---

Translations of the Greek text of Aristotle's *Politics* are taken from C. Lord, *The* Politics *of Aristotle* (Chicago, 1984).

1. Montesquieu, *De l'esprit des lois,* bk. 3, chap. 3.
2. K. Polanyi, "Aristotle Discovers the Economy," in *Trade and Market in the Early Empires,* ed. K. Polanyi, C. M. Arensberg, and H. W. Pearson (Glencoe, Ill., 1957), 65.

relevant phenomena (such as a market in which prices are set by the free interaction of supply-and-demand factors) simply did not yet exist, and hence could not be observed. For example, a standard history of economics by Alexander Gray judges that although "Aristotle . . . went further than any other thinker in antiquity in the direction of detaching a separate science of economics,"[3] nevertheless

> the ancient world, even as represented by Athens, was in many ways but a poor soil for any kind of economic speculation; and consequently, unless to those who are fanatically determined to find everything in antiquity, adumbrations of economic theory among the Greeks will rather appear in the form of incidental observations, thrown off in the pursuit of a more worthy end.[4]

In particular, Gray alleges two causes why economics could not develop in ancient Greece. First was the predominance of ethical and political inquiry in the context of the comprehensive society of the ancient *polis:*

> Economics was not merely the handmaiden of Ethics (as perhaps she should always be); she was crushed and blotted out by her more prosperous and pampered sister, and later excavators, in search of the origins of economic theory, can only dig out disconnected fragments and mangled remains.[5]

Second, the existence of a slave class and the relegation to it of important sectors of economic activity resulted in a contempt for work among the thinkers of ancient Greece:

> To the Greek mind nearly all the activities of modern society would have appeared unworthy and debasing. . . . If the "ordinary business of life" was thus despised, it is hardly reasonable to expect that its study should be regarded as a subject worthy of sustained and independent investigation.[6]

Another view is that the market was already coming into existence in Aristotle's time, but that Aristotle himself was too aristocratic in his prejudices or too idealistic in his approach to social reality to evaluate it realistically, or perhaps was simply too inattentive to notice. Joseph Schumpeter, for example, explains what he views as the limitations of Aristotle's economic thought partly as follows:

> Nothing would be easier than to show that . . . the economic facts and relations between economic facts which [Aristotle] considered and evaluated appear in the light of the ideological preconceptions to be expected in a man who lived in, and wrote for, a cultivated leisure class, which held work

3. A. Gray, *The Development of Economic Doctrine* (London, 1934), 22.
4. Ibid., 13.   5. Ibid., 14.   6. Ibid., 14–15.

and business pursuits in contempt and, of course, loved the farmer who fed it and hated the money lender who exploited it.[7]

Similarly, M. I. Finley insists that

> nowhere in the *Politics* does Aristotle ever consider the rules or mechanics of commercial exchange. On the contrary, his insistence on the un-naturalness of commercial gain rules out the possibility of such a discussion, and also helps explain the heavily restricted analysis in the *Ethics*. Of economic analysis there is not a trace.[8]

Ultimately, the reason for this lack of interest may be found in the view, held by Aristotle but given its fullest expression by Xenophon in *Ways and Means*, that "what we call the economy was properly the exclusive business of outsiders."[9]

In either case, Aristotle's remarks about economics tend to be seen as precursors of the corresponding theorem of modern economics; as such, they may be treated respectfully, in deference to Aristotle's reputation, or scornfully, in view of the large gap between the Aristotelian dictum and the modern theorem. However this may be, the interest in Aristotle's economics, on this basis, would be from the point of view of the prehistory of economic ideas, which are, of course, better understood now than they possibly could have been by Aristotle.

If our goal, however, is to understand Aristotle, to say nothing of the possibility of learning from him, then these views are deficient in that they take as given that the approach of modern economics is the standard to which Aristotle must be compared and in terms of which his economic ideas must be understood as either foresighted, wrongheaded, or, in Finley's view, simply nonexistent. According to this approach, economics is the study of the "economy," which is seen as a social structure, theoretically separable and, to a large extent, practically separate from the state, and governed by its own laws. Economics looks at the effects of outside forces (such as political interference, technological change, environmental changes) on the economy, but it treats those factors as just that—forces from the "outside" that affect the economy, but do not change the laws by which it operates. On the other hand, economics does not look at the effects the economy might have in other realms, as politics or "culture," for example.

Clearly, Aristotle cannot be understood at all if we are unwilling to put aside this view of economics, at least for the moment. We must keep

---

7. J. A. Schumpeter, *History of Economic Analysis*, ed. E. B. Schumpeter (New York, 1954), 60.

8. M. I. Finley, "Aristotle and Economic Analysis," *Past and Present* 47 (1970): 18.

9. Ibid., 25.

in mind that while some form of economic activity (in the sense of the interaction between man and his physical environment by means of which he satisfies his material needs) is a necessity, these activities need not form their own sphere of human life; they can be part and parcel of other facets of society. In fact, Polanyi argues that the separation of the economy from other facets of society was a development that, historically, took place in the ancient Greece of Aristotle's time. He claims: "In Aristotle's writings we possess an eye witness account of some of the pristine features of incipient market trading at its very first appearance in the history of civilization."[10] For Polanyi, this unique historical perspective accounts for the worth of Aristotle's writings on economics:

> It may seem paradoxical to expect that the last word on the nature of economic life should have been spoken by a thinker who hardly saw its beginnings. Yet Aristotle, living, as he did, on the borderline of economic ages, was in a favored position to grasp the merits of the subject.[11]

Whether or not Polanyi's claim with respect to the history of the market economy should be accepted and whether or not the breadth and direction of Aristotle's thought can be explained in this manner, it will be argued here that Aristotle's importance as an economic thinker resides precisely in the fact that he very carefully evaluates the political effects of the "emancipation" of the economy. While his thought has not come down to us in as systematic or clear a form as we might wish, this essay will attempt to show that it can, nevertheless, be reasonably well understood and that we have more to work with than "disconnected fragments and mangled remains."

ARISTOTLE'S APPROACH TO ECONOMICS

Our first task must be to identify the approach Aristotle took to the study of economics, since, as noted above, it is not the same as that of modern economics. A good beginning point is Aristotle's own description of economics as a *practical,* as opposed to a *theoretical,* science, one that is closely related to, and indeed forms a part of, the overarching practical science, namely, political science.

According to Aristotle, economics is a kind of prudence (*phronēsis*).[12] As such, it deals with the "human things" (*ta anthrōpina*) and with deliberation about the ways of attaining the human good by means of human

10. Polanyi, "Aristotle Discovers the Economy," in *Trade and Market,* ed. Polanyi, Arensberg, and Pearson, 67.
11. Ibid., 78–79.
12. *Eth. Nic.* 1141b30–32.

action.[13] Unlike theoretical science (*epistēmē*), it does not deal with those things that exist "by necessity," that is, that cannot be other than they are.[14] Aristotle's distinction between *phronēsis* (prudence or practical science) and *epistēmē* (theoretical science) bears a surface resemblance to, but is actually quite different from, the distinction between pure and applied science with which we are familiar from modern science. In the current view, a pure science attempts to understand a given realm of phenomena; it ultimately results in the discovery of a set of laws that "govern," that is, precisely describe, those phenomena. An applied science then applies those laws to particular situations, thereby enabling man to manipulate the phenomena so as to produce a desired result.

In the case of modern economics, the goal is to discover those laws that "govern" such phenomena as markets, prices, and levels of production. To the extent that economics can be "applied," it is possible to turn those laws into conditional prescriptions for action in a given situation: to reach result X, do Y. Economics does not prove, or even assert, that result X is "good" in any sense. In the case where X equals "prosperity," this distinction, whatever its theoretical interest, appears to those engaged in government and politics to be a mere quibble. (On the other hand, to the extent that someone might claim that he regards equality of income, or the suppression of the putatively evil consequences of affluence, as more important than prosperity, then no amount of economic reasoning can gainsay him.)

For Aristotle, the situation is entirely different: as a practical science, economics must be concerned with the human good and with the human actions necessary to attain it. As the beginning of the *Nicomachean Ethics* makes clear, this ultimately means that economics must be a part, in some way, of political science.[15] In other words, the economic phenomena will always be discussed and analyzed in the light of the political context and, in particular, of their consistency with a political regime based on the best principles.

Thus Aristotle's economics cannot be an analysis of the free play of economic forces; rather, the key question is whether such an "emancipa-

13. Ibid., 1141b8–12.

14. Ibid. Aristotle's discussion of *epistēmē* (theoretical science) at *Eth. Nic.* 1140b31–32 emphasizes the importance of the distinction between those things that are "by necessity" (i.e., that cannot be other than they are) and those that can be changed by human action and hence may be fit subjects for deliberation.

15. *Eth. Nic.* 1094a26–b3. In this passage, Aristotle seems to say that economics is subordinate to political science, while in the passages in Book 6 cited above, he seems to regard both economics and political science as parts of prudence or *phronēsis*. The key difference is whether prudence or political science should be regarded as the architectonic practical science, the one that deals with the complete human good.

tion" of economics is good or bad. This does not mean, however, that Aristotle's inquiry is of a hopelessly utopian or idealistic nature. As will become clear, Aristotle knew not only that there were strong forces tending to "liberate" the economy from its appropriate status as a subordinate part of the polity, but also that under some circumstances there might be political advantages to accommodating them. His resistance to these forces is based on neither blindness nor stubbornness, but rather on a consideration of the effects of various economic arrangements on the overall political goals of a society.

ARISTOTLE'S INQUIRY INTO ECONOMICS

Natural Acquisition

As we would expect from the above, Aristotle's main inquiry into economics takes place in the context of his discussion of politics; in particular, it is part of his discussion of the status of the political community or city (*polis*) with respect to the households it contains and, ultimately, with respect to nature.[16] Aristotle presents himself as a defender of the city against those who would deny its dignity or its natural status. In the course of the discussion he rebuts the contentions of those who, like the Eleatic Stranger in Plato's *Statesman*, deny the existence of essential differences between the household and the city or between political government and economics understood as the management of a household (*oikonomia* in its original sense). He also refutes those who, like the Sophists, argue that the city and its laws lack all natural status but exist only by convention, that is, by human agreement.

Aristotle's discussion of economics is thus undertaken to investigate the truth of certain assertions about the city and the relationship between political life and other human activities. His purpose in isolating economic phenomena to the extent that he does in the first book of the *Politics* is to defend the naturalness of the city's economic foundation (as part of his defense of the city's naturalness) and, at the same time, to point to the essentially political realm that lies beyond economics.[17]

Aristotle distinguishes between the city and the household in the course of his "natural history" of the city. The household is described as

16. Outside of the *Politics,* Aristotle's most important discussion of a major economic topic is found in Book 5 of the *Nicomachean Ethics,* where, in the context of a discussion of "political justice," he takes up the question of justice in the exchange of goods among the artisans of a city. (In addition, there exists a three-book work, entitled *Oeconomica,* which was traditionally attributed to Aristotle but which is now generally believed to be spurious.)

17. For a discussion of the importance of the question of the city's naturalness, and of Aristotle's nuanced handling of it, see W. H. Ambler, "Aristotle's Understanding of the Naturalness of the City," *Review of Politics* 47 (1985): 163–85.

"the partnership constituted by nature for [the needs of] daily life" (1252b13–14).[18] The village, and, *a fortiori*, the city are "for the sake of nondaily needs" (1252b16); the city strives to reach a level of full self-sufficiency. Despite some difficulties, Aristotle proceeds, for the bulk of the first book, on the assumption that the city, as opposed to the household, is the source of virtue and justice.[19] Although Aristotle retains, in a formal sense, the notion that economics is primarily the management of the household in terms of the relationship with its dependent parts (wife, children, and slaves), the greatest part of the discussion of the household is nonetheless devoted to the provision of food and the other material necessities of life, in other words, to economic needs in the modern sense of the term.[20]

Thus the acquisition of property becomes a main theme of the first book, and the general term *chrēmatistikē* is introduced. This term refers to the art of acquiring property; property, however, is understood as those things that are capable of being evaluated in terms of money,[21] and so *chrēmatistikē* means something like "money-making ability" or "business expertise." The question of whether *chrēmatistikē* is a part of economics or merely a separate and subordinate activity gives rise to its division into a natural part and an unnatural part; the natural part is a part of economics, while the unnatural part is not.[22]

This division rests on the fundamental tenet that nature provides the things that man needs to survive; those modes of acquisition that merely take from nature what it stands ready to provide are natural, while those that make possible the accumulation of money without having direct recourse to the natural sources of useful things are unnatural.

Aristotle attempts to defend this fundamental principle by comparing

18. This and similar references appearing within the text are to Aristotle's *Politics*.

19. As regards the difficulties mentioned, at 1253a18, Aristotle states that "partnership in these things [i.e., good and bad and just and unjust] is what makes a *household* and a *city*" (emphasis added). Thus it appears that virtue and justice are not the exclusive preserve of the city, despite the implication of Aristotle's discussion of virtue and justice at 1253a1–17. See Ambler, "Naturalness of the City," 171.

20. Our use of the word *economics* is not so different from ordinary Greek usage as one might conclude from Aristotle's insistence on treating the proper conduct of the marital, paternal, and master-slave relationships as the core of *oikonomia*. As he notes at 1253b12–13, some hold "business expertise" (*chrēmatistikē*) "to be [identical with] household management [*oikonomia*], and others its greatest part."

21. *Eth. Nic.* 1119b26.

22. Aristotle's usage is by no means consistent. Sometimes the term *chrēmatistikē* refers to both parts and sometimes only to the unnatural part. There are some cases (mentioned in W. Newman, *The Politics of Aristotle*, vol. 2 [Oxford, 1887], 165, note to 1256a1) in which the term seems to refer to the natural part only, but then it must be so qualified (e.g., *chrēmatistikē kata physin*, "chrematistics" according to nature, and *oikonomikē chrēmatistikē*, economic "chrematistics"). On the other hand, the unnatural part is "particularly" and "justifiably" called *chrēmatistikē* (1256b40–41).

the various kinds of life led by different groups of men (nomadic, hunting, and agricultural, for example) with the various kinds of life led by the animal species; in each case, the source of food seems to be the major determinant of the kind of life led. For instance, the grazing animals are generally solitary. As Aristotle remarks, "the differences in sustenance have made the ways of life of animals differ" (1256a21–22).

The situation is similar with respect to human beings. For instance, the nomads, living off their flocks, must move from place to place as new pasturage must be found; farmers, on the other hand, remain in one place. Nature seems to provide for the different groups of men, just as it does for the different species of beasts; if we regard the compatibility between the animals' behavior and their mode of obtaining food as due to nature, how can we deny to nature the credit for that same compatibility in the case of the various groups of men?

The similarity between animals and men with respect to their obtaining food is, however, only superficial. In the case of animals, nature may be said to provide for their nourishment in that their instincts are consistent with their environments and their internal constitutions. In the case of man, however, the different modes of obtaining food must be learned; furthermore, since there is no guarantee that any particular mode will suffice, it may be necessary to combine two different ones.[23]

Perhaps influenced by the difficulties with the analogy between nature's provision of food for the animals and for man, Aristotle adduces another natural phenomenon that seems to indicate a natural providence: humans, as well as all other animals, have food provided for them in their infancy, whether as milk or in some other form. Aristotle claims that there must be a similar providence for adult human beings as well. Aristotle's conclusion is nevertheless tentative:

> One must suppose both that plants exist for the sake of animals and that the other animals exist for the sake of human beings—the tame animals, both for use and sustenance, and most if not all of the wild animals, for sustenance and other assistance, in order that clothing and other instruments may be got from them. (1256b15–20)

A further "scientific," if hypothetical, proof is added:

> If, then, nature makes nothing that is incomplete or purposeless, nature must necessarily have made all of these for the sake of human beings. (1256b20–22)[24]

23. "There are also some who live pleasantly by combining several of these in order to compensate for the shortcomings of one way of life, where it happens to be deficient with regard to being self-sufficient" (1256b2–4). Thus Aristotle acknowledges a difficulty in the simple view of nature's providence for man: what man, as compared with the animals, lacks in instinct, he makes up for in adaptability.

24. Since the phrase "all of these" (*auta panta*) appears to include the wild animals, it

The discussion of natural acquisition concludes with the observation that expertise in such acquisition "is by nature a part of expertise in household management [*oikonomikē*]" (1256b27–28). Its goal is the acquisition of those goods "a store of which is both necessary for life and useful for partnership in a city or a household" (1256b29–30). In this connection, Aristotle takes exception to Solon's verse "of wealth no boundary lies revealed to men" (1256b33–34). Against this view, Aristotle claims that a limit is set by the material requirements of the good life; any goods possessed in excess of that optimal amount are of no use and hence cannot be considered true wealth. To support this claim, he relies on the analogy of the other arts, in which tools of an optimal size and number are required: bigger or more tools would be of no use, and would perhaps even be a hindrance, to the practitioners of the art. "Wealth is the multitude of instruments belonging to expert household managers and political [rulers]" (1256b36–37).

Aristotle's argument in favor of the existence of a natural limit to wealth depends on the analogy between household management and the arts, that is, on the assumption that household management is itself an art, indeed an art (or perhaps *the* art) that is directed toward the good life. In this sense, it would be an architectonic art, which would assign a proper place to all subsidiary arts and activities, including, of course, acquisition.[25] In view of Aristotle's distinction between natural acquisition and acquisition that is not natural but that "arises rather through a certain experience and art" (1257a4–5), one must wonder whether Aristotle's reliance on an art of household management does not represent an important qualification of his theory of natural acquisition.

The connection between natural acquisition and the natural limit on wealth becomes clearer when we remember the context of that discussion. So far, Aristotle has discussed only the acquisition of food; here there seems to be a natural limit imposed both by the limited amount of food necessary and useful to sustain life (absent a great variety of foods and a culinary art devoted to preparing them in especially tempting ways, resources devoted to food would be clearly limited) and the in-

---

implies a correction of the previous assertion. Aristotle now asserts that *all*, and not just *most*, wild animals exist for the sake of man. However, the limiting of the scope of that assertion seems eminently sensible: what use can be made by man of the scorpion, for example? One might answer that all of these animals can be observed by man and hence "used" by him as objects of contemplation and as means of knowing the cosmos, but this clearly takes us beyond the realm of economics in any meaning of the term.

25. On architectonic arts, see *Eth. Nic.* 1.1. In *Politics* 1 Aristotle speaks of both household managers and political rulers as users of wealth, whereas in the beginning of the *Ethics*, wealth is given as the goal of household management or economics (*oikonomikē*). Wealth, and thus economics, seems to enjoy a higher status in *Politics* 1 than elsewhere in Aristotle's works.

ability to store most foods for long periods of time because of spoilage.

In this context, the assertion of a natural limit on wealth seems to be derived from the natural characteristics of both man and the goods that are naturally useful to him. What Aristotle seems to be doing is extending a principle originally grounded in the characteristics of man's obtaining food to wealth generally, even to wealth that can be stored and whose consumption is not strictly limited by man's physical capacities. In this less obvious context, the principle must rely on the notion of the good life, the goal of the art of household management (and, indirectly, of all other arts), which limits the amount of wealth that can be used to any advantage.[26]

Unnatural Acquisition

Aristotle traces the origin of the unnatural mode of acquisition to what appears to be a slight flaw in nature's providence as described in the discussion of natural acquisition: the natural fact that, for whatever reasons, "human beings have either more or fewer things than what is adequate" (1257a16–17). The result is barter; Aristotle's example (the exchange between two households of wine for grain) suggests that the trade results not from a conscious division of labor but from accidental excesses and deficiencies.[27]

26. Aristotle's procedure may be profitably compared with that followed by John Locke in his *Second Treatise of Civil Government*. Starting with a similar observation about the natural limitations on wealth, Locke attempts to find a way around them. In his presentation, the limitation is caused by the perishability of the "truly useful . . . supports of life" (sec. 47); accordingly, "it was a foolish thing, as well as dishonest, to hoard up more than [one] could make use of" (sec. 46). To overcome this limitation on accumulation, Locke introduces money, something durable and valuable that can be hoarded indefinitely without spoiling. By exchanging "the truly useful but perishable supports of life" for money, an individual can accumulate wealth without limit. In order, however, to reach this result, Locke had to ignore the question of the use to which the accumulated money might be put. It is obvious that food that spoils before it can be consumed is useless; but what of money that is in excess of the requirements of the best life? Presumably, Locke would argue that for reasons of security or the insatiability of the human desire for pleasure, there could be no optimum amount of wealth. In any case, this tendency toward the unlimited accumulation of money was understood by Locke to have beneficial effects for society even if, in and of itself, it was an irrational manifestation of greed. It serves as an incentive for the most effective utilization of resources; this was particularly important in the case of landowning aristocrats who might otherwise not have been interested in producing the greatest possible amount of food from their lands.

27. It should be noted, however, that Aristotle has already indicated that natural providence can fall short and some people must exercise two modes of natural acquisition in order to survive. This implies the possibility of a conscious division of labor in that an alternative method of achieving the same result would be a system of barter between the practitioners of the various modes of acquisition. But Aristotle's emphasis on self-sufficient households makes this a less attractive explanation of the origin of exchange than that given in the text.

From this rudimentary barter, the more sophisticated forms of business expertise (*chrēmatistikē*) developed *kata logon,* "reasonably enough" (1257a31). Aristotle describes this development as follows:

> For as the assistance of foreigners became greater in importing what they were in need of and exporting what was in surplus, the use of money was necessarily devised. For the things necessary by nature are not in each case easily portable; hence with a view to exchanges they made a compact with one another to give and accept something which was itself one of the useful things and could be used flexibly to suit the needs of life, such as iron and silver and whatever else might be of this sort. (1257a31–38)

Finally, coins were made of these substances and were stamped with characters showing the amount of the coin to obviate the need for weighing and assaying the metal with each transaction.

The principal feature of this "historical" account of the development of money is its emphasis on foreign trade; domestic trade is considered at first to be only a form of barter, "in order to support natural self-sufficiency" (1257a30). In this regard, the *Politics* differs from both the *Nicomachean Ethics* and Plato's *Republic.*

In the first city discussed in the *Republic,* the need for money is connected with domestic commerce, while foreign commerce is carried on by means of barter.[28] Indeed, the very existence of this first city derives from the economic relations among the citizens, and its heart is the market where they sell what they produce and buy what they need. In the *Nicomachean Ethics* as well, the use of money seems connected with commerce in general (the examples have to do with the exchange of products among the artisans of a city) rather than with foreign commerce specifically. The general context, a discussion of justice in commercial transactions among citizen-artisans as a mode of association within the city, is more reminiscent of the *Republic* than of the *Politics.*[29]

In addition, one might note that Aristotle's account of the origins of money seems inherently self-contradictory. As he notes, the metal (iron or silver, for instance) first used as money is itself something inherently useful; in fact, it is hard to see why the trading partner would originally

28. *Rep.* 371b; by the "first city," I mean the city described by Socrates and Adeimantus in *Republic* 369b–72d. It is also called the "city of sows" (by Glaucon) and the "true city" (by Socrates). On foreign trade, see *Republic* 370e–371a, where Socrates observes that "just to found the city itself in the sort of place where there will be no need of imports is pretty nearly impossible." Socrates implies that the necessary foreign trade will be carried on by barter when he describes the following: "If the agent [entrusted by the city to procure imported goods] comes empty-handed, bringing nothing needed by those from whom they take what they themselves need, he'll go away empty-handed, won't he?" (This and all other translations from Plato's *Republic* are taken from A. Bloom, trans., *The* Republic *of Plato* [New York, 1968].)

29. *Eth. Nic.* 1133a20 and context.

have accepted it in exchange unless it were. Thus this example of a transaction that introduces the use of money proves to be more an example of barter. It is only after money exists in a given region that imports from that region can be financed by the exportation of the metal of which such money is composed, independently of the demand for the metal as a commodity. And, as Aristotle notes soon after giving this account, the defining characteristic of money is not the inherent usefulness of the metal from which it is minted, but rather its status as an agreed-upon medium of exchange. He observes that "when changed by its users, [money] is worth nothing and is not useful with a view to any of the necessary things; and it will often happen that one who is wealthy in money will go in want of necessary sustenance" (1257b12–14).[30] Be this as it may, Aristotle then argues that it was the development of money, due to its role in necessary foreign trade, that led to the development of the (domestic) commercial form of business expertise (*to kapēlikon* [*eidos tēs chrēmatistikēs*]), which he takes to be the unnatural form of acquisition par excellence.

Aristotle's complex history of these phenomena seems designed to present commerce as something marginal to the city. Every possible concession to the economic self-sufficiency of the household is made; to the greatest extent possible, the city is seen as having no economic purpose or aspect. This procedure may be understood in the context of Aristotle's defense of the naturalness of the city. The city has no intrinsic dependence on money and business expertise; those unnatural elements enter only because the city develops trade relations with foreign cities and peoples. While this exchange is at first a form of barter intended to remedy accidental deficiencies, it gives birth to the use of metals as money.

The existence of money provides the starting point for the unnatural form of the art of acquisition that goes by the specific name of business expertise (*chrēmatistikē*); it is characterized by the seeking of the greatest possible amount of wealth, that is, money or goods that can be valued in money. The culmination of this development is usury,[31] which, Aristotle says, "is most reasonably hated because one's possessions derive from money itself and not from that for which it was supplied. For it came into being for the sake of exchange, but interest actually creates more of it" (1258b2–5).

Having sketched the development of the unnatural mode of ac-

---

30. Aristotle thus returns to the view of Plato's *Republic*, which takes money to be a "token for the sake of exchange" (*symbolon tēs allagēs heneka*) that facilitates domestic (retail) trade (371b).

31. Aristotle uses the term *obolostatikē*, which implies the loan of small sums of money, presumably for consumption purposes, rather than for investment in profit-making enterprises.

quisition from its "natural" origins, Aristotle returns to the question of whether business expertise is part of economics. He is unable to reach a firm conclusion, remarking that "in the case of goods [business expertise] belongs to the household manager [*oikonomos*] in a sense, but in another sense not but rather to the subordinate expertise. This should be available above all, as was said before, by nature" (1258a32–35). But while it makes sense to say that the household manager should look to the health of the members of the household, not by attending to it himself, but rather by procuring the services of a doctor (thus subordinating, in a sense, the medical art to the art of the household manager), one cannot treat business expertise as a similar subordinate art; if you do not have money to begin with, you cannot hire a "business expert" to make some for you. Aristotle's preferred solution (namely, that nature should provide) seems to mean, in practical terms, that one should inherit a self-sufficient estate from one's father. As we shall see below, Aristotle is not as unaware of the impracticality of this advice as might appear on the surface.

In any event, this problem in the elaboration of the distinction between natural and unnatural acquisition seems to lead Aristotle to view the issue in another manner. Unnatural acquisition seems of necessity to allow for the unlimited accumulation of wealth in the form of money. But, Aristotle asks, can money truly be regarded as wealth? He adduces the view, by which he appears to be persuaded, that money is "altogether [by] law, and in no way by nature" (1257b11–12); money can lose its value by demonetarization,[32] and one can imagine a case (such as a famine, for instance) in which a "wealthy" man might starve to death. The story of Midas makes this point in mythical form.

But if wealth cannot be considered to be the same as money, perhaps it can be viewed as the total of a man's useful possessions; is wealth so understood capable of indefinite increase? In theoretical terms, as noted above, the Aristotelian answer must be in the negative: in looking to its end—the good life—the art of household management (*oikonomikē*) imposes a limit on the amount of possessions that can truly be useful and that hence can be considered wealth.

Aristotle notes, however, that for all practical purposes, the opposite is the case, pointing out that "thus in one way it appears necessary that there be a limit to all wealth; yet if we look at what actually occurs we see that the opposite happens—all who engage in business increase their money without limit" (1257b32–34). Thus the original distinction between natural and unnatural modes of acquisition seems to give way to another, similar but not identical, distinction—that between wealth

32. See p. 85 above.

understood as something inherently limited (to what is useful for the good life) and wealth understood as something inherently unlimited (measurably in money). What before seemed blameworthy as an *unnatural mode* of acquisition now seems blameworthy as *unlimited* acquisition.

Ultimately this situation has a moral, rather than economic, cause: some men are less concerned about living well than they are about assuring mere survival against any and all contingencies, no matter how remote, while others seek the good life in the pursuit of bodily pleasure. In both cases, it appears that there is no limit on the amount of wealth that can be usefully amassed in the pursuit of these goals.

Natural and Unnatural Acquisition: A Theoretical Critique

As already noted, the division between natural and unnatural acquisition rests on the fundamental tenet that nature provides for man's needs. Not untypically,[33] Aristotle's formulations of this principle are tentative and hypothetical:

> One must *suppose* both that plants exist for the sake of animals and that the other animals exist for the sake of human beings. (1256b15–17; emphasis added)

> *If,* then, nature makes nothing that is incomplete or purposeless, nature must necessarily have made all of these for the sake of human beings. (1256b20–22; emphasis added)

This basic principle is supported by analogies with the situation of the other animals and of the newborn of each species. These analogies, while suggestive, are hardly conclusive or even persuasive; they could just as easily lead to the view that man is singularly *un*provided for.[34] To survive, man requires an adaptability that the other animals, who seem more fitted by nature to obtain food, do not; a child's dependency on adults lasts a particularly long time compared with that of the offspring of other species, outlasting the natural provision for dependency (mother's milk) and requiring other help.

To examine, then, these assertions, we turn to Aristotle's *Physics*, his exposition of "the science of nature."[35] The things that exist by nature appear to be those that have within themselves a principle ("beginning," *archē*) of motion and rest.[36] (Motion is here used as a comprehensive term to include locomotion, growth, decay, or other qualitative change.)

---

33. For the similar situation regarding Aristotle's assertion of the city's naturalness, see Ambler, "Naturalness of the City," 164.

34. Cf. Protagoras' "myth" in Plato's *Protagoras.*

35. *Ph.* 184a15.

36. Ibid., 192b8–15.

The prime examples of natural beings are the living things, which are responsible for their own motion and growth. The most interesting natural phenomenon seems to be the natural growth of living things, by means of which they attain their mature form. Innumerable changes occur as the acorn becomes an oak tree, as the baby becomes a man. These changes are not caused by an external agent, although they may require favorable external conditions.

Because of the regularity of its occurrence, this process of change and growth cannot be understood as accidental. While there are occasional monstrous births, these are exceptions to the general rule according to which the young of each species grow into mature beings of that species, resembling their parents. This is taken, by Aristotle, to reflect a purposiveness in nature, according to which the adult form of each being acts as a final cause of the being's growth; nature then comes to refer both to the process of growth and to the final form. The expression "the nature of man" refers then primarily to the qualities of the fully developed man, the man in whom the entire natural process of growth has taken place.[37]

This natural purposiveness is the basis of Aristotle's teleology; the end (*telos*) directs the process of growth, which must then be seen as being for the sake of that end. In the case of living things, the various parts of the being, which come into existence in the course of its development, are

37. In *Physics* 2.8, Aristotle attempts to prove that nature is a final cause, that is, that nature is purposeful and seeks an end. He presents first the opposing view, according to which natural events occur by chance, or without any purpose or end. From this point of view, the appropriateness of the various bodily organs to the functions they serve must be considered as coincidental; those creatures whose organs are appropriately formed survive, while the others perish. Thus, according to Empedocles, in whose name this view is put forward, there were once such monsters as "man-faced oxen," but they did not survive. Aristotle counters that the birth of such monsters is a rare event (if it occurs at all), rather than a normal one, as the Empedoclean thesis requires. In the absence of a reason why the birth of monsters would have been a more common occurrence in the past than now, one must conclude that the birth of viable organisms cannot be attributed to chance alone. Despite his appearing to ignore the possibility that this regularity is due to necessity rather than purpose, Aristotle is nevertheless aware of the view that nature acts "as Zeus drops the rain, not in order that wheat might grow, but from necessity—for the vapor becoming cold it is necessary that the condensate descend and, this happening, it incidentally causes the wheat to grow" (*Ph.* 198b18–22). Aristotle deals with this view at length in *Physics* 2.9 and concludes that necessity of this sort can be attributed to beings only in consequence of the natural motions of the materials of which they are composed, such as the natural downward motion of earth and the natural upward motion of fire. In this respect, the main difference between Aristotelian and modern physics is the possibility, in the latter, of a necessity that results not from the inherent qualities of the material, but from an abstract relationship between two or more objects, as, for example, gravitational or electromagnetic forces.

seen in terms of their contribution to the existence and functioning of the completed being. As W. D. Ross puts it in his discussion of Aristotle's biological writings,

> Aristotle's teleology is, it will be seen, an "immanent" teleology. The end of each species is internal to the species; its end is simply to be that kind of thing, or, more definitely, to grow and reproduce its kind, to have sensation, and to move, as freely and efficiently as the conditions of its existence—its habitat, for instance—allow.[38]

This view certainly differs from that taken in the *Politics*, as Ross notes:

> In *Pol.* 1256b15–22, Aristotle adopts the Socratic position that plants exist for the sake of animals, and the lower animals for the sake of man. But there he is not writing biology.[39]

In general, Aristotle argues that the various species exist for their own sake without any ties between them; he certainly never says that the prey exist for the sake of the predators or the plants for the sake of the herbivorous animals.[40] We will return to the question of why, in that case, "one must suppose" that the opposite is true.

Natural Slavery

The most important mode of natural acquisition is farming, for, as Aristotle notes, "the type of human being that is most numerous lives from the land and from cultivated crops" (1256a38–40). But, unlike the nomadic existence, which Aristotle describes as being "without exertion and amid leisure" (1256a32), farming involves hard work. This could be seen as a failure of nature to take care of man; Aristotle replies that natural providence is operative here as well, since nature has provided a group of men, the natural slaves, for whom such bodily toil is the best of which they are capable. These men, according to Aristotle, are natural slaves. As he explains,

> the naturally ruling [*archon*] and ruled [*archomenon*] [join together] on account of preservation [*sōtēria*]. For that which can foresee with the mind is the naturally ruling and naturally mastering element, while that which can

38. W. D. Ross, *Aristotle*, 5th ed. (London, 1949), 126.
39. Ibid., 126 n. 2.
40. While there are some cases where the species is seen as subordinate to the genus of which it is a part (see *Metaph.* 1033b33, where Aristotle counters his initial judgment that the begetting of a mule by a horse and an ass is "against nature" with the observation that "the closest genus, common to the horse and the ass, is not named, but would be perhaps both, like the mule"), in no case is the existence of one species understood as being for the benefit of another.

do these things with the body is the naturally ruled and slave; hence the
same thing is advantageous for the master and slave. (1252a30–34)

Note that what must join together, according to Aristotle, is a naturally ruling "element" and a naturally ruled "element" (*archon* and *ar-
chomenon* are in the neuter gender and hence do not particularly refer to
human beings). While this gives Aristotle's statement a more scientific
cast, it raises the question of whether these two "elements" must be, or
even can ever be, two different people, a master and a slave.

Aristotle's detailed discussion of slavery proceeds under three general
headings: art, nature, and law. Under the first heading, he considers
household management as an art (*technē*), albeit of a special kind: he
distinguishes between it and the specialized ("definite," *hōrismenē*) arts.
Every artisan must possess the proper tools in order to practice his art;
the tools may be inanimate or animate (subordinates and slaves). This
section of the discussion ignores the difference in legal status between
subordinates and slaves. Aristotle claims nevertheless that it makes clear
the nature and capacity (*dynamis*) of the slave as someone who belongs
entirely to someone else, a tool of action that is separable from its owner.
However, it clearly does not address the key question of whether any
such slaves exist by nature; the next section of the discussion takes up
this issue.

Aristotle claims that this question can be investigated either theoretically ("to discern by reasoning," *tōi logōi theōrēsai*) or empirically ("to
learn from what actually happens," *ek tōn ginomenōn katamathein*). The
theoretical part of the argument (1254a21–b24) finds that the ruler-
ruled relationship permeates all of nature and concludes that "the
same must of necessity hold in the case of human beings generally"
(1254b14–16). Aristotle asserts that this must be the case whenever
there is "a single common thing" (*hen ti koinon*) made up of many parts;
this is true even in the case of nonliving things; for example, harmony is
the ruling principle of a musical scale. This example poses a problem,
however: why may not the ruling element (*to archon*) be a principle of
law, rather than a person, the master? Furthermore, the assertion is only
that a ruling element is necessary; there is no assurance that it is provided by nature.

Aristotle adduces three examples in which a natural relationship of
ruling and being ruled exists among living things: the rule of the soul
over the body, and, within the soul, of the intellect over the desires; the
rule of man over the (tame) animals; the rule of male over female. Of
these, the sole explicit example of despotic rule is the rule of the soul
over the body. However, it is not clear whether this sort of ruling is

analogous to human ruling (that is, to ruling over someone who could conceivably disobey) or whether it is ruling only in the metaphorical sense in which one might say that the moon rules the tides, that is, gives rise to a force that inevitably causes the tides to behave as they do. We note that of those apparent exceptions, the morally unsound, Aristotle says only that, in their case, the body "is held to" rule the soul; it may in fact be impossible for this to occur, and it may be necessary, in such cases, to trace the defect to the soul (1254a39–b2).

The example of the rule of man over the (tame) animals seems, therefore, more in point; this is emphasized later at 1254b25, where Aristotle says that a similar use is made of slaves and tame animals. In addition, the benefit that comes to the animal from being ruled by man is said to be preservation (*sōtēria*), which was earlier said to be the purpose of the master-slave relationship.

Whereas the first example seemed defective in that the relationship between the soul and the body is not analogous to that between two separate individual beings, the second seems defective in that it ignores the difference between even the most intelligent and trainable of brutes and the stupidest of men, a difference to which Aristotle makes the following allusion in the conclusion of this section: "For he is a slave by nature . . . who participates in reason only to the extent of perceiving it, but does not have it. (The other animals, not perceiving reason, obey their passions.)" (1254b20–24)

The third example seems to bear least on the problem at hand. As Aristotle expresses it, "the relation of male to female is by nature a relation of superior to inferior and ruler to ruled" (1254b13–14). No mention is made of any benefit that accrues to the female as a result of this rule. The sort of superiority involved is hinted at by the words used, *kreitton* and *cheiron*, which carry connotations of superiority and inferiority with respect to strength and bravery. Is Aristotle suggesting that, in this case, where the need for the union is undeniably natural, nature fails to provide a hierarchical ordering principle other than force? In any case, Aristotle had earlier (1252a34–b1) warned against the identification of the female and the slave, a warning that seems to point out the inapposite character of this example.

Having stated his general principle and given some specific examples, Aristotle concludes that

> those who are as different [from other men] as the soul from the body or man from beast—and they are in this state if their work is the use of body, and if this is the best that can come from them—are slaves by nature. (1254b16–19)

This conclusion, however, is difficult to interpret. In any strict sense, it is obviously impossible for two men to differ from each other as much as the body does from the soul: if the soul is taken to be the source of the individual's motion, then it would appear that the slave would have no source of motion within himself, he would not even be alive.

Similarly, as noted above, Aristotle's view is that there is a significant difference between even the stupidest man and a brute. A natural slave would have to be someone almost totally lacking in reason; this would seem to be impossible or, at any rate, so improbable as to be practically irrelevant. Aristotle further explicates his conclusion by adding that "they are in this state [i.e., are natural slaves] if their work is the use of the body, and if this is the best that can come from them" (1254b17–19). This explanation raises the question of whether the improvement of the natural slave's even limited mental abilities might not be intrinsically better than the "use of the body." At the end of the first book Aristotle asserts that a slave ought to possess a certain sort of moral virtue; this implies that the "use of the body" cannot be the best of which the "natural slave" is capable.

Perhaps because of these difficulties in establishing the existence of natural slaves, Aristotle turns to a consideration of the relation of slavery and law. In this respect, Aristotle is willing to grant that those who attack slavery have a point. He recognizes that the justice that he claims characterizes natural slavery may not exist in the case of legal or conventional slavery.

Actual slavery seems to rest on "a certain agreement by which things conquered in war are said to belong to the conquerors" (1255a6–7). While Aristotle refers to this agreement as a "law" (*nomos*), it is clearly a law of a special kind, being an agreement among cities rather than the law of a given city. Aristotle clearly has some sympathy for those who challenge the justice of this law,

> as they would challenge an orator—on a motion of illegality, on the grounds that it is a terrible thing if what yields to force is to be enslaved and ruled by what is able to apply force and is superior in power. (1255a7–11)

Aristotle's method of confronting the discrepancy between the basis of actual slavery and his own view is typical of his general approach to the practical sciences. Rather than abandon the natural standard and proclaim, with the Sophists, that the institutions of the city rest solely on convention (agreement) or force, he attempts to reconcile the two positions by showing how the popular one reflects, albeit only partially, the true situation:

The cause of this dispute—and what makes the arguments converge—is that virtue, once it obtains equipment, is in a certain manner particularly able to apply force, and the dominant element is always preeminent in something that is good, so that it is held that there is no force without virtue. (1255a12–16)[41]

Aristotle deals similarly with the other convention underlying actual slavery: the enslavement of the children of slaves. This position, too, he regards as reflecting, although not attaining, an understanding of the true situation:

> When they speak in this way, it is by nothing other than virtue or vice that they define what is slave and what is free, who well born and who ill born. For they claim that from the good should come someone good, just as a human being comes from a human being and a beast from beasts. (1255a39–b2)

However, as Aristotle notes, this convention is as little deserving of total support as the one that allows conquerors to enslave the conquered. In fact, the two conventions are not consistent with each other; the latter suggests that the "well born" should be free, while the former would allow the possibility of their enslavement if through the accidents of war they happened to be captured by their inferiors.

Although Aristotle concludes this discussion with a reassertion of the mutual benefits of natural slavery for the master and the slave, he must now recognize that the situation is different in the case of conventional slavery:

> There is thus a certain advantage—and even affection of slave and master for one another—for those [slaves] who merit being such by nature; but for those who do not merit it in this way but [who are slaves] according to law and by force, the opposite is the case. (1255b12–15)

Natural Slavery: A Theoretical Critique

As the above discussion makes clear, even as presented in the *Politics*, a large part of Aristotle's case for natural slavery is not very convincing. The main difficulty seems to be that the differences in soul between men are not great enough (that is, they are not similar to the differences between soul and body or between man and beast) to justify natural slavery

41. As noted in the Lord edition of Aristotle's *Politics*, this passage, due to its obscurity, has been variously interpreted. In any case, it seems clear that Aristotle is trying to provide a rationale for the conventional view that points toward his own view that superiority in virtue constitutes the natural claim to rule; as the immediate sequel makes clear, he realizes that this effort can enjoy only a very limited success.

as Aristotle understands it.[42] The doctrine of natural slavery becomes even more questionable when viewed in the light of Aristotle's views on nature as a whole.

On two occasions, Aristotle specifically refers to what nature wishes or intends (*bouletai*) with respect to natural slaves. First, he tells us that

> nature indeed wishes to make the bodies of free persons and slaves different as well [as their souls]—those of the latter strong with respect to necessary needs, those of the former straight and useless for such tasks, but useful with a view to a political way of life (which is itself divided between the needs of war and those of peace); yet the opposite often results, some having the bodies of free persons while others have the souls. (1254b27–34)[43]

Secondly, he notes that those who deny that a "well born" person can be properly considered a slave

> claim that from the good should come someone good, just as a human being comes from a human being and a beast from beasts. But while nature wishes to do this, it is often unable to. (1255b1–4)

Taking these two statements together (and they are the only ones in which Aristotle says that nature fails to achieve what it "wishes" to do), it would appear that Aristotle believes that nature intended there to be not one species of human beings, but rather two.

But we have already noted that the existence of self-propagating species is the prime phenomenon on which Aristotle bases his notion of the purposiveness of nature. Consequently, it hardly makes sense for him to claim that nature could fail to achieve its intention, not with respect to single cases (where necessity or chance might prevent the individual from attaining its natural end), but with respect to an entire species. In fact, Aristotle never denies that human beings form one species; and since it is the existence of species that indicates to us nature's intention, it is clearly impossible for us to know of an unfulfilled natural intention to arrange the species themselves differently from the way they are in fact arranged.

ECONOMICS AND POLITICS

We have described Aristotle's doctrines of natural acquisition and natural slavery and discussed the various theoretical difficulties to which

42. One might perhaps say that the situation would be otherwise in the extreme case of a mentally defective person who could not be said to "participate in reason." But such a case would be very rare, and such a person would be practically useless as a slave. He could certainly not be said to be "a partner in [the master's] life" (1259b39–40).

43. This explains, incidentally, why the "ruling element" and the "ruled element," whose conjunction Aristotle had said was necessary for preservation (1252a30–31), cannot be the soul and body of the same human being.

these doctrines are subject. In this section, we will examine the extent to which these economic doctrines inform Aristotle's discussion of practical politics, in terms both of his critique of existing regimes and of his positive prescriptions for political practice.

Sparta and Crete: The Problem of Slavery

Aristotle's critique of the actual regimes of the "cities that are said to be well managed" (1260b30–31) begins with this economic consideration: "It is agreed that any [city] that is going to be finely governed must have leisure from the necessary things; but in what manner it should have this is not easy to grasp" (1269a34–36). In Sparta and Crete, this goal was accomplished by means of a serf class; in the former city, at least, it occasioned numerous rebellions and had a major effect on the character of the regime.

The serf class in Sparta, the helots, posed a perpetual threat due to their readiness to form an alliance with any external enemy who indicated an intention and ability to invade Spartan territory. Even in the absence of an external enemy, the policing of this class was a burdensome task that required the city to remain on a perpetual war footing.[44] (According to Plutarch, the Spartans employed a "secret service" to kill the "sturdiest and best" of the helots, presumably in order to destroy whatever leadership may have developed among them.)[45]

Aristotle blames this preoccupation with military matters for the neglect of the education of the women and the regulation of their way of life; instead, they lived in a dissolute and luxurious manner, the opposite way of life from that which the regime, in the name of military virtue and efficiency, forced on the men. It seems that the legislator, being concerned only with war, did not pay sufficient attention to the women, considering their way of life to be, in the main, irrelevant to his purposes.[46]

44. Crete's avoidance of this problem was due to chance, namely, its favorable (isolated) geographic position. Nevertheless, Aristotle notes that this advantage cannot be trusted to last, since "only recently has foreign war come to the island and made evident the weakness of the laws there" (1272b20–22).

45. Plut. *Lyc.* 24.

46. Aristotle recounts an anecdote according to which Lycurgus tried to bring the Spartan women under some sort of public discipline but gave up when they resisted his rules; his greater success in subjecting the men to his rigid laws is traced to the fact that due to the long military campaigns they had undertaken, the men were already used to harsh discipline. This is the only reference to Lycurgus by name in the chapter on Sparta; elsewhere, Aristotle refers to "the legislator." This almost total silence about the famous Lycurgus, the effect of which is hardly mitigated by the mention of his name in connection with an important failure of his policy, is noteworthy. Aristotle's criticism of Sparta will point to several instances in which the results produced by the regime were the opposite of the original intention.

Consequently, the Spartan women were deficient even in that virtue to which the city was most devoted, bravery, and "this became clear during the Theban invasion: they were not only wholly useless, like women in other cities, but they created more of an uproar than the enemy" (1269b37–39). But the real harm was caused by the indirect influence their desire for luxury had on the city by means of their influence on the men. This influence was exceptionally great in Sparta; Aristotle goes so far as to say that, in effect, women ruled many areas of life in that city. He traces this mainly to the warlike character of the Spartans, observing that "most stocks that are fond of soldiering and war" are dominated by women (1269b25–26).

As a result, the men became more concerned with amassing wealth than the legislator had intended. Due to certain loopholes in the property laws (involving, characteristically, the possibility of providing large dowries and, in the absence of male heirs, bequeathing estates to daughters), it was possible for some women to come into the possession of large amounts of land. As the land became concentrated in fewer and fewer hands, the number of citizens who could afford the required contribution to the common meals diminished. Since partaking in the common meals was a prerequisite for the enjoyment of citizenship rights, the citizen body of Sparta decreased in size. This reduction in the number of citizens proved to be a severe military liability; thus the prime goal of the legislator, the founding of a regime dedicated to military strength, was frustrated.

Aristotle ignores the regulations by which the legislator had hoped to disinterest the Spartans in wealth. According to Plutarch, the regulations substituted iron for silver and gold in the currency so as to make foreign trade impossible and, generally, to hinder all business activity.[47] (Aristotle does note, at 1294b18–29, that the Spartan men, rich and poor, shared a common way of life. This, too, was designed to disinterest the Spartans in wealth; it failed in that it did not include the women.)

This feature of the regime is perhaps alluded to in Aristotle's final criticism of the Spartiates. The public finances are poorly managed, and the city on occasion found itself without the necessary resources with which to carry on a large-scale war. Ridding the city of business activity seems in this sense to have reduced its war-making potential. Since the citizens own neither gold nor silver (or, at any rate, cannot admit to owning any), the city cannot replenish the public treasury by taxation.[48]

47. Plut. *Lyc.* 9.
48. The connection between the poor public finances of Sparta and the prohibition on gold and silver is hypothetical, since, as noted above, Aristotle ignores this famous prohibition in his discussion of the Spartan regime. The reason he gives for the Spartan financial problem is that "they are very backward in paying [special war] taxes. For because most of

Aristotle's main criticism of Sparta is, therefore, that the attempt to provide leisure for the citizens led the city to become so warlike as to make it unable to use its leisure wisely; consequently, the city was secure while at war but became corrupt and overly given to luxury once its foreign position had become securely established (1271b3–6). As he explains further,

> most cities of this [warlike] sort preserve themselves when at war, but once having acquired [imperial] rule they come to ruin; they lose their edge, like iron, when they remain at peace. The reason is that the legislator has not educated them to be capable of being at leisure. (1334a6–10)

This situation is reflected in the fact that the corruption of the regime began with the nonwarring part of the city, namely, the women.

In the entire course of the discussion of Sparta, Aristotle nowhere asks whether the institution of helotry was in accordance with the standards of natural slavery as set down in *Politics* 1; perhaps he considers it obvious that it was not. He does, however, tacitly criticize Spartan practice in his discussion of the proper goal of the best regime in *Politics* 7 and 8. In denying the possibility that indiscriminate imperialism could properly be the city's goal, he asserts that "one should not try to exercise mastery over all things but only over those that are to be mastered, just as one should not hunt human beings for a feast or sacrifice, but that which is to be hunted for this" (1324b38–40). In this, Aristotle appears to recur to the natural slavery doctrine set forth in the first book; indeed, we might be tempted to say that the Spartan difficulties arose because they enslaved the neighboring populations indiscriminately, instead of being guided by the doctrine of natural slavery and enslaving only those who were suited for such a condition. As the discussion of the best regime in the seventh and eighth books makes clear, however, we would be well advised to resist this temptation.

Aristotle's thematic treatment of slavery in the best regime occurs at *Politics* 1330a25–33. In the best case (and in imitation of Sparta), all those who farm the land will be slaves. They are not all to be of the same stock (thereby differing from the helots), nor ought they to have a spirited character. This second requirement, like the first, is important for

---

the land belongs to the Spartiates, they do not scrutinize each other's payments of such taxes" (1271b13–15). (In this sentence, Aristotle uses the word *Spartiates* instead of the more usual *Lakon* for Spartan. The former term appears in only two other places in the chapter on Sparta. The implication is that there was a small class of non-Spartiate Lacedaemonian landholders who had subordinate political status; this class could not have been identical with the helots, who worked the land of the Spartiates. The financial situation could have been eased if this class had been larger and richer, since it could have easily been made to pay its taxes fully and promptly.

the sake of avoiding rebellion; as such, it seems no more than common sense.

To see its wider import, we must consider Aristotle's earlier tripartite division of the peoples of the world (1327b23–29). He distinguishes among the Asians, who are intelligent and skillful (*technika*) with respect to their souls but who lack spiritedness; the Europeans (and, generally, those inhabiting cold places), who are spirited but lacking in intelligence and art; and the Greeks, who are spirited *and* intelligent.[49] The demand that the slaves be unspirited is equivalent, in this context, to a demand that they be taken from among the intelligent and skillful Asians; yet such people could not be considered as natural slaves according to the standards of the first book.

This shift in perspective brought about by the consideration of the role of spiritedness is subtly prepared by an earlier passage in which Aristotle explains as follows why some monarchies can securely exercise almost despotic powers: "It is because barbarians are more slavish in their characters than Greeks (those in Asia being more so than those in Europe) that they put up with a master's rule without making any difficulties" (1285a19–22). The first dichotomy (barbarian-Greek) is that which Aristotle says approximates or points toward the distinction between natural slaves and natural freemen (1252b7–9 and 1255a28–31), while the second (Asian-European), that between the intelligent and the spirited, is that discussed in the seventh book.

In the course of the *Politics*, the basis of slavery shifts from the intrinsic suitability emphasized in the first book (the lack of foresight) to the practicality or, perhaps, even the inevitability, emphasized in the seventh book, of the enslavement of those who are unwilling to risk their lives for their freedom. (Aristotle's first requirement, that the slaves not be of the same stock, is also of this order; it speaks to the feasibility of the institution without saying anything of its justifiability in terms of the characters of the enslaved.)

Even more striking, as regards the natural slavery doctrine of the first book, however, is Aristotle's (unfulfilled) promise, in the course of the description of the best regime, to explain "why it is better to hold out freedom as a reward for *all* slaves" (1330a33–34; emphasis added). The slaves are not to be natural slaves at all.[50]

49. The principle of the division appears to be climate: the Europeans are grouped together with those who inhabit cold places, while the participation of the Greeks in the good qualities of both Europeans and Asians parallels their middle position geographically (and hence climatically). This hypothesis would explain how the non-Greek Carthaginians could have the free regime for which they are praised: any people enjoying a moderate climate (like that of Greece) would share in its natural advantages.

50. L. Strauss, *The City and Man* (Chicago, 1964), 23.

Aristotle's prescriptions with respect to slavery in the best regime seem to be designed to bestow on the citizens the advantages of freedom from economic concerns without necessitating the extremely warlike character of Sparta. To do so, he appears to jettison the natural slavery doctrine, which, as we have seen, suffered from major weaknesses in its original presentation.

Toward the end of the discussion of natural slavery in *Politics* 1, Aristotle makes the strange assertion that

> it is evident, at any rate, that if they [sc., natural freemen] were to be born as different only in body as the images of the gods, everyone would assert that those not so favored merited being their slaves. But if this is true in the case of the body, it is much more justifiable to make this distinction in the case of the soul; yet it is not as easy to see the beauty of the soul as it is that of the body. (1254b34–39)

In other words, because of the failure of nature to make human excellence immediately visible and persuasive in the form of godlike images, even natural slavery will necessitate warfare in order to enslave "those human beings who are naturally suited to be ruled but unwilling" (1256b25).

Leaving aside, for the moment, the questions of whether there would be sufficient numbers of such men and whether they would be sufficiently useful, we confront the problem of Sparta. The attempt to create a society on this basis requires the cultivation of a warlike character that is pernicious for the city's good order and that ultimately undermines even itself. To solve this dilemma, Aristotle moves even farther from the natural slavery doctrine in an attempt to find a feasible way of maintaining the institution of slavery without having the city's military requirements dominate all other considerations.

Carthage: The Role of Wealth and Acquisition

The constitution of Carthage, discussed primarily in *Politics* 2, presents us with an example of a regime based on principles that are the opposite of those of Sparta. It openly holds wealth in high regard, and even those holding political offices do not refrain from business activity (1316b5–6). Conversely, it does not attempt to provide leisure for its citizens and possesses no subject class similar to the helots of Sparta or the "subjects" (*perioikoi*) of Crete.[51] The necessary work of the city is carried on, in the main, by the body of poorer citizens, the *dēmos*. Nevertheless, Aristotle joins Carthage together with Sparta and Crete as regimes "which are justly held in high repute" (1273b26).

51. Aristotle does not mention whether slavery exists at Carthage; it may, but, in any case, it does not have the economic or political importance that it had in Sparta or Crete.

Whereas the constant uprisings of the helots indicated a defect in the Spartan regime, the Carthaginian regime is praised for the fact that the *dēmos* has remained faithful to it. In this context, in fact, Aristotle introduces a new standard by which to judge regimes. In the discussion of Sparta, Aristotle had focused on the provision of leisure for the citizens as a, if not the, key political desideratum. This focus shifts at the beginning of the discussion of Carthage, where Aristotle remarks that "it is a sign of a well-organized regime if the people [*dēmos*] voluntarily acquiesce in the arrangement of the regime, and if there has never been factional conflict worth mentioning, or a tyrant" (1272b30–34). In other words, in Carthage, as opposed to Sparta, the relationship between the well-off and the rest of the population is determined by politics rather than by warfare.

While their poverty prevents them from holding any of the most important offices of the city, the Carthaginian poor exercise considerable political power in the city through an assembly of some sort to which matters may be referred by the kings and the senate. This assembly exercises greater powers than the comparable assemblies of the cities of Crete.[52] In fact, at one point, Aristotle refers to Carthage as a democracy (1316b5–6).[53]

Despite its democratic features, the Carthaginian regime inclines toward oligarchy by virtue of a pervasive opinion that honors wealth and considers that the leaders of the city should be chosen from among those who possess it. This is connected with the fact that the city itself does not undertake to provide leisure for its citizens, even for those who hold

52. Compare 1273a6–13 with 1272a10–12, where Aristotle says that the Cretan assemblies could only ratify proposals put before them. Plutarch (*Lyc.* 6) describes the Spartan assembly as similarly limited in authority.

In particular, Aristotle notes the relative freedom of speech enjoyed by the Carthaginian *dēmos:*

> And when the [king and senators] propose something, it is granted to the people not only to hear out [and approve] the opinions of the rulers, but they have authority to come to a decision of their own, and whoever wishes is permitted to speak against the proposals—something which does not exist in the other regimes. (1273a10–14)

53. This reference is often rejected as spurious, since it contradicts Aristotle's reference to the Carthaginian constitution as oligarchic at 1273b18. At 1293b14–16, the constitution is called aristocratic (albeit in a subsidiary sense, as is clear from the preceding discussion) because it pays attention to virtue as well as to wealth and the *dēmos*. (The passage 1316a29–34 also implies that the Carthaginian constitution is aristocratic.) At 1320b5, Carthaginian practice is cited as an example of how the rich may prevent moderate democracies from degenerating into extreme ones. It is possible to avoid rejecting these contradictory readings as spurious by considering the following: "The defining principle of a good mixture of democracy and oligarchy is that it should be possible for the same polity to be spoken of as either a democracy or an oligarchy" (1294b14–16). Carthage seems to pass this test.

office; therefore, only the wealthy would have the time to devote to public concerns. As an extreme consequence of this situation, the offices of
king and general are available for purchase; an almost inevitable result is
corruption, as those who have paid for their offices attempt to reimburse
themselves for their original expense when they have the opportunity to
do so.

In the absence of a subject class, the *dēmos* must perform most of the
necessary tasks for the city; despite its power in the assembly, it does not
in fact rule the city, nor are the poorer citizens eligible for the highest
honors. The instability and discontent that could result from this situation are remedied by emigration, which acts as a safety valve and keeps
the *dēmos* from rising up against the rulers of the city. Aristotle mentions
this Carthaginian practice approvingly in the course of a chapter discussing policies by which the rich may keep moderate democracies from degenerating into extreme ones (1320b4–7). The rich equip and send out
to the surrounding territories the destitute and/or ambitious members
of the *dēmos;* these emigrants are able to establish themselves and perhaps even become rich themselves (1273b18–21). In this manner, the
rich prevent the growth of an idle urban mob that, having the time to
spend on public affairs and having nothing to lose and everything to
gain by disturbing the existing relationships, could become a force for
extreme democracy.

Although Aristotle praises this expedient, he regards it as a defect of
the regime that it is forced to resort to it. To the extent that the success of
this policy depends on chance (the avoidance of an economic or military
misfortune that would prevent implementation of the policy), the regime may be said to be flawed. The avoidance of factional conflict should
be the result of the arrangements laid down by the legislator, not of
chance. Nevertheless, it is striking that Aristotle reserves what appears to
be his highest praise for a regime that openly honors wealth and in
which the leading citizens carry on business activities.[54] The natural economic doctrines appear to have been totally abandoned. In any case, we
are forced to consider what the natural economic standard is intended to
mean in the context of a political reality that appears to be more complex
and variegated than would appear from the discussion of the economically self-sufficient households of the first book.

54. In particular, compare 1271b18–19, "concerning the regime of the Lacedaemo-
nians, then, let this much be said; for these are the things one might particularly criticize,"
with 1272b24–25, "the Carthaginians are also held to govern themselves in a way that is
fine and in many respects extra-ordinary compared to others." Although Aristotle never
explicitly ranks the Carthaginian, Cretan, and Spartan regimes with respect to each other,
the contrast between the faithfulness of the Carthaginian *dēmos* and the frequent uprisings
of the helots is striking.

SUMMARY AND CONCLUSION

Summary of the Argument

In the first book of the *Politics,* Aristotle develops a doctrine of "natural economics" based on the fundamental tenet that nature provides food and the other necessities of life for man, just as it provides for the different species of animals (through a compatibility between their instincts, their ability to digest food of a certain kind, and their environment) and for the young of each species (through the provision of milk, albumen, or similar substances). To the extent that toil is required for the agricultural way of life (as opposed to, say, the nomadic), this is not to be seen as a failure of nature's providence, since nature also supplies a class of men, the natural slaves, for whom such bodily toil is the best way of life of which they are capable.

Aristotle uses the doctrine of "natural economics" in his defense of the city's naturalness, in which he states that "every city, therefore, exists by nature, if such also are the first partnerships [namely, the village and the household, as well as the husband-wife and master-slave partnerships of which the latter is constituted]" (1252b30–31). Aristotle argues that the city is a natural being, ignoring, for the sake of his argument, the differences among cities in terms of regimes (a major theme in the remainder of the *Politics*), as well as the affinity between the city and the "unnatural" forms of acquisition, such as commerce and money lending.[55]

In the course of the development of "natural economics," Aristotle provides several indications that the doctrine is not his last word on the subject. For example, the fundamental tenet of natural providence is stated as a supposition. Similarly, the following key conclusion regarding natural slavery, at 1254b16–19, also has a hypothetical character: "Accordingly, those who are as different [from other men] as the soul from the body or man from beast . . . are slaves by nature." Thus, "natural economics" is not presented as scientific doctrine.

In fact, if we look at Aristotle's writings on biology and on nature generally, we see that the view of "nature" presupposed by "natural economics" does not accord with that presented in these more theoretical works. In particular, Aristotle's view of nature seems to depend heavily on the phenomenon of the existence of species, distinct types of animals and plants that reproduce themselves while preserving their distinctive characteristics. In reproducing itself, each species produces young, immature beings, which then grow and develop into the mature form. In its

---

55. For a fuller development of this point, see Ambler, "Naturalness of the City," 174. Consider, in this regard, Aristotle's admission (at 1259a33–35) that cities may have to engage in business practices (such as monopolies) that are decidedly "unnatural."

fundamental sense, nature is the process by which the young of each species mature into the adult form, which is then understood as its "nature" and as the cause of the developmental process that resulted in it.

Thus it is anomalous to maintain that one species exists for the sake of another; the view of self-sustaining species whose causation is immanent (that is to say that the species is the cause of the individuals that compose it) is incompatible with the view of "natural economics" that plants exist for the sake of animals and that the other animals exist for the sake of man. Similarly, if we can understand nature's purposes from the species themselves, then the view that nature wishes or intends (*physis bouletai*) the existence of two separate species, masters and slaves, in place of the one human species that does exist cannot be seriously maintained.

Finally, when we look at the rest of the *Politics*, we discover that the natural economic standard is nowhere alluded to, let alone used to judge the characters of the various regimes discussed. For example, it appears that the overly warlike character of Sparta may be blamed on the constant need to keep its vast subject population under effective control; this defect is ultimately the cause of the regime's corruption. Thus it is understandable that in the discussion of his view of the best regime Aristotle tacitly assumes that the slave population will not be comprised of natural slaves, but rather of intelligent, but unspirited, Asians to whom eventual freedom can be held out as a reward for faithful service.

The fact that the natural economic standard could not be directly applied to political life as it existed in Aristotle's time is clear even by the end of the first book of the *Politics*. Having "discussed adequately what relates to knowledge [*gnōsis*]," Aristotle turns to "what relates to practice [*chrēsis*]" (1258b9–10). As he had already conceded at the end of his discussion of "the unnecessary sort of expertise in business," we may nevertheless be in "need" (*chrēsis*) of it (1258a14–16). Thus we are somewhat prepared for the fact that with respect to farming Aristotle merely refers the reader to treatises by others, but himself relates two examples of "the ways some have succeeded in business" and recommends that a more complete collection of instances be undertaken (1259a3–5).

Nevertheless, it is easy to attribute Aristotle's recounting of the monopolistic "killings" made by the eminent philosopher Thales and an anonymous Sicilian to his desire to be comprehensive, to catalogue everything. However, as noted above, Aristotle's discussion of the proper relationship between true economics (that is, household management) and business expertise seems to end in the suggestion that to be a real householder or *oikonomos*, one ought to inherit a self-sufficient estate from one's father. The practical discussion of business expertise may be interpreted as Aristotle's silent recognition of the impracticality of this advice.

While the idea that a naturally good man might have to resort to commercial trickery of some sort (such as monopoly) to rectify nature's error in not providing for him remains implicit, Aristotle explicitly notes that "many cities need business and revenues of this sort, just as households do, yet more so" and that therefore "it is useful for political [rulers] also to be familiar with these things" (1259a33–35). In other words, Aristotle makes it clear that he is not recommending the codification of his natural economic standard into a legal code. There is, for example, no reason to suppose that he would have favored laws banning the lending of money at interest, such as existed during the Christian Middle Ages.

These observations merely raise the question of what the import of Aristotle's "natural economics" is supposed to be. If it is not to be regarded as scientific truth or as a legislative model or even as a guide to action for individuals in any simple sense, what purpose is it intended to serve?

The Addressees of the Politics

In raising again the question of the kind of study that Aristotle takes economics to be, we must first ask whom Aristotle intended to address in the *Politics*. Since economics is for Aristotle a "practical" science, that is, one devoted primarily to action rather than to knowledge, our understanding of an economic doctrine will depend on the kind of person Aristotle intended to advise and on how the nature of that kind of person affects the manner in which the advice is given. Unfortunately, Aristotle does not explicitly discuss the issue of the book's "addressees" in the *Politics;* he does, however, deal with the question in the *Nicomachean Ethics*. We turn to that work, therefore, for a general sense of what is meant by an "addressee."

Of particular interest is Aristotle's contention that the young should not study political science (the inquiry of the *Ethics* having been earlier described as "a kind of political science").[56] One of the reasons he gives is that their study would be in vain, since, being led by their passions, they would be unable to follow the precepts that they learned in the course of their study. Since "the end [of the study of political science] is not knowledge but action,"[57] it would be pointless for those who would be unable in any case to improve their actions to learn how they should act. The knowledge of political science or ethics, separate from action, does not appear to be a worthwhile goal.

As Aristotle develops his doctrine in the *Ethics*, however, it becomes clear that habituation is an important prerequisite for moral virtue. If the young should not study ethics because, being led by their passions,

56. *Eth. Nic.* 1094b10–11.
57. Ibid. 1095a6.

they would be unable to follow its precepts, it would seem that the old, as well, should not study it, since their habits are already formed. Aristotle addresses this problem in the tenth book of the *Ethics,* where the transition from ethics to politics in the narrow sense is prepared. The force of law is necessary to regulate both the education of the young (to inculcate proper habits) and the actions of the old (to prevent the force of that habituation from degrading).[58] One exception, however, to the necessity for the force of law is admitted: speeches (*logoi*) have the power to exhort and encourage generous youth and to cause those of good innate character and who truly love the noble to be possessed by virtue.[59]

Yet the *Ethics* itself is a "speech." It is certainly not a law that can enforce compliance with its prescriptions by means of rewards and punishments. If the book has as its primary purpose not the theoretical one of the transmission of knowledge of a certain kind, but rather the practical one of making men good, then it would seem that among its primary addressees must be, the remarks of the first book cited above notwithstanding, the "generous youth" described above.[60] Since the purpose of the book is not so much to instruct them as to persuade them, the interpreter of the *Ethics* would have to keep in mind that some, if not all, passages have a primarily rhetorical function.

As we have noted, economics is, like ethics, a practical science and is hence concerned with guiding men to correct actions.[61] Thus, in examining Aristotle's economic doctrines, we must be alive to the possibility that certain passages may serve a primarily rhetorical function, that is, they may be intended primarily to influence the reader to behave in a certain way rather than to instruct him.

The Rhetoric of the Politics

To understand this problem better, it may be useful to compare it with a more extreme case of rhetoric of this sort, the first part of Socrates' "noble lie," at the end of the third book of Plato's *Republic*.[62] Here we find

58. Ibid. 1179b32–1180a5.
59. Ibid. 1179b4–11.
60. Among the other addressees might be those adults already possessed of a good habituation; in this case, the book's purpose would be not so much to make men good as to refine the notions of virtue already held by basically good men.
61. Whereas in the beginning of the *Nicomachean Ethics* we are told that the end of the study of ethics is not knowledge but action, in the first book of the *Politics* goals of both sorts are typically cited as the ends of the study (1253b15–18 and 1258b9–10). Furthermore, the practical goal of economics is given as use or need (*chrēsis, chreia*) rather than action. The implication seems to be that the relation between the practical science of economics and "physics" (the theoretical knowledge of nature) is somewhat closer than that between ethics and "physics."
62. *Rep.* 414d–e. Strictly speaking, only this first part of the tale (*mythos*) Socrates tells is called a lie.

an example of a lesson about nature (in this case, about the earth and its relationship to a particular group of men) that is propagated for the sake of its effects on the citizens' behavior. This lie is designed to be told to the citizens of a particular city and is of a rather extreme character.

Aristotle's books, on the other hand, are accessible to the citizens of many different cities and would in any case be unable to propagate so fantastic a story. For one thing, they cannot isolate the reader from other, contradictory accounts, whereas the propagation of the "noble lie" seems to depend on the city, and its ability to censor the stories told to the young, already being in existence.[63] Thus Aristotle's teachings will have to be much more plausible than the "noble lie" even if they do not coincide in all respects with the truth as he would attempt to establish it in his theoretical writings.

The doctrine of natural acquisition is an example of this. While it does not correspond to the teachings about nature in the *Physics,* it nevertheless enjoys some inherent plausibility by virtue of the analogy Aristotle draws between the survival of the various animal species and that of primitive men such as hunters and nomads. It establishes a standard according to which the various modes of acquisition may be judged. Farming, hunting, and the raising of livestock are adjudged natural modes of acquisition; "business" in the sense of commerce, money lending, and practicing an art for wages are adjudged unnatural. The doctrine of natural acquisition encourages a trust in natural providence; since nature takes care of man's basic material needs, there is no reason for man to concern himself overmuch with their satisfaction. Instead of being constantly concerned with mere life, man should focus his attention on what is necessary for the good life.

This doctrine can be reasonably addressed only to an aristocratic class whose property is sufficient to take care of their basic economic needs and to provide them with the wealth necessary for taking an active part in the public life of the city. Directed to such a class, the doctrine is an attempt to persuade its members to concentrate on political activity (or on more noble uses of leisure) rather than to attempt to increase their wealth. That Aristotle conceives this to be a serious political danger is made clear in *Politics* 5. Since all aristocratic regimes have an oligarchic character, the notables tend to grasp for wealth (1307a34–35). This tendency not only harms the aristocrats themselves but leads to political instability as well: the common people are much more likely to abide the rule of an aristocracy when they think that the aristocrats are not using their superior political position for the sake of amassing wealth (1308b31–1309a9, 1318b17–21). (It might be objected that political

63. *Rep.* 415d.

problems would arise only when the aristocrats use their public offices to enrich themselves [such as through graft], whereas Aristotle seeks to dissuade them from any kind of money-making activity, honest or dishonest. Aristotle seems to have little faith that the money-making spirit, once active in the aristocracy, would be able to confine itself to legal channels or that the aristocrats would be willing to compete on equal terms with ordinary citizens. As Montesquieu describes this latter problem, in an aristocracy, "it is necessary that the law prohibit [the aristocrats] from engaging in commerce: merchants so well connected would gain all sorts of monopolies.")[64]

But if the opposition to the unlimited acquisition of wealth is Aristotle's main purpose in discussing economics, we must still ask why he chose to proceed by distinguishing between natural and unnatural modes of acquisition, rather than by directly making the moral argument emphasizing money's role as a means to the good life, but not an end in itself. An advantage of this second course would be that the message would be applicable to everyone, not only to the members of an aristocracy. With respect to a poorer person, the teaching would be that while it is reasonable to attempt to acquire some property, one must always keep in mind that the ultimate goal is to be able to forget about economic concerns and shift one's attention elsewhere after the requisite amount of property has been attained. Indeed, it is difficult to see how else to interpret Aristotle's assertion that a concern with wealth is in one sense the duty of the household manager (*oikonomos*), but in another, that of a subsidiary art (1258a32–34).

The answer to this question points directly to the rhetorical function of the natural economics doctrine. Apparently, Aristotle did not believe that merely preaching the moral argument against the unlimited pursuit of wealth would be likely to have very much effect, especially if, at the same time, one gives a qualified approval to business activity within certain limits.[65] Aristotle must present his arguments against the unlimited

64. *De l'esprit des lois,* bk. 5, chap. 8.
65. The unlimited pursuit of wealth is a manifestation of the vice of illiberality, according to the scheme of virtues and vices set forth in the *Nicomachean Ethics.* Illiberality bears some relation to cowardice, the former involving the excessive accumulation and preservation of the means to life and the latter the excessive concern for the preservation of life itself. Illiberality is more innate in man (that is, ingrained in his nature, *symphyesteron*) than the opposite vice of prodigality, and tends to grow worse with age. Whereas illiberality is incurable, prodigality can, if subjected to the proper influence and training, transform itself into liberality. Both of these assertions derive from the same phenomenon, the tendency to husband one's resources with more caution as one grows older. If the discussion of liberality in the *Ethics* is to have any practical effect, it must be to guide the prodigal youth on the path toward true liberality by teaching him to distinguish between noble and ignoble uses of money. The generally more pervasive problem of illiberality is ignored,

pursuit of wealth in such a manner as to be convincing to his aristocratic addressees. He must therefore argue from premises that they are likely to accept; these premises not only form the basis of a convincing demonstration, but also help establish Aristotle's credit with his audience.[66]

The basic premise or prejudice from which Aristotle proceeds is the aristocratic contempt for the tradesman—his constant concern for small sums of money (or as Adam Smith put it, his abiding by the "pedlar principle of turning a penny wherever a penny was to be got"),[67] his sedentary and unmanly way of life, his dependence on the arbitrarily given or withheld custom of his patrons, and the obsequiousness that dependence can engender.

For an expression of this contempt, we may turn to these remarks by Plato's Adeimantus:

> There are men [i.e., the tradesmen] who see this situation and set themselves to this service; in rightly governed cities they are usually those whose bodies are weakest and are useless for doing any other job. They must stay there in the market and exchange things for money with those who need to sell something and exchange, for money again, with all those who need to buy something.[68]

This is Adeimantus' only long response to a Socratic question in the course of founding the first city. It seems to denote a special contempt for the tradesman. Adeimantus' response to questions concerning merchants are straightforward and short.[69] The missing element of pettiness would seem to be crucial. Aristotle's procedure attempts to identify the two activities under the heading of business by transforming the objectionable feature from the element of pettiness to the concern with money. Concern with money must be seen as inherently petty.

This transition is facilitated by the natural economic standard Aristotle introduces. Money is conventional and hence is a symbol of the economic interdependence of men in the city. This notion of economic interdependence goes against the grain for a proud aristocrat who would prefer to believe that in his relations with others (particularly his fellow

---

presumably as being relatively less important in the case of the work's prime addressees, the noble and generous youth. In the *Politics*, on the other hand, Aristotle must tackle the harder problem of illiberality.

66. *Rh.* 2.21.15–16.

67. A. Smith, *Inquiry into the Nature and Causes of the Wealth of Nations* (New York, n.d.), 391.

68. *Rep.* 371c–d.

69. Ibid. 370e–371a.

citizens) he is acting voluntarily and from a desire for honor, rather than from necessity and for the sake of material need.[70]

By this rhetorical means, Aristotle attempts to present the unlimited pursuit of wealth as something beneath the dignity of the aristocrat; his effort, however, extends only to those modes of acquisition that fall under the general heading of "business." The possibility of an individual or a city enriching itself by political and military means, not to mention tyrannical or imperial means, seems to remain. The cultivation of liberality and moderation with regard to wealth is, in the final analysis, a political problem; one must attempt, as Aristotle says in the second book of the *Politics*, to contrive that "those who are respectable by nature will be the sort who have no wish to aggrandize themselves, while the mean will not be able to" (1267b6–8).

One is tempted to conclude that Aristotle opposes business activity not because of its injustice but because of its justice (as compared with the other methods of increasing wealth suggested above). While robbery, for example, cannot be tolerated by any city as a regular means of an individual's increasing his wealth, business clearly can be; the political necessities no longer automatically restrain the unlimited pursuit of wealth. Precisely what a modern thinker like Locke finds so attractive about money and business, that it allows each individual to pursue his economic self-interest without necessarily coming into conflict with his fellow citizens or with the city, is what to Aristotle appears to be its most insidious characteristic. His doctrine of natural economics opposes such an attempt at a reconciliation between individual self-aggrandizement and the city's interests, which would tend to bury the moral issue of the role of wealth in human life.

In a similar manner, Aristotle's doctrine of natural slavery seems to be designed to keep alive a moral issue that Aristotle did not believe capable of solution. In this context, we must first observe that Aristotle's "intellectual" opponents on this question, the conventionalists, were by no means abolitionists, as is most clearly shown by their belief that not only slavery, but the city itself, existed only by convention. Their view was rather that the individual should free himself from any inward belief in the majesty or rightness of these institutions, the better to be able to manipulate them in his own interest. Consequently, the practical alter-

---

70. "Expertise in exchange is justly blamed since it is not according to nature but involves taking from others" (1258a40–b2). As appears from Aristotle's inclusion of piracy among the *natural* modes of acquisition (1256b1), the "blame" involved in "taking from others" does not result from a sense that one is cheating or stealing from the others, but rather that one is dependent on them.

natives seem to have been slavery as understood by Aristotle (namely, natural slavery), as understood by the conventionalists (that is, having no basis in nature but resting only on force), or, in accordance with the common Greek view to which Aristotle alludes at 1255b29, as resulting from the racial superiority of the Greeks over the barbarians. By choosing as he does, Aristotle is able to establish a standard by which the existing institution may be judged. As we have noted, he is reticent to apply this standard himself; to do so would seem to condemn the institution entirely, as well as any likely replacement. It is nevertheless clear that in some cases the divergence between the natural standard and the actuality would become so great as to appear to the most casual reader; the addressees of the book would be encouraged, for example, to manumit any slave who showed superior intellectual abilities. According to the conventionalist understanding, on the other hand, there would be no incentive to free such an individual, since his enslavement would be no less just or more anomalous than the enslavement of anyone else. Similarly, the "racist" understanding would tend to blind masters to the existence of any superior individuals among their slaves.

In this regard, then, Aristotle's doctrine of natural slavery seems to serve the same purpose as his discussion in the sixth book of the *Politics* of the various ways in which democratic and oligarchic regimes can be moderated and thereby increase their chances for stability. In both cases, the sorts of "reforms" that Aristotle recommends seem to a reader who is used to considering the grand idealistic schemes of modern political thinkers intolerably small and cautious; on the other hand, because Aristotle is careful to link them with the interests of his addressees, as those addressees can be brought through Aristotelian rhetoric to see them, he may have felt that the smallness of the steps he discusses would be balanced by the higher probability of their being taken.[71]

For Aristotle, economics is a practical science, directed toward action rather than knowledge. Since wealth is not an independent goal, there is no independent science of economics; one cannot issue prescriptions with respect to the attainment of wealth without considering whether the actions recommended would be advisable from other points of view.

Since the unlimited desire for wealth is a moral and political fault that is deeply rooted in man's constitution, it must be a major goal of any

71. "Aristote est le défenseur de l'esclavage, mais il en est aussi le réformateur" (M. Defourney, *Aristote: Études sur la "Politique"* [Paris, 1932], 36–37). Using a historicist approach, Defourney analyzes Aristotle's doctrine in the light of the economic situation of the time. While this enables him to get at the practical side of Aristotle's intention with sense and understanding, it prevents him from asking whether Aristotle might not have seen beyond the immediate situation and the practical proposals he makes in the light of it.

practical science to combat it; hence Aristotle's economics, unlike, for instance, the science of economics as defined by Adam Smith, which "proposes to enrich both the people and the sovereign,"[72] is more concerned with limiting man's desire for wealth than it is with showing him the means of fulfilling it.

72. Smith, *Wealth of Nations*, 397.

FOUR

Aristotle's Political Sociology: Class, Status, and Order in the *Politics*

Josiah Ober

For one investigating the *politeia* [regime]—what each sort is and what its quality—virtually the first investigation concerns the *polis* [city], to see what the *polis* actually is. . . . and the *politeia* is a certain arrangement of those who inhabit the *polis*. But since the *polis* belongs among composite things, and like other composite wholes is made up of many parts, it is clear that the first thing that must be sought is the *politēs* [citizen]; for the *polis* is a certain multitude of *politai* [citizens]. Thus who ought to be called a *politēs* and what the *politēs* is must be investigated.[1]

The central importance of sociology to political analysis is made explicit in Aristotle's introduction to the third book of the *Politics*. The attempt to classify how relations of power among social groups affect the political regime is a central theme of the *Politics*. Moreover, the intimate and inseparable connection of the *organization of the residents of the polis*—especially, but not uniquely, the citizens—with the regime and with the identification and definition of the *polis* itself is assumed throughout the *Politics*. Failure to take this assumption into account renders the *Politics* incomprehensible. R. Osborne has rightly commented that "it is the impossibility of divorcing the *politeia* from the society that makes it evident to Aristotle that to change the *politeia* changes the polis; to his modern critics, however, who have no difficulty driving a wedge between state

I would like to thank Carnes Lord, Barry Strauss, James Allard, Mogens Hansen, and Adrienne Mayor for their helpful comments on various drafts of this essay. Its timely completion was made possible by a grant from the Research Office of Montana State University. Translations of passages of the *Politics* are adapted from the translation of C. Lord, *The* Politics *of Aristotle* (Chicago, 1984).
    1. *Pol.* 1274b32–1275a2.

and society, Aristotle's remarks become opaque."[2] Here I do not intend to debate those who fail to recognize the importance of sociology to Aristotle's political thought, but rather to attempt to define the analytical categories he employed in describing and explaining the relationship between society and regime.

In an important section of his massive study, *The Class Struggle in the Ancient Greek World*, G. E. M. de Ste. Croix argues that economic class is the fundamental analytical category of Aristotle's political sociology, observing: "Aristotle, the great expert on the sociology and politics of the Greek city, always proceeds on the basis of a class analysis and takes it for granted that men will act, politically and otherwise, above all according to their economic position."[3] Ste. Croix concludes that Aristotle's conception of the political role of class was virtually identical to that of Karl Marx. This conclusion supports the further assumption that since the most astute and systematic contemporary observer of Greek political behavior employed "Marxist" categories, a Marxist analysis of ancient Greek history is valid. Aristotle becomes a key not only to understanding ancient political philosophy, but to a historical understanding of the political sociology of antiquity.

Ste. Croix's definition of the term "class" is detailed and precise.[4] For Ste. Croix, class is determined by property ownership or nonownership, since property (especially agricultural land) was the primary means of economic production in antiquity. The relationship between classes is inevitably one of *"exploitation by the propertied class of the non-propertied"* (Ste. Croix's italics).[5] This exploitative relationship results in class struggle—

2. R. Osborne, Demos: *The Discovery of Attika* (Cambridge, 1985), 9. The "embeddedness" of the political order in the social order is a central tenet for most modern political sociologists; see, for example, S M. Lipset, "Political Sociology," in *Sociology Today*, ed. R. K. Merton et al. (New York, 1959), 82–83, who emphasizes the error of "trying to deal with state and society as two independent organisms" by pointing out that "the state is just one of many political institutions, and . . . political institutions are one of many clusters of *social* institutions." He asserts, in addition, that "the relationship between political institutions and other institutions is the special province of political sociology." For further discussion of the history and current state of political sociology, especially in the United States, see P. C. Washburn, *Political Sociology: Approaches, Concepts, Hypotheses* (Englewood Cliffs, N.J., 1982). Compare the approach of N. Luhmann, discussed in note 36 below.

3. G. E. M. de Ste. Croix, *The Class Struggle in the Ancient Greek World from the Archaic Age to the Arab Conquests* (Ithaca, N.Y., 1981), 79; see 69–80 generally. The following sheds light on Ste. Croix's definition of "fundamental": "All I am saying is that [class] is the fundamental [category of analysis], which *over all* (at any given moment) and *in the long run* is the most important, and is by far the most useful to us, in helping us to understand Greek history and explain the process of change within it" (45; Ste. Croix's italics). Cf. his use of the term on pp. 74, 75, 79.

4. Ste. Croix, *Class Struggle*, 42–69.

5. Ibid., 68.

although that struggle may not be political, overt, or even consciously perceived by the participants on either side. When the struggle does become overt, an individual's class interest will typically determine his political actions. Hence political behavior is determined by economic class; the wealthy property owners are ranged against those who do not own significant amounts of property, and the former will attempt to use the political process to protect their property. If the propertied are successful, the resulting political order will be an oligarchy. The poor will attempt to use the political process to defend themselves against exploitation by the rich; if they are successful, the result is some form of democracy.[6] Ste. Croix does not suppose that class is the only category useful in describing or analyzing ancient society, but he does believe that it is the only category that can explain social change.[7] Thus he is scornful of attempts by others to use as a primary analytical device any sociopolitical category other than class. M. I. Finley's use of the category of status in his book *The Ancient Economy* is singled out by Ste. Croix as an example of the erroneous use of nonclass categories.[8]

Finley specifically rejects the notion that class, in either its Marxist or non-Marxist sense, is, by itself, adequate to explain the interwoven, crisscrossing categories of Greek and Roman society.[9] Although Finley never attempts a precise definition of status, which, he remarks, is "an admirably vague word with a considerable psychological element," what he means by status is made quite clear by the examples he cites—especially the example of the social position of the Roman freedman Trimalchio (described by Petronius in the *Satyricon*).[10] Trimalchio was extremely wealthy but was excluded by his slave birth from the highest Roman social circles. His inferior status vis à vis the traditional senatorial aristocracy was recognized by all parties, and Trimalchio made no attempt to become a senator. Status was further defined by occupation;

6. Ibid., 71–74, 96–97. Ste. Croix's definition of "exploitation" is "the appropriation of part of the product of the labour of others: in a commodity-producing society this is the appropriation of what Marx called 'surplus value'" (43).

7. Ste. Croix, *Class Struggle*, 45. For the purposes of political sociology, I employ the following definitions: *describe:* "to say what important social groups exist in a society or polity and how the membership of each group is to be defined"; *analyze:* "to say how social groups relate to one another and to the political order"; *explain:* "to say why the relationships between groups and of groups to the political order remain static or change over time." I think these are approximately the definitions Ste. Croix employs.

8. For Ste. Croix's scorn for the category of status, see Ste. Croix, *Class Struggle*, 80–98; on Finley's use of the category, 90–94.

9. M. I. Finley, *The Ancient Economy* (Berkeley, 1973), 48–51. Ste. Croix, *Class Struggle*, 58–59, considers Finley's understanding of Marxism inadequate, but that need not concern us here.

10. Finley, *Ancient Economy*, 51; on status and its relationship to class and order, 35–61.

those who (openly at least) engaged in various forms of nonagricultural economic activity (including merchants, traders, moneylenders, and craftsmen) were frequently regarded as of lower status than those whose class was similar but whose wealth was derived entirely from their landed estates. According to Finley, then, an individual's status may be determined by his birth and occupation, as well as by his wealth. Status is a more fluid category than is class; status does not require the concepts of exploitation or struggle, but it does require consciousness; that is, a general consensus by the members of society about which descent/occupational groups are to be accorded what place in the social hierarchy. Hence, in contrast to the materialistic Marxist determination of class, status is determined ideologically. Finley's preference for the category of status over class has been traced to the influence of the sociological theories of Max Weber.[11] Thus the disagreement between Ste. Croix and Finley over the most appropriate categories for describing and explaining ancient society reflects a broader debate between Marxian and Weberian modes of social analysis.

Finley does not deal directly with Aristotle's *Politics* in *The Ancient Economy*, but he does treat the *Politics* extensively in his later book, *Politics in the Ancient World*. Here Finley employs the term "class" instead of "status" and concentrates more on the sociopolitical importance of wealth than on that of birth or occupation. Finley still rejects the "bad habit" of assuming that analysis based on economic class must be Marxist. He obviously considers Ste. Croix's turning "Aristotle into a Marxist" to be misleading, and he uses the term "class" more loosely than does Ste. Croix.[12] Although his discussion of the significance of economic class in the political analysis of the *Politics* has much in common with that of Ste. Croix, Finley specifically states that his use of the term "class" rather than "status" in this volume does not represent a change in his assessment of the relative analytic value of class and status as defined in *The Ancient Economy:*

> In that book I argued that 'status' and 'order' [for which see below] are preferable to 'class' in analysing the ancient economy. My return in the

11. See B. D. Shaw and R. P. Saller's introduction to M. I. Finley, *Economy and Society in Ancient Greece* (New York, 1983), xvii–xviii. Ste. Croix, *Class Struggle*, 91, considers Finley's classification by status "virtually identical" with Weber's. In *Ancient History: Evidence and Models* (New York, 1985), 88–103, Finley criticizes Weber's discussion of charismatic leadership at Athens and of Greek law but reiterates his conviction that Weber's analysis of the ancient economy and social structure is "without parallel" (90). Finley took a more juridical/legal approach to the question of status at the lower end of the hierarchy in his 1960 article "The Servile Statuses of Ancient Greece," in *Economy and Society,* 131–49.

12. M. I. Finley, *Politics in the Ancient World* (Cambridge, 1983), 1–10; on Ste. Croix, 10, with n. 26.

present work to 'class' (in the sense intended in ordinary discourse, not in
a technical sense, Marxist or other) does not imply a change of view. I
merely find the conventional terminology more convenient, and harmless,
in an account of ancient politics.[13]

Because the difference in terms of social categories between Finley's two
works is apparently terminological rather than substantive (despite the
greater emphasis Finley gives to wealth as a determinant of political behavior in *Politics in the Ancient World*), it seems legitimate to use Finley's
Ancient Economy description of status in this investigation into Aristotle's
sociological categories.[14]

Both Finley and Ste. Croix recognize the existence and descriptive
value of a third social category: "order" (or estate). Relative to classes
and status groups, orders—the category, like "status," is Weberian in origin—are rigid, and they are typically juridically defined: the members of
the various orders in a society are assigned specific privileges, duties, or
disadvantages by legal enactment.[15]

The three categories adopted by Finley and Ste. Croix as the most
useful models of sociological analysis provide a point of departure for
this investigation into Aristotle's political sociology: Did Aristotle recognize any or all of these social categories? Did he find any or all of them
useful for the description, analysis, or explanation of politics? And finally, if the answer to these questions is affirmative, did he consider any
one category of primary importance? Establishing the parameters of the
investigation in these terms may appear perverse to those who reject the
notion of analyzing the ancient world or its literary products in any but
ancient terms. For some, no doubt, the inquiry ends with the determination that there are no terms in the *Politics* that correspond exactly to the
words "class," "status," and "order" as defined above. However, classical
Greek philosophers were limited in their technical terminology; the absence of precise terminological analogues to class, status, and order in
the *Politics* does not *ipso facto* preclude the possibility that Aristotle recognized the significance of these concepts.[16]

Furthermore, if the political sociology of the *Politics* is to be used
in the study of Greek social history, we must ask whether Aristotle's

13. Finley, *Politics in the Ancient World*, 10 n. 29.

14. Finley assumes that status considerations were of major concern to Aristotle and his
contemporaries in his article "Aristotle and Economic Analysis," *Past and Present* 47 (1970):
3–25.

15. Ste. Croix, *Class Struggle*, 42, 94; Finley, *Ancient Economy*, 45–48.

16. Cf. Ste. Croix, *Class Struggle*, 35 and 80, where Ste. Croix observes that if the Greeks
did not have a word for a given concept, the phenomenon may not have existed in Greek
times, and objects to the category of status on the grounds that there is no straightforward
Greek word for "status." But Ste. Croix is unable to come up with a single Greek word that
suits his conception of "class."

thought has any point of connection with the best and most sophisticated modern analyses of society. If so, Ste. Croix's indirect premise—that Aristotle can provide some guidance in deciding which modern categories can fruitfully be used in historical analyses of sociopolitical activity in antiquity—is validated. If Aristotle's social categories have no analogues in modern sociological literature, historians must choose between Aristotle's analytic categories and modern categories. And this means they must face a dilemma: on the one hand, they risk using the possibly erroneous and idiosyncratic notions of a single observer; on the other, they risk misinterpreting ancient societies by the employment of inappropriate, anachronistic social models.

A corollary aim of this essay is to investigate the *degree* of societal differentiation that Aristotle recognized as existing within the *polis*. This problem is of central importance in assessing the value of the *Politics* to modern political philosophy. S. T. Holmes, in a seminal article, has argued that the "relatively undifferentiated character of the Greek social order" was a critical factor in Aristotle's (and other Greeks') equation of society with *politeia* and in his emphasis on the duties, as opposed to the rights, of citizens. Aristotle's political theory, Holmes suggests, was based on a form of social organization unique to classical Greek antiquity. Therefore, ancient political philosophy can shed no direct light upon the sociopolitical organization of modern states, with their high degree of structural differentiation and consequent emphasis on legality and negative freedoms. For Holmes, then, the modern separation of political systems from the social environment and of government from polity renders Aristotle's political thought obsolete.[17] Holmes's argument loses some of its force, however, if it can be shown that Aristotle's political theory assumes the existence of a relatively highly differentiated social order.

Two other methodological considerations must be briefly noted. The structure of the *Politics* is complex. In some books Aristotle is concerned with empirical description of the basic types of commonly existing regimes: oligarchy, democracy, and tyranny. He also attempts to define and analyze the "better" regimes, of which the commonly existing regimes are "debased" forms: aristocracy, "polity," and kingship (see especially 1279a22–b10). Finally, Aristotle attempts a description of the best of possible regimes: an achievable ideal *polis*. This last endeavor is sometimes difficult to extricate from the second, qualitative analysis, since Aristotle's best achievable regime is a version of aristocracy, one of the "better" regimes. It is extremely important for our purposes to define the literary context of Aristotle's various discussions of political sociol-

17. S. T. Holmes, "Aristippus in and out of Athens," *American Political Science Review* 73 (1979): 113–28, especially 116, 126.

ogy, since the categories of social analysis he employs vary according to whether he is engaged in empirical description or philosophical analysis.[18]

We must also remain sensitive to the ideological climate in which the *Politics* was written. Aristotle lived most of his adult life in democratic Athens. Some aspects of his discussion in the *Politics* are best understood by assuming that Aristotle was consciously engaged in a dialogue with the ideology of democratic egalitarianism. This ideology, while not described in existing philosophical texts, was clearly enunciated in the "constitution" of the Athenian state. Briefly stated, the Athenians recognized as citizens all free, adult males, born of Athenian parents. The citizens collectively determined state policy through mass meetings of the Assembly and resolved legal questions in the people's courts. In both the Assembly and the courts simple majority voting determined the issue. With few exceptions any citizen could fill any state office; most offices were annual and filled by sortition, thus maximizing the numbers of citizens holding office and eliminating relative levels of probable ability as a primary criterion in the selection of officials. Undergirding these constitutional arrangements was the conviction that mass decisions were better than individual decisions and that all citizens, regardless of their social position, were of equal political worth.[19]

Turning to Aristotle's social categories of analysis, we may begin with class. If we leave exploitation and struggle aside for the moment, it is beyond doubt that in the *Politics* Aristotle employed the category of "class" in its ordinary modern sense—a division of society according to wealth distribution. Aristotle refers to the populace divided into two parts (*moria*): the "rich" (usually *euporoi* or *plousioi*) and the "poor" (usually *aporoi* or *penētes*). By the "rich," Aristotle clearly means individuals who own sufficient property so that they are free from the need personally to engage in labor. Hence the rich constitute a leisure class, living from the labor of others, usually slaves.[20] The "poor," on the other hand, are not necessarily propertyless, but they possess insufficient property to permit them a life of leisure; the "poor" man is not typically impoverished, but he must work for a living. He may be characterized as a man

18. Cf. Finley, *Politics in the Ancient World*, 126; id., "Aristotle and Economic Analysis," 5.

19. The single most important authority for the constitution of Athens in the fourth century B.C. is the Aristotelian *Athēnaiōn Politeia* 42–69; cf. the massive commentary of P. J. Rhodes (Oxford, 1981). On the egalitarian nature of Athenian democracy, see, for example, A. H. M. Jones, *Athenian Democracy* (Oxford, 1957), 46–48. On the order and date of composition of the *Politics*, R. Weil, *Aristote et l'histoire: Essai sur la "Politique"* (Paris, 1960), is still very useful.

20. E.g., 1315a31–34, 1318a26–b1; cf. *Rh.* 1361a12–16. On the classical Greek terminology of wealth and poverty, cf. Finley, *Ancient Economy*, 40–41; for an assessment of the constitutional significance of these terms in Athens, see V. Gabrielsen, *Remuneration of State Officials in Fourth-Century B.C. Athens* (Odense, 1981), 119–26.

who owns an ox instead of slaves and whose human labor force consists of his family (1252b9–12; cf. 1323a5–6). In this case the *oikos* (family unit) is based economically on subsistence farming and is essentially autarkic in that the labor of the members of the *oikos* produces goods consumed directly by the *oikos*.[21] Other "poor" men, who owned property insufficient to feed themselves and their families, worked as wage laborers; Aristotle refers to these individuals as *thetes*.[22] Hence Aristotle's definition of the "rich" necessarily implies (in Ste. Croix's terms) exploitation of the labor of others, but Aristotle's "poor" includes both those whose labor was exploited and those whose labor was not directly exploited.

Aristotle also refers in several passages to a "middle" element in society (*hē mesē*). The middling citizens (*hoi mesoi*) promote stability in any state, and in a "polity" (the "better" form of democracy) they are a majority. In the context of his discussion of the best form of government that could be achieved in most *poleis* (as opposed to the ideal achievable regime discussed in Books 7 and 8) Aristotle states that in practical terms this segment of the populace is the best, since they are neither excessively rich (and hence arrogant and incapable of being ruled) nor excessively poor (and hence humble and covetous and incapable of ruling) (1295b1–1296b12). Aristotle states that the citizens of a "polity" should be those who could afford to possess hoplite armor, but he was unable to define the size of assessment necessary for this purpose (1297b1–3). In a related passage, however, he suggests a middling citizen should have a "middling and sufficient" (*mesē kai hikanē*) amount of property (1295b40). "Sufficient," we may suppose, to avoid the necessity of manual labor. Since subsistence farmers were elsewhere defined as poor (see above), it appears that those of the "middle" represent the lower rungs of the leisure class.[23] At any rate, Aristotle's *hoi mesoi* are certainly not

21. On the large numbers of subsistence farmers in Attica in the fourth century, see J. Ober, *Fortress Attica: Defense of the Athenian Land Frontier, 404–322 B.C.* Mnemosyne Supplementum 84 (Leiden, 1985), 19–28; E. M. Wood, *Peasant-Citizen and Slave: The Foundations of Athenian Democracy* (London and New York, 1988). Cf. V. N. Andreyev, "Some Aspects of Agrarian Conditions in Attica in the Fifth to Third Centuries B.C.," *Eirene* 12 (1974): 445–56; G. Audring, "Über Grundeigentum und Landwirtschaft in der athenischen Polis," in *Hellenische Poleis*, vol. 1, ed. E. C. Welskopf (Berlin, 1974), 108–31.

22. E.g., 1278a13. On the difficulties of separating subsistence farmers from landless *thetes* and from *banausoi* in the sources, see Y. Garlan, "Le travail libre en Grèce ancienne," and E. C. Welskopf, "Free Labor in the City of Athens," in *Non-Slave Labour in the Greco-Roman World*, ed. P. Garnsey (Cambridge, 1980), 6–22 and 23–25, respectively. Cf. also A. Fuks, "*Kolonos misthios*: Labour exchange in Ancient Athens," in *Social Conflict in Ancient Greece* (Jerusalem, 1984), 303–5.

23. Cf. 1288a12–15, where members of the *politikon plēthos*, the citizen population of a "polity," are defined as *euporoi*. Cf. C. Lord's note ad loc. (*The Politics of Aristotle* [Chicago, 1984]).

satisfactorily explained in terms of modern notions (Marxist or other-wise) of the mercantile/manufacturing middle class or petite bour-geoisie.[24] The concept of the middle element is of limited scope in the *Politics*. For the most part reserved for the description of the rare regime of "polity," it has a relatively insignificant place in Aristotle's empirical description of the commonly existing "debased regimes" or in his ideal state. Through most of the *Politics* Aristotle depends on a rich/poor di-chotomy in his analysis of classes of free persons. This dichotomy is a very significant aspect of Aristotle's sociopolitical thought, and the em-phasis he places upon it suggests that a relatively high degree of class stratification and tension typically existed within the Greek *polis*.

In his discussion of oligarchy and democracy Aristotle employs class as *a* fundamental (if not *the* fundamental) concept in explaining political behavior. In several passages, highlighted by both Ste. Croix and Finley, Aristotle explicitly defines the two regimes of democracy and oligarchy as the products of class interests. In discussing the basic division of re-gimes into the better and debased types (1279b17–19) Aristotle states specifically that oligarchy is the rule of the well-to-do and democracy is the rule of the poor. This means that democracy and oligarchy must be formally defined, respectively, as the rule of the poor and the rule of the rich, not as the rule of the many and the rule of the few (1279b20–39; cf. 1290a30–b20). The minority status of the rich in an oligarchy and the numerical superiority of the poor in a democracy, although nearly universal, were epiphenomenal (*sumbebēkos* 1279b36) for Aristotle's ana-lytical purposes. If there were a society in which the rich were many and the poor few, it would be a democracy if the poor minority ruled and an oligarchy if the wealthy majority ruled, since "what makes democracy and oligarchy differ is poverty and wealth" (1279b39–1280a4). Hence, the regimes of oligarchy and democracy are *dependent* upon the exis-tence of class differentiation. If a leveling of property takes place, the regime becomes a different one, so that those political theoreticians who eliminate differences in property ownership would destroy the existing regime (1309b38–1310a2). Aristotle's discussion here of the defining principles of democracy and oligarchy is clearly and explicitly founded on the category of class. Aristotle implies that social differentiation is *prior* to constitutional development (in debased regimes, at least) and his analysis is, in its materialistic determinism, similar to some aspects of Ste. Croix's Marxism.

Although he does not deal analytically with the concept of class con-sciousness, Aristotle obviously considered that rich and poor individuals

24. Finley, *Politics in the Ancient World*, 10–11, with n. 31 (referring to the passage cited in the preceding note) cogently argues that the middle class is not a useful analytic category for Aristotle. Cf. the similar conclusions of Ste. Croix, *Class Struggle*, 71–72.

were, typically, aware of the political significance of class. In his discussion of the techniques used by tyrants and demagogues to gain popularity, for example, he notes that both tyrants and demagogues incited revolution and gained the trust of the poor majority by attacking the privileges and property of the rich (1304b15–1305a7). In terms of political activity, then, Aristotle's class-based analysis would seem to lead to the conclusion that the political actions of a class-conscious individual are predetermined. In Ste. Croix's formulation, the existence of a significant number of class-conscious individuals within a socially differentiated community should result in class conflict as each class attempts to use the political process in order to protect and advance its own interests.

Aristotle never draws the foregoing conclusion in quite those terms. He is certainly clear about the likelihood and consequences of class conflict: after the conflict of virtue and vice, the conflict between poverty and wealth is the primary cause of factional conflict (*diastasis*), and all other causes are of lesser significance (1303b13–17; cf. 1265b10–12). And when factional conflicts between rich and poor do erupt, the poor, when victorious, invariably establish democracies; the rich, narrow oligarchies (1296a21–32). In existing democracies, attempts by the poor majority to confiscate the property of the rich are a cause of antagonism between classes and ultimately can lead to civil war, as occurred, for example, in Rhodes in 390 B.C. (1302b24–25, 1304b20–1305a7). The existence of extremes in wealth and poverty is especially productive of conflict, as in the aristocratic regime of Sparta during the Messenian Wars (1306b36–1307a1). And even in the ideal city, the exacerbation of poverty could cause civil war and crime (*stasis* and *kakourgia* 1265b10–11). But Aristotle also recognized numerous causes of factional conflict that had nothing much to do with class (consider the examples cited at 1302a16–1304b18, for instance), and he did not regard class conflict, even on an "unconscious" plane, as inevitable. Class conflict, and even resentment, could be avoided if the rich treated the poor justly. It was not so much their poverty that the poor resented, or even their relative lack of political power, but the tendency of the rich (especially in an oligarchy) to act illegally (1297b6–10, 1308a3–11, 1308b31–38, 1310a6–12).

Aristotle specifically rejected the arguments of Phaleas of Chalcedon, who asserted that all civil conflicts arise over the question of property and that property equalization is therefore an adequate means of avoiding factional conflict. Aristotle attacked Phaleas both by asserting that equalization was impracticable and on the grounds that the just desire for *inequality* by the "refined types" (*charientes*) would result in continued conflict (1266a31–1267b21). Aristotle thus rejects narrowly materialistic approaches to lessening class differences in favor of the development of a rapprochement between the classes on the basis of legal (rather than social) justice.

Aristotle's rejection of materialistic solutions to the problem of potential class conflict demonstrates that major differences exist between Aristotle's and Marx's approaches to the sociology of politics. But Aristotle's statements regarding the importance of class in the analysis of democracy and oligarchy, along with his definition of the rich as a leisure class who live from the labor of others, show that he was able to think along lines similar to certain aspects of Ste. Croix's version of Marxism. Aristotle is, furthermore, sufficiently explicit in his hints about class consciousness and in his description of the origins of class conflict to allow us to set aside the question (although it is crucial to other parts of Ste. Croix's argument on the nature of ancient society) of whether or not consciousness and overt conflict are necessary to a class-based analysis of society; Aristotle recognized the political significance of class consciousness and the reality of class conflict. The questions remain whether Aristotle *always* proceeds on the basis of a class analysis and whether class was *the fundamental* category used by Aristotle in constructing his political sociology.

Early in Book 4, after a somewhat confused discussion of various possible social categories, Aristotle seems to allot class a primary role in his discussion of the various "parts" of the *polis*. Aristotle here begins by suggesting that the population of the *polis* could be divided in a variety of ways: by households, by class (rich, poor, and middle), or by military service. The *dēmos* (those who are not in the leisure class) is then subdivided into farming, marketing, and "banausic" elements; the *gnōrimoi* (here the leisure class) are subdivided into the more and less wealthy. In addition to divisions according to wealth, Aristotle notes possible divisions based on family and on virtue (1289b27–1290a1). A bit later in the same book (1290b40–1291b2) Aristotle attempts another complex categorical division of the "parts" of the *polis:* farmers, *banausoi*, merchants, laborers, and soldiers; then (after a digression and a possible lacuna), wealthy liturgists, magistrates, those who deliberate and judge. Aristotle notes that the memberships of these various "parts" often overlap, "but it is impossible for the same persons to be poor and wealthy. Hence these are particularly held to be [*malista einai dokei*] parts of the *polis:* the wealthy and the poor" (1291b2–8). This last sentence suggests that class indeed precedes other categories in the hierarchy of analytical categories. Aristotle then states, "Further, on account of the fact that the former are for the most part few and the latter many, these parts [wealthy and poor] appear to be (*phainetai*) [the most] opposed parts of the city. Accordingly, regimes are instituted on the basis of the sorts of preeminence associated with these [parts], and they consider there to be (*dokousin einai*) two sorts of regimes: democracy and oligarchy."

The crux is, of course, that the sentences quoted above are a summary by Aristotle of the political thinking of ordinary people ("held to be," "they consider"). Aristotle himself found the two-regime (democracy/oligarchy) scheme inadequate and potentially misleading. He states specifically and repeatedly that there are not just two, but several (*pleious*), basic sorts of regimes (1290a24–29, 1291b14–16; cf. 1289a8–10). Nevertheless, Aristotle did not consider the common opinion on this subject to be completely useless. The discussion of "parts" of the city in Book 4 comes in the context of Aristotle's analysis of democracy and oligarchy. It appears that Aristotle agreed with the general opinion that class was the single most useful category for analysis of democracy and oligarchy, but his rejection of the notion that all regimes are simply variants of oligarchy and democracy leaves open the possibility that he did not find class fundamental for analysis of all possible or existing regimes.

Furthermore, Aristotle did not find the category of class fully adequate in and of itself to describe the political sociology of oligarchic and democratic regimes. Although in Books 3 and 4 Aristotle makes it clear that he regards oligarchy and democracy as founded on the principle of class, he notes that the masses may be subdivided into the farmers, artisans, marketing types, seafaring types (sailors in the fleet, overseas traders, ferrymen, fishermen), laborers without leisure, and metics. The notables (*gnōrimoi*) are again subdivided by possession of more or less wealth, but also by good birth, virtue, and education (1291b14–30). He also mentions in passing (1296b26–30) that each variant form of democracy depends on the prominence of a different social group: farmers in the first (best) sort, banausic types (craftsmen or artisans), and wage laborers in the last (worst) sort. Wage laborers can be regarded as a separate class from farmers, but *banausoi* could be quite wealthy (see below), and Aristotle seems to be linking the predominance of low-status persons, as well as of poor persons, with radical democracy. In the detailed treatment of the varieties of democracy in Book 6 (1317b39–41) Aristotle associated other characteristics with each regime, stating that oligarchy was defined by (*horizetai*) noble birth (*genē*), wealth, and education (*paideia*) and that democracy therefore appears on the surface (*dokei*) to be defined by the opposite of these characteristics: lack of noble birth, poverty, and "vulgarness" (*banausia*).[25] The distinction between a good democracy, based on a large population of subsistence farmers, and a bad one, with a population of banausic types, merchants, and wage laborers, who live a mean life and engage in no tasks involving virtue,

---

25. Cf. *Eth. Nic.* 1131a24–29 (cited by Finley, *Ancient Economy*, 5): democrats define merit as the status of the free man; some oligarchs define merit as wealth, others as noble birth; supporters of aristocracy associate merit with *aretē*.

is considerably elaborated (1319a19–28). Similarly, in his discussion of ways in which oligarchies can be preserved, Aristotle notes that the masses are divided into four "parts"—farmers, banausic types, merchants, and wage laborers (1321a5–6)—and that one way to bring individual members of the masses into the citizenship body is to co-opt those who have refrained from engaging in banausic activities for a certain length of time (1321a28–29). Class remains important, but other social distinctions, which can best be understood in terms of status, have been added.

A significant blurring of the sharp emphasis on class is perceptible in the discussion of the defining principles of democracy earlier in Book 6. The central defining principle of democracy is freedom (1317a40–b16; cf. 1318a2–10). According to Aristotle, democrats believed this meant two basic rights: first, the right of the majority of citizens to determine policy by voting in the Assembly and, second, "to live as one desires . . . since not living as one desires is characteristic of a person who is enslaved." Democratic voting rendered rich and poor individuals equals, and so might be regarded as a denial of the primacy of economic class. Aristotle, however, notes that majority decision making left the poor in control of the state and so, links voting to class interests. But the second aspect of the democratic principle of freedom—to live as one desires— relates in this context more directly to status.

In class terms, slaves and the poorest citizens of a democracy might be similar. An agricultural slave and a landless free agricultural laborer had virtually the same relationship to the conditions (that is, the means and labor) of economic production. The labor of both was exploited by the wealthy landowner, and the work each did might be identical. But even the poorest citizen was clearly and consciously of higher status than the slave; because he had been born of citizen parents, he could exercise a citizen's political prerogatives. Birth and the status it conferred was therefore of overwhelming importance for those at the lower end of the social hierarchy. Aristotle too assumed that free birth was a proper prerequisite for citizenship in any regime. Hence for Aristotle, as for the poor Athenian citizen, descent was an essential status characteristic and one that was distinct from economic class.[26]

Aristotle saw other status considerations as important as well. While the average citizen in a democracy probably regarded his birthright to

26. On class as a relationship to the conditions of production and on what those conditions consisted of, see Ste. Croix, *Class Struggle*, 43. On the importance of free birth to the Athenian citizenry, see Aeschin. 3.170; Lys. 30.2, 5–6, 27–28, 30. The doctrine of "natural slavery," most fully enunciated at 1254a15–1255b15, but taken for granted throughout the *Politics*, eliminates the possibility that Aristotle could have approved of freed slaves becoming citizens.

have greater status significance than the work he did, for Aristotle an individual's occupation had considerable status value, and occupation status could have political ramifications, especially in an aristocratic regime. Aristotle regarded certain occupations—manufacturing, trading, wage labor, professional acting, and musical performance—as inherently low status. Individuals in these occupations engaged in activities whose end product was "consumed" by someone else or by the community (*koinōnia*). Aristotle regarded the man who worked for the benefit or pleasure of others—rather than for himself, his *oikos*, or his friends—as acting like a slave, since a slave always engaged in activity for the good of another.[27] By acting like a slave, that individual partook of the necessarily low social status of the slave.

Participation in "slavish" activities did not have direct political significance for most citizens of a democracy.[28] Nor was such activity necessarily politically significant in an oligarchy, where citizenship was based on the principle of wealth. Aristotle notes that although many oligarchic regimes forbade citizens to engage actively in business (*chrēmatizesthai* 1316b3–5), a successful trader or manufacturer could become wealthy enough to qualify for citizenship in an oligarchic regime (1277b33–1278a25). Where wealth alone determined citizenship, the origins of that wealth were unimportant. Occupation status was, however, of great significance to an aristocratic regime.

The importance of status considerations to aristocrats is hinted at in the discussion of oligarchically inclined "polity." Here Aristotle notes that such regimes were commonly called aristocracies, because of the fact that the "better off" (*euporōteroi*) citizens often possess education and good birth as well as wealth (1293b34–39). Hence Aristotle implies that an aristocrat is typically regarded as possessing this particular constellation of attributes. For Aristotle, however, the defining characteristic of an aristocracy was an emphasis on virtue (*aretē*). Since in an aristocracy the right to hold office was one defining characteristic of the citizen, those utterly lacking in virtue could never be citizens in any sort of aristocracy, and in the purest form of aristocracy officeholders were selected *solely* on the basis of their virtue, as opposed to their wealth or other

27. On the concept of *banausia* (translated by Lord, *The Politics of Aristotle*, Glossary, s.v. "vulgar," as "vulgarness") see, for example, 1337b18–22; 1258b25–27, 33–39; 1260a41–b2; 1277a36–37; 1277b33–1278a13; 1277a32–b7; 1341b8–18. Cf. S. C. Humphreys, "Economy and Society in Classical Athens," *Annali della Scuola normale superiore di Pisa*, 2d series, 39 (1970): 1–26, especially 14–15.

28. Athenian politicians attacked each other on the basis of each others' lowly occupational background (e.g., Dem. 18.258–60; 19.98, 200; Andoc. 1.146), but politicians were held to a stricter code of behavior than ordinary citizens; see J. Ober, *Mass and Elite in Democratic Athens: Rhetoric, Ideology, and the Power of the People* (Princeton, 1989), 314–32.

characteristics (1293b1–20; cf. 1326b13–16). Aristotle might appear to have replaced social criteria and categories with purely moral ones, but the possibility of an individual's possessing political virtue, and hence political rights in an aristocracy, was directly linked to status considerations. According to Aristotle, engaging in slavish, banausic activities made living a life of virtue impossible. Therefore anyone who engaged in banausic occupations was automatically excluded from citizenship (1319a20–32). In these terms, participating in even the highest economic level of "banausic" activities, where the amount of wealth accumulated would place the participant in the top economic class in the community, permanently excluded the participant from the political body just as surely as engaging in wage labor. Aristotle's distinction between citizen requirements in oligarchies and aristocracies demonstrates that status was not simply a mask for class.

The inadequacy of class in the analysis of aristocracy is also obvious in Aristotle's rejection of the definition of aristocracy as the simple mix of the wealthy and the poor in political rule—such a mix was defined as "polity." Aristocracy (in its nonideal form) pertained when the variables of freedom, wealth, and virtue, along with the secondary variable of good birth (secondary because it combined virtue and old wealth), were successfully mixed (1294a9–29; cf. 1301b1–4). As we have seen, freedom, virtue, and good birth are all subsumed more readily under the category of status than under that of class. The distinction between class and status categories helps to explain Aristotle's terminology for the higher social groups in Greek society. The *plousioi* and *euporoi* were members of the upper economic classes *tout court;* the *charientes* and *epieikeis* were members of the highest status group in society, wealthy indeed, but distinguished from other rich men by their birth, education, and way of life.[29]

Since Aristotle's ideal state was a form of aristocracy, we should expect that status considerations would weigh heavily there. As an aristocracy, the ideal state was grounded in political virtue, the underlying principles of which are given in Books 3 and 4. The central importance of political virtue is justified by the assumptions that the purpose of the *polis* is for the citizens to live well, that a political community exists for undertaking noble actions, and that those who excel in political virtue (and so live better lives and engage in more noble actions than others) deserve a greater share in the community than those who are highest born, most free, or wealthiest (1281a1–7). Aristotle here specifically elevates virtue *qua* virtue over considerations of class and ordinary (birth/occupation)

29. Cf. Lord, *The* Politics *of Aristotle*, Glossary, s. vv. "well off," "refined." The latter group, the rich who were also "refined," was at least one of the primary intended audiences of the *Politics;* see C. Lord, *Education and Culture in the Political Thought of Aristotle* (Ithaca, N.Y., and London, 1982), 32–33.

status, but, as we have seen, Aristotle's formulation of citizen requirements in an aristocracy renders political virtue inseparable from status
considerations. Those who were much superior to others in virtue would
be treated unjustly if made political equals with their inferiors; indeed,
they could not justly be made subject to the same set of laws. Such
individuals were typically driven out of depraved regimes (for example,
through ostracism) but were the natural leaders of the best regime
(1283b34–1284b34; cf. 1287a32–b6).

In Books 7 and 8 Aristotle proceeds to establish the details of the best
regime, which will exist in a moderate-sized *polis* (1326a5–b25). The
residents will include farmers, artisans (*technitai*), warriors, wealthy men,
priests, and those able to judge concerning what was necessary and advantageous for the state (1328b19–22). Not all of these categories of
persons were to be citizens; as in any aristocracy, those living banausic
and mercantile lives are excluded on status grounds; their ignoble (*ag-
genēs*) occupations are contrary to the development of political virtue
(1328b39–41). Hence, as expected, Aristotle uses the category of occupational status in defining his ideal regime. But farmers, who would
not be automatically excluded by their occupation, are also barred from
citizenship. The reason is that subsistence farmers, though autarkic,
lacked sufficient leisure to develop virtue or to engage in political activity
(1328b41–1329a2). The exclusion of farmers from citizenship demonstrates that Aristotle mixed class together with status considerations in
constructing his ideal state.

The importance of class in the ideal state is also evident in the arrangement whereby all property will be owned by the citizens (1329a17–24,
1329b36–37). The farmers will be a mixed stock of unspirited natural
slaves or barbarians with slavish natures, and so, of course, be excluded
from property ownership (1329a24–26, 1330a25–33). The banausic
types necessary to the economic maintenance of the state will possess no
share in the *polis* (1329a19–20). The monopoly of property, along with
the partially communal nature of real estate and agricultural slaves
(1330a9–18), will ensure that the citizens constitute a leisure class, freed
from the necessity of having to work at an unsuitable, low-status occupation in order to make a living.[30] Extracting the surplus of the labor of
noncitizens will permit each citizen to participate full-time in those political activities suitable to his age-group.

The education of the citizens, the subject of the fragmentary Book 8,
was an important aspect of the social organization of the ideal state. Education was to be a concern of the state and standardized for all citizens
(1337a21–26). Even as small children, the citizens are to be kept as

30. On the importance of leisure to the rulers of the good state, see 1273a31–34,
1273b6–7.

much as possible away from the company of slaves, so as to avoid the taint of "illiberality" (*aneleutheria*) that contact with slaves might inculcate (1336a39–b2). The isolation of the citizens from all low-status activities is to be ensured by their formal education, which will avoid any teaching of proficiency in "illiberal" or banausic tasks (1337b4–13). Expertise in musical performance (as opposed to music appreciation) was also forbidden, on the grounds that professional musicians typically were banausic and laboring types (1339b8–10, 1340b40–1341b18). After his education, the citizen of the best state served sequentially as a soldier, a political decisionmaker and officeholder, and as a priest. Each stage in the citizen's career (along with such ancillary concerns as the right to procreate) was strictly regulated according to age categories.

The citizen body would of course be perpetuated on the basis of birth; Aristotle takes for granted that only the sons of citizens would be allowed political rights. Although Aristotle had some doubts about whether excellent parents could be counted upon to produce equally excellent progeny (1255a32–b5; cf. 1261a14–24, 1271a16–21, 1286b22–25), he was uncompromising in advocating a limitation on additions to the citizen body; only the most depraved of democracies allowed those who were not citizens by birth to achieve citizenship (1319b5–11, 1326a27–28).

In constructing his ideal state, Aristotle certainly made use of the categories of economic class and status, but, even taken together, class and status do not adequately define the social organization of Aristotle's state. The social system on which the regime was based was designed to be inflexible and was to be maintained by the laws (Books 7–8 passim). The rigidity of the sociopolitical regime and the strict legal definition of the society of the best state suggest that Aristotle was using as his operative principle something similar to Weber's sociological category of "order." In Aristotle's state the farmers were the lowest order; as natural slaves, they had no rights and only economic duties. The banausic and mercantile types, excluded from the franchise by their participation in slavish activities rather than by being "natural" slaves (cf. 1260a41–b2), would provide a second order. They would engage in all the economic activity (besides the farming itself) necessary to the maintenance of the *polis*. Presumably the slaves and banausic types would be treated justly, and so would not grow to resent their condition; in any event they were not to be armed, and so would not be particularly dangerous.[31] The

31. Concerning their just treatment, see Aristotle's comments, cited above, on preserving oligarchic regimes by just treatment of the lower classes; on their lack of arms, see 1329a9–12. Regrettably, Aristotle's promise to discuss the proper treatment of slaves (1330a32) is not fulfilled in the extant version of the *Politics*.

highest order was the citizenry, a relatively homogeneous elite standing above the rest of the residents of the state in terms of class and status: the citizens' membership in the highest order was theirs by birthright, their leisure purchased by the exploitation of the labor of the lower orders, their homogeneity in terms of class and ideology reinforced by communally held property and a standardized, status-conscious education, their superior position guaranteed by both "nature" and the laws.

Aristotle's ideal state may appear to be a conscious contradiction of the egalitarian principles of the Athenian democracy. In contrast to the Athenian refusal to allow class or occupation-status concerns to determine citizenship, Aristotle denies citizenship to all but the members of a narrow order. But although his ideal state as described in Books 7 and 8 is indeed ideologically far distant from Athens, it would be incorrect to suppose that the argument of the remainder of the *Politics* was uncompromisingly antidemocratic. Aristotle (1297a7–12) disapproved of those who, in philosophical discussions of possible states, suggested giving too much power to the rich and who believed that it was just to deceive the *dēmos*. For Aristotle, the self-aggrandizement (*pleonexia*) of the rich was actually more destructive to the *polis* than that of the *dēmos*. It is not surprising, therefore, to find him stating (1289b4–5) that democracy was the best of the three debased regimes.

In Book 3 Aristotle actually embraces (if with some reservations) one of the most important doctrines of the egalitarian democracy: that the collective judgment of the masses—those who possessed neither property nor special virtue—could yield decisions superior to those made by individuals or small groups of "experts."[32] But, unlike the Athenians, Aristotle found it necessary to separate the social requirements for decision making from the requirements for high office holding. High offices, he believed, should be reserved for the necessarily small virtuous elite (1281a2–1282b14; cf. 1277b25–30). Hence, while accepting the Athenian assumption that good political decisions could be made by a democratic assembly, he rejected the Athenian notion that no special skill, education, or training was necessary for performing the duties associated with the various offices of the state.

By drawing a sharp distinction between the criteria for good decision

32. 1281a39–1282a41; cf. 1284a30–34, 1286a26–b7. As regards Aristotle's interest in economic class, it is worth noting that at the end of this section (1282a39–41) Aristotle further justifies his egalitarian argument by commenting that the property assessment of the multitude would collectively be greater than that of the elite few. The Athenian belief in the superiority of mass decisions is implicit in the constitution (simple majority voting pertained in both the Assembly and the law courts) and in the ideological statements of Athenian orators (e.g., Dem. *Exord.* 45; cf. Thuc. 6.39.1f. [speech of Athenagoras of Syracuse]).

making and good individual action as officeholder, Aristotle appears to be trying to balance elitist and egalitarian principles. This is closely related to his various attempts, in the *Politics* and *Nicomachean Ethics,* to define a just form of equality that would balance the "arithmetical" notion of equality as inherent in the principle of "one man, one vote" and the notion that the superior (in property or virtue) deserved a proportionately greater say in affairs of the state.[33]

A truly just form of proportionate equality, which would balance the rights of the majority against the legitimate privileges of the superior minority, ultimately eluded Aristotle, and his failure to find the balance is reflected in the rigid orders of the "ideal state." Aristotle could not bring the notion of proportionate equality into line with his conviction that true citizenship required that a citizen be, by turns, ruler and ruled (see, for example, 1277b13–16), because he insisted upon defining rule in terms of office holding (1275a22–24, b18–21, for instance). His willingness to accept the doctrine of wise mass decisions, along with his comment (1283b30–34) that a multitude might justly claim their right to govern on the basis of the superiority of their *collective* virtue, suggests that he might have defined ruling as participating in voting in the Assembly for legislation that would be binding upon the entire populace. This would have left the way open to the development of a constitution embracing both mass decisions and elite officeholders. Aristotle seems to be heading in this direction in his discussion (1295a25–1297b34; cf. esp. 1298b5–11) of how to establish the regime of "polity," which would balance oligarchic and democratic tendencies and in which property assessments would be specifically designed to ensure that "those sharing in the regime would be more numerous than those not sharing in it" (1297b4–6). He offers another possible way around the difficulty in Book 5 (1308b38–1309a14), suggesting that by eliminating the profits of office holding it might be possible to effect a practical combination of aristocracy and democracy, since the poor would avoid standing for offices that offered no possibility of profit. His discussion of the "farm-

---

33. 1280a22–24, 1282b14–1284a3, 1287a13–17, 1296b15–34, 1301a25–1302a15; *Eth. Nic.* 1132b33–34ff. Cf. Finley, *Politics in the Ancient World,* 137; and especially F. D. Harvey, "Two Kinds of Equality," *Classica et mediaevalia* 26 (1965): 113–20, 126–29, who argues that Aristotle's failure to resolve the problem was at least in part due to his unwillingness to abandon traditional notions of the justice of privileges accorded to the highborn and wealthy (117). Perhaps so, but Aristotle was working within a context in which even the democratically minded citizens of Athens believed in these notions (see below). Hence Aristotle rightly assumed that privileges for the elite would pertain, in some form or other, in every conceivable *polis*. If his aim was to define an ideal state that could exist in practice, he had to consider how to balance elite and mass. See also C. Mossé, "Citoyens actifs et citoyens 'passifs' dans les cités grecques: Une approche théorique du problème," *Revue des études grecques* 81 (1979): 241–49.

ers' democracy" in Book 6 (1318b6–1319a19) incorporates elements of both these approaches, and this regime earns his praise as one that is "finely governed" (1318b33) in that the masses elect members of the elite to offices, resulting in the elite ruling without error while the masses get no less than their due, "something that is most beneficial for regimes" (1319a1–4).

But in constructing his ideal state, Aristotle avoided the problem of proportionate equality altogether by legally excluding from political activity all those whose class or status rendered them unfit for office holding. Those who remained as citizens would be sufficiently similar in virtue, and, by legal enactment, sufficiently similar in property, to obviate the necessity of achieving a complicated balance between quantitative and qualitative equalities. The political sociology of Aristotle's ideal state is, in the end, based upon exclusionary and elitist principles. Aristotle's social thought thus has affinities not only with the theories of Karl Marx, but also with those of the elitist philosophers of the early twentieth century—Gaetano Mosca, Robert Michels, and Vilfredo Pareto. In common with modern elitist thinkers, Aristotle assumes that only a small minority of the members of society are naturally capable of ruling, that the members of the elite are conscious of their superiority and able to form a cohesive ruling group, and that the masses can (and, in the view of many elitists, should) be permanently excluded from access to political power without the state's incurring a serious risk of revolution.[34]

The Athenians too struggled with the problem of balancing egalitarian and elitist principles. Their solution was different. By eliminating class and occupational status requirements for the exercise of full political rights, they achieved legal equality for all members of a very large citizen body. At the same time, however, the Athenians continued to allow certain circumscribed political privileges to individual members of an elite of wealthy and highly educated citizens whose attainments could facilitate the practical functioning of the state.[35] Aristotle's regime is ulti-

34. The relatively small size of Aristotle's ruling elite is suggested at 1332b29–33. Cf. the concise treatments of classical elitist theory in M. N. Marger, *Elites and Masses: An Introduction to Political Sociology* (New York, 1981), 63–86; J. Burnham, *The Machiavellians* (New York, 1943), 81–115 (Mosca), 135–68 (Michels), 171–220 (Pareto). For a fuller exposition, see L. Mosca, *The Ruling Class*, ed. and trans. A. Livingston (New York, 1939); R. Michels, *Political Parties*, trans. E. and C. Paul (New York, 1962); V. Pareto, *The Mind and Society*, 4 vols., trans. A. Bongiorno and A. Livingston (New York, 1935). Aristotle's links with the "classical elitists" should not be overemphasized; he seems to see domination of the elite as both less inevitable and more desirable than they; nor would Aristotle have been partial to Pareto's theory of the circulation of elites (co-option to the elite of capable individuals from the lower classes).

35. This is the central argument of Ober, *Mass and Elite*. Cf. the brief, but stimulating, treatment of the problem in R. Seager, "Elitism and Democracy in Classical Athens," in *The Rich, the Well Born, and the Powerful*, ed. F. C. Jaher (Urbana, Ill., 1973), 7–26.

mately elitist, but he recognized the validity of some egalitarian principles; the Athenian state was ultimately egalitarian, but the Athenians
recognized the efficacy of granting certain privileges to members of the
elite.

At the heart of Aristotle's political sociology, just as at the heart of
Athenian political ideology, is the attempt to resolve the claims of elite
and masses for a just share in the regime. The fact that Aristotle and the
Athenians struggled with the same basic sociopolitical question is significant and must be borne in mind in assessing the value of the *Politics* for
the historical analysis of ancient society. Aristotle not only used categories of social analysis similar to those employed by modern students of
political sociology, he used these categories in order to deal theoretically
with the same central problem of political participation that concerned
his contemporaries on a practical plane. Hence there seems no reason to
question Ste. Croix's indirect proposition that Aristotle's analysis may
serve as a guide to the employment of modern sociological models in attempting to define the nature of politics in antiquity. On the other hand,
Ste. Croix's argument that Aristotle's political sociology supports a Marxist analysis to the exclusion of other models appears incorrect. Aristotle
employed status and order categories as well as the category of class. Although the question of whether he regarded any one of these as fundamental remains open, he does explain some social conflicts (and therefore, at least by implication, some social changes) in nonclass terms, and
he does not invariably proceed on the basis of a class analysis.

We may also suggest that Aristotle's emphasis upon the wide variety of
distinct political roles that were played by members of various class and
status groups in different regimes casts some doubt upon Holmes's argument that the putative undifferentiated character of *polis* society under-
pinned the Greek theoretical and practical linkage of political society
and polity. It is, of course, impossible to measure quantitatively societal
differentiation in antiquity, but I have no doubt that modern societies
are indeed *more* structurally differentiated than were Greek *poleis*. Aristotle himself supposed that a *polis* would desire "to be made up of equal
and similar persons to the extent possible" (1295b25–26), and the citizens of his ideal state are indeed undifferentiated. But his emphasis in
the *Politics* on the implications for the political regime of social unequals
acting as political equals (especially in democracies) tends to support the
argument that there was in reality a very significant degree of societal
differentiation in some ancient Greek *poleis*.[36] The difference in the de-

36. Holmes's differentiation argument ("Aristippus," 114 n. 4) is based in part on the
systems-theory sociology of Niklas Luhmann, some of whose most important work has now
been collected and translated by Holmes and C. Larsmore in N. Luhmann, *The Differentiation of Society* (New York, 1982). Luhmann argues that modern political systems are quite

gree of differentiation of modern and ancient societies is indeed an important variable in assessing both. The lower level of differentiation in Greece is at least in part responsible for the lack of ancient concern for negative freedoms of citizens. But the difference remains a matter of degree and is not sufficiently immense to obviate, *a priori*, the contemporary usefulness of ancient political philosophy or practice.

Can we make a positive argument that Aristotle's political theory has modern relevance? His ideal society is certainly not a satisfactory model for modern states, or even for a classical *polis*. Aristotle himself noted that the tendency of an aristocracy to deprive all but the *epieikeis* of honors (offices) was comparable in injustice to forced property redistributions under democratic regimes (1281a13–32). In terms of the classical *polis*, Aristotle's abandonment of the search for proportionate equality within a broad-based citizenry in favor of a scheme that denied citizenship to all but a narrow, socially homogeneous elite must be seen as a grave failure.

I would suggest, however, that Aristotle's ordered ideal state was not an inevitable or organic outgrowth of the sociopolitical principles discussed in Books 3 and 4, but was, at least in part, a response to a newly emerging political order.[37] By the late 330s B.C. Philip's and Alexander's conquests had rendered truly free *poleis* rare (at least in terms of freedom of choice in foreign policy), and the average Greek was already on his way to becoming less of a *zōon politikon*. The wave of the future was, to a prescient observer, indeed the divorce of the social from the overtly political: the end of the classical *polis*. Aristotle seems to be anticipating

---

highly differentiated from the social environment, and so relatively autonomous (138–52). This differentiation "takes place primarily at the level of roles" (140). In "simple societies" the political and social roles are conflated, so that, for example, "one who fails as a neighbor cannot be trusted as a warrior" (140). I would suggest that the Athenians, at least, were able to apply a degree of political role differentiation. The case of Demosthenes is one example; although he advocated the policy that led to the disastrous loss at Chaeronea in 338 and displayed personal cowardice in the course of the battle, he was nonetheless selected for the honor of delivering the oration over the fallen (Aeschin. *In Ctes.* 3.175; Dem. *De Cor.* 18.285). On the other hand, I think Luhmann may overestimate the degree of role differentiation in modern political life, at least at the important level of elected officials; cf. the problems experienced by American vice presidential candidate Geraldine Ferraro in 1984, when her husband's personal financial irregularities were brought to light. For an examination of the effects of social differentiation on the history of classical and Hellenistic Greece, see A. Fuks, "Patterns and Types of Social-Economic Revolution in Greece from the Fourth to the Second Century B.C.," in *Social Conflict*, 9–39; many of Fuks's other essays in this collection are also relevant to the issue.

37. This argument does not necessarily imply anything substantive about the order of composition or proper arrangement of the books of the *Politics*, on which see Lord, *The Politics of Aristotle*, 13–17; cf. the refinement of Jaeger's sequential composition theory (i.e., that Books 7 and 8 are much earlier than the other books) in Weil, *Aristote*, passim.

the developed Hellenistic cities of Asia and Africa in his attempt to create a new form of *polis* that would preserve the *politēs/politeia* linkage for a narrow and socially homogeneous citizen elite of Greeks who would be supported by the labor of naturally slavish barbarians.[38]

If the foregoing hypothesis is correct, Aristotle foresaw a radical rupture between political and socioeconomic roles, between polity and society, and this is the central factor that Holmes and others have identified as distinguishing the modern world from the world of the *polis*. Aristotle's ideal state, as I have suggested, does not provide a satisfying method for healing that rupture because it abolishes social diversity within the citizen body. The failure of the "ideal state" to provide a model for modern political life should not, however, be seen as a failure of the entire undertaking of the *Politics*—which was, at least in part, an attempt to define how the links between regime and society could provide a political basis for moral community in a socially diverse world. The world of the *polis* indeed differs from our own in terms of scale, but that scale difference, which has already been rendered less significant by modern telecommunications, should not blind us to the similarities. I would suggest that man remains a "political animal"—not in the sense that he should live in a *polis*, but because isolation from political partici-

38. On the internal political structure of the Hellenistic city, see the comments of A. H. M. Jones, *The Greek City* (Oxford, 1940), 157–69; E. Will, "Pour une 'anthropologie coloniale' du monde hellénistique," in *The Craft of the Ancient Historian: Essays in Honor of C. G. Starr*, ed. J. W. Eadie and J. Ober (Lanham, Md., 1985), 273–301. The composition date of ca. 333 B.C., suggested by Lord, *The Politics of Aristotle*, 15, is not too early for Aristotle to have seen the handwriting on the wall, although obviously the political consequences of the Macedonian hegemony would have been clearer a decade later. Aristotle's recognition of the changing realities facing the *polis* is demonstrated by his suggestions for dealing with modern military threats (1330b32–1331a2). Aristotle specifically states (1327b20–33; arguing on the basis of thoughtfulness and spiritedness) that the inhabitants of the ideal state must be Greeks. And barbarians were more slavish in *ēthos* than Greeks and therefore (at least under some circumstances) justly dominated by those who were natural rulers (1285a19–22, 1324b36–37). Aristotle also states that it is evident that in the ideal state all property must belong to citizens if the farmers "must necessarily be slaves or barbarian subjects" (1329a24–26). This may simply relate to his comment (1330a25–33) that it is *ideal* to have as farmers those who are slaves by nature or barbarians with slavish characteristics, since these will be unlikely to revolt. It may, however, also reflect a realization on Aristotle's part that the agricultural workers in the new *poleis* that would eventually be established in the East would in fact be barbarian *perioikoi*. My hypothesis throws into question the frequent assertion (see, for instance, Finley, "Aristotle and Economic Analysis," 18) that Aristotle ignored the consequences of the careers of Philip and Alexander for the *polis*. On Aristotle's attitude toward the political effects of Macedonian hegemony in Greece and in Persia, see Lord, *Education and Culture*, 193–95, with the literature cited. My hypothesis may be seen as a variant of Lord's theory (*Education and Culture*, 33) that the ideal state was intended as practical guidance for aristocrats living in a state where they do not constitute the ruling class in a political sense.

pation and action robs human life of some part of its meaning and satisfaction. Holmes may be correct to state that "in modern society there is no longer any question of morally and humanly fulfilling participation for the mass of citizens inside the political system,"[39] but this is a sad state of affairs and one in need of correcting. The questions of how to balance the social privileges of the elite against the political rights of the masses, of how the social diversity of the community affects the exercise of political power, of how the social and the political can together provide meaning and fulfillment for the citizenry, seem to me to be issues as urgent for residents of modern democratic regimes as they were for Greeks in the late fourth century B.C. Aristotle may not provide us with final answers, but his discussion of these problems deserves our attention.

39. Holmes, "Aristippus," 126.

FIVE

The Aetiology of Justice

David K. O'Connor

The guiding question of Aristotle's approach to moral and political philosophy is, What is the most choiceworthy focus for a human life? He
identifies this focus as activity expressive of virtue, both moral and intellectual. Within this framework, Aristotle conceives of vice as primarily a
kind of misorientation. The vicious person is one who focuses too much
on bodily pleasures or honors at the expense of virtue. In contrast, most
contemporary moral philosophy is guided by a concern with how we
should treat other human beings. More specifically, it is concerned with
the difference between egoistic and altruistic ways of treating others.
The central concern in this approach to moral philosophy is "the possibility of altruism," not the best focus for a human life. It has a correspondingly different conception of vice; selfishness, rather than misorientation, becomes the primary criterion of viciousness.

One might think that these two approaches simply complement each
other. Perhaps Aristotle is concerned with the good of the individual,
while modern moral philosophy is concerned with how to treat other
people. In this view, there would be a convenient division of labor between Aristotle's attempt to understand (personal) happiness and our attempts to understand (interpersonal) ethics. But as is so often the case,
the convenient does not coincide with the true. Aristotle devotes an entire book of the *Nicomachean Ethics* to *the* social virtue, justice. One could
try to interpret this to mean merely that in this book he crosses over
from prudential to ethical concerns, adopting our guiding question and

An earlier version of much of this paper was part of my dissertation in the Stanford Philosophy Department, 1985. I am grateful for a Mrs. Giles Whiting Dissertation Fellowship
that supported my research and for the help and encouragement of my director, Julius
Moravcsik, and my readers, Stuart Hampshire, Richard Pruitt, and Jean Roberts. I also
thank Carnes Lord and Paul Vander Waerdt for their comments. Translations are my own.

leaving aside his own. But in fact Aristotle's account of justice is as much concerned with the proper orientation of a human life as his treatments of, say, courage, temperance, and liberality. At no point does he take selfishness, rather than misorientation, as the root of vice, not even when he discusses justice.

The present study will attempt to put some flesh on the bare bones of these claims. I will have two goals in mind throughout this paper. First, I want to give an accurate and detailed exegesis of a central but relatively neglected part of Aristotle's moral philosophy: his account of the relation between justice and the other moral virtues. I hope to show how his account of justice harmonizes with his general emphasis on proper orientation as the root of virtue. Second, I want to make more clear what kind of alternative Aristotle offers to contemporary approaches to justice. I do not claim that Aristotle is superior in emphasizing orientation rather than altruism in his account of justice. But I do claim that his perspective is coherent and powerful and should at least give us pause before we take the modern approach for granted.

Aristotle begins his account with a distinction between two senses of justice. In one sense, justice "seems to be the chief [*kratistē*] virtue, more wondrous than morning star or evening star." When it is used this way, justice refers to complete or perfect virtue and includes all the other virtues.[1] In its second sense, justice refers to only one species of virtue within the genus of justice.[2] Justice in this sense is one particular virtue on a par with courage, temperance, mildness, liberality, magnanimity, and the like, and refers only to a part of virtue, and not to the whole of virtue.[3] Using the somewhat inaccurate but conventional terms, we will call the inclusive kind of justice universal justice, the partial kind of justice particular justice.

There are two questions raised by this characterization of justice that we need to address. First, how does universal justice include the other moral virtues? After all, magnanimity (in the *Nicomachean Ethics*) and nobility (*kalokagathia* in the *Eudemian Ethics*) are also inclusive virtues.[4] We want to know what is distinctive about the way universal justice includes the other virtues. Second, what distinguishes particular justice both from the rest of (universal) justice and from the rest of the moral virtues? We want to know why Aristotle singles out particular justice for special attention within justice and also why particular justice is a part of universal

1. *Eth. Nic.* 1129b25–29.
2. See *Eth. Nic.* 1130a33–b5.
3. Ibid. 1130a14–15.
4. See *Eth. Nic.* 1123b29–30, 1124a1–4; *Eth. Eud.* 1232a30–32, 1248b8–13, 1249a16. Magnanimity and nobility seem to be more than just the sum of the virtues, but that does not affect the point at issue here.

justice in a different way from the other moral virtues included in universal justice.

The key to understanding Aristotle's answers to these two questions is the contrast he draws between two perspectives we can take on virtue. Aristotle contrasts justice (universal and particular) with the rest of the moral virtues, declaring that justice is virtue "in relation to others" (*pros heteron*), while the rest are virtues simply (*haplōs*).[5] I will call virtue considered in relation to others relational virtue, and virtue *haplōs* I will call simple virtue. The section entitled "Two Perspectives on Virtue" explains this distinction and applies it to our first question of how universal justice includes the other virtues. As we will see, the perspective of simple virtue focuses on what sort of psychic state (*hexis*) a particular virtue is, while the perspective of relational virtue focuses on how a given psychic state manifests itself in community life with other people. Universal justice includes all the simple virtues to the extent that they cause people to be good members of a community. I compare the relational and simple perspectives on virtue to two different perspectives we can take on health and disease, namely, symptomological and aetiological perspectives. Simple virtue focuses on a person's psychic state in the way a doctor might focus on the underlying causes of a disease; relational virtue focuses on the political manifestations of virtue and vice, as we might concentrate on the symptoms of a disease.

In the next section, "Particular Justice and *Pleonexia*," we will go on to our second question and see both why particular justice is an especially important part of universal justice and why it is distinct from any of the other virtues. Particular justice is especially important because it includes those simple virtues the lack of which is most destructive of community life, namely, the virtues concerned with wealth and honors. But it is still distinguished from the virtues it includes by taking the relational perspective. Like the simple virtues, particular justice is identified by a specific aetiology. But unlike them, it is concerned with misoriented desires for wealth and honors as producers of breaches of community rather than as disordered psychic states. This combination of aetiological and symptomological aspects of particular justice will explain the puzzling fact that the vice opposed to particular justice (*pleonexia* "graspingness") seems to refer "to a class of motives, rather than to any single motive."[6]

After laying out the structure of Aristotle's account of justice, I turn in the final section, "Particular and Distributive Justice," to a comparison between Aristotle's analysis of justice and the dominant contemporary

5. *Eth. Nic.* 1130a12–13, 1130b1–2.
6. B. Williams, "Justice as a Virtue," in *Essays on Aristotle's Ethics*, ed. A. O. Rorty (Berkeley, 1980), 199. The same criticism is made by W. F. R. Hardie, *Aristotle's Ethical Theory* (Oxford, 1978).

approach. To this end we will consider in some detail Bernard Williams's perceptive argument that Aristotle's account seriously misdescribes the phenomena of injustice. Williams's attack hinges on his own conception of the psychic state that makes a person just. His basic disagreement with Aristotle concerns the underlying aetiology of injustice: Aristotle emphasizes a certain class of misoriented desires (especially for wealth and honors), Williams a certain kind of indifference to others grounded in partiality to ourselves. Where Aristotle sees primarily a symptom of misdirected desire, Williams sees a failure of altruism. I try to show that Aristotle's position has more resources than Williams allows and that an Aristotelian approach to justice is a more plausible alternative than might first appear.

TWO PERSPECTIVES ON VIRTUE

Aristotle distinguishes universal from particular justice by identifying two different vices that oppose justice. On the one hand, we call the man who is unfair (*anisos*) or grasping (*pleonektēs*) unjust. The virtue opposed to this vice is particular justice, and the man who is just in this sense can be called fair (*isos*). On the other hand, we call the man who is a lawbreaker (*paranomos*) unjust. The law-abiding man (*nomimos*) is, accordingly, called just, in the universal sense.[7] Aristotle regards injustice of the first kind as a part of injustice as lawbreaking, for "everything unfair is against the law, but not everything that is against the law is unfair."[8] Thus to understand the nature of the virtue of particular justice, we will first need to consider the viciousness of lawbreaking.

"Since the lawbreaker is unjust and the law-abiding man just," says Aristotle, "everything that is according to the law [*panta ta nomima*] is just in a way [*pōs*]."[9] It is only just "in a way" because this sense of justice is different from justice as fairness, being more inclusive. Indeed, Aristotle goes on to say that this kind of justice includes the whole of virtue and that it is complete virtue.[10] This may strike us as a very extravagant claim. No doubt law-abidingness is in general a praiseworthy character trait, but we would not be very likely to think that in it "all virtue is summed up."[11] The difficulty is caused by the very different conceptions that we and Aristotle have of the purpose of law.

We are likely to think of law as more or less limited in its objectives.

---

7. *Eth. Nic.* 1129a32–34.
8. Ibid. 1130b12–13. This passage is very corrupt in some of the manuscripts. I follow the text of Bywater and Stewart.
9. *Eth. Nic.* 1129b11–12.
10. Ibid. 1129b26, 30, 1130a8–10.
11. See *Eth. Nic.* 1129b29–30.

Through a system of publicly enforced regulations, we try to guarantee the conditions of public order and safety necessary for individuals to pursue their own happiness. Aristotle was aware of a conception of law much like this, but he rejected it.[12] If law were limited to the requirements of such a "social contract," it could not provide the structural principles of a real *polis*. The requirements to avoid harming one another, to keep contracts, and the like, while indispensable to a political community, serve only the lower needs of human beings. The *polis*, however, is understood by Aristotle to be the architectonic community, the one that embodies the most important and complete ends at which humans aim.[13] As Aristotle often puts the point, the *polis* is for the sake of the good life, not merely for the sake of the requirements of living.[14]

The result of this conception of the *polis* and of the architectonic nature of its end is a much greater demand on law in Aristotle's account of justice than in our own. The laws must not only guarantee the necessary conditions for each individual's pursuit of happiness, but actually direct and educate him in being happy, that is, in achieving *eudaimonia* by living well.[15] Of course, living well means for Aristotle living in accordance with virtue: the *polis* is for the sake of fine actions (*kalai praxeis*).[16] As a result, Aristotle assumes that laws will have a very wide sphere of interest. He goes so far in one passage of the *Nicomachean Ethics* as to say that "the laws give commands about everything."[17] Certainly everything that pertains to virtue or the virtues will come under their directives. With this understanding of the purpose and extent of law, it is not at all surprising that justice as law-abidingness is thought of as in some sense including all the other virtues. As Aristotle puts it, "in one way [namely, with regard to universal, rather than particular, justice], we call just what produces and preserves *eudaimonia* and its parts [namely, the particular virtues] for the political community."[18] Insofar as the virtues come within the purview of the art of lawmaking, so far are they included within universal justice.

It is the inclusive nature of the end of the *polis*, then, and the resulting

12. See especially *Pol.* 3.9, in particular 1280b5–12. Such passages show that attributions to Aristotle of such a limited conception of law are groundless, despite D. J. Allan, "Individual and State in the *Ethics* and *Politics*," in *La "Politique" d'Aristote*, Entretiens sur l'antiquité classique 11 (Geneva, 1965), 55–95. The same objection applies to the account of law in A. MacIntyre, *After Virtue: A Study in Moral Theory* (Notre Dame, 1981), 141–42, and the account of justice in S. Hampshire, *Two Theories of Morality* (Oxford, 1977), insofar as they are intended to be interpretations of Aristotle.

13. The classic statements of the architectonic nature of the *polis* open the *Politics* and *Nicomachean Ethics*.

14. See especially *Pol.* 1252b29–30.

15. See *Pol.* 1280a31–34, among many passages.

16. *Pol.* 1281a1–3.   17. *Eth. Nic.* 1129b14–15.   18. Ibid. 1129b17–19.

inclusiveness of the laws that provide its framework, that explains the inclusiveness of universal justice. "The law directs us to live in accordance with each of the virtues, and forbids us to live in accordance with each of the vices." [19] For example, the law commands acts of courage (like holding one's place in battle), acts of temperance (like avoiding adultery and rape), and acts of mildness (like not striking or slandering others).[20] But if this were all there is to say about the relation between universal justice and the particular virtues, Aristotle could have said simply that universal justice is complete virtue, without adding that it is virtue "in relation to others." It is this addition, however, that points to what is distinctive about justice. How does virtue in relation to others differ from virtues like courage, temperance, and mildness?

Aristotle answers this question by deploying his common distinction between being the same thing and being the same in definition or essence. Complete virtue is different from universal justice because "though both are the same [thing], what they are [*to einai*] is not the same. Considered in relation to others, [this thing] is justice, while considered as a particular sort of *hexis*, it is simply [*haplōs*] virtue." [21] The point of this distinction is most easily grasped if we consider one of Aristotle's illustrations of the general principle. Suppose there is a white ruler on a desk.[22] There is only a single object on the desk, but that object is both straight and white. If I need something to draw a line, I will ask you to hand me the straight thing. If I need a color sample, I will ask you to hand me the white thing. In either case, you will hand me the same thing, but the descriptions that the ruler had to satisfy in the two cases are very different. In relation to drawing lines, I view the ruler as something straight; in relation to comparing colors, I view it as something white. There is only one thing on the desk, but there are two perspectives from which I can view it.

Virtue viewed from the two perspectives, which I earlier referred to as relational and simple virtue, is also one thing. Simple virtue is considered from the perspective of what sort of *hexis* it is. From this point of view, the focus is on the psychic structure of the virtuous person. More specifically, the focus is on his susceptibility to feelings or emotions (*pathē*) and on how his feelings motivate his actions.[23] This is especially evident in the way the vices are individuated. Different vices are the result

19. Ibid. 1130b23–24.   20. Ibid. 1129b19–23.   21. Ibid. 1130a12–13.

22. I take this example of one thing that is both white and straight from *Eth. Eud.* 1219b35–36. Other interpretations of this passage are possible, but the point of my example is unaffected by these differences.

23. For examples of general statements of this approach, see *Eth. Nic.* 1106b16–21, 1107a3–6, 1109a22–24. This is also clear in the accounts of the particular virtues in *Eth. Nic.* 3–4.

of different kinds of temptation, of seduction by various kinds of pleasures.[24] Since different people have natural inclinations to different
kinds of pleasure, we must learn where our tendencies lie in order to
correct for them.[25] Aristotle compares this to the kind of medical treatment that takes place by means of contraries.[26] Considered simply, a virtue is a mean state between too much and too little susceptibility to some
particular kind of pleasure, as health is a mean between extremes of dry
and wet, hot and cold, and the like. It should not surprise us that virtue
is considered from this point of view. It is the perspective taken on all of
the particular virtues up to the account of justice, where Aristotle first
introduces the second perspective.

Aristotle contrasts this second perspective on virtue with the view of
virtue as a particular sort of *hexis*. If relational virtue does not focus on
the psychic structure of virtue, and thus not on the feelings and motives
of virtuous action, what does it focus on? What are we looking for when
we look at virtue "considered in relation to others"? We must be guided
here by the intimate connection between law and relational virtue. In
particular, we must be guided by the fact that law aims at the common
good of the *polis*, at least insofar as it is well constituted;[27] for though law
aims at happiness, and hence at virtue, it aims at happiness, and hence at
virtue, from its own point of view. The laws require the virtues and the
actions in accord with virtue with a view to their contribution to the common good of the entire community of citizens, and not primarily with a
view to the perfection of the individual. That is not to deny that the laws
require the citizens to develop the moral virtues. But "the things that
produce the whole of virtue are established by law [*nomima*]" only insofar
as they "are legislated [*nenomothetētai*] concerning education for the common good [*peri paideian tēn pros to koinon*]." [28]

I propose that when Aristotle says that universal justice is virtue in
relation to others (*pros heteron*), he has in mind the kind of perspective on
moral virtue that the legislator and the law have on moral education,
which they consider insofar as it is "for the common good" (*pros to
koinon*). In this interpretation, relational virtue focuses on the way that
virtue makes people able to share in community life. This contrasts with
the focus of simple virtue on psychic structure, but it does not conflict
with it. Simple virtue looks to the feelings that accompany and motivate
action, especially the pleasures and pains that define the mean. Rela-

24. *Eth. Nic.* 1104b9–11 is a general statement of the point, which is amply illustrated
in the accounts of particular virtues.
25. *Eth. Nic.* 1109b1–4.
26. Ibid. 1104b16–18.
27. See *Eth. Nic.* 1129b14–17, 24–25. Of course, this is a central theme of *Pol.* 3.9–13.
28. *Eth. Nic.* 1130b25–26. See also *Pol.* 1283a37–40, where Aristotle describes justice
as "community-directed virtue" (*koinōnikē aretē*).

tional virtue looks to the actions themselves with a view to their consistency or inconsistency with the common life of the community. From the first perspective, a person is identified as virtuous or vicious primarily because of the ends that he pursues and the underlying psychic states responsible for this pursuit. From the second, he is identified primarily by the extent to which his pursuit of happiness shows itself to be in harmony with his common life among his fellow citizens. Of course, the kind of end he pursues will determine how good a partner he will be in the shared life of the *polis;* but this does not reduce the second perspective to the first. Neither do these two accounts of the nature of virtue compete with each other, any more than the two descriptions of the white ruler compete. The perspective of simple virtue looks to the psychic causes of action, the perspective of relational virtue to the public manifestation in community life of these underlying causes.

Aristotle's example of the inclusion of the particular virtues of courage, temperance, and mildness within universal justice illustrates these two perspectives.[29] Considered simply as dispositions of a particular sort, these virtues are distinguished from the corresponding vices by being means with regard to certain feelings that serve as motives for action. Courage is concerned with fears, especially fear of death in battle; temperance is concerned with animal pleasures; and mildness is concerned with anger. But the laws are concerned with these virtues because actions motivated by their corresponding vices result in breaches of community and thus unfit a man for shared life. The coward endangers his fellow soldiers' lives; the profligate corrupts his fellow citizens' wives and daughters; the hothead offends their honor and persons. It is these breaches of community on which relational virtue focuses, rather than on the psychic misorientations that motivate them. Furthermore, these examples show that many different psychic causes can manifest themselves as universal injustice by motivating breaches of community. Universal justice includes all the particular virtues to the extent that all of the various kinds of vice lead to such breaches.

This inclusion of breaches of community motivated in many different ways under universal injustice is very clear in the *Rhetoric.* As part of the knowledge useful for prosecution and defense speeches, Aristotle discusses injustice in a broad sense more or less equivalent to universal injustice: the voluntary infliction of harm on another in breach of the law.[30]

29. See *Eth. Nic.* 1129b19–23.
30. *Rh.* 1368b6–7. Though they overlap, universal injustice and the voluntary infliction of harm against another's wish should be distinct. For example, unlawful acts among "consenting adults" would be unjust according to the former standard but not the latter. In general, there is no reason to think that law, with its orientation toward happiness and virtue, would be limited to proscribing the infliction of harm on others. However, Aristotle seems not to have distinguished the two; see also *Eth. Nic.* 5.8–9.

He says the following about the motives of injustice so defined:

> The reasons people choose to harm [others] and do base things contrary to
> the law are vice and incontinence. For when people have either one vice or
> many, they are unjust [*adikoi*] with regard to whatever they are vicious. For
> example, an illiberal person [is unjust] with regard to money, a licentious
> person with regard to bodily pleasures, a soft person with regard to taking it
> easy, a coward with regard to dangers (for he deserts those in danger with
> him because of fear), an honor lover [*philotimos*] because of honor, a sharp-
> tempered person because of anger, a victory lover because of victory, a bitter
> person because of revenge, a thoughtless person because he is deceived
> about the just and unjust, a shameless person because of contempt for repu-
> tation. In the same way with other [causes of vice], a particular person [is
> unjust] with regard to a particular underlying [cause of vice].[31]

Notice especially the last sentence of this passage. Injustice corresponds to
the whole depressing variety of ways that human lives are misoriented, at
least to the extent that misorientation leads people to harm one another.

We can see now why universal justice does not include the particular
virtues simply as their summation. The law-abiding citizen must have
and practice all of the virtues, and so he must have the proper psychic
dispositions with regard to the whole range of moral feelings. But when
we describe such a person as just (rather than courageous, temperate, or
mild), we focus on how these dispositions fit him for sharing the common life of the community, rather than on the quality of the dispositions
themselves. What fits him for common life is the same thing as what
makes him simply virtuous, but it is considered from two different perspectives. The vicious person, whether his vice be cowardice, intemperance, or hotheadedness, is characterized by a misorientation in his
psychic state, his particular vice depending on his particular kind of misorientation. But all of these psychic misorientations will display themselves in breaches of community, and thus every particular vice will be
included within universal injustice.

I think it is helpful to summarize Aristotle's account of this relation
between universal justice and the particular virtues with a medical analogy. We may identify a sick person's disease in two different ways. We
may focus on the underlying causes of the disease, and so identify the
disease by its aetiology. For example, we might say the sick person has a
viral infection as opposed to a bacterial infection. Alternatively, we can
focus instead on the symptoms produced by the underlying infection,
and so identify the disease by its symptomology. For example, we might
say the sick person has a sore throat as opposed to aching joints. In an
analogous way, the lawgiver or moral philosopher may focus on either

31. *Rh.* 1368b12–24.

the psychic causes of vice or its political manifestations. Breach of community is caused by particular vices in the way that a single symptom can be caused by a number of different underlying diseases. In looking to the psychic causes of vice, the perspective of simple virtue is aetiological. In looking to the political manifestation of vice, the perspective of relational virtue is symptomological.

It is this shift from an aetiological to a symptomological perspective that accounts for the distinctive features of Aristotle's treatment of justice. There is no new temptation to vice, different from those that Aristotle has treated in the first four books of the *Ethics*, that becomes the subject matter of the fifth book's account of justice and injustice. Rather, virtue is here viewed in a different light, from the lawgiver's perspective of the common good rather than the agent's perspective of his individual good, so to speak. A good man's justice (in the universal sense) is just the way that his virtue is displayed in his relations with others. Like the other vices, injustice is caused by misorientation to inappropriate ends. But the other vices are identified primarily by which improper end is pursued: intemperance by bodily pleasure, hotheadedness by revenge, excessive ambition (*philotimia*) by honor. Injustice, on the other hand, is identified primarily by the manifestation of the underlying misorientation as a breach of community. Such a breach is like a symptom that can be caused by a number of different underlying diseases. In Aristotle's account, the symptomological unity of injustice (as conflict with others) goes along with its aetiological multiplicity, for the motives that lead men into conflict with their fellow citizens are as various as vice.

This account of the relation between relational and simple virtue is fundamentally at odds with interpretations like those of Thomas Aquinas, Troels Engberg-Pedersen, and Terence H. Irwin.[32] None of these three commentators takes Aristotle's treatment of justice as virtue *in relation to others* to imply a shift to a symptomological perspective. Instead, they take Aristotle to be modifying his earlier aetiological accounts of the virtues given in the third and fourth books of the *Nicomachean Ethics*. In particular, all three attribute to Aristotle the view that in performing a just act, the agent chooses the act as a contribution to the *common* good rather than his individual good. But in such interpretations, Aristotle's explicit statement that relational and simple virtue are the same thing (*Eth. Nic.* 5.1.1130a12–13) becomes a puzzle. Thomas deals with the puzzle simply by denying that they are really the same thing; he claims

---

32. For Thomas's interpretation, see, for example, his commentary on *Eth. Nic.* 1130b25–26. See also Engberg-Pedersen, *Aristotle's Theory of Moral Insight*, (Oxford, 1984), 42–62; T. H. Irwin, "Aristotle's Conception of Morality," in *Proceedings of the Boston Area Colloquium in Ancient Philosophy*, vol. 1, ed. John Cleary (Lanham, Md., 1986), 127–40.

that just acts are chosen under the aspect of the common good while virtuous acts of other sorts (courageous, temperate, mild, etc.) are chosen
under the aspect of the agent's own good. Engberg-Pedersen and Irwin,
on the other hand, claim that virtuous acts of *every* kind are chosen
under the aspect of the common good. They believe that Aristotle's repeated statements that virtuous actions aim at "the fine" (*to kalon*) imply
this, since they take an essential feature of aiming at the fine to be aiming
at the common good. I do not find their interpretation of the fine persuasive;[33] I prefer to think that the aetiological accounts of virtue in the
third and fourth books are not essentially incomplete and do not depend
on a link between the fine and the common good nowhere made explicit
in the *Nicomachean Ethics*. Aristotle is not modifying his earlier accounts
of the motives and psychic structure of virtue and vice when he discusses
virtue in relation to others. He is shifting to a different point of view, one
that focuses on the manifestation of virtue and vice in community life.

The fact that Aristotle's account of virtue in relation to others is symptomological rather than aetiological should alert us to an important difference between his approach to "interpersonal" virtue and most modern approaches. Philippa Foot gives a lucid description of the modern approach in the following passage:

> Virtues such as justice and charity . . . correspond not to any particular
> desire or tendency that has to be kept in check but rather to a deficiency of
> motivation; and it is this they must make good. If people were as much
> attached to the good of others as they are to their own good there would be
> no more a general virtue of benevolence than there is a general virtue of
> self-love. And if people cared about the rights of others as much as they
> care about their own rights no virtue of justice would be needed to look
> after the matter.[34]

The problem with this passage is that it is intended as an interpretation
of *Aristotle's* view of justice. It is true that the virtue of law-abidingness
(that is, universal justice) does not correspond "to any *particular* desire or
tendency that has to be kept in check," as, say, temperance does to bodily
pleasure and mildness to anger. But this is not because injustice is caused
by a particular deficiency of motivation (rooted in our partiality to ourselves). It is simply a consequence of the fact that justice is identified by a
particular symptomology of vice, not by a particular aetiology. Universal
injustice does not correspond to one particular kind of psychic misorien-

33. Engberg-Pedersen and Irwin both admit that there is nothing like an explicit account of *to kalon* in the *Nicomachean Ethics* that makes the common good an essential feature of it. I believe the coherence of my interpretation of relational virtue removes much of
the motivation for reading such accounts of the fine into the *Nicomachean Ethics*.

34. P. Foot, "Virtues and Vices," in *Virtues and Vices* (Berkeley, 1978), 9. Foot has been
influenced here by Thomas.

tation because *many* kinds of misorientation can underlie the breaches of community that characterize relational vice. Foot identifies injustice psychically by its connection to various kinds of egoism. Aristotle identifies it "politically" by its connection to failures of community.

As a result of this difference in approach, Foot sees a fundamental division of virtue, each kind corresponding to a different kind of temptation to vice, where Aristotle sees only one basic kind of temptation. Foot draws a distinction between the interpersonal virtues, which must make good a deficiency of motivation caused by egoism, and what we may call the intrapersonal virtues, which must moderate various desires. From the aetiological point of view, this splits virtue into two different parts. Once this split has been made, it is quite natural to contrast the moral interest expressed through interpersonal (or other-regarding) virtues with the merely natural or prudential interest expressed through intrapersonal (or self-regarding) virtues. How altruism is possible becomes the fundamental moral problem. Aristotle does not base his account of justice on such an aetiological division. He regards all vice as caused by various kinds of misoriented desire; there is no special aetiology, rooted in our partiality to ourselves, that accounts for injustice. Interpersonal virtue does not have a distinctive aetiology, but only a distinctive symptomology. Since interpersonal and intrapersonal virtue (that is, relational and simple virtue) are one thing, albeit considered from different perspectives, the distinction between moral and prudential interest cannot arise. Thus for Aristotle the fundamental problem of interpersonal virtue (and so of justice) is not the aetiological one of the possibility of altruism. Instead it is the political one of whether there is a kind of community in which the good man and the good citizen are identical.[35]

One might try to defend Foot's interpretation by limiting it to particular justice. Such a defense might hold that in Aristotle's account of *particular* justice, virtue is opposed primarily by unrestrained egoism rather than misdirected desire, even if in his account of universal justice it is not. We can already see that this line of defense must be wrong. Particular justice is a part of universal justice. Both are relational, rather than simple, virtues because they view virtue symptomologically rather than aetiologically and not because they are concerned with a different cause of vice from the other virtues. But we still must explain what part of relational virtue par-

---

35. Aristotle's treatment of this problem is beyond the scope of this paper. Because the content of the moral virtues, especially justice, varies as regimes (*politeiai*) vary (see, for instance, *Pol.* 1309a36–39), inferior regimes may not be able to tolerate the best human beings (see, for example, Aristotle's discussion of the political necessity of ostracism in *Politics* 3.13). But even in the best regime, people of especially outstanding virtue may be hard to satisfy (see *Pol.* 1284b25–34, for example, for the possibility of monarchy in the best regime). For a discussion of this second issue, see P. A. Vander Waerdt, "Kingship and Philosophy in Aristotle's Best Regime," *Phronesis* 30:3 (1985): 249–73.

ticular justice is. Universal justice is complete virtue because it is concerned with all of the motives of vice (though as sources of breaches of
community rather than as species of psychic misorientation). As we will
see in the next section , particular justice is concerned with only a special
subclass of the motives of vice. This limited aetiological focus distinguishes it from universal justice, while its symptomological perspective
distinguishes it from the simple virtues concerned with the same motives.
In the final section, we will use this interpretation to bring out the contrast
between Aristotle's approach to justice and most contemporary approaches. In particular, we will examine Bernard Williams's criticisms of
Aristotle's account of justice as a particular virtue, for Williams brings into
sharp focus the central difference between Aristotle and ourselves.

PARTICULAR JUSTICE AND PLEONEXIA

The central point of the previous section, to repeat it once more, was that
Aristotle's distinction between relational and simple virtue is a distinction
between two perspectives on virtue, one aetiological, one symptomological. We have also noted that particular justice is a part of relational virtue, and so should be a species of virtue viewed symptomologically. It is a
special case of justice as law-abidingness, since it too is concerned with
the manifestation of virtue in relation to others. But so far we have left
open which part of universal justice it is, except to note that Aristotle
identifies it with *to ison*, which we can translate as "fairness." For the
present-day reader, justice as fairness probably first brings to mind the
theory of justice of John Rawls, in which a kind of impartiality is the core
of justice. Yet in the previous section I claimed that Philippa Foot was
wrong to find some sort of egoistic partiality at the root of universal injustice. *A fortiori* it must also be wrong to identify a form of impartiality
with any of the parts of universal justice, including justice as fairness.

No doubt this last claim has a paradoxical ring to it. We would take
it as a matter of course that the vice opposed to fairness is unfairness,
and would immediately assume that unfairness has its source in egoism. Since universal injustice includes *any* breach of community, no
matter what its motivation, we might expect particular injustice to cover
breaches of community caused specifically by unfairness or partiality.
But Aristotle does not analyze it this way. As we will see, particular injustice does concern only those acts of (universal) injustice that have a
specific aetiology; but this specific aetiology is not some form of partiality
or egoism. Instead, Aristotle restricts particular injustice to acts of (universal) injustice motivated by the desire for profit or gain (*kerdos*), or
more precisely, for the pleasure that comes from gain.[36]

36. *Eth. Nic.* 1130a24, 27–28, 31–32, b3–4.

Aristotle labels this motive "graspingness" (*pleonexia*). This misdirected interest in gain is what Aristotle opposes to fairness, not partiality to oneself. Indeed, he introduces the notion of unfairness (*to anison*) in the first place simply to solve a terminological shortcoming of graspingness:

> The unjust man [in the particular sense] does not always take more [*to pleon*], but also less in cases of simply bad things. But because the less bad also seems to be good in a way, and graspingness [*pleonexia*] is concerned with the good, such a man seems to be grasping [*pleonektēs*]. So let him be [called] unfair [*anisos*]; for [unfairness] includes what is common [to taking more of a good thing and less of a bad thing].[37]

It is clear that unfairness is introduced here only because Aristotle felt that the etymology of *pleonexia* made it unnatural to apply it to taking less of unpleasant burdens as well as more of goods. The aetiology of that part of relational vice that constitutes particular injustice is an improper interest in a certain class of goods, not primarily some form of egoism.

The goods that Aristotle picks out as the objects of pursuit of the unfair (*anisos*) or grasping (*pleonektēs*) man are those he sometimes calls goods of fortune or external goods, the chief of which are honor and wealth.[38] The improper pursuit of these goods produces the breaches of community that characterize the part of relational vice that Aristotle identifies with particular injustice. He has already treated the improper pursuit of these goods from the perspective of simple virtue in his accounts of magnanimity and liberality. A comparison of these accounts of the particular virtues concerned with honor and wealth will help to illustrate how the aetiological and symptomological approaches to virtue fit together.

The magnanimous man is characterized by disdain for and detachment from those things that excite the concern of most people. His only real concern is for the honor that comes from great and dangerous undertakings, and even then his desire is ambivalent, for there are few people whose opinion he really cares about. Thus he is detached not only from a concern for what most people value, but also from a concern for most people.[39] Yet the magnanimous man is a paragon of virtue. In particular, Aristotle tells us that he will not commit injustice (*adikein*), since "for the sake of what would he to whom nothing is great do base

37. Ibid. 1129b6–11; I agree with Vermehren's change of *esti* to *estō* in line 10, since Aristotle appears to be giving a stipulative definition rather than merely describing the common use of the word *anisos*.

38. Ibid. 1129b1–4.

39. See especially *Eth. Nic.* 1124b28–1125a2.

things [*aischra*]?"[40] This is a perfect illustration of how the magnanimous man's aetiological excellence manifests itself as symptomological excellence; his virtuous psychic disposition guarantees that he will play his proper role in his relations with his fellow citizens. The pursuit of the kind of honor that the magnanimous man desires detaches him from concern for most of his fellows, but it also detaches him from concern with those things for the sake of which people do injustice.

The relation between the particular virtues concerned with wealth (namely, liberality and magnificence) and justice presents a similar case. Liberality is the virtue concerned with giving and taking things whose value is measured by money. It is concerned especially with appropriate giving,[41] and so "people who give are called liberal, while those who take [wealth in the appropriate way] are not praised for liberality, though they are praised for justice."[42] Still, Aristotle believes that the proper attitude to wealth, which is the basis of liberality, is responsible for propriety in both giving and taking,[43] with the result that the aetiologies of liberality and justice are virtually identical. The liberal man's limited interest in money distinguishes him from those who do injustice. Indeed, it makes him their target. They find him a good partner (*eukoinōnētos*) in affairs concerned with money, "for he can be treated unjustly, since he does not honor money."[44] The attitude that keeps him liberal and just in giving and taking also causes him to be less diligent in guarding his money than those whose improper honoring of it leads them to treat him unjustly.[45]

We will find more evidence that justice is related to liberality as symptom is to underlying aetiology if we consider Aristotle's account of the vices opposed to liberality. Since liberality concerns both the giving and taking of wealth, there can be excess and deficiency in either. Thus, it is possible to go wrong in four distinct ways: one can combine excessive giving of wealth with either excessive or deficient taking, and similarly for deficient giving. I summarize Aristotle's classification of the corresponding vices in the following table:

| | | TAKING | |
		excessive	deficient
GIVING	excessive	greedy wastefulness	foolish wastefulness
	deficient	gain-loving illiberality	miserly illiberality

---

40. *Eth. Nic.* 1123b32.   41. Ibid. 1119b25–27.   42. Ibid. 1120a19–20.
43. Ibid. 1120b31–1121a1; see also 1121a30–32.
44. Ibid. 1121a4–5.   45. Ibid. 1120b14–20.

Though all of these vices are opposed to liberality, Aristotle treats those that involve excessive taking differently from those that do not.[46] We have already seen that liberality is especially concerned with giving, while justice is more concerned with taking. Aristotle's analysis of these vices shows why this should be so.

We begin with those who give away wealth in an excessive way. Both the greedy waster and the foolish waster give more than they should and give to inappropriate people for improper reasons. But while the foolish waster is simply careless about preserving his wealth, and so tends to spend himself into poverty,[47] the greedy waster's desire to spend drives him to try to replenish his wealth from whatever sources are available.[48] It is exactly this base willingness to get money out of everything and everybody that Aristotle says makes a man grasping (*pleonektikos*).[49] *Pleonexia* both defines the aetiology of particular injustice and motivates the greedy waster to exploit his neighbors. Excessive giving without excessive taking is not so much vicious as foolish, for it benefits others even while it ruins the giver.[50] But wastefulness coupled with greediness is a powerful motive for cheating others for gain, and thus for particular injustice.

This contrast between the forms of wastefulness that do and do not lead to harm to others, and thus that do or do not lead to injustice, is explicit when Aristotle considers the properly illiberal vices corresponding to deficient giving. Deficient giving is more common than excessive giving, says Aristotle, because most people are money lovers (*philochrēmatoi*).[51] But money loving takes two different forms, depending on whether or not it is conjoined with excessive taking. The less vicious form of illiberal giving is that of the miser. Such people are unwilling to part with their own wealth for the sake of virtuous action, and this makes them illiberal. But they are also unwilling to go after other people's possessions, because either they are ashamed to do so or are afraid of punishment.[52] Aristotle contrasts such people with those who combine deficient giving and excessive taking. The vice of this latter sort of person Aristotle calls shameful pursuit of gain (*aischrokerdeia*), and he says that these people will put up with blame for the sake of gain (*kerdos*).[53] A de-

46. Aristotle does not distinguish clearly between deficient and merely nonexcessive wealth taking in his classification. (Contrast his explicit treatment of the deficient taking of honors in *Eth. Nic.* 1125a19–27.) He seems to regard deficient taking as going along with the wasteful fool's general carelessness about money. The illiberal miser is not said to be deficient in obtaining wealth. This will not affect the distinction I draw below between the vices that do and the vices that do not imply injustice, since neither deficient nor merely nonexcessive taking implies harming others, as does excessive taking.

47. *Eth. Nic.* 1121a16–19.   48. Ibid. 1121a30–b3.
49. See *Eth. Eud.* 1221a23–24.   50. *Eth. Nic.* 1121a25–30.
51. Ibid. 1121b12–16.   52. Ibid. 1121b21–31.
53. Ibid. 1122a2–3, 8–9.

sire for money drives them to seek wealth from every kind of base occupation, like pimping and loan-sharking.[54] Their willingness to engage
in such activities, all for the sake of gain, is why we call such people unjust.[55] Because of their misdirected interest in money, they are motivated
to take advantage of others, a motivation held in check only through
shame and fear.

We see, then, a consistent difference between Aristotle's treatment of
the illiberal vices that involve excessive taking of wealth and those that
do not, which is based on the fact that the latter, but not the former,
involve taking advantage of others. Aristotle characterizes excessive
taking as unjust, while excess or deficiency merely in giving are less
vicious, since they do not involve harm to others. He cites the same underlying aetiology of vice in his discussion of liberality as he does in his
account of justice: a misdirected concern for gain (*kerdos*). From the perspective of simple virtue, this mistaken honoring of wealth is the focus
of illiberality. But Aristotle does not deny that it makes a difference
whether this psychic misorientation actually leads to injustice. From the
perspective of relational virtue, neither the foolish waster nor the illiberal miser is vicious, since neither manifests his psychic misorientation by
harming others. As Aristotle observes of excessive and deficient giving
when he discusses magnificence, "these *hexeis* themselves [of excessive
and deficient giving] are bad [*kakai*], but they are not much blamed,
since they are neither harmful to one's neighbors nor too unbecom-
ing."[56] Considered simply as a particular sort of *hexis*, love of money (or
carelessness about money) is a vice; but it is vicious in a special way when
considered as the motive for harming others, that is, as the motive for
injustice.

It is because he is taking this symptomological approach to particular
justice that Aristotle treats it as a different sort of mean from the other
virtues. While the other virtues are means between two vices, acting
justly is a mean not between two vicious ways of acting but between
doing and suffering injustice.[57] Aristotle takes this "external" view of the
mean as applied to justice because he is thinking primarily of how virtue
is *manifested* in relations with others and only secondarily of how it is
motivated in the individual. He focuses on the median symptom rather
than the median psychic state. Considered simply as a disposition (*hexis*)
of a certain sort, the just man's virtue *is* a mean between two vices. (*Which
mean it will be depends on what is at stake in a particular case, since in-*

---

54. Ibid. 1121b31–34.   55. Ibid. 1122a6–7.   56. Ibid. 1123a31–33.
57. Ibid. 1133b30–1134a1. MacIntyre is wrong when he says that justice is a mean between two vices (*After Virtue*, 145). See also *Eth. Eud.* 1221a4, where in the table of virtues
and vices the just (*to dikaion*) is the mean between gain (*kerdos*) and loss (*zēmia*), whereas the
other virtues are means between two psychic states.

justice has a number of distinct motives. For example, in money matters, the good man's justice may be a manifestation of his liberality, while in a matter of honor it may be a manifestation of his magnanimity.) But this dispositional mean is manifested by the just man's satisfaction with what the law commands with a view to the common good, and especially by his satisfaction with a median amount of external goods. From the perspective of justice, the mean is in the external fact of cooperation rather than in the internal fact of motivation, so to speak.

I believe that this symptomological focus also explains the otherwise puzzling fact that *pleonexia* includes desires for both money and honor. Aristotle's general approach to the particular virtues associates each of them with one particular kind of temptation to vice. In other contexts, Aristotle does not treat the pleasures of honor and wealth as comparable temptations. In the first place, love of honor is of higher rank than love of wealth, since pleasures of the soul are higher than those of the body.[58] In the second, many people who are tempted by honors are not tempted by money, and vice versa.[59] When he treats the virtues aetiologically, Aristotle clearly distinguishes between the vices that spring from the pursuit of honor and those that spring from love of money. Why then in his account of particular justice does he treat the desire for money and the desire for honor as the one unified motive of *pleonexia* when he habitually distinguishes them in other contexts?

I suggest that what unifies these two different kinds of desire when they are viewed symptomologically is that both honor and wealth are competitive goods, what Aristotle calls "things people fight over" (*perimachēta*).[60] As temptations that lure an individual from the good life, they are different; but as threats to the shared good life of the citizens of a *polis*, they are importantly the same. Both by nature are ordered toward (and hence limited by) the life of virtuous activity. But when they are pursued as ends themselves, this natural limit gives way to an insatiable desire that leads to injustice and ultimately to civil conflict (*stasis*).[61] Such conflict is the ultimate symptom of an underlying moral disease within the members of a community. Furthermore, honor and wealth also seem to be the most *common* objects of misorientation, and thus the most com-

---

58. On the relative rank of the pleasures of honor and wealth, see *Eth. Nic.* 1117b28–31.

59. For Aristotle's usual distinction between honor and wealth as motives, see, for example, *Pol.* 1266b38–1267a2, 1308a9–10, 1311a4–7, 1315a17–20; *Rh.* 1372b2–8 and 18–21.

60. For the description of honor and wealth as competitive goods (*perimachēta*), see *Eth. Nic.* 1169a20–22; *Eth. Eud.* 1248b27.

61. For a striking example of this sort of analysis, see *Pol.* 2.7, especially 1266b28–1267a17 and 1267a37–b9: the only protection against *stasis* is public education of the desires for wealth and honor, "for the nature of desire is without limit."

mon temptations to (universal) injustice.[62] Not only is their pursuit inherently divisive, but it is also particularly tempting. For both of these reasons, desires for honor and wealth are especially important to the problem of justice, that is, the problem of virtue in our relations with one another, and this justifies Aristotle's special focus on them as motives of injustice.

Thus particular justice is distinguished from universal justice, which is *complete* virtue, by its focus on just one particular class of important causes of injustice. In this it resembles the other particular virtues rather than universal justice, since a particular aetiology is relevant to its identification. But only one kind of temptation is included in the identifying aetiologies of the other virtues (fear for courage, bodily pleasure for temperance, honor for magnanimity, for example), while particular justice has what from the point of view of simple virtue would be at least two very different aetiologies. This aetiological multiplicity is justified because particular justice, like universal justice, is virtue considered in its manifestation in relations with others, so that its unity is primarily symptomological, not aetiological. *Pleonexia* is uniform when considered in relation to the symptoms it produces even though it is complex when considered simply in itself as a motive.

The connections between universal justice, particular justice, and the rest of the particular virtues are summarized in the following table:

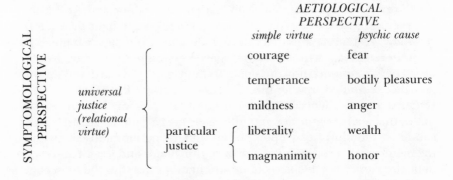

		AETIOLOGICAL PERSPECTIVE	
		simple virtue	*psychic cause*
		courage	fear
		temperance	bodily pleasures
SYMPTOMOLOGICAL PERSPECTIVE	*universal justice (relational virtue)*	mildness	anger
	particular justice	liberality	wealth
		magnanimity	honor

We can see that Aristotle's account of particular justice bears out his claim that it is one part of universal justice. It is the part concerned with an especially important subclass of all the motives that result in breaches of community. Particular justice is distinguished from the other particular virtues not by a distinctive aetiology, but by its different perspective on a certain class of aetiologies. From the perspective of simple virtue,

62. See *Pol.* 1271a16–18.

the cause of injustice must be sought in the same place as the causes of the particular vices concerned with external goods. For example, one and the same psychic misorientation characterizes the illiberal and the unjust man. But from the perspective of relational virtue, the question is whether or not an individual's psychic misorientation unfits him for community life. At the aetiological level, what unfits someone for community life is not some form of egoistic partiality. It is rather some form of teleological misdirectedness. The unjust man is primarily one whose ends necessarily limit the extent to which he can pursue them in common with others. He is not primarily an egoist, but a money grubber or honor grubber. His selfishness is the consequence of the (improper) end that he pursues.

This approach to justice makes Aristotle's account very different from modern accounts. In the next section, we will consider Bernard Williams's critique of Aristotle's account of justice as a virtue, for it provides a striking illustration of this difference. As we shall see, the fundamental issue raised by Williams is whether or not distributive justice has a special aetiology of its own. If so, Aristotle's symptomological approach fails to capture it. More specifically, if distributive injustice is psychically grounded in a form of partiality, then Aristotle is wrong to explain it primarily as a symptom of an underlying misorientation. Our examination of this problem will make clearer what kind of alternative Aristotle's approach to justice offers us, and what differences it makes for moral philosophy.

PARTICULAR AND DISTRIBUTIVE JUSTICE

Bernard Williams's understanding of justice (in the narrow sense, in which it is one particular virtue) is strikingly similar to Foot's. He too thinks that injustice is distinguished from the other vices by the fact that "this vice, unlike others, does not import a special motive, but rather the lack of one," namely, a lack of concern with promoting just distributions.[63] But unlike Foot, Williams sees that this is not Aristotle's understanding of the aetiology of injustice, and he tries to show that Aristotle's understanding is defective. In particular, he claims that Aristotle overassimilates "the vice of *adikia* [injustice] . . . to the other vices of character [by seeking] a characteristic motive to go with it,"[64] when in fact it is

63. Williams, "Justice as a Virtue," in *Aristotle's Ethics*, ed. Rorty, 198.

64. Ibid. Because Williams limits himself to considering particular justice, his account misses Aristotle's reason for treating *pleonexia* as a unified motive despite its multiplicity from the aetiological point of view. Thus Williams overstates the assimilation of particular injustice to the other vices here; but his contrast between Aristotle's focus on justice's defining motives and his own focus on its defining lack of a motive is unaffected by this overstatement.

distinguished from the other vices precisely by a characteristic *lack* of certain motives.

The cause of Aristotle's mistake, thinks Williams, is that he requires an act to be the product of some particular identifying motive for it to count as an act of a particular type of vice.[65] For example, a necessary condition for an act's being intemperate is that it be the product of lust and for an act's being cowardly that it be the product of fear. This is the result of Aristotle's motivational or aetiological focus in his analysis of the particular virtues of temperance, courage, and the like. Applying this general framework to justice, Williams points out that acts that are unjust in the narrow sense have as their characteristic motive the desire for gain. He believes that this leads to the absurd consequence that any act that is unjust (in the narrow sense) must be motivated by *pleonexia*. Otherwise, given the necessary connection between act type and motive, the act will not count as unjust. This is "obviously false," says Williams, since "there are acts that are unjust, and in the 'particular' sense, but which are the products of fear, jealousy, desire for revenge, and so on." Aristotle's motivational or aetiological approach leads him astray here, thinks Williams, since "we can identify certain intentional acts as unjust in the particular sense . . . without referring to their motive. Indeed," he continues, "we are helped by Aristotle in doing this, by his drawing our attention to such basic cases as the intentional misdistribution of divisible goods."[66]

Williams cites the following passage as a particularly clear illustration of how Aristotle's link between particular injustice and *pleonexia* leads to error:

> It is apparent that he who distributes [too much] commits injustice, but not always he who gets too much [*to pleon*]; for it is not he to whom the unjust amount belongs who commits injustice, but he who voluntarily produced [the unjust amount]. This is because the source [*archē*] of the action is the one who distributes, not the one who receives. . . . If a man knowingly decides unjustly [in a dispute between two parties], he too takes too much [*pleonektein*] of gratitude [*charis*] or revenge [*timōria*]; for he who decides unjustly for the sake of these has too much [*pleon*] just as if he shared in the unjust gain [*adikēma*].[67]

Aristotle here describes a corrupt judge and offers an account of his motivation. Williams calls this account "nonsense" and "a desperate device." "What would it be," he asks, "to get the right amount of gratitude or re-

65. Williams, "Justice as a Virtue," in *Aristotle's Ethics*, ed. Rorty, 191.
66. Ibid., 192–93.
67. *Eth. Nic.* 1136b25–29, 1136b34–1137a4.

venge?"[68] There is no tolerable sense in which the judge's *motive* can be included within *pleonexia*, thinks Williams, even though his *act* is clearly a case of particular injustice. The solution is to realize that the injustice of a particular act does not depend on its issuing from any particular motive. It depends rather on the act's being an intentional misdistribution of divisible goods, something that can be motivated by a great many things besides *pleonexia*.

But the specific example that Williams describes as nonsense will seem much less nonsensical when we realize that both gratitude and revenge (or punishment) are connected in important ways to honor. Gratitude simply is a kind of honor, while taking revenge is a way to restore one's honor, to avoid being humiliated and treated like a slave.[69] If their inclusion in *pleonexia* stretches the concept, it does not stretch it very far. Aristotle is thinking of the kind of judge who is corrupted by a delight in approval that leads him to "give someone a break" when he shouldn't or who "throws the book" at someone as an act of self-assertion, as if to say, "You can't get away with that around *me*." Such judges are corrupted by immoderate desire as surely, though perhaps not as basely, as the man who takes a bribe. This explanation is no "desperate device," but rather an interesting and revealing analysis of a case where the wrong kind of concern for honor can lead one to commit an injustice.[70]

Of course, the explanation of this particular case does not put to rest Williams's objection to Aristotle's linking of the particular vice of injustice and *pleonexia*. A defender of Williams might say, "Suppose I accept your claim that gratitude and revenge can be referred to honor in such a way that Aristotle's corrupt judge is a case of *pleonexia* after all. Still you must admit that what makes the judge's act unjust (in the particular sense) is that it is an intentional misdistribution of divisible goods, and not that it is motivated by *pleonexia*. This will be obvious if we take a judge who is corrupted by lust and who for sexual favors renders an unjust decision involving the distribution of goods. His act will be un-

68. Williams, "Justice as a Virtue," in *Aristotle's Ethics*, ed. Rorty, 192, 193.

69. For the association of gratitude and honor, see *Eth. Nic.* 1163b1–5; *Eth. Eud.* 1242b19–21; *Rh.* 1378b26–34. For revenge, see, for example, *Eth. Nic.* 1126a3–8, 1132b34–1133a1; *Eth. Eud.* 1231b10, 19–20, 25–26.

70. Though I think this shows that we can understand Aristotle's corrupt judge as motivated by *pleonexia*, it should be noticed that Williams is too quick to assume Aristotle intends the judge as an illustration of particular injustice. The entire discussion in *Eth. Nic.* 5.8–9 concerns what Aristotle calls *haplōs to adikein* ("doing injustice in the most basic sense"), namely, voluntarily harming someone (see 1136a31 and 1135b11). This sense of injustice is much broader than particular injustice, including, for example, striking someone in anger (1135b19–23). Aristotle intends the corrupt judge to illustrate only this broad sense of injustice; whether or not the judge is motivated by *pleonexia* is irrelevant to Aristotle's point in the passage.

just (in the particular sense) even though his motive has nothing to do with *pleonexia*. Aristotle's conception of acts of particular injustice as motivated by *pleonexia* is obviously defective, since it will exclude paradigmatic cases of injustice like that of the lustful judge."

To see what is at stake in this criticism it will help to consider the different ways that Aristotle and Williams would organize cases of vice manifested in relations with others. In the first place, there are cases of intentional misdistribution that Williams, but not Aristotle, would include as cases of particular injustice. Consider three corrupt judges, one lustful, one greedy, one overly fond of honor (whom for brevity we will call ambitious). Suppose all three intentionally misdistribute goods when they render their decisions, the lustful judge for sexual favors, the greedy judge for a bribe, and the ambitious judge for the sake of some honor, such as political advancement. Williams would seem to be committed to considering all three judges unjust in the particular sense, since they all intentionally misdistribute divisible goods. But Aristotle would count only the greedy and the ambitious judges as unjust in this sense, since the lustful judge is not motivated by *pleonexia*.[71] The lustful judge would of course be unjust in the *universal* sense, since his internal intemperance manifests itself externally as a breach of the bonds of community. But intemperance does not have that especially potent tendency to produce breaches of community that (I have argued) leads Aristotle to treat greed and ambition together as *pleonexia*. Aristotle does not single it out for the special attention he gives the other two in his account of virtue in relation to others.

A second important difference between Williams's approach and Aristotle's can be seen in cases that do not involve misdistribution at all and that Aristotle, but not Williams, would count as cases of particular injustice. In addition to the three corrupt judges, consider three corrupt seducers, one who commits adultery out of lust, one for the sake of money, the third out of ambition. Williams would not count any of the seducers as unjust in the particular sense, since their actions have nothing to do with distributing goods. Aristotle, however, uses precisely the difference between the lustful and the greedy seducer to illustrate the difference between universal and particular injustice.[72] The greedy seducer's action clearly involves harm to another, so it fulfills the broad symptomological conditions of universal injustice; and its motive falls within *pleonexia*, so it also fulfills the aetiological conditions of particular injustice.

71. If we say a public official is corrupt, we are usually thinking of his greed and ambition rather than his illicit sexual habits. This is a reflection of the emphases behind Aristotle's way of categorizing the corrupt judges.
72. *Eth. Nic.* 1130a24–27 with 1129b21–22.

These different categorizations are summarized in the following table:

		MOTIVE		
		lust	greed	ambition
ACTION	misdistribution	W	AW	AW
	adultery		A	A

A = Aristotle's cases of particular injustice
W = Williams's cases of particular injustice

As we can see, Williams finds a unity in all the cases of misdistribution. From Aristotle's point of view, this unity is purely symptomological: though the lustful judge manifests his viciousness in the same circumstances as the greedy and ambitious judges, the cause of his action, its aetiology, is entirely different. On the other hand, Williams distinguishes the greedy judge, who is characterized by particular injustice, from the greedy seducer, who is not; he makes the same distinction between the ambitious judge and seducer. Again, to Aristotle this distinction would seem to be purely symptomological: there is a single aetiology, a single moral disease, underlying the political "symptoms" of judge and seducer. Why prefer the symptomological focus of Williams's categories to the aetiological focus that structures Aristotle's account?

Williams's response would be that his organization of the phenomena does not lack an aetiological basis. He finds a kind of basis that Aristotle does not consider. Aristotle unified greed and ambition in *pleonexia* despite their difference *qua* motives because of their similarity *qua* especially important producers of vice in relations with others. But since lust does not share this status with them, Aristotle separated the lustful judge from the other two. Williams's way of unifying all three judges does not depend in this way on finding relevant similarities among their motives. Instead, they are united by their common *lack* of a motive, or put the other way around, by an indifference they all share, namely, an indifference to promoting just distributions.[73] Such an indifference is at the basis of the corruption of all three judges and in fact is operative in any case of intentional misdistribution. The "symptom" of intentional misdistribution is always associated with the indifference to just distributions that constitutes the vice of particular injustice. Because he believes there is such a specific kind of indifference that operates in the distribution of goods, Williams can treat the lustful judge and the greedy judge as manifestations of a single underlying aetiology.

73. See Williams, "Justice as a Virtue," in *Aristotle's Ethics*, ed. Rorty, 197–98.

Appeal to this same aetiological basis could justify a distinction between
the greedy judge and the greedy seducer. We saw that Aristotle considered both as examples of particular injustice. Both manifest their viciousness in relations with others, and so fulfill the broad symptomological
requirements to count as unjust, whether in the universal or the particular sense. Further, the motives of both the greedy judge and the
greedy seducer belong to that restricted class of motives that fulfill the
aetiological requirements to count as particular injustice; and so Aristotle counts both judge and seducer as unjust in the particular sense.
Williams's aetiological basis of particular injustice, however, distinguishes between the judge and the seducer, for there is a specific kind
of indifference, namely, an indifference to just distributions, that is
operative in the one case but not in the other. Here again, because
Williams finds a special moral disposition that comes into play in the context of distribution, his organization of the phenomena is different from
Aristotle's.

Williams, then, need be no more content than Aristotle to give a
purely symptomological basis to his account of particular justice. He
does not identify acts of particular injustice merely as intentional mis-
distributions of divisible goods. Williams, like Aristotle, looks for something in the soul, for a cause that unifies the symptoms. From Williams's
point of view, the defectiveness of Aristotle's account derives from his
obliviousness to the real cause of injustice. This obliviousness is itself in-
duced by Aristotle's theoretical commitment to treat vice primarily as a
matter of misplaced motives. This commitment leads him to look for the
aetiology of injustice in the wrong place and to miss its distinctiveness,
for it depends precisely on a certain lack of motive.

Aristotle, however, finds no reason to think that the greedy and ambitious judges share anything more than the external symptoms of their
actions with the lustful judge. All three will misdistribute goods, true
enough; but they are no more alike in their souls than two men who
commit adultery, one for money, one for sexual pleasure. Both a lustful
adulterer and a greedy adulterer could be said to share an "indifference
to licitness in sexual relations," but this indifference has two distinct
causes in their souls. In the same way, Aristotle would say that the "indifference to just distributions" shared by the lustful and greedy judges has
no aetiological unity. Furthermore, from Aristotle's point of view, there
is no aetiological distinction between the greedy judge and the greedy
seducer. It is true enough that the judge can be said to be "indifferent to
just distributions"; but this indifference does not have a different source
from the indifference to virtue of the greedy seducer. There is no special
kind of indifference that distinguishes the judge from the seducer.
Rather, the same underlying misdirectedness in both men manifests itself in two different contexts in a failure to share in the community.

This is not to deny that the context of the distribution of goods is especially important to Aristotle's account of particular justice. The distribution of the very goods that so attract the fancy of the grasping man (*ho pleonektēs*) is, so to speak, the natural context for the indulgence of his viciousness. The grasping man pursues external goods like wealth and honor without regard for their appropriate place in the good life as equipment for virtue. He is not mindful of the fact that such things are useful only up to a point, and his mistaken indulgence motivates him to be unfair, that is, to fail to be satisfied with his share of good in the community.[74] Thus it is no accident that most of Aristotle's account of particular justice is devoted to an examination of justice in the distribution and exchange of goods. Indeed, it would not be unreasonable to take special notice of the importance of this context by restricting the fullest and most proper sense of particular injustice to it alone. For example, we might say that while the greedy judge and the greedy seducer are both unjust in the particular sense, the greedy judge is so in the strictest sense. This would add a symptomological restriction to the aetiological restriction that distinguishes particular from universal justice.

Even if we were to accept this restriction (and Aristotle himself does not indicate that he accepts it), the link between the typical context of injustice and the cause of injustice is not so tight for Aristotle as it is for Williams. For Williams, the intentional misdistribution of divisible goods has a very specific aetiology in a very specific kind of indifference, and presumably has an equally specific cure in the development of a very particular kind of sensitivity to the just claims of others. For Aristotle, injustice in distribution can have as many different causes as there are kinds of misorientation, though typically it will be caused by *pleonexia*. Each of these different kinds of motive for viciousness requires its own cure. There is no unified sensitivity to just claims that can serve the purpose.

Aristotle and Williams agree that injustice in the distribution of goods can have many motives. But for Aristotle, this is merely a special case of the aetiological indeterminacy of universal injustice. For Williams, it is a consequence of the fact that the single source of this manifestation of injustice is precisely a *lack* of motive, that is, a special kind of indifference to just distribution. Thus Williams is willing to treat all acts of misdistribution as cases of one kind of injustice, which he somewhat misleadingly links to Aristotle's conception of particular injustice. From Aristotle's point of view, Williams is wrong to think that there is a special moral sensitivity relevant to distributions. He would think Williams had made a mistaken and empty postulation of a single cause to explain an incidental unity of symptoms. He would agree that distribution of goods

74. See *Eth. Nic.* 1129b3–4, 1137a26–30, 1138a29–31.

162 DAVID K. O'CONNOR

is the most important context of particular justice. But he would not agree that it is the only context, nor that all cases of misdistribution are cases of particular injustice.

In the final analysis, we are left with two very different accounts of the relation between virtue and community. Williams's criticisms of Aristotle rely on his claim that the aetiology of particular injustice is unified. He can take this position because, unlike Aristotle, he believes that "the notion of a fair distribution is prior to that of a fair or just person."[75] Since a just distribution is characterized without reference to the just man, it makes sense to define the just man as "one who is disposed to promote just distributions, look for them, stand by them, and so on, because that is what they are."[76] In other words, it is possible to think of the promotion of just distributions as itself a motive of the just man. The lack of such a motive will then be exactly the indifference that characterizes particular injustice.

Aristotle's account of the relation between just distributions and the good man's motives does not allow this tight aetiological connection. The just man's virtue can be considered from two different perspectives. From the perspective of individual virtue, the just man is simply the good man who has control of his desires for external goods like money and honor. His life is devoted to virtuous activity, and so he pursues the external goods not as ends themselves but as means. The external goods are the equipment of happiness for him, not its constituents. This defines a limit to his interest in them and to the effort he will devote to pursuing them. He will be satisfied with a "median" amount of these goods, which neither falls short of what is required for virtuous activity nor exceeds this measure. From the perspective of virtue in relation to others, the just man's limited interest in external goods makes it possible for him to share with others, since he is not bent on getting as much as he can from them. He will be satisfied with a "median" amount in the sense that he demands an amount sufficient for living well and virtuously (and thus won't accept being deprived unjustly of a share commensurate to his virtue) but not an amount that brings him into conflict with the reasonable claims of others.

Since justice is virtue considered in relation to others, it is this second, "external" mean that is of primary importance. This is why justice is a mean primarily between suffering and committing injustice, not between too little and too much concern for external goods. But this "interpersonal" mean is in no sense prior to the "intrapersonal" mean defined by the requirements of virtuous activity. Indeed, it is defined with refer-

75. Williams, "Justice as a Virtue," in *Aristotle's Ethics,* ed. Rorty, 196–97.
76. Ibid., 197.

ence to the "intrapersonal" mean; for the aim of the community is to promote the virtue (and thus the happiness) of each of its members. In a sense, then, the just man is conceptually prior to the just distribution: he is prior *qua* virtuous simply, not *qua* just. As a result, in Aristotle's view an indifference to just distribution is based on an underlying misorientation, since a man's unwillingness to abide by the mean in his relations with others is just the "political" manifestation of his failure to abide by the mean psychically. There is no standard of justice in distribution independent of the standard of the active life of virtue and thus nothing to ground Williams's unified treatment of all intentional misdistribution as particular injustice.

In summary, Aristotle offers an approach to justice that is very different from modern accounts that make some form of impartiality, and thus of altruism, their central feature. Such accounts divide virtue into two realms. One is concerned with the intrapersonal excellences. For example, temperance and courage would be primarily intrapersonal virtues, focusing on the proper habituation of our dispositions toward fears and pleasures. The other is the interpersonal realm, a category that would include justice (and such virtues as benevolence). These virtues are not primarily concerned with particular kinds of pleasure and pain, as are the intrapersonal virtues. Instead, they correct for or moderate the tendency of our desires to be egoistic. In one way or another, they force us to see things from the other person's point of view (for example, from behind a veil of ignorance or as a sympathetic ideal observer). From the aetiological perspective, these two kinds of virtue are independent. The psychic capacity through which we are just (for example, a Rawlsian sense of justice) is different from the particular capacities for pleasure and pain that are the concern of intrapersonal virtue. The development of the interpersonal virtues, which are the basis of community, can thus proceed independently of intrapersonal excellence: the self-indulgent man may well be a just citizen, and the temperate man may well fail to be sensitive to the just claims of others.

Aristotle does not think of justice and other interpersonal virtues (such as *philia*) as having a different aetiological basis from the particular virtues concerned with pleasures and pains. He does not see two realms of virtue, but one fundamental kind of human excellence viewed from two perspectives. Injustice and other breaches of community are not caused by a special incapacity linked to egoism (such as a poorly developed sense of justice). They are the "political" or interpersonal symptom of psychic or intrapersonal misorientation. Someone with an insatiable desire for money or honors will necessarily find himself at odds with others. Thus for Aristotle the self-indulgent man is at least potentially the unjust man, and the cure for his self-indulgence would also be the cure for his injustice. The only guarantee of good citizenship is the proper psychic disposition toward the pleasures and pains that motivate human action.

I do not propose to prove that one or the other of these frameworks is the correct one. It is enough if we see the alternative that Aristotle provides. He replaces our aetiological focus on the possibility of altruism with a symptomological focus on the possibility of a truly *common* good, one whose pursuit is not "something to fight about." He refers failures of a community to the ends its members pursue within and through it rather than to the baneful effects of insufficiently controlled egoism. The obstacles to and limitations of community life are to be found in the same sorts of misorientation that account for simple vice. Virtue serves community primarily by orienting individuals toward the end of virtuous activity, an end that can really be common and shared.

SIX

Women, Soldiers, Citizens: Plato and Aristotle on the Politics of Virility

Stephen G. Salkever

Interpretations of Platonic and Aristotelian texts play an increasingly important role in several debates concerning central issues in contemporary political life. Particularly in the years since the publication of Hannah Arendt's *The Human Condition,* the study of Plato and especially Aristotle has been seen as a key element in the critique of liberal individualism and of the modern tendency to confuse technical rationality and practical reason.[1] For Arendt, Hans-Georg Gadamer, and Alasdair MacIntyre, Aristotle has significance as a guide to formulating an understanding of politics as a way of life rather than as a mere instrument for the protection of prepolitical rights. Plato's role in this contemporary debate is less clear; while surely no liberal individualist, he appears to some modern writers to present an unattractive antipolitical counterpart to Aristotle, who is now seen as the defender of the "deep beliefs"[2] that constitute the political order against the dissolving critique of theoretical wisdom.

Plato and Aristotle have also received attention in considerations of the sources of the tendency to identify masculinity and humanness (or human virtue) in the tradition of Western political thought and practice.

Translations are my own, though greatly aided by the translations of the *Nicomachean Ethics* by M. Ostwald (Indianapolis, 1962) and T. Irwin (Indianapolis, 1985), and of the *Politics* by H. Rackham (Cambridge, Mass., 1959) and C. Lord (Chicago, 1984).

1. H. Arendt, *The Human Condition* (Chicago, 1958), 36; for an especially vehement critique of liberal individualism, see A. MacIntyre, *After Virtue: A Study in Moral Theory* (Notre Dame, 1981); a more moderate approach is taken by R. Beiner, *Political Judgment* (Chicago, 1983); notable among those who have analyzed the modern tendency to confuse technical rationality and practical reason is Hans-Georg Gadamer, who gives a good, brief summary of his use of Aristotle in "Hermeneutics and Social Science," *Cultural Hermeneutics* 2 (1975): 307–16.

2. M. C. Nussbaum, *The Fragility of Goodness* (Cambridge, 1986), 320.

Here, however, their relationship to the tradition being criticized is generally reversed; Plato is sometimes cited as an early opponent of a prevailing misogyny, while Aristotle is almost inevitably identified as the champion of male domination.[3]

These two ways of reexamining Aristotle—from the perspective of the question of the meaning of citizenship and from the perspective of gender valuation—have proceeded independently of one another. The separation of the questions of citizenship and of gender is unfortunate, since in the view of both Aristotle and Plato, as I will try to show, the two issues are inextricably mingled. Furthermore, Plato and Aristotle are very much in agreement concerning these questions. There is in fact an essential connection between participatory politics and male domination, at least insofar as such politics is shaped by our recollection of the Periclean political culture that formed the point of departure for the philosophizing of Plato and Aristotle. Both philosophers identify this connection and are similarly critical of the way of life it supports. As a result, while neither Plato nor Aristotle can be called feminists, insofar as feminism is taken to be a position that asserts the equal rights of women and men contrary to existing practice, both can be seen as urging a significant improvement in the status of women relative to the norms of their time. The source of their opposition to Greek misogyny is, I will argue, not to be found in any theory of the rights of individuals, but in the significant reservations each holds concerning the view that the best human life is that of the committed citizen, the life that cares most for the things of the city or political community. Properly understood, the Platonic-Aristotelian project is in part an attempt to call attention to a deep psychological connection between republican virtue and misogyny, a connection otherwise simply ignored by later writers in the tradition, whether liberal or republican.

It is difficult to speak with assurance concerning the actual practices of Greek political life in the fifth and fourth centuries; but it is by no means hard to see that the language in which that political life was articulated placed a very high value on both political activity and maleness. So much is clear from Pericles' funeral speech, in which it is observed

3. See J. B. Elshtain, *Public Man, Private Woman* (Princeton, 1981); and especially S. M. Okin, *Women in Western Political Thought* (Princeton, 1979), who relies heavily on G. E. R. Lloyd's *Aristotle: The Growth and Structure of His Thought* (London, 1968). Lloyd there states without much text argument (the book is intended as a popularization for the beginning student) that Aristotle tends to support the majority view in politics and ethics. His later *Science, Folklore, and Ideology* (London, 1983) explains flaws in Aristotle's biology by reference to Aristotle's acceptance of "the ideological presuppositions of contemporaries concerning the differences between men and women" (105). Again, this assertion is made without considering any of Aristotle's discussions of gender in political and ethical contexts.

that women should be quiet and remain at home and "we [Athenians] alone think of one who does not participate in public affairs not as a quiet man, but as a useless one."[4] For Pericles, human happiness is impossible outside of an autonomous *polis*, and the existence of such a *polis* depends on the courage or stoutheartedness of its citizens, for "happiness depends on freedom, and freedom depends on being courageous [*eupsychos*]."[5] Arendt's recollection of this tradition stresses the special status of courage among the Greek political virtues. "Courage," Arendt remarks, "therefore became the political virtue par excellence, and only those men who possessed it could be admitted to a fellowship that was political in content and purpose."[6] The Greek word most frequently used to express this quality is *andreia*, the virtue of the *andres* or real males, a word ordinarily translated as "courage," but perhaps more tellingly rendered by "virility" or "manliness." In a world dominated by war and the threat of war, it is perhaps not surprising that an aptitude for battle constituted a chief requisite for free citizenship. As Michael Shaw puts it, speaking of the Greek political understanding, "the first necessity of society is that it be autonomous; to gain this autonomy, society's members must put hatred above love, in order that enemies may be repelled."[7]

The equation of virility and political virtue in prephilosophic Greek political thought is further reinforced by the habit of drawing a sharp dichotomy between the world of the household or family and that of the *polis*, by the association of *oikia* with women and *polis* with men, and by the designation of the *polis* as clearly superior to and even threatened by the household. As Arendt says, "according to Greek thought, the human capacity for political organization is not only different from but stands in direct opposition to that natural association whose center is the home (*oikia*) and the family."[8] Moreover, "the public realm stands in the sharpest possible contrast to our private domain, where, in the protection of family and home, everything serves and must serve the security of the life process. . . . Courage liberates men from their worry about life."[9] This tendency to polarize *oikia* and *polis* and to articulate their relationship in terms of the imagery of conflict is associated in speech, whatever may have been the case in political practice, with the tendency similarly

4. Thuc. 2. 40.   5. Ibid. 2. 43.   6. Arendt, *Human Condition*, 36.
7. M. Shaw, "The Female Intruder: Women in Fifth Century Drama," *Classical Philology* 70 (1975): 266; see 255–66 generally.
8. Arendt, *Human Condition*, 24.
9. H. Arendt, "What Is Freedom?" in *Between Past and Future* (New York, 1961), 156 and 143–71 generally. In *The Human Condition* Arendt also notes that women and slaves had the same status among the Greeks since both were kept within the *oikia*, hidden from public view (72–73). Compare Aristotle, who craftily attributes this Greek view exclusively to barbarians (*Pol.* 1252b5–6).

to oppose female and male and to define human virtue in terms of the hard-won triumph of the latter member of each of these pairs. Thus Froma Zeitlin characterizes "the misogynistic tradition which pervades Greek thought" as "a bias which both projects a combative dialogue in male-female interactions and which relates the mastery of the female to higher social goals." [10] The Greek political imagination, then, revolves around a norm of manly valor, according to which courageous citizens display their patriotism by the spirit of anger (*thymos*), with which they pursue not peace or justice but honor (*timē*) and fame (*kleos*), a norm that takes its substance from a contrast with the idealized life of women, who toil in silence and seclusion, like slaves. [11]

The republican political imagination of Periclean Athens depends upon the polarized opposition of male, war, and *polis* on the one hand and female, peace, and family on the other. Both the tone and the content of the brief advice to the women of Athens at the end of Pericles' funeral oration make this clear:

> If it is necessary for me to recall anything of feminine virtue for those of you now widowed, I shall signify all by this brief exhortation: great will be your repute if you do not become worse than your proper nature, and especially she of whom the least is said, whether of her virtue or her flaws, in the reports of the men. [12]

This association of politics, publicity, and virility has not been ignored by latter-day admirers of the virtues of ancient republics, such as Machiavelli (whose *virtù* is a wholly adequate translation of *andreia*) and Arendt.

But what of the first political philosophers—Socrates, Plato, and Aristotle? What is the relationship of their thought to the political context from which it arose? According to Arendt, the first philosophical understanding of politics is essentially a reflection of prephilosophic opinion. She comments, "The true character of this *polis* is still quite manifest in Plato's and Aristotle's political philosophies, even if the borderline between household and *polis* is occasionally blurred, especially in Plato." [13] It is part of Arendt's rhetorical strategy to suggest that her notion of politics as sharply antithetical to the household is present in Aristotle, if not in Plato, and that the republican virtue she finds in Greece is preserved in Aristotle's reflections. "According to Greek thought," she notes,

10. F. I. Zeitlin, "The Dynamics of Misogyny: Myth and Mythmaking in the *Oresteia*," *Arethusa* 11 (1978): 149–81.

11. Shaw, "Female Intruder," 256–57.

12. Thuc. 2.45. That Thucydides is not himself inclined to admire exaggerated maleness is indicated in his discussion of *stasis* in 3.82.

13. Arendt, *Human Condition*, 37.

the human capacity for political organization is not only different from but stands in direct opposition to that natural association whose center is the home (*oikia*) and the family. The rise of the city-state meant that man received besides his private life a sort of second life, his *bios politikos*. Now every citizen belongs to two orders of existence; and there is a sharp distinction in his life between what is his own (*idion*) and what is communal (*koinon*).[14]

Arendt's footnote ad loc. reveals, however, that she is quoting Werner Jaeger rather than Aristotle. Arendt's insistence on attributing a non-Aristotelian view of politics to Aristotle has led to understandable misreadings of both Arendt and Aristotle.[15] Jürgen Habermas, for example, displays excusable and edifying confusion in his statements that Arendt's "emphatic concept of praxis is more Marxist than Aristotelian" and, two pages later, that Arendt's concept becomes useful "only if we extricate it from the clamps of an Aristotelian theory of action."[16]

But Aristotle, like Plato, is less inclined to celebrate Periclean Athens than either Arendt or Marx. In the remainder of this essay I will try to show that the critical disposition of Plato and Aristotle toward Greek political culture is especially evident in each's attitude toward women. Both accord women and womanly activities a greater dignity than does their tradition (or its modern adherents)—a revaluation that stems from a deep opposition to the view that the virtues of the best human life are most clearly displayed in the practices of war and the pursuit of undying glory. Plato and Aristotle's objection to this tradition is based on their shared view that it reflects a mistaken assessment of human needs and of the best or most human life.

The elevation of women via the "first wave" of *Republic* 5 is well known. Women guardians are said there to be the equal of men *but* weaker in every respect, including in the practice of traditionally feminine arts.[17] But this is only the most explicit, and, I think, certainly not the most interesting, of the various instances in Plato in which we can see in operation

14. Ibid., 24.

15. Arendt is a wonderfully intelligent reader of Aristotle, though not always a scrupulous one. In *The Human Condition*, she attributes to him the view that the central function of politics is conversation among citizens (27), the view that politics is the route to immortality (56), and strangest of all, the view—again, one *she* holds—that "being" is simply a name for common appearance (199). A mixture of sharp perception and odd formulation is exhibited in her critical comment that Aristotle is the first "materialist" for holding that *to sympheron* ("interest") "does and should reign supreme in political matters" (*On Revolution* [New York, 1963], 14).

16. J. Habermas, "Hannah Arendt's Communications Concept of Power," *Social Research* 44 (1977): 13 and 15. On the basis of a doubtful reference to *Politics* 1257a8, Arendt herself suggests that Aristotle may have been almost as decisive an influence on Marx as Hegel (*Human Condition*, 254 n. 4).

17. *Rep.* 455c–d.

the intention to elevate the status of women and feminine things. Socrates is consistently, and sometimes violently, critical of the common Greek notion that the best teachers of virtue are either Athenian gentlemen, like Pericles and Themistocles (in the *Meno* and *Gorgias*), or Homer (in the *Republic*) or philosophers like Anaxagoras (in the *Phaedo*). When speaking of his own teachers, he inevitably refers to women: Diotima in the *Symposium* (who is both female and a foreigner), Phaenarete in the *Theaetetus,* and Aspasia in the *Menexenus.*[18] Similarly, in dialogues specifically concerned with human excellence or virtue, the *Meno* and the *Protagoras,* he pointedly refers to priestesses as well as priests as his sources for the recollection *logos* and claims, contrary to obvious fact, that in Sparta and Crete there are many women, as well as men, who can be proud of their education.[19] His own particular technical expertise, he tells us in both the *Theages* and the *Symposium,* is in erotics, the science of love, a subject he learned from Diotima.[20] Furthermore, Plato continually uses female arts as images or metaphors for Socratic activity; midwifery in the *Theaetetus* and weaving (in the Eleatic Stranger's account of the statesman's art) in the *Statesman* are two examples.[21]

In all these instances, we can see a consistent project of critique and revaluation at work. By means of unobtrusive insinuation, rather than manly didactic confrontation, Socrates subverts his noble interlocutors' instinctual disposition to see maleness and the virile arts of politics and war as components of a coherent ideal of human excellence. However,

18. *Symp.* 204e; see also *Phd.* 78a. Socrates refers as well to Kallikrate as a potential teacher in *Theages* 125e and to Sappho in *Phaedrus* 235b–c. The only major exception to this rule is Prodicus, but he is not someone likely to be mistaken for an Athenian gentleman. See also the illuminating conversation between Socrates and Theodote in Xenophon (*Mem.* 3. 11). For references to Xenophon's Socrates on women, see S. R. L. Clark, "Aristotle's Woman," *History of Political Thought* 3 (1982): 177–91.

19. *Meno* 81a; *Prt.* 342d.

20. *Thg.* 128b; *Symp.* 177d–e.

21. A. W. Saxonhouse, "The Philosopher and the Female in the Political Thought of Plato," *Political Theory* 4 (1976): 195–212, especially 208. Socrates also swears frequently by a foreign god, the Egyptian dog, a device that serves to cast further doubt on his virility and his Greekness. I suspect that more evidence for this point could be developed by noting the occasions in which Socrates' *elenchos* works by unobtrusively substituting the evaluative terms "good" and "bad" (*agathon* and *kakon*) for the terms "noble" and "base" (*kalon* and *aischron*); see, for example, the refutation of Polus in *Gorgias* 476e–477a, a ploy that the manly Callicles recognizes as a subliminal attack on Greek convention (482e–483a; he objects to the fact that it is hidden, not to the fact that it is an attack). Conventionally, many things may be called good that are not called noble (including womanly activities), but Socrates insists that all truly noble actions must be good (*Prt.* 358b), a critical component of the claim that no one willingly does evil, and something Socrates learned from Diotima (*Symp.* 201c and 205e–206a). The point of the argument for the unity of the virtues in the *Protagoras* is not to make a theoretical statement, but to oppose the ordinary Greek sentiment that *andreia* is somehow on a different plane from the other virtues (394d).

Plato is surely not consistently profemale. Even in the *Republic* (outside of Book 5), women are not regarded as equals, but are relegated to the household, presented as frivolous or as temptresses. Frequent instances of this kind of depiction occur throughout the dialogues. How can we account for this apparent inconsistency?

Arlene Saxonhouse says that the inconsistency is only apparent and that it appears because we are asking Plato the wrong question—namely, Do you think women are the equal of men or not?[22] But there is no good reason to think that this question formed any part of Plato's agenda. Rather, as Saxonhouse says, Socrates argues and intimates the need to elevate the status of women in order to attack the ordinary Greek attachment to maleness, the tendency to identify virtue or excellence (*aretē*) with virility or courage.[23] The tension between Socrates and the norm of *andreia* can also be seen in the *Meno* and the *Gorgias,* where Meno and Callicles express their difference from Socrates by defining virtue as virile participation in public affairs.[24] Socrates' friends, as well as his enemies, suspect the philosopher of unmanliness or cowardice (*anandria*).[25] It is hardly surprising that any Greek, no matter how well disposed, would have doubts about Socrates' virility, given the association of *andreia* with an active political life combined with Socrates' statements that his own life is of necessity private rather than political and that a first-rate philosopher is someone who doesn't even know the way to the *agora* or other centers of political activity and the strikingly paradoxical claim (relative to standard Greek usage) that real politics (of which he is the only true practitioner) is practiced not in the Assembly or the courts, but in private, behind closed doors.[26] Even Socrates' friends must have been troubled by his proud assertions that he has no honor (*timē*) in the city and is thus no gentleman.[27] Most shocking of all is the claim that the love of honor has approximately the same moral status as vulgar money grubbing, a claim repeated by Aristotle in his critique of Sparta.[28]

For Saxonhouse, Socrates' women in Books 5 and 6 of the *Republic* are images of the philosopher and emblems of the claims of the private life against those of the *polis*, which is here identified with war, battle, and

22. Saxonhouse, "Philosopher and Female in Plato," 196.
23. Ibid., 210.
24. *Meno* 71e; *Grg.* 485a–486d.
25. *Cri.* 45d–46e; *Grg.* 485c–d.
26. *Ap.* 31c–32a; *Tht.* 173c–d; *Grg.* 521d.
27. *Thg.* 127b; see T. Pangle, "Socrates on the Problem of Political Science Education," *Political Theory* 13 (1985): 112–37.
28. *Rep.* 1. 347b; this remark is made in passing to Glaucon, who accepts it without comment, although he later (*Rep.* 8. 548c–549a) is identified as one whose life exhibits the spirited love of victory and honor, tempered in his case by his skill in music. Aristotle (*Pol.* 1269b23–24) connects the love of money and of honor in Sparta.

death.[29] Saxonhouse develops an elaborate set of correspondences that seem to me to be generally reasonable: female, philosopher, private life (the *oikia* or household for women, the beautiful city in speech for the philosophers), peace, play, and life *versus* male, citizen, public life (the *polis* in action or deed as opposed to speech), war, seriousness, spiritedness, and death. This opposition is not to be understood as simply antagonistic—as in the prephilosophic Greek view concerning the relations of private and public, male and female—but as expressing both tension and mutual need or interdependence.[30] The core of the relationship is not, for Plato, the question posed by the needs and the capacities of the two genders relative to one another; these serve only as metaphors for the definitive interdependent opposites that are the ground for the Platonic critique of the Greek civic culture, philosophy and politics.

I believe that Aristotle's position is very similar to Plato's. This means first of all that Aristotle, as much as Plato, must be read as a critic rather than as a mirror or glorifier of Greek opinion in general and the politics of virility in particular. This is contrary to what is probably the most generally held view, which is that "the philosophy of Aristotle, unlike that of Plato, is a codification of general social practice, a systematization of social values."[31] It is surely contrary to Arendt's claim that Aristotle's definition of humans as political animals "only formulated the current opinion of the *polis* about man and the political way of life" by insisting on a profound separation of the *polis* (and men's affairs) and the *oikia* (and womanly business).[32] Some critics, like Susan Moller Okin, go even farther and say that Aristotle does not merely reflect the Greek view of politics but attempts to transform Greek prejudices against women into transcendent truths by arguing that the differences between the sexes are natural (biologically inherited) rather than conventional or cultural.[33] I agree with Okin and not with Arendt in holding that Aristotle's biology is absolutely essential to and inseparable from his political thought, but this biology does *not* result in a theory of orthogenesis or in a kind of theodicy that bestows the blessings of the gods on any particular group of humans; rather, Aristotle's biology lays the ground for a style of political

29. Saxonhouse, "Philosopher and Female in Plato," 205–11.

30. See A. W. Saxonhouse, "Men, Women, War, and Politics: Family and Polis in Aristophanes and Euripides," *Political Theory* 8 (1980): 65–81, especially 65; and Shaw, "Female Intruder," 256–57.

31. M. B. Arthur, "Review Essay: Classics," *Signs* 2 (1976): 394.

32. Arendt, *Human Condition*, 27.

33. Okin, *Women in Western Political Thought*, 73–74. A challenge to such views in terms of Aristotle's orientation toward prevailing opinions in general is found in Nussbaum, *Fragility of Goodness*, chap. 8; and relative to the status of women in particular in A. W. Saxonhouse, *Women in the History of Western Thought* (New York, 1985) chap. 4.

thought that is explicitly *critical* of some of the most important Greek political institutions and opinions, among them the notion that virtue and
slavishness are biologically inherited, the idea that virility or courage is
the foremost human virtue, and the Periclean opinion that all quiet
people and cities are useless.[34]

In particular, he does *not* say that our status as political animals is the
most important thing about us, the characteristic that essentially distinguishes us from other animals; thus he is in no way committed to the
view that political activity is—relative to the possibilities of human nature, to say nothing of the divine—an end in itself. Although Arendt's
claim that "the twofold Aristotelian definition of man as a *zōon politikon*
and a *zōon logon echon,* a being attaining his highest possibility in the faculty of speech and the life in a polis, was designed to distinguish the Greek
from the barbarian and the free man from the slave" may accurately de-
pict the underlying sense of Periclean political culture, it seriously dis-
torts Aristotle.[35] This view, that Aristotle defines humans as equally political and rational, is frequently repeated by readers much less adept
than Arendt, but it cannot be supported by the relevant text. Rather, Aristotle's position is that we are political animals *because* we are rational
animals; our political character is less fundamental than our potential rationality, for, as Aristotle explains, "the reason why the human being is
more a political animal than any bee or herding animal is clear; for nature, as we always say, makes nothing in vain, and the human alone
among the animals has *logos.*"[36] Our rationality explains us; our political
character does not—at least not to the same degree. We do need to live

34. For the first idea, *Pol.* 1255a28–b4; see also *Rh.* 1390b14–31; for the second, *Pol.*
1334a11–34; for the third, *Pol.* 1325b16–21. Other important views criticized by Aristotle
are the opinions that public education in virtue is unnecessary (*Pol.* 1310a12–36) and that
statesmanship and mastery are one and the same (*Pol.* 1252a7–9, 1324b32–33). Readers
of Aristotle commonly err in believing his practice of beginning his inquiries with "repu-
table opinions" (*endoxa*) prevents him from transcending or criticizing those opinions. For
a solid defense of Aristotle against this charge, see J. Barnes, "Aristotle and the Methods of
Ethics," *Revue internationale de philosophie* 34 (1980): 490–511.

35. Arendt, "Tradition and the Modern Age," in *Between Past and Future,* 22–23. She
adds that the two "definitions" supplement each other (*On Revolution,* 9). But the terms are
not equally definitive.

36. *Pol.* 1253a7–9. For the distinction employed here between a mere fact (*to hoti,* "a
that"), such as our being political animals, and a fact that explains (*to dioti,* "a because
that"), such as our being rational or deliberative animals, see *Nicomachean Ethics* 1095b2–8.
The point here is that rationality is prior to civility for human beings, in the same way that
civility is prior to the family in *Politics* 1253a18–19. Moreover, in *History of Animals*
488a8–488b25, Aristotle notes that several animals in addition to humans are political (he
lists bees, wasps, ants, and cranes), but that we alone are deliberative (*bouleutikon*) since we
alone can recollect. See L. Berns, "Spiritedness in Ethics and Politics: A Study in Aristotelian Psychology" *Interpretation* 12 (1984): 334–48, especially 40–41.

in cities, not as an end in itself or as an expression of our humanness, but because it is generally the case that by living according to laws and customs we can develop our biologically inherited potentiality for living rationally.

Polities that do not adequately serve the goal of rational development are not, strictly speaking (that is, in terms of biological, rather than political, language), *real* polities at all.[37] According to Aristotle, the greater part of the so-called cities have no definite goal at all, while the most coherent of them (Sparta, Crete, Carthage) make the typically Greek error of thinking that the purpose of political life is ruling over outsiders, or war, rather than rational development. Strictly speaking, therefore, there are no real polities, either in Greece or elsewhere. This is hardly theodicy, nor ideological mirroring of Greek opinion. The work of Aristotle's teleological or functionalist biology is thus not to endorse but to criticize the political life of his time, a political life that Arendt and many others among us find so attractive, and to criticize it on grounds quite similar to those we found operating in the Platonic critique of the politics of virility.

Nonetheless, there can be no doubt that Aristotle's biology seems to give women a rank even lower than the rank they held in classical Greek society.[38] This appears most strongly in Aristotle's account of reproduction in the *Generation of Animals*. In the bisexual production of embryos, Aristotle says, the male semen supplies the form of the potential offspring, while the female semen (which he identifies with menstrual blood) supplies the matter. Menstrual blood is defined as semen that is lacking in form or *ergon* (it is *ou katharon alla deomenon ergasias*).[39] Female children are produced when form cannot fully master or rule (*kratein*) matter, such as when the parents are either too young or too cold (heat being required for the imposition of form).[40] Females are thus, to an extent, lacking form, and hence can be described as imperfect (*ateleia*—unfinished, lacking the *telos*) human beings. Furthermore, sex differences are especially marked in humans; females are much colder, weaker, and shorter-lived than males, among humans more so than any other ani-

---

37. *Pol.* 1280a31–b8. The frequency of Aristotle's use of the word *physis* and related terms at the beginning of the *Politics* is striking. According to Wayne Ambler, "words based on the root 'nature' are used 86 times in Book 1; no other section of *Politics* or the *Nicomachean Ethics* is similarly focussed on nature" ("Aristotle on Acquisition," *Canadian Journal of Political Science* 17 [1984]: 487–502).

38. According to Lloyd Aristotle is more guilty of underestimating the significance of the female than are the majority of Greek medical writings dealing with the contributions of each sex to reproduction (*Science, Folklore, and Ideology*, 107).

39. *Gen. An.* 728a26–27.

40. Ibid. 767b10–13.

mal.[41] A sign of this is said to be the great pain that childbearing causes human females, unlike females of other species. However, Aristotle says, this fact may be at least partly explained by the unnecessarily sedentary way of life of Greek women; in tribes where women are more active, birth is easier.[42] Thus Aristotle is at least partly open to the possibility that certain of the gender-linked characteristics we see are caused by culture rather than nature; and in general it does not make sense to say that his biology is "metaphysical" or in any way intended as rigidly deterministic rather than empirical.[43] Still, it must be noted that for Aristotle the inferior status of women is to some degree a matter of biological, rather than cultural, inheritance.[44]

Now, if we follow Lloyd in holding that the biological writings about gender difference are intended to support prevailing Greek ideological presuppositions about male superiority, we will expect to find Aristotle's political writings claiming that women are to be treated as mere matter needing to be ruled entirely by male form.[45] And yet this is not the case. Nor is the male-female relationship within the household or family treated by Aristotle as being merely and solely for the purpose of generation. It is here that the difference between Aristotle and Arendt (or the Arendtian reading of Aristotle) is most significant; the sharp functional distinction between *polis* and *oikia* along the lines of meaningful activity

41. *Hist. An.* 608a21–28.

42. *Gen. An.* 775a30–35; also *Pol.* 1335b11–16.

43. A substantial number of recent studies have vigorously attacked the notion that Aristotle's biology is *a priori* and overly deterministic, among them those of A. Gotthelf, "Aristotle's Conception of Final Causality," *Review of Metaphysics* 30 (1976): 226–54; M. C. Nussbaum, "Aristotle on Teleological Explanation," in *Aristotle's De Motu Animalium: Text with Translation, Commentary, and Interpretive Essays* (Princeton, 1978), 59–106; and D. W. Balme, "Aristotle's Biology Was Not Essentialist," *Archiv für Geschichte der Philosophie* 62 (1980): 1–12. Even Lloyd, who holds that Aristotle's sexual biology is distorted by the ideological assumptions he brings to the study, finds that in general Aristotle reworks traditional assumptions in the light of his independent empirical theorizing, Lloyd points out that "while [Aristotle] adopts many of the classes embedded in his own natural language, he does not do so uncritically, but modifies existing usages and introduces substantial new coinages where he sees a need" (*Science, Folklore, and Ideology*, 54).

44. *Metaphysics* 1058a29–b5 sets an interesting *aporia* concerning the *degree* to which sexuality defines an animal. It is less than a species difference, but is it any more than a difference in color? The conclusion is that sexuality is an "attribute proper to the animal, but in its matter and body, and not relative to its substance [*ousia*]" (1158b21–23). The logic of contraries, rather than sexuality, is the central concern of this section of text, but it does suggest that Aristotle is not convinced that there is a radical—relative to the possibilities of human nature—biological difference between male and female. Clark, "Aristotle's Woman," notes this passage but seems to conclude that the weight of the passages from the biological works favors the view that Aristotle shared the typical prejudices of the Greek male.

45. Lloyd, *Science, Folklore, and Ideology*, 104–5.

versus mere generation is an Arendtian (and arguably a Greek), rather than an Aristotelian, crux. For Aristotle, the *polis* is indeed prior to the *oikia,* relative to the needs and capacities that define the human form or function (just as, for example, rationality is prior to civility), but both *polis* and *oikia,* when truly, rather than nominally, such, aim at that virtue or excellence that is distinctly human. As Aristotle expresses it, "humans alone have a perception of good and bad, just and unjust, and other things, and it is a community of this that makes an *oikia* and a *polis.*"[46] The most significant or final cause of *oikia* and *polis* alike is the development of human rationality or "living well" (*eu zēn*), even though both arise from (have as efficient causes) lesser (relative to specifically human characteristics) concerns[47]—procreation in the case of the family and security or living (*zēn*) in the case of the *polis.*[48] In Book 1 of the *Politics,* the political relationship (one of equality under laws and customs) is not defined in opposition to or in contrast with the household or the male-female relationship, but rather in contrast with the unequal relationship of natural master and natural slave. Particular humans are said to be fit to be slaves (and so unfit for citizenship) *to the extent that* their difference (in terms of biologically inherited needs and capacities) from other humans is as great as the difference between human and beast or between form and matter. So, form is to matter as natural master to natural slave and *not* (in the *Politics*) as male is to female. Men and women are not as different from one another as humans and beasts—but why not? Aristotle's biology would appear to require that they must be, and the language of the *Politics* (especially the consistent deployment of the distinction between nature and convention) makes it abundantly clear that that work must be understood through the categories developed in the biological works.

The analogy between woman and beast, however, is treated in the *Politics* as a mistake characteristically made by barbarians, who are said to

46. *Pol.* 1253a15–18.

47. It is also quite possible that Aristotle's discussion of reproduction itself invests procreation with a dignity much greater than that accorded it by those who see life, with Arendt, as "mere life," those whose notion of the human depends on treating all that is animal as mechanical and dull (see my "Beyond Interpretation: Human Agency and the Slovenly Wilderness," in *Social Science as Moral Inquiry,* ed. N. Haan et al. [New York, 1983], 195–217). J. Lennox, "Aristotle and the Functions of Reproduction" (Paper presented to the Society for Ancient Greek Philosophy, 1982), presents an interesting argument that, for Aristotle, the function of reproduction is to guarantee organisms "that they will share or participate as far as possible in something everlasting and divine" (10–11). For Aristotle, as for Diotima's ladder, the continuities between animal and human are at least as important as the discontinuities.

48. *Pol.* 1252a26–30, 1252b29–30; see M. P. Nichols, "Women in Western Political Thought," *Political Science Reviewer* (1983): 241–60, especially 251.

treat women and slaves in the same way.[49] Among barbarians, we are told, women and slaves have a similar order (*taxis*), are subordinated to their rulers in the same way. Aristotle says that this is wrong, an error— but then how are women subordinated? Aristotle's solution to this problem does not ignore his biology; rather, he places the issue squarely in a biological context by considering which traits (needs and capacities) involved in the relationship are decisively human and ascertaining the purpose or purposes of the male-female relationship relative to the goals (*telē*) that distinguish the human form from that of other biological species. The most decisive of these traits is (not courage but) the capacity for living according to a rational perception of one's overall interest as a particular human, rather than living according to whim or temporary passion or preference. In *Politics* 1.1260a13, Aristotle says that both males and females have this deliberative capacity (*bouleutikon*), but that females possess it without force or authority (*akyron*).[50] Thus, the male being stronger (as a rule) with respect to that capacity that is decisively human (not physical strength), males should rule over females. But the question remains, How—that is, with what kind of rule (since there are, contrary to ordinary opinion, many kinds of rule)?[51]

Aristotle's answer is that this rule should be political rather than despotic (the way masters should rule over slaves) and that the appropriate biological metaphor for the rule of males over females is thus *not* that of the soul (form) ruling over the body (matter), but the rule of one aspect of soul or form over another, the way in which reason (*nous*) rules over desire (*orexis*) (and it should be recalled here that *nous* and *orexis* are interdependent with respect to good *praxis* or action).[52] The way in which *nous* governs *orexis* is said to be a rule that is accomplished through giv-

---

49. *Pol.* 1252b5–6; a similarly rhetorical use of "barbarians" as a device for loosing the Greeks from their prejudices is found in Antiphon's *On the Truth*, where it is said that human differences are only by convention, not by nature, and that the only people who disagree with this are barbarians, not Greeks.

50. A. Saxonhouse, "Family, Polity, and Unity: Aristotle on Socrates' Community of Wives," *Polity* 15 (1982): 202–19, suggests that Aristotle's meaning here is intentionally ambiguous, noting that "whether this want of 'authority' in the woman's deliberative capacity inheres in the soul itself or becomes manifest in groups of men who would scorn it coming from a woman is unclear in the text" (208). There is a similar ambiguity in one of the first propositions of the *Politics*, the claim that the *polis* is the "most authoritative" (*kyriōtatē*) of all human associations (*Pol.* 1252a5). The whole issue of who or what must be the authoritative element (*to kyrion*) in the *polis* is treated as an *aporia* that is never adequately resolved in theory (*Pol.* 1281a11–39). That *to kyrion* can mean simply powerful or effective control without any suggestion of legitimacy is surely suggested by the way the term is used in *Politics* 1325a35. Cf. Clark, "Aristotle's Woman," 179–80.

51. *Pol.* 1252a7–9.

52. Ibid. 1260a3–7; *Eth. Nic.* 1139b4–5, 1144b29–30; see Berns "Spiritedness in Ethics and Politics."

ing advice rather than orders, by persuasion rather than command, and is called by Aristotle political or monarchical rule, rather than despotic.[53] Males, he concludes, are generally fitter to rule, but only as permanent political rulers. Ordinarily, of course, political rule means taking turns ruling; this detail is not present here, however, although other elements of political rule are, including rule in the interest of both rulers and ruled (which is only incidentally present in the case of slaves), rough equality of ruler and ruled, and the presence of an impersonal legal authority that limits and informs the will and actions of the rulers.[54] Women should not rule, but they should be ruled as fellow citizens—that is, as needing the same things from the political relationship as males—and *not* as children or slaves, whose needs and hence whose status is entirely different from the needs and status of those who rule them.

But what do women need that is to be supplied by the political relationship? For Aristotle, mature human beings as such need politics because they need a stable order within which they can become rational animals in actuality.[55] That is, human beings need politics not as a way of protecting their rights against the community or for security generally, but as a context for moral development or the development of those virtues or excellences whose *potential* expression humans inherit biologically. In general, Aristotle's understanding of the purpose of politics is as different from the Arendtian or civic republican position as it is from the liberal individualist position.[56] Women need politics (as slaves and children do not) because they require education in virtue as much as men do—even though the virtues or potential excellences of women are not the same as the virtues of men. Socrates denies this differentiation of virtues in the *Meno*, and Aristotle explicitly disagrees with Socrates on this score.[57] But *how* different, for Aristotle, are the virtues that characterize the well-developed male and the well-developed female? The important

53. *Eth. Nic.* 1102b29–1103a1; *Pol.* 1254b5–6.

54. *Pol.* 1259b1–5.

55. Rationality is understood by Aristotle as the most important human good (and thus, in teleological terms, the definitive human attribute) and not simply as a means for achieving other goods. Mary Midgley gives this entirely Aristotelian account of rationality: "'Rational' includes references to aims as well as means; it is not far from 'sane'. . . . Rationality, like all our practical concepts, belongs to the vocabulary of a particular species with particular needs" (*Beast and Man: The Roots of Human Nature* [Ithaca, N.Y., 1978], 71). I discuss a similar concept of rationality in "Who Knows Whether It's Rational to Vote?" *Ethics* 90 (1980): 203–17.

56. See my "Beyond Interpretation," in *Social Science as Moral Inquiry*, ed. Haan et al.; and "Aristotle's Social Science," *Political Theory* 9 (1981): 479–508, especially 492–95, for discussion of the Aristotelian view that the character of political life is essentially multifunctional: politics must be concerned with security (*zēn*) and sociality (*syzēn*) as well as with virtue (*eu zēn*), and these goals are not always mutually compatible.

57. *Pol.* 1260a22.

thing here, it seems to me, is that they are much less different than they are for the Greek tradition generally, and surely much less different than the virtues of the two sexes as defined by Pericles.[58] For Pericles, males are articulate fighters, and females silent homebodies. Aristotle speaks directly to the extent of the differentiation of the virtues in *Rhetoric* 1.2–7, where the virtues of males are said to be *sōphrosynē* (moderation) and *andreia* (virility), and the virtues of females are *sōphrosynē* and *philergia* (industry) without slavishness (*aneleutheria*). *Sōphrosynē* is thus *the* common human virtue, although a woman's moderation (mixed with industry) will be different from a man's (mixed with virility).[59] On the whole, the Aristotelian position is that *sōphrosynē*, like justice, is a more elevated virtue than courage or virility to the same degree that leisure is of greater worth than business, and peace than war.[60] The virtue whose potential expression the two sexes share is of infinitely more importance and worth than the one that divides them.

Plato's several discussions of the proper ordering of moderation and courage have much the same countercultural tone as do Aristotle's re-valuations. This can be seen in the last third of the *Gorgias*, in which Socrates defends *sōphrosynē* by elevating it above the claims for *andreia* put forth by the manly Callicles, Socrates' chief rival in commitment to excellence and erotics.[61] The conventional Greek notion of courage, the ideal of the citizen soldier who stands fast in battle and faces his enemies unafraid, is criticized by the Athenian Stranger in the first book of the *Laws* (630a and ff.) in the context of a critique of the views of the poet Tyrtaeus (identified there as Athenian as well as Spartan) that anticipates Aristotle's point in *Politics* 7 by reducing such courage from first to fourth (and last) place among the virtues. Plato seeks further to invest the term *andreia* with new meaning in the *Republic* by saying that the virtue of the spirited defender of the city is courage only in a qualified, "political," sense;[62] true courage has apparently nothing to do with soldier-

58. The polarization of virtues by gender seems so extreme to Arthur that she characterizes it with the odd term "dimorphism" in her discussion of the "mutual exclusivity of social roles" in both ancient and modern Greece ("Review Essay," 386). In his objection to Socrates' answer to Meno, Aristotle cites Sophocles' "silence adorns a woman" with seeming approbation. But as Nichols points out, the context of this remark in the drama—mad Ajax addressing sane Tecmessa—suggests at least the possibility of some irony at work here, especially given the plethora of other possible citations ("Women in Western Political Thought," 252–53).

59. According to MacIntyre, "*sōphrosunē* is for the Greeks *the* womanly virtue" (*After Virtue*, 128). Cf. J.-P. Vernant, *The Origins of Greek Thought* (Ithaca, N.Y., 1982), 84–94.

60. *Pol.* 1334a13–16.

61. *Grg.* 481c–482c, 486e–488b.

62. *Rep.* 430a–c. Aristotle makes precisely the same point in his discussion of courage in *Nicomachean Ethics* 1116a15–29, where the willingness to endure danger for the sake of the laws and honor is said to be political courage or the courage of citizens and is associated

ing or citizenship and is instead described as persistence in following abstract arguments wherever they lead.[63] The same claim is advanced in the *Phaedo* and in the *Meno,* where Socrates makes the clearly non-Greek claim that "we will be better and manlier if we believe that one must search for the things one does not know."[64] Like the Aristotelian discussions, all of these claims are a very long way from Pericles' funeral speech and from Arendt's favorite Heraclitean maxim, that the people "should fight for the *nomos* as for the city wall."[65]

After Aristotle distinguishes male and female virtue in *Rhetoric* 1, he goes on immediately to stress the common human need for education in virtue, and for this education to be carried out both in private and in public, remarking that "it is necessary for both the common *and the private* alike to seek to establish such qualities in men and women—for places where women are base, as Sparta, are half unhappy."[66] Here Aristotle joins together, as subjects for criticism, the Greek tendency to link virtue exclusively with maleness and the tendency to consider what occurs in private as beneath notice and irrelevant to the achievement of virtue or excellence. He makes the very same points relative to Sparta in Books 2 and 7 of the *Politics,* in which he argues that the Spartan laws and customs are deficient both because they neglect the education of women and because they rest on a mistaken conception of what virtue is; they express the view that *andreia* and *aretē* are one and the same. When we recall that for Aristotle Sparta stands as one of the very few *poleis* even to attempt moral education (the rest being mostly heaps of laws and customs developed in response to particular problems and interests and without any overall goal or purportedly desirable way of life in view) and when we note that the Spartan love of victory in war is not an accidental difficulty but seems to follow naturally from the fact that political *philia* (friendship) and patriotism are based on *thymos* (spiritedness) and the love of honor,[67] we can see that the neglect of women's education by the Spartan *nomoi* is no local accident but follows from the good Greek patriot's view that there are, in fact, no womanly virtues so elevated or difficult as to require political development. Aristotle disagrees.

---

with Homeric usage, but is said only to resemble real courage, rather than being the thing itself. See Berns, "Spiritedness in Ethics and Politics," 343–45, for an excellent discussion of this section.

63. *Rep.* 503b–504a.
64. *Phd.* 68c; *Meno* 86b.
65. Arendt, *Human Condition,* 63 n. 2.
66. *Rh.* 1361a7–11.
67. *Pol.* 1327b40–1328a1; see C. Lord, "Politics and Philosophy in Aristotle's *Politics,*" *Hermes* 106 (1978): 336–57, especially 348. One might say that for Aristotle political friendship is to true friendship as political courage is to true courage. Friends love the same things, and political men love honor (*Eth. Nic.* 1095b22–23).

But why should women require this moral development if they are not normally fit to be full participants in political life (which requires the exercise of the status of ruling as well as being ruled)? If women's lives are best lived in the sphere of the *oikia*, rather than in the "public space," then why can't they simply be ordered about and controlled (for their masters' good) like slaves or like children (for their own good) rather than being educated and habituated by laws, like free males? Now, if the purpose of the *oikia* were simply to serve as a procreative unit, there would then be absolutely no reason why women—mere procreators or, perhaps, only necessary instruments of procreation—should be educated rather than mastered. But this is resoundingly not the case; for Aristotle, the *oikia* is not simply a procreative *taxis* or order; its purpose is not, as we see from the *Politics,* utterly distinct from that of the *polis.* Aristotle makes the case for continuity of function most clearly in the *Eudemian Ethics,* where he states that "the source and springs of friendship, political order, and justice are in the *oikia.*"[68] It is for this reason that Aristotle insists on drawing a sharp distinction between the status of women on the one hand and that of slaves and children on the other.

The *Eudemian Ethics* stresses the similarity of *oikia* and *polis* as forms of living together that distinguish humans from other animals as follows:

> The human being is not only a political but also a familial [or economic] animal [*zōon politikon kai oikonomikon*], and does not, like other animals, couple occasionally with any chance male or female, but is uniquely not solitary but communal [*koinōnikon*] toward those who are his natural kin; and thus there would be *koinōnia* and a kind of justice even if there were no *polis.*[69]

A similar passage in the *Nicomachean Ethics* is prefaced by the remark that friendship between male and female seems to be especially according to nature among humans and by the comment that friendship between husband and wife can be based on virtue (as the best friendships are) rather than on mere utility or episodic pleasure.[70] A consequence of this is that marital relations can be either just or unjust; when the husband's rule encompasses all the affairs of the *oikia,* the rule is said to be unjust or oligarchic.[71] More importantly, the *oikia* as such is a relation-

68. *Eth. Eud.* 1242a40–b1.
69. Ibid. 1242a22–27. The clear difference between Aristotle's ethology and Rousseau's in the *Second Discourse* is important. For Rousseau, there is absolutely no connection between family life and the virtues of civil men, largely because there is nothing humanizing about family life (at least not so far as the *Discourses* and the *Social Contract* are concerned; *Emile* and *Julie* tell a different and much more Aristotelian story). It is interesting to note the modern republican tendency to accept Rousseau's political claims as true while ignoring the fact that the biological thesis that supports them is palpably false.
70. *Eth. Nic.* 1162a16–17.
71. Ibid. 1160b35–1161a1.

ship that can be evaluated, as can the *polis,* in terms of its justice. Sche-matically, one might say that Aristotle's intention here is to demytholo-gize and problematize political life (recall Pericles' evocation of Athens as a source of perpetual immortality and greatness) by making—in the lan-guage of his biology—a case for the dependence of "political animal" upon "rational animal" on one side and for the functional similarity of the attributes "political" and "economic" on the other.

When Aristotle speaks of justice, he is not referring to some abstract or transcendent principle or rule but characterizing a kind of order that makes the development of human virtue, or the rational or deliberative capacity most broadly understood, possible; justice could not apply to an order whose only purpose is the preservation of human life.[72] Thus while the *polis* is indeed more important than the *oikia* from the perspec-tive of those needs and potentialities that define humanity, it is equally clear that the perception of the human good relative to individuals—the presence of which distinguishes a rational from a disorderly life—is a perception developed both within the *oikia* and within the *polis.* Aris-totle's claim here is not a description of the usual practices of societies but follows from his functionalist biology; he is making an argument about the relationship between a particular order or activity (the *oikia*) and the specific need or potentiality that we inherit biologically, which is the cause of our being a recognizably separate species. That is, just as we can say that the need and capacity for living rationally or according to choice (*kata prohairesin*) is distinctly human—since nonhuman animals can live neither according to choice nor in a disorderly (*ataktōs*) way[73]— so we must say that the activities and associations through which we have the possibility of realizing the capacities and satisfying the needs that de-fine us are also distinctly human. For Aristotle, this includes the family as well as the *polis.*

72. No specifically human virtues could be expressed in such activities or orders: we may eat or sleep well, but not justly (*Eth. Nic.* 1102b2–12). The notion of the just family points up a very clear difference between Aristotelian and Arendtian politics. For Arendt, familial life is as nonhuman an activity as sleeping, and justice is not a political virtue in the way that courage is. A similar criticism of Arendt is made by H. F. Pitkin, "Justice: On Re-lating Public and Private," *Political Theory* 9 (1981): 327–52, especially 338–39.

73. *Pol.* 1280a32–34. In saying this, Aristotle is not at all glorifying humanity but pre-senting the problem that characterizes us as a biological species: we need to form or accept a conventional order if we are to live well (since we do not inherit one biologically), and yet our strongest desires are for a disorderly life (*Pol.* 1319b31–32). I discuss this aspect of Aristotle's biological politics in this volume in "Aristotle's Social Science," pp. 24–30. In ad-dition to being uniquely deliberative, recollecting, familial, and mimetic (*Poet.* 1448b5–9) creatures, we can thus also be summed up as the peculiarly problematic animal (*Eth. Nic.* 1176a2–15). Biologically, humans are, for Aristotle, "dualizers" or boundary crossers in respect to their mode of life (*His. An.* 487b33–488a18; for discussion of dualizers in gen-eral, see Lloyd, *Science, Folklore, and Ideology,* 44–53; for this passage, see C. Lord, "Aris-totle's Anthropology," 55–56, in this volume).

Aristotle's elevation of the status of women above that status accorded them by his culture, while less marked than that of Plato, stems from a similar concern: the defense of the importance of the private life, and in Aristotle's case the family, as necessary not simply for procreation or bare living, but for the development of human excellence, rationality, and happiness (*eudaimonia*). This promotion of the *oikia* has, I think, two sources, one negative and one positive, one based on an awareness of the dangers inherent in the political life, the other based on hopes for an increased emphasis on moral education (*paideia*) within the Hellenic world. The negative reason stems from Aristotle's fear that excessive commitment to the *polis* will always be accompanied by that love of victory that is dangerous to rationality and the other more human virtues, such as moderation and justice; the positive reason is contained in the Aristotelian propositions that a sense of shame is a necessary precondition for the development of the capacity for deliberative living and that this rationalizing sense of shame is best developed in the family. I would suggest, in fact, that *the* function of the family is not procreation (or security) but the development of this indispensable sense, without which decent political life as such is impossible. Familial life, then, has crucial political importance in two respects: it prepares us for political life and at the same time provides a separate focus of attention and care that can check those dangers of excessive civility that seem always to threaten to turn the most tightly knit cities into armed camps. It is thus desirable that a certain tension be maintained between public and private, and especially necessary for political philosophy to defend the claims of the private against the louder voices coming from the public sphere. In all of this, there is great agreement between Plato and Aristotle.[74]

The positive argument for the natural importance of the household is based on the view that people who are not capable of being ashamed are

74. Aristotle is much more emphatic and explicit about the value of the family than Plato. However, Socrates is usually well acquainted with and much interested in the family connections of his interlocutors. A nice, brief instance of this concern is found at the beginning of the *Theaetetus* (144b–c), where Socrates is presented as being well aware of Theaetetus' parentage, in marked contrast to the boy's teacher, the very theoretical Theodorus, who is indifferent to it. More direct evidence is supplied by the exchange between Euthyphro and Socrates in *Euthyphro* 4b–e, in which Socrates opposes the "Platonic" position that family ties are irrelevant where justice is concerned. See also Xenophon *Memorabilia* 3.6, in which Socrates is shown dissuading young Glaucon from even thinking of a political career until he is capable of managing the affairs of his household. Still, the major components of the Socratic defense of privacy are Socrates' own irony, his habitual concealment, and his preference for enclosed spaces like private homes and wrestling schools, in contrast to the public man's love of the market and the Assembly. He also frequently calls attention to the way in which public virtue depends upon private support, something noticeable especially in those cases when such support is clearly fictitious, as in his claim that the Spartans would be nothing without the secret tutelage of their hidden sophists (*Prt.* 342a and ff.).

not open to persuasion and deliberation; the only motive such people have for not living childishly or according to momentary or episodic passionate attraction is the fear of punishment.[75] The sense of shame, the habitual disposition to worry that one's initial response to a situation might be wrong, or the fear of disgrace is a necessary prelude to mature deliberation and *paideia*.[76] Fear as such, as long as it is not hopeless dread, has the effect of making people deliberate and thus of humanizing them. For Aristotle, as for Hobbes, "fear makes people deliberate" (*phobos bouleutikous poiei*).[77] It is for this reason that rule by the middle class, and especially the rural middle class, is said to be preferable to rule by the very rich or the very poor.[78] Those of moderate means are subject neither to *hybris* nor to envy or hopelessness, and so unlike the overly wealthy, the overly manly, and the fearlessly immature in general, they are open to *logos* and are not likely to be swept away.[79] Such people are, then, in a middle position with respect to their confidence in their ability to rule.

But the development of a decent sense of shame is neither automatic nor easy; most people, Aristotle notes, tend to respond to a fear of punishment rather than disgrace, are thus not open to argument, and so are guided or restrained not by shame but only by legal threat.[80] Shame is

75. Another, and, I think, complementary, way of stating the case for the importance of the family in Aristotle is to see it as the locus for the formation of a sense of separate personal identity (as opposed to being merely a fractional part of the whole), a sense necessary for fully deliberative animals. For this interpretation see M. C. Nussbaum, "Shame, Separateness, and Political Unity: Aristotle's Criticism of Plato," in *Essays on Aristotle's Ethics,* ed. A. O. Rorty (Berkeley, 1980), 395–435; and also Saxonhouse, "Family, Polity, and Unity," who says that Aristotle insists on the importance of the family "from concern for affectionate ties of care and love between human beings. He insists that the sense of oneself as an individual, as different in form, must be prior to a sense of oneself as a political equal" (218). This is a strong and perhaps a surprising claim, but it is fully consistent with the Aristotelian proposition that we are deliberative animals *before* we are political animals; the priority is understood here not, of course, in time, but in relation to our essential humanness.

76. The sense of carefulness or hesitancy that belongs to the modest person is nicely expressed in the definition of shame in the *Magna Moralia* 1193a7–10, where it is observed that a person capable of shame "will not, like the shameless person, say and do anything in any way; nor like the shy person, hold back in every thing in every way; but will do and say what is appropriate." A related definition is given in *Rhetoric* 1383b12–14, where shame (here *aischunē*) is described as "a certain pain or uneasiness about past, present, and future bad things that bring disgrace [*adoxia*]." See also *Eth. Nic.* 1128b10–13 on the fear of disgrace.

77. *Rh.* 1383a6–7.

78. *Pol.* 1295a25–1296a21.

79. On the overly manly, see *Rh.* 1389a25–26; on the fearlessly immature, *Eth. Nic.* 1095a2–11.

80. *Eth. Nic.* 1179b20–1180a32.

very much like a virtue (such as moderation), as it is an intermediary between two extremes—in this case, shamelessness and shyness. In both
versions of the *Ethics*, shame is described as being "like a virtue" but not
quite the same thing, since virtues (and vices) refer to relatively stable
personality traits (*hexeis*) in mature people, and shame or modesty (like
righteous indignation—*nemesis*) is better conceived as a feeling (*pathos*).[81]
Like the virtues, however, shame (or modesty) is demonstrated in a tendency to respond to certain situations in certain ways and can be represented by a mean that indicates a norm rather than a quantitative average. "Shame is a mean between shamelessness and shyness: one who
cares about no one's opinion is shameless, one who cares about everyone's opinion is shy, while the modest person [*aidēmōn*] cares about the
opinion of those who seem decent."[82] Being prone to this sort of feeling
involves a certain immaturity and lack of reflection,[83] and so it is more
properly praised in young people than in adults, who might be expected
to respond more thoughtfully to the kind of situations in which shame is
worth praising as a motive for genuinely virtuous actions.[84] As an antic-
ipation of practical wisdom, shame—though still a *pathos*—is much more
reasonable than *thymos* or spiritedness.[85]

The *oikia* and the *polis* are both places in which a sense of shame can
be developed, but the *oikia* is even more suited to this than is the *polis*,
since parents are likely to be better at this kind of moral education than
public officials. As Aristotle remarks, "Just as laws and customs prevail
in . . . cities, so do ancestral *logoi* and habits prevail in *oikiai*, and even
more, because of kinship and benefits, and there love and willingness to
obey are by nature."[86] The natural love that makes the family the important site of moral *paideia* does not flow simply from the dependence children feel toward their parents as a source of the greatest benefits; it also
flows from the love parents feel toward their children as emblems of pa-
rental activity, of the *energeia* that defines the actors as whatever they are.
Thus animals are said to care for their children not out of altruism but
because actors love their own activity most of all, and children are tangi-

81. Ibid. 1108a30–b2; *Eth. Eud.* 1233b17–1234a27.
82. *Eth. Eud.* 1233b27–29. "Seem" decent, since modesty, like the moral virtues, never
guarantees practical wisdom. See note 76 above.
83. According to *Eudemian Ethics* 1234a25, it is "without choice [*prohairesis*]," but this
may not be Aristotle's final opinion, since it is not mentioned in the *Nicomachean Ethics*, and
since several traits presented as virtues in the *Nicomachean Ethics*, such as truthfulness, wit-
tiness, and friendliness, are said in the *Eudemian Ethics* to be, like shame, feelings.
84. *Eth. Nic.* 1128b15–21.
85. Genuine virility, Aristotle says, differs from the quality of being a good soldier because it follows from a desire for the noble rather than from anger. This modest virility is
much more to be praised than spirited virility (*Eth. Nic.* 1116a27–30, 1116b23–31).
86. *Eth. Nic.* 1180b3–7.

ble expressions of that activity.[87] For this reason, parents love children immediately, but children love their parents only as they come to develop perception and understanding.[88] Moreover, just because the basis of natural *philia* is the love we feel for our own activity, mothers are said to love their children more than fathers do, "because they think children are more their work [*ergon*]; for people define work by its difficulty, and the mother suffers more pain in the genesis of the child." [89] The fact that, on the basis of the biology of reproduction, Aristotle regards mothers as being wrong about whose *ergon* the child chiefly is seems to be irrelevant here; at any rate, Aristotle does not mention it at all in either the *Eudemian Ethics* or the *Nicomachean Ethics*. The point of these discourses, as of the ethical and political works generally, is not theoretical precision, but to persuade listeners to act well (a concept whose meaning for Aristotle is strictly biological, at least relative to the species, although in a scheme of final causes, reproductive biology is not biology's most fundamental part). Given that intention, the lesson here is plain: since women love their children so much, their role as educators is crucial; and since their role, and that of the *oikia* as such, is what it is, the moral development of women must be accorded a higher priority and status than it is given by the barbarians, by the Spartans, by Pericles, or by anyone who asserts that the political life is the only truly human activity.

As regards the negative account, my argument is that there is for Aristotle an important empirical connection between a sense of political unity and commitment and the exaggerated love of victory, a connection that is drawn very clearly in Book 7 of the *Politics* and that is evident in the linking of military and political activities in Book 10 of the *Nicomachean Ethics*.[90] Political, as opposed to natural, friendship is said to rest on *thymos* and to demand *andreia*, and good political people will treat honor (*timē*) as the goal of political life.[91] But if moderation is a greater virtue than virility, as it is for both Plato and Aristotle, then some counterweight is required to oppose our wrongheaded, and unnatural in one sense, attraction to fully committed citizenship. This connection between politics and war is an empirical and contingent matter, even though it is widespread and its roots can be understood. Even though it is because of, and not simply in spite of, the *polis* that we live always in the precincts of battle, it is not humanly impossible to imagine a quiet and moderate *polis*, and so it is reasonable to attempt to identify resources that can oppose the politics of virility.[92] In *Politics* 7 and *Nicomachean Ethics* 10, the theoretical or philosophic life is presented as just such a counterweight.[93]

87. *Eth. Eud.* 1241a40–b7.   88. *Eth. Nic.* 1161b24–26.   89. *Eth. Eud.* 1241b7–9.
90. *Eth. Nic.* 1177b6–15.   91. Ibid. 1095b22–23.   92. *Pol.* 1324b41–1325a7.
93. This is Lord's argument in "Politics and Philosophy."

The life of the *oikia,* like that of philosophy, can provide an attachment to an order different from the *polis* with a similar end in view. Aristotle's insistence on the importance of the family as a focus of regard is most apparent in his criticism in Book 2 of the *Politics* of the *Republic's* proposed abolition of the biological family. The lesson suggested by this is that Aristotle sees the greatest danger to a decent political life as stemming not from the reluctance to get involved in public affairs, but from the unbridled love of the city. This, and not Tocqueville's individualism or some Machiavellian or Arendtian identification of the private life as a source of corruption and idleness, is the danger Aristotle addresses. His appreciation of the merits of a tension between private and public concerns is thus profoundly anti-Periclean in its respect for the dignity of the family and the private sphere, in its refusal to identify virility and virtue, and in its acknowledgment of the endemic dangers of political life.

These dangers are clearest in Aristotle's account of the regime he calls polity (*politeia,* the generic name for all regimes). Polity is a regime in which the people (the *dēmos* or *plēthos*) rule in the common interest. Such a regime is said to be closer to democracy than to oligarchy, and so provides Aristotle with some reason for hope concerning the possibilities of democratic political life. But it is especially here, because of the way in which the common interest in virtue is perceived, that the line between politics and war becomes most blurred. Polity, in Aristotle's own words,

> is the name common to all regimes, and it is reasonable to call it this, because while it is possible for one or a few to be virtuous, it is difficult for a large number to reach a high standard in all forms of virtue—with the conspicuous exception of military virtue, which is found in a great many people. That is why in this regime the warriors are the most authoritative element [*kyriōtaton*], and those who bear arms [*ta hopla*] share in the regime.[94]

The fact that the Greek democracies are hoplite democracies is surely no accident for Aristotle (as it is not historically), precisely because virility (or at least a semblance of it) is the easiest of the virtues, both to see and to practice.[95] It is also a virtue that serves us very badly when the order imposed by war ceases, for, as Aristotle explains, "manliness possessing power is boldness" (*andreia gar dynamin echousa thrasos estin*), and "boldness is a quality of use in none of the affairs of daily life, but only, if at all, in war."[96] Both the ease and the low rank of courage for Aristotle are easily explained. Courage is the virtue that requires the least delibera-

94. *Pol.* 1279a38–b3.
95. See Vernant, *Origins of Greek Thought,* 62–68.
96. *Pol.* 1312a19 and 1269b34–36, respectively.

tion and thought; it is, in fact, a virtue whose expression is clearest when there is the least possibility for deliberation.[97]

The significance of the diametrical opposition between the Aristotelian and the Arendtian positions concerning the ease and rank of virility or courage among the virtues should now be plain. Arendt, of course, is by no means alone in thinking about the hopes for a truly political life in terms of an imagery of warfare *sans* bloodshed. Among us, the political problem is often conceived as the problem of discovering some "moral" equivalent of war, a project that presupposes that the best and most truly human qualities are likely to shine forth under extreme pressure. This is Machiavelli's view: if a republic is always prepared for war, "there will always be a demand for citizens of repute, as there was in Rome in its early days."[98] It is also Nietzsche's: "war and courage have accomplished more great things than love of the neighbor," and "it is the good war that hallows any cause."[99] Neither Arendt nor Machiavelli nor Nietzsche, nor Hegel in his characterization of the struggle between lord and bondsman as the primary political interaction, are bloodthirsty lovers of war.[100] But they agree in holding that a certain tense spiritedness, characteristic of the virile warrior, is the hallmark of truly human, truly political activity. Aristotle's imagery is very different. The figure who represents the peak of moral virtue, the great-souled person (*megalopsychos*), does strangely little and is quite slow to do even that much and is, above all, not tense or tightly strung, owing to a sense that nothing much in the realm of action is very great (*oude syntonos ho mēden mega oiomenos*).[101] Just as Plato attempts, against his culture, to transfer the laurel of *andreia* from the soldier to the philosopher intent upon his or her researches, so Aristotle seeks to replace the vision of the bold warrior with that of a beast who combines magnitude and a certain gentleness. The Spartans, he tells us toward the end of the *Politics*, aim only at courage, and so fail to produce even that. Real courage has nothing of savagery about it but goes "rather with the gentler and more lion-like characters."[102]

Those who see Aristotle's biology as providing a pseudoscientific apology for male supremacy are as mistaken as those who read his social science (*politikē*) as a stirring call for a participatory politics of communal identity. The error in both instances comes from failing to see how Aris-

97. *Eth. Nic.* 1117a19–22.
98. *Discourses*, bk. 3, chap. 16.
99. *Thus Spoke Zarathustra*, part 1, sec. 10.
100. On Hegel's account, see Berns, "Spiritedness in Ethics and Politics," 3.
101. *Eth. Nic.* 1125a15.
102. *Pol.* 1338b17–19.

totle strives to undermine, rather than support, the evaluative distinction between public things and private things. For Aristotle, our human identity—as beings who can come into our own through living reasonably—requires both *polis* and *oikia*, and the latter even more (in one sense) than the former. This argument, itself thoroughly biological in character (in that its first premises are statements about the nature of human beings, about the problems and capacities that compose our distinct biological heritage), serves as the ground for the Aristotelian derogation of the Greek attachment to virility and the love of honor and to the extreme hierarchy and differentiation of gender roles that is the consequence of that attachment. It is his biology, in fact, that provides the basis for his high valuation of women, who were not highly valued by the culture in which Aristotle lived.

If doing justice to Aristotle were all that is at stake here, the matter would be of little interest. But the issues involved are of more general significance for us. The Platonic and Aristotelian discussions of women bring to the fore two important points that are otherwise inaccessible. The first is that the prephilosophic or Periclean attachment to the public world is in large measure a commitment to the identification of virtue with masculinity or virility. The second is that the first people to philosophize about politics, Plato and Aristotle, reject this attachment on the grounds that it reflects and conceals a false, or only partially true, conception of human *aretē*. The various ways in which Plato and Aristotle suggest an elevation or revaluation of the status of women are thus not based on any sort of answer, affirmative or negative, to the question of whether the rights of women should equal those of men. Instead the goal is to subvert the prevailing conception of the best human life—a conception that had been revived for us, against classical political philosophy, by Machiavelli, by Nietzsche, and by Arendt—and to replace it with a novel, more complex, and surely less masculine one. This reading of Plato and Aristotle enriches our political vocabulary and indicates that we have some resources against a republican communitarianism saturated by the imagery of war other than the doubtful attractions of the commercial republic.

One of the difficulties posed by the political alternative implicit in the Platonic and Aristotelian critique of Periclean Athens is that the philosophers' solution to the human problem is so much less definite and vivid than the one celebrated by the politicians. At any rate, we can at least say that the best generally accessible human life, for them, is surely not that of the citizen-soldier, whose horizons are those of the city and whose life is a quest for *timē* and *kleos* regardless of the cost that must be borne in private. Rather, the best life open to most of us at least some of the time

might be that of the moderately detached householder and/or philosopher (understood in the broad, nontechnical sense of *Politics* 7), who is
sometimes a citizen and sometimes not.[103] If we keep this in mind, we may
be able to avoid the illusion of easy virtue that the imagined flash of battle
stimulates, and preserve those places (such as families and other schools)
within which human *paideia* can occur. The discussion of women in Plato
and Aristotle reflects this concern and makes it accessible to us, and it is in
this light that we can most profitably understand that discussion.

103. An excellent discussion of the broad characterization of philosophy and its political possibilities is provided by Lord, "Politics and Philosophy," who describes it as follows:
"Philosophy in the broad sense does not necessarily exclude theoretical speculation, but its
core is traditional culture; and traditional culture means above all literary culture. The
core of that philosophy which is politically relevant is, in the language of Aristotle and his
contemporaries, music" (355). Aristotle's proposal is to emphasize traditional literary culture more than is usually done but, as Lord says, "only in order to support more effectively
a way of life that is the antithesis of tradition" (357).

SEVEN

Superlative Virtue: The Problem of Monarchy in Aristotle's *Politics*

W. R. Newell

Recent interpreters of Aristotle's writings hope to find in them a communitarian alternative to contemporary liberalism. Although these interpretations vary considerably, they share the hope that the recovery of Aristotelian political philosophy could mitigate the *a priori* individualism of the liberal tradition without detracting from its broader democratic impulse. Notable among such interpretations is the recent study by Ronald Beiner, who follows the work of Hans-Georg Gadamer in looking to Aristotle for a philosophy that recognizes communal "discourse" rather than "technical expertise" as constituting our political essence. Both believe that a recovery of Aristotle's emphasis on the "context of mutual agreement" immanent in a healthy society can help to offset the alienating tendencies of the modern technological state.[1]

Although these are serious and thought-provoking studies, what is absent from them is a consideration of Aristotle's reflection on the good

I am grateful to the National Humanities Center, where I was a Fellow during the 1985–1986 academic year, for its support during the writing of this article. I also wish to thank Kerry H. Whiteside for his comments on an earlier version presented at the Annual Meeting of the Northeastern Political Science Association, November 15, 1985, in Philadelphia. The translations of Aristotle are my own.

1. See especially R. Beiner, *Political Judgment* (Chicago, 1983); and H.-G. Gadamer, *Truth and Method* (New York, 1975); id., "On the Scope and Function of Hermeneutic Reflection," in *Philosophical Hermeneutics*, ed. and trans. D. E. Linge (Berkeley, 1976); id., *Reason in the Age of Science*, trans. F. G. Lawrence (Cambridge, 1983). For other attempts to adapt Aristotelianism to a broadened conception of contemporary community, see W. A. Galstone, *Justice and the Human Good* (Chicago, 1980); and A. MacIntyre, *After Virtue: A Study in Moral Theory* (Notre Dame, 1981). For a thoughtful critique of MacIntyre, see B. Yack, "Community and Conflict in Aristotle's Political Philosophy," *The Review of Politics* 47 (1984): 92–112. For a recent treatment of a number of themes connected with this paper, see P. A. Vander Waerdt, "Kingship and Philosophy in Aristotle's Best Regime," *Phronesis* 30:3 (1985): 249–73.

and bad potentialities of monarchical rule as he analyzes the prospects
for achieving and sustaining political community. Beiner's analysis of
Aristotelian prudence, for example, rightly suggests that prudent judgments can be understood by nonexpert citizens. But while Beiner hopes
to make Aristotelian prudence the basis for wider and more meaningful
participation, Aristotle himself never attributes the capacity for making
prudent judgments to more than a few leaders in any given time or
place. Beiner concedes this difficulty in a footnote, but he does not ex-
plore the implications it would have for his main argument that we need
to combine the universalism (both logical and political) of Kant with the
"heteronomy"—the richness of experience and responsiveness to circumstance—of Aristotle.[2] For if Aristotle does not believe that even a siz-
able minority, let alone a majority, of people in a community are capable
of exercising prudent political judgment, what grounds are there for
drawing upon his conception of prudence to justify wider and more
meaningful political participation? Gadamer, in discussing Aristotle's
transition from ethics to politics, rightly observes Aristotle's belief that
custom and tradition help provide the context for a harmonious social
existence. But he makes no mention of Aristotle's further argument that
custom and tradition are not sufficient for habituating most people to
become virtuous and cooperative citizens; coercion and punishment by a
prudent ruler will also be needed.[3]

As a consequence of ignoring Aristotle's commendation of the uses of
monarchical rule, Beiner and Gadamer offer a rather one-sided interpretation from which Aristotle emerges as too sanguine about the prospects for communitarian harmony and participation. This has the effect
of misstating the grounds on which Aristotle actually does commend
what he calls the "political community." To be sure, Aristotle's political
philosophy emphasizes the desirability of communities governing themselves. Most of his arguments and illustrations point in this direction.
But Aristotle makes this recommendation in the light of the possibility
that he also raises that the best form of government is not a political community at all, but a monarchy run with a rational efficiency that leaves
little or no scope for citizen participation. Beiner and Gadamer tend to
treat the expert, constructivist dimension of politics as the alienating alternative to the context of mutual agreement. They see political "discourse" as something that flowers naturally when it is released from the
constraints placed on it by the technical reasoning that buttresses the
modern state. But in Aristotle's view, good government draws not only
on the everyday experience of the nonexpert majority, but on a certain

2. Beiner, *Political Judgment*, 48, 63, 68, 103, 177–78.
3. Gadamer, *Reason in the Age of Science*, 47, 81, 92, 131–36.

kind of technical reasoning (*technē*) and construction (*poiēsis*) at the disposal of expert rulers. The prospects for adapting Aristotle's political thought to the search for a new communitarian philosophy depend not on omitting this technical and inegalitarian side of it, but on understanding how Aristotle is able to arrive at a preference for political community in full awareness of what he takes to be the monarchical claim.

In what follows, I will demonstrate the importance of the monarchical dimension of Aristotle's political thought for understanding the character and limits of his preference for political community by examining the problem of what Aristotle calls "superlative virtue" in the *Politics*.[4] In Aristotle's presentation, the public claims of the "best man" to rule monarchically constitute an especially revealing test case for the political community's claims to be able to govern itself; for here the community's aims are at loggerheads not merely with selfish desires—which Aristotle has no difficulty repudiating—but with the highest degree of virtue. As I will argue, Aristotle has a way of resolving this problem in favor of what he takes to be the requirements of "politics" and the political community. But although the cumulative message of the *Politics* is Aristotle's en-

---

4. Although I have employed the familiar translation of the Greek word *aretē* as "virtue," it is helpful to note here that the Greek word has a broader range of meanings than its English counterpart. Literally, it means "excellence." Thus it can make perfect sense in Greek to speak of the "virtue" of a carpenter, doctor, rhetorician, or general, meaning their talent for what they do. This can strike modern readers as unusual, because we generally take "virtue" to mean something completely disinterested, the capacity to rise above one's own desires, ambitions, and preferences for the sake of the general good. We would be inclined to think that a general's talent to conquer people or a rhetorician's ability to persuade them to see an argument as being stronger than it really is are too prone to belligerence, deceit, self-aggrandizement to be considered properly virtuous. The Greek *aretē* certainly can have the connotation of self-denial and preference for the common good above one's own, and it often does have this meaning in the works of Plato and Aristotle. But its meaning is not restricted to this, and virtue is never categorically defined in this way, so as to exclude all other meanings. Plato and Aristotle often use the word in its more colloquial sense as a talent that may well result in advantage, honor, and reputation for its possessor. This makes it difficult to state at the outset a general definition of Aristotle's view of virtue from which all specific instances of it could be rigorously derived. The plasticity of the Greek word gives "virtue" a shifting meaning. For instance, "superlative virtue," the theme of this paper, could also be translated as "too much virtue," "excessive virtue." To our moral reasoning, this sounds almost like a contradiction in terms, like "harmful benefit." For Aristotle, however, as we will see, it is quite conceivable that a ruler could have an excessive, overbearing amount of "excellence" from the viewpoint of those under his rule. Psychologically, Aristotle observes, the "best man" may well be prey to anger and passion; only laws are capable of being purely disinterested. Thus one has to follow the different meanings of virtue throughout Aristotle's texts, noting the ways in which Aristotle acknowledges the various "excellences" that people contribute to their communities and contrasting this plural meaning with the "superlative virtue" that the rare individual of prudence will occasionally come along to demonstrate.

dorsement of political community, the claim of superlative virtue to monarchical authority undulates throughout it, leaving this endorsement a
nuanced and conditional one.

THE PROBLEM: WHOSE RULE IS "BEST"?

The problem of superlative virtue in the *Politics* comes clearly to light in
Aristotle's equivocal definition of the best claim to rule.[5] In the sixfold
classification of constitutions presented in Book 3, the "correct" constitutions are monarchy, aristocracy, and polity, while the "deviations" are tyranny, oligarchy, and democracy. Aristocracy means, literally, "rule of the
best" with respect to virtue (1279a–b; 1278a15–20), making it the "best
constitution" (1284b20–30; 1293b1–10). But Aristotle also argues in
Book 3 that the rule of the best could be monarchical. In fact, if the "best
man," a man of "superlative virtue" (*aretē hyperbolē*), were to appear, even
an aristocracy—indeed, especially an aristocracy—should give him complete authority, since virtue is its principle of justice (1284a–b; 1286a5–
10). Strictly speaking, then, it appears that the rule of the best—aristocracy—is monarchy, rather than the self-governing community that bears
this name in the sixfold classification.[6] Some commentators regard this
aspect of Book 3 as a rather puzzling relapse into Platonism, as if Aristotle
had suddenly conceded the possibility of the Platonic philosopher-king.[7]
It is all the more puzzling because when Aristotle turns, in Books 7 and 8,
to the full analysis of the "best constitution," he proceeds to describe an
aristocratic *community*—as if he had never admitted that, strictly speaking,
the most virtuous form of rule was monarchical (1325b30–40; 1326b9).

We can make sense of this apparent inconsistency by relating it to
some broader issues in the *Politics*. The case of the individual possessing
"superlative virtue" is part of an extended discussion of the meaning of
justice in Book 3. The core of this argument is the section on ostracism,
where Aristotle says that to exclude the man of superlative virtue from
monarchical authority bespeaks "a certain political justice" (1284b17)
but would not conform to the "absolutely just" (1284b25). However, in
order to understand the full bearing of Aristotle's distinction between
"absolute" justice and "political" justice, we should first consider what he
means by "political." I will begin, therefore, by examining Aristotle's way
of distinguishing between political and other kinds of authority. As we
will see, this turns out to be a distinction between a political community

5. For the *Politics*, I use *The* Politics *of Aristotle*, edited and translated with an introduction, two prefatory essays, notes critical and explanatory by W. L. Newman (Oxford, 1950).

6. Newman, *The* Politics *of Aristotle*, vol. 3, xxix.

7. See T. J. Saunders, ed. and trans., *The* Politics, (New York, 1981), 210, 220; Sir David
Ross, *Aristotle* (London, 1960), 255.

whose members possess enough virtue to be able to govern themselves and a prudent monarch whose virtue is so outstanding that he deserves to rule the city with the same kind of authority that a master exercises over a household. However, the claim of superlative virtue to exercise this kind of authority leads to the destruction of the city understood as a community of diverse contributions and interests. Having shown the tension between political community and monarchy, I then turn to Aristotle's consideration of what happens when the claim to possess superlative virtue rears its head in the midst of the political community itself.

Political and Monarchical Authority

The association that aims at the supreme good, according to Book 1 of the *Politics,* is the political community (*koinōnia politikē*).[8] The member of this community is a citizen who holds office in alternation with other citizens. A political community, in other words, is one where, by natural endowment and condition of life, people are equal—or, at least, no one is sufficiently superior to the others to be entitled to hold office permanently. The other kinds of rule, although they are associations, are thus not political associations, but varieties of monarchical rule: the king or royal ruler, household manager, and master. Aristotle is at pains to point this out because some hold the view that these forms of rule do not differ in kind, but only in number. If this were so, Aristotle argues, it would mean that statesmanship, kingship, mastery, and household management could be conflated. However, the three types of one-man rule have more in common with each other than they do, taken together, with the political community. As we soon learn, household management and the mastery of slaves are both required by the household (*oikos*) in order to secure the necessities of life. As for kingship, some have evidently thought that the city itself could be ruled like a household—a view that in Book 2 Aristotle attributes to Plato's *Republic* (1261a10–22). From the very outset of the *Politics,* then, and with Plato in mind, Aristotle is disputing the argument that all human associations, public and private, could be organized by a single royal "science" (*epistēmē*) of governing (1252a).[9] A city ruled like a household, in which the monarch's subjects do not participate in rule but passively carry out the tasks assigned them,

8. The "political community" (*koinōnia politikē*) is Aristotle's most general term for a community of shared rule, in contrast with monarchy. The "constitution" (*politeia*) is the more specific ordering of, and distribution of offices and authority within, the city in accordance with a correct or deviant interpretation of justice. "Constitution" is also the name of *one* of the six "constitutions." I translate it in the familiar way as "polity" to avoid confusion. The meanings of these terms are discussed more fully as they emerge from the text.

9. Cf. Newman, *The* Politics *of Aristotle,* vol. 2, 101; Pl. *Statesman* 259; Xen. *Mem.* 3.4.12, 3.6.14.

is the alternative that Aristotle is concerned to prevent from overwhelming self-government by citizens in a political community.[10]

The distinction between political and monarchical rule sheds light on the long discussion of the household that completes Book 1 (1253b–1260b). Beiner and Gadamer share the view advanced by Hannah Arendt and Jürgen Habermas that the aim of this discussion is to establish the superiority of public, communal existence over the private household's concerns with material necessities and comforts.[11] This is one of its aims. But focusing on this aim alone misses what for Aristotle is the more problematic and extended part of the investigation: can the household's forms of rule be applied to managing not only one's private affairs, but to entire cities? When Aristotle poses the question of whether the art of household management is identical with the acquisition of wealth, he is not only concerned with private households. This question is one of his ways of exploring more fully the possibility that there is a "science" of mastery that would swallow up not only the management of private households but statesmanship and kingship as well—an error, he points out, "which we raised at the beginning" (1253b15–20). The discussion of the household and its place vis-à-vis the city thus doubles back to that alluring prospect of a single monarchical science of governing.[12] Moreover, whereas Aristotle is certain that the life of citizenship is better for a human being than absorption in private money making and acquisition, he is not nearly so categorical in asserting the superiority of the "political community" to a certain version of the household as a pattern for government.

The analysis of the household begins with the rule of a master over slaves. According to Aristotle, the tools, including slaves, that the master employs are either for production (*poiēsis*) or action (*praxis*). The epitome of productivity is the "architectonic" rule of a master craftsman (*architektōn*) over a ranked division of labor, his slaves being "tool[s] serving tools." Ideally, Aristotle suggests, tools would direct themselves automatically to fulfill their part of the master craftsman's plan. The fanciful comparison of such tools to the legendary self-moving statues of Daedalus implies that just as the most productive tools would be animate, the most productive slaves would be inanimate, or as close to automatons as human beings could become. Perfect productivity, in other words, would abstract from all action. But a slave is, rightly considered, an instrument

10. For a discussion of Xenophon's conception of universal monarchy in contrast with the Aristotelian conception of political community, see W. R. Newell, "Tyranny and the Science of Ruling in Xenophon's *Education of Cyrus*," *The Journal of Politics* 45 (1983): 889–906.

11. H. Arendt, *The Human Condition* (Chicago, 1958), 22–37; J. Habermas, *Theory and Practice*, trans. J. Viertel (Boston, 1974), 42, 48.

12. Cf. Newman, *The Politics of Aristotle*, vol. 1, 145.

for action rather than production (1254a1–10). It is like a bed, which provides nothing beyond its use, rather than like a shuttle, which produces a commodity. A slave is thus someone who by nature belongs to a master as an instrument of action. In this way, Aristotle tries to prevent the identification of mastery with the open-ended acquisition of wealth.

As to whether the authority of master over slave can be justified quite apart from the question of its economic consequences, Aristotle argues that this is a matter of distinguishing natural slavery from merely conventional or legal slavery. Despite the attention this particular passage has understandably received from commentators,[13] we should bear in mind that Aristotle is not only, or even mainly, concerned with the frequent injustice of conventional slavery (which he admits), but to distinguish political rule over naturally equal citizens from the rule of a master over slaves even when the latter would be just. Though some details of the argument justifying natural slavery are drawn from private life, in its conclusion we are reminded that its main target is that error discussed during the initial distinction between political and other kinds of authority: "all [forms of] rule are not [the same], although some say they are" (1255b15–20).

The first conclusion Aristotle draws, then, about the art of household management is that it should not be identified with productivity. Were this identification to be made, the inflated desires such productive arts would serve in private life could, Aristotle observes, fuel an ambition for power and status in public life. Someone who is unable to fulfill his desires in private life will seek to do so "by other means" like "courage" or "generalship" (1285a5–15)—that is, by political and martial daring. Aristotle underscores the danger by depicting a tyrant in this context as someone who disposes of an entire city as his private property and business enterprise (1259a23–37). The productivity of the private household must therefore be circumscribed by the requirements of the common good. The proper use of wealth is to enable the heads of households to pursue public affairs and philosophy.

Although this might seem to dispose of the claim of the household as a model for good government, it is, however, far from the whole story.

13. The degree to which Aristotle believed that conventional slavery coincided with natural slavery—or whether he believed such a coincidence ever occurred—is a much-argued question. See, for example, Ross, *Aristotle*, 241–42; L. Strauss, *The City and Man* (Chicago, 1964), 22–23; M. P. Nichols, "The Good Life, Slavery, and Acquisition: Aristotle's Introduction to Politics," *Interpretation* 11 (1983): 171–84; R. G. Mulgan, *Aristotle's Political Theory* (Oxford, 1977), 42–45; N. D. Smith, "Aristotle's Theory of Natural Slavery," *Phoenix* 37 (1983): 109–22; W. W. Fortenbaugh, "Aristotle on Slaves and Women," in *Articles on Aristotle*, ed. J. Barnes, M. Schofield, and R. Sorabji (London, 1977), 135–39.

The question remains as to whether some form of one-man authority besides the exploitive, tyrannical kind might be more beneficial for the city than the "political community." This leads to the more complex level of Aristotle's investigation, which Beiner and Gadamer omit. If there are not enough people in any given city who are naturally talented enough to be able to pool their abilities and govern their own affairs, a monarch who organized them into their respective functions might be a superior alternative to a self-governing community. Anticipating this objection, Aristotle argues that "nature" will provide "human beings" fit for citizenship just as it can be expected to provide both household managers and statesmen with the material necessities. Statesmanship, therefore, does not need to "make" or produce (*poiein*) human beings fit to live in a city, just as weaving does not produce wool but "uses" wool already provided for it (1258a20–30). At most, statesmanship must be able to distinguish between the good and bad people already present. The derogation of "making" in favor of "using" what has already been provided recalls Aristotle's earlier criticism of the household devoted wholly to productivity, epitomized by the rule of a master craftsman over a ranked division of labor. Just as the household does not need to be given over to the "architectonic" organization of the arts, Aristotle implies, neither does the city.

In light of what has preceded, Aristotle goes on to make the startling remark that "the ruler must have complete moral virtue, for the work [he does] is, taken absolutely, that of a master craftsman, and reason [*logos*] is a master craftsman" (1260a10–20). Until now we have received the impression that Aristotle prefers shared rule to monarchical rule and that the monarch's skill in "producing" people fit to live in a city need not override the community's claim to be able to govern itself. Has Aristotle now reversed himself to endorse the "architectonic" pattern of rule? In order to clarify the terms of this remarkable assertion, we must turn to some references outside of Book 1 and to the *Nicomachean Ethics.*

In Book 3 of the *Politics,* we learn that while rulers and ruled may share certain virtues, one virtue is peculiar to rulers alone. This is prudence or practical wisdom (*phronēsis*). Prudence, therefore, demonstrates why the virtue of a good citizen rarely coincides with that of a good man, since prudence cannot be exercised by citizens who do not themselves rule. Only in an aristocracy, where the citizens are also rulers, can the virtue of a good citizen and a good man coincide. Prudence is, at all events, uncommon, characteristically exercised by "one" or "one with others." Aristotle emphasizes its rareness with two illustrations. (1) The ruled do not need prudence for understanding political affairs but can get by with "true opinion." This presumably enables them to understand the prudent judgments of their rulers without sharing the capacity to make them. Aristotle likens this relationship between ruler and ruled to that between a pipe player and his pipes. (2) Aristotle's example of the prudent ruler here is Jason, who could not bear to retire from tyranny into private life because he had such a "hunger" to rule. All in all, a large gulf separates the virtue of the ruler from the virtue of the citizen (1277a15–25, b25–32).

The virtue of the "best man," Aristotle observes later in Book 3, is "superlative" specifically with respect to "political capacity" (1284a10). Prudence is similarly characterized in Book 6 of the *Ethics* (1180b25–1181a10), and the discussion there clarifies a number of the terms we have encountered. Prudence is both the chief intellectual virtue apart from wisdom and the condition for the possession of all the moral virtues. The rare individual who possesses it will therefore possess such virtues as liberality, moderation, and courage, while people possessing one or more of these lesser virtues will not necessarily achieve prudence. Prudence is not an art (*technē*) because it does not "make" or "produce" (*poiein*) things. It is not a science (*epistēmē*) because it does not deal with permanent conditions, but with variable ones (1140a25–b10). However, prudence is something considerably more precise and skillful than instinct, improvisation, or even debate among informed citizens; for prudence must be guided by an "architectonic" faculty for "statesmanship," applying this faculty according to "correct reason" (1141b10–30, 1144b10–25). Aristotle's example of prudent statesmanship here is Pericles (1140b7–10), whose predominance over the Athenian democracy Thucydides compares to a monarchy in all but name (Thuc. 2.65.9).

The characterization of prudent statesmanship as an "architectonic" faculty guided by correct reason suggests that the gap between technical and scientific reasoning on the one hand and prudence on the other is not as wide as it might appear. As we observed in Book 1 of the *Politics*, Aristotle regards the architectonic organization of the arts as the optimal one for technically skilled production (*poiēsis*). Moreover, although "intelligence" (*nous*) is initially characterized in the *Ethics* as the source from which "science" intuits the first principles of deductive proofs, Aristotle later suggests that "intelligence" also furnishes prudence with an intuition of the particulars with which it must deal (1143b1–10). In Book 10 of the *Ethics*, when Aristotle discusses the transition from ethics to government, the distinction between art and science on the one hand and prudence on the other is further relaxed. This appears to parallel Aristotle's contention that we must turn from ethics to government because persuasion is not enough to make most human beings prefer virtue to vice; for most people, "force" and law are also required. The prudent ruler is now said to have to know "statesmanship" with the same acuity as scientists know science and artisans know art, so as to be able to "make

[*poiein*] people better" (1179b–1180a10, 1180b20–1181a10). In other
words, the transition from questions of ethics to questions of government and rule leads to less emphasis on persuasion and the voluntary
aspect of citizens' habituation to virtue and to more emphasis on the
need to supplement persuasion with regulation and punishment. As this
transition occurs, prudence moves correspondingly closer to (though it
never coincides with) *poiēsis* and *epistēmē*.

These modulations in the meaning of prudent statesmanship take us
back to the underlying debate between Aristotle and Plato. Aristotle will
not abandon the distinction between prudence as a kind of skilled judgment of experience and the pure expertise of scientific and technical
knowledge. In contrast with Plato, Aristotle will not allow the sphere of
practical statesmanship to be assimilated entirely to a monarchical science of rule. This parallels his unwillingness to see the sphere of public
life obliterated by the monarchical science of household management.
His examples of prudent statesmen, though individuals of rare ability,
are flesh-and-blood, actual rulers like Jason and Pericles rather than the
totally disinterested and ideal prototype of Platonic monarchy. On the
other hand, however, Aristotle is willing to modify the distinction between prudent statesmanship and technical reasoning as he moves from
the formation of a gentlemanly character in the *Ethics* to the frequent
need in wider political practice for more direct and coercive modes of
habituation.

Let us return to the passage from the *Politics* with which this excursus
began (1260a10–20): if the ruler in the "absolute" sense, who rules according to "reason" and "complete moral virtue," is to pattern his rule on
that of the master craftsman, then it would seem that politics ought indeed to be organized according to the ranked division of labor; for this
is the master craftsman's way of organizing the household. In Book 2 of
the *Politics,* we learn that Aristotle interprets Plato's *Republic*—the city,
as the Platonic Socrates put it, "according to reason" (*Rep.* 369a)—as functioning according to just such a division of labor. In this context, Aristotle observes that just as it is more productive for shoemakers always to
do the same job rather than rotating their jobs with others, so would it be
"better" if the rulers of the political community were "always . . . the
same" (1261a30–b10). When consulting the criterion of the good, in
other words, Aristotle seems to be at one with Plato on the best form
of rule.[14] Where that is not possible because "all are naturally equal,"
he continues, the members of the community should rule and be ruled
in turn.

14. *Beltiōn* ("better") being the comparative of *agathos* ("good").

But even if the ranked division of labor between ruling and ruled were possible, it is difficult to reconcile Aristotle's approval of it in the context just cited with the main drift of his arguments in favor of shared participation in ruling. The way to make sense of this, however, is to keep before us the fundamental distinction he makes between political and nonpolitical associations. The *Republic*, Aristotle argues, is so unified owing to its hierarchy of labor that it is like a single household rather than a city; for the nature of the city is differentiation. Diverse contributions, selfish interests, and conflicting views of justice comprise its fragile unity. Returning to Book 1, we find a variation on this argument. Although he has just spoken of moral virtue in its "completion," Aristotle now criticizes Socrates for having held that virtue is the same in every soul and differs only in the amount of it each soul possesses (cf. Pl. *Meno* 71–73; *Eth. Nic.* 1144b–1145a). Instead, different kinds of virtue are distributed in varying degrees among men, women, and children, depending on which virtue, and how much of it, is needed for their tasks as slaves, servants, family members, or citizens—tasks that will vary further with the particular kind of constitution under which they live (1260a–b).

Summing up the results of this analysis of Aristotle's distinction between political and monarchical rule: Aristotle argues that although there is such a thing as a good form of household rule, it is not a city and that although there is such a thing as "absolute" rule employing "complete moral virtue," it need not assimilate the lesser and diverse varieties of virtue that make the city go. Thus, while the reasonable ruler may indeed be the ruler in the "absolute" sense, reason need not assert its claim to rule where nature has supplied people of sufficient, diverse virtues to govern themselves. Where human nature is not deficient, the "architectonic" rule of reason would be unnecessarily and unjustly coercive. Even where human nature were so deficient as to require this kind of rule, however, it would still be *unpolitical* rule, destructive of the city and citizenship. With these arguments in mind, we can now consider how Aristotle treats the claim of superlative virtue to monarchical authority when it presents itself among the other claims to authority that contend in actual political life. What happens, in other words, when the man of "superlative virtue" rears his head in the midst of the community of shared rule?

Equality, Inequality, and Political Justice

The "best man's" claim to authority is taken up in the midst of a discussion of the meaning of justice in political argument. According to Book 3 of the *Politics*, justice is equality for equals and inequality for unequals. But while there is agreement on the comparative quality of things, there is disagreement over who really deserves which things. Our own interests are inextricably involved when we argue about what constitutes just treatment. Hence, for example, the partisans of oligarchy mistake their superiority in wealth for superiority in all contributions to the political community. The partisans of democracy mistake their equality in free birth for the equality of human beings in every respect. Thus, Aristotle says, "all adhere to a kind of justice, but they only proceed so far, and do not discuss the whole of justice" (1280a5–15). The decision about the meaning of justice, commonly a blend of the arguers' self-interest and a "part" of justice, generates the distinctions among constitutions.

In Book 3, however, Aristotle raises doubts about the adequacy of his own sixfold classification of constitutions. In effect, he asks, is not even this variety of possible decisions about how to constitute the political community too limiting of the possible meanings of equality and inequality, each one too exclusive and narrowly based within itself? There are other qualities (for instance, ancestry and family background) that contribute to the city's survival and pursuit of the good life besides those contained in the six principles.[15] How, then, can we judge precisely a person's equality or inequality in comparison with other people so as to know who is entitled to "offices"? Distinguishing equality from inequality in a politically relevant way, it transpires, is a problem for which we need "political philosophy" (1282b).

Aristotle offers this illustration of the problem (1282b20–1283a30). Some would argue that if people are equal in other respects, any remaining superiority will suffice to justify the unequal distribution of offices. To this he responds that not all forms of superiority justify superior *political* authority. Using an analogy, Aristotle argues that a superior pipe player will always deserve the best pipes. This will be the case even where another person is superior to the pipe player in birth or good looks in a greater proportion than the pipe player is superior to that other person in pipe playing, and even supposing looks and birth to be greater goods than pipe playing. In other words, the diverse contributions that people make to the city are not commensurable. They cannot be superadded so as to arrive at a ranked hierarchy of who deserves what. This is in keeping with Aristotle's criticism, noted earlier, of the Socratic argument for the unity of virtue—the notion that virtue is the same for all people, varying only by the amount each person possesses. If this were the case, it would be possible to conclude that the second man is more entitled to

15. In Book 4, where the most inclusive constitution, polity, is discussed in detail, Aristotle observes that not only are there many claims to virtue, but they may coexist in the same people, making it even more difficult to decide precisely who is equal and unequal in a politically relevant way. "The same people [may be] soldiers, farmers and artisans, as well as councillors and judges, and indeed everyone thinks they are capable of holding most of the offices" (1291b1–10).

the best pipes than the best pipe player, because his superior birth and looks add up to more "superiority" than the pipe player's musical talent.

Of course, in another sense the analogy does point toward the unity of virtue and monarchical rule; for even though the contributions of different types of people cannot be added up in one overriding claim to rule, apparently *one* person could possess enough virtue to make this claim from the outset; for the best pipe player does unambiguously deserve the best pipes. Earlier in Book 3, as we observed, Aristotle makes this point more explicitly by comparing the relationship between an outstandingly virtuous ruler and his subjects to that between a pipe player and his pipes (1277b25–30). Here, though, the drift of the argument is toward inclusiveness. Hence, returning from the analogy to the problem of justly distributing political authority, Aristotle concludes that neither the well-born, the free, the wealthy, the educated, nor the virtuous— taken together, in combinations of two or more, or separately—can claim *all* political honors and influence, although they are certainly entitled to a share of them.

The specific mention of "education and virtue," the concomitants of aristocracy (cf. 1283a35–1288b), makes it clear that Aristotle is not just speaking of virtue in the relative sense of the many talents that keep the city going. While allowing that education and virtue have the "most just" (1283a20–25) claim to political authority, he maintains that even these do not deserve "inequality in all." It therefore transpires that "all such constitutions," including aristocracy, are "deviant" because in each case the ruling part mistakes superiority in one quality for superiority in all. We are not surprised to learn this about the regimes previously described as deviant because they do not rule for the common good but only for the ruling part's advantage. But it is surprising to learn that virtue itself can push its claim to authority too far.[16]

But this is just what Aristotle means, and his reason for it is "political" in the sense discussed in the examination of political and monarchical authority above. Here we should bear in mind that the most inclusive of the correct constitutions—most conveniently translated as "polity"—is both specifically distinguished from rule according to virtue (aristocracy) and given as its own particular name the name common to all six principles of rule (*politeia*, or "constitution" 1279a35–b). Although it is the least virtuous of the correct constitutions, polity is evidently closest to

16. As Newman notes (*The* Politics *of Aristotle,* vol. 3, xxii–xxiii), the problem cannot be solved by assuming that "all such constitutions" refers only to tyranny, oligarchy, and democracy or to those in which authority is claimed on the basis of something other than virtue. See also the discussion in R. G. Mulgan: "A Note on Aristotle's Absolute Rule," *Phronesis* 19:1 (1974): 66–69; and id., "Aristotle and Absolute Rule," *Antichthon* 4 (1974): 69–90.

what Aristotle takes to be the practical aim of "constitutional" government as such, which is the inclusion within the political community of as
many diverse and conflicting interests and abilities as possible.[17] Indeed,
a city that excludes too many people from rule will be "full of enemies"
and hence unstable, making both mere life and the good life impossible
to sustain (1281b25–35). The derogation in this context of the politics of
virtue in favor of the "constitutional" politics of inclusiveness helps to explain Aristotle's remark that we have to consider what will happen when
all six claims to rule "are present in one city" (1283b1–5). This appears
to mean that the sixfold schema, though useful as a heuristic device, is
too abstract and that there will seldom, if ever, be a precise "fit" between
real cities and the six principles of rule (cf. 1292b10–25). Cities as we
observe them in practice are more likely to be a kind of political cauldron
in which all the claims are contending for power at once. Even in cities
that do fit one of the classifications closely, there are other claims seeth-
ing beneath the surface, waiting for their opportunity. Far from being
able to stabilize the political community, therefore, each of the constitutions (with the probable exception of polity) is likely to be felt as a despotic imposition by those whom it excludes. Aristotle underscores this
deficiency by arguing that, pushed to its extreme, each principle of rule,
as it were, self-destructs, ruining the self-interest and authority of its
very claimants and necessitating a more inclusive approach to power
sharing. Thus, the oligarchs must, in order to live up to their own principle, give way to the one or few richest in their midst or to the common
people if they are collectively richer than the oligarchy. Those claiming
to be equal by free birth will have to yield to the freest-born by background and ancestry. Those who claim to rule through virtue will have
to yield to the one or few most virtuous in their midst (1283b5–1284a).

Up to this point, Aristotle's argument seems strongly to favor a broad
definition of contributions to the city and a broad claim to public authority. In a rather abrupt shift, however, he goes on to argue that there
may be "one" whose virtue is so outstandingly superior to all other virtues as to make him like a "god" among "human beings," and who cannot even be considered "a part of the city" (1284a1–15). This is in keeping with the preceding, which might appear to deny any such claim, if
one bears in mind that Aristotle's denial of supremacy to any one virtue,
and the overall derogation of virtue in favor of "constitutional" rule, was

17. Polity is the most inclusive and stable of constitutions because it blends the principles of democracy and oligarchy that, between them, include the most people and are the
source of the most explosive and prevalent of conflicts, namely, rich versus poor. Consider
S. R. L. Clark, *Aristotle's Man: Speculations on Aristotelian Anthropology* (Oxford, 1975),
104–5; J. H. Randall, *Aristotle* (New York, 1968), 263–64.

made squarely within a "political" context as that term was discussed earlier. The point here, by contrast, is that the man of "superlative virtue" is literally not political, not "a part of the city."[18] Here, then, we are looking at the other conclusion from the pipe player analogy, which Aristotle did not draw when stressing the limited claims of various kinds of virtue to political authority. Although the diverse contributions in any given political community cannot be ranked so as to establish an entitlement to exclusive authority, some rare individuals possess a degree of virtue so overwhelming that it cannot be included within this balancing and blending of claims in the first place. This is the "best man" with that rare kind of prudence that sets him apart from the rest.

Although Aristotle recognizes the force of this claim to rule, we should note that he does not present superlative virtue as an exclusively or self-evidently beneficent quality from the perspective of the political community. Superlative virtue certainly can be taken to mean rule in the "absolute" sense, rule according to reason by one who possesses complete moral virtue. But even a reasonable or prudent ruler, Aristotle implies here, could be partly motivated by an ambition for honor and perhaps even desire, appearing to his subjects like a predatory lion among the hares. We recall that the examples of prudence offered in Book 3 and in the *Nicomachean Ethics* were Jason and Pericles—men scarcely devoid of ambition and certainly accustomed to having things done their way. Whether purely benevolent or willing to rule benevolently in exchange for certain advantages, such a ruler will in any case be hard for the "equals" making up a political community to bear, just as the Argonauts found Hercules too heavy for their ship to stay afloat (1284a15–25).

The questionable desirability of superlative virtue from the perspective of the political community—the question of whether such a ruler's talents and beneficence could ever outweigh the overbearing quality of his authority—is emphasized by Aristotle's initial discussion of it in the context of ostracism. In Aristotle's presentation, ostracism is a typically democratic practice because the claim of superlative virtue to absolute authority exists in a starker contradiction with democracy, whose principle is absolute equality, than with any other regime. But the question of how to accommodate such a claim is a problem for all regimes, according to Aristotle, the correct as well as the deviant. Ostracism is in fact analogous to the practice of tyrants in "lopping off," like the tallest blades of grass, the leading citizens who might rival them. Despite his usually

18. The language recalls Book 1, where someone who is self-sufficient enough not to be "a part of the city" is said to be either a beast or a god (1253a25–30).

strong condemnation of tyranny, in this connection Aristotle does not
consider the critics of tyranny to be "absolutely correct" (1284a25–40);
for the other regimes—"even the correct ones"—must likewise lop off
the outstandingly virtuous. In this sense, he seems to imply, all regimes
contain an element of tyranny, an uncompromising suppression of the
best title to rule, and in this they are adhering to "a certain political justice," although not to "absolute justice." The community as political community, as a differentiated unity, cannot tolerate the unified authority of
the "best man" except at the price of its own being—any more than a
painter can allow one part of his painting to be disproportionately large
or a chorus master can allow a performer whose voice is "nobler and
more powerful" than all the rest (1284b1–30).

But when the constitution's own principle of rule is "the best," there
appears to be an insurmountable problem in principle; for neither the
deviant constitutions (which are nakedly based on the rulers' self-
interest) nor polity (which aims at a blend of diverse interests and contributions) espouse virtue as their exclusive and undiluted claim to authority. But how can an aristocracy consistently reject the rule of one
"surpassingly virtuous"? For *it* to do this, Aristotle argues, would be like
"claiming to rule over Zeus." In an important qualification of his claim in
Book 1 that statesmen need not "make" human beings because nature
will provide sufficient numbers of them capable of governing themselves, Aristotle now adds that superlative virtue and its claim to authority also flow from nature (1284b20–35). In the case of this one constitution (that is, aristocracy), one-man rule overrides "political" rule
strictly in keeping with a correct principle of "political" rule itself. In
other words, the aristocrats' claim to authority over the political community lays bare, in an especially revealing way, the inability of "political justice" altogether to live up to the requirements of "absolute justice."
Thus, while allowing that other constitutions may need to ostracize individuals of superlative virtue, Aristotle depicts the claims of the "best
man" as being particularly embarrassing for aristocracy. Within the sixfold classification, aristocracy is a peculiar sort of halfway house between
the deservingness of superlative virtue and the necessity for inclusiveness. On the one hand, aristocracy is likely to exclude too many people,
in comparison with polity. On the other hand, since aristocracy recognizes virtue as the only claim to rule, its failure to embody the highest
degree of virtue is more glaringly unjust than in the case of constitutions
that judge people's contributions and interests less rigorously and with a
greater view to stability. Thus Aristotle concludes in what sounds almost
like a quotation from Plato's *Republic* that "it remains for all to obey such
a man gladly, so that men of this sort are kings in the cities forever" (cf.
Rep. 473d).

Superlative Virtue and Justice

The discussion of monarchy that completes Book 3 is a recapitulation of the problem of how to reconcile competing claims for authority—how to judge between the equal and the unequal—in light of the admitted possibility of superlative virtue. Aristotle's presentation of virtuous monarchy recalls his discussion in Book 1 of rule in the "absolute" sense, the "architectonic" rule of reason; for this monarchy of the "best man" is a form of household management (1285b20–1286a). Moreover, alone of the correct constitutions, monarchy is in principle lawless, since its ruler "acts in all things according to his own will" (1287a1–10, 30–40).[19] It is an emphatically "unpolitical" form of rule, that is, incompatible with any notion of civic community. Since the view of justice it embodies—the outstanding merit of one person—can in no way be shared or participated in by the members of a local community, it is also universalistic in principle, and so capable of swallowing up whole cities and "nations."

Aristotle raises some possible objections to virtuous monarchy from the "constitutional" perspective on the city as an association "composed of many [people]" (1286a25–35). Thus he suggests that the "multitude" by pooling its judgments may frequently be a better judge of public affairs than the expert, in the sense that a banquet provided by many hands will be superior to one provided by a single individual. Whereas one man—even, apparently, a virtuous ruler—can be corrupted by "anger" or some "other such passion," it is more difficult for everyone in a crowd to be led astray at once. If the "majority"—relative to the monarch—are actually of "sound soul," that is to say, an aristocracy, then they will resist the tendency of a "multitude" to split into factions and will therefore be altogether preferable to the rule of one (1286a35–b10).

Some would argue, moreover, that it is simply "against nature" that one man should rule, because the city is composed of equals (1287a10–15). Thus a community where law rules and offices are rotated is preferable to monarchy; for although man is a political animal possessing reason (1253a1–10), he is an animal nonetheless, and to allow even the "best man" absolute power unconstrained by law may offer too much temptation to the "wild beast" (*thērion*) within him of desire and spiritedness (*thymos* 1287a25–40). Thus we are reminded again that—at least from the perspective of the political community—the "best man" may mix his benevolent expertise with the leonine qualities of a lord and master. The rule of law, by contrast, is like intelligence divested of such passions. Moreover, although experts admittedly must sometimes override the law (just as a doctor must sometimes depart from prescribed treatment), expertise can be used for unjust ends (just as a doctor knows best

---

19. Cf. Newman, *The* Politics *of Aristotle*, vol. 3, 28; Pl. *Statesman* 292b–303c.

how to kill a patient). Thus the rule of law is on the whole preferable to the rule of an expert, a "mean" between (apparently) absolute monarchy and the spontaneous impulses of the multitude (1287a40–b).

Still, it is important to note that these are not so much Aristotle's own arguments as hypothetical objections presented for our consideration. Aristotle concludes by stating that where men are equal, monarchy is neither just nor advantageous, even if the monarch is (relatively) "superior in virtue"—"except in a certain case." This is the case, as at the outset, of the man of "superlative" virtue, who should not rule "in alternation" like citizens, but "absolutely." Having rehearsed the objections, Aristotle does not find them sufficient. While an absolute monarch should not rule over equals, where he is "outstandingly" unequal, they are plainly no longer (even relatively) equal (1288a1–30).

Aristotle brings us full circle to the problem of distinguishing equality from inequality and argues, somewhat startlingly, that this problem is solved by the claim of superlative virtue to monarchical authority. We are reminded that all the other constitutions, including aristocracy, make claims to authority based on different kinds of inequality. However, while they all urge the justice of these claims, only monarchy meets the requirements of "the whole of justice," of justice in the "absolute" sense. Whereas the partiality and exclusiveness of the other claims led Aristotle earlier to back away from the sixfold classification and to stress the need to blend as many competing claims as possible, in the case of superlative virtue he appears to regard the equal and unequal as reconcilable. This claim is commensurable with all the others if only in the negative sense that all the other claims are incommensurable with it. But this kind of monarchy, based on the principle of household management, is, in accordance with the distinctions between kinds of rule made at the beginning of the *Politics*, unpolitical. The one constitution that meets the requirements of justice is not itself a political community. Thus, although we are reminded in conclusion that to ostracize such a man would never be in accordance with "absolute justice," we remember that it is in a sense "politically just" to do exactly that.

CONCLUSION

Although Aristotle continues to include monarchical rule among the possible meanings of aristocracy—the "rule of the best"—throughout the rest of the *Politics* aristocracy has mainly the meaning of a political community of the virtuous (1289a26–38, 1293a35–b7, 1294a9–29). In Books 7 and 8, where the "best constitution" is prescribed in detail, it has exclusively this meaning. On the basis of the preceding analysis, several reasons can be suggested for this ambiguity. First of all, aristocracy in the latter sense, while extremely rare, is in Aristotle's view relatively closer to practical possibilities, and thus more easily emulated, than the rule of a "godlike" monarch. Oligarchies, for instance, can sometimes qualify as "loose" aristocracies, a blend of wealth and virtue (1249a9–29). Polity, the correct regime that Aristotle believes has the best chance of setting a standard for actual practice, can encourage the awarding of offices on the basis of virtue, the aristocratic principle of distribution (1294a35–b14).

The other reason for Aristotle's equivocal definition of aristocracy is, in my view, the danger that he believes is posed to public life by the advancement of a merely presumptive claim to superlative virtue. As we saw in Book 1, Aristotle cautions against perverting the proper use of the household or monarchical form of rule into a tyrannical exploitation of the city. In real life, Aristotle later remarks, most people are not even aware of the distinction between monarchy and tyranny but tend to identify all government with "mastery"—the exploitation of the ruled by the ruler (1324b22–41).[20] Thus the claim to possess superlative virtue could be used as a powerful rhetorical camouflage by those who aim at tyranny.[21] Even someone who really does possess the knowledge to govern—and here Aristotle departs notably from the Platonic presentation of monarchy—may be vulnerable to a desire for honor, to excessive anger, and to an intolerance for even a reasonable and well-intentioned airing of views.

Precisely because Aristotle is willing to mute the claim of superlative virtue, however, we might ask whether we cannot push him further in this direction and abandon his concern with superlative virtue while retaining his endorsement of political community. My answer is that a conception of political community that excluded superlative virtue would not be an Aristotelian conception of political community. This is because Aristotle's understanding of politics, while trying to give inclusiveness and diversity their fair weight, is inegalitarian in principle. According to

20. See C. Lord, *Education and Culture in the Political Thought of Aristotle* (Ithaca, N.Y., and London, 1982), 190–91.

21. In this light, we can see Hobbes as arguing that Aristotle did not go nearly far enough in this direction. For Hobbes, admitting even the possibility of superlative virtue promotes political instability; for the presumptive claim, once admitted as a possibility, is always open to recognition and acceptance, meaning that the "vainglorious" have a convenient pretext for their ambition. Hobbes's presentation of the state of nature is meant to convince us that no claim to superior virtue can outweigh our fundamental equality in vulnerability to violent death. Paradoxically, this demands a Sovereign with powers far outstripping any that Aristotle would have attributed to virtuous monarchy. For Hobbes, even fear of death at the whim of the Sovereign, let alone resentment at his failure to recognize merit or to rule beneficently, is preferable to a state of open contention for power based on competing claims to virtue. If the protection of life, rather than the possession of virtue, is the only admissible claim to absolute authority, the result is a Sovereign who cannot, in practice or principle, be distinguished from a tyrant. See T. Hobbes, *Leviathan*, ed. C. B. Macpherson (New York, 1979), 226, 240, 700, 722; J. Laird, "Hobbes on Aristotle's *Politics*," *Proceedings of the Aristotelian Society* 43 (1943): 1–20.

Aristotle, man fulfills his nature in political life by pursuing virtue. Virtue for Aristotle is, as we have seen, on a kind of sliding scale between monarchy and slavery. Between these extremes of excellence and helplessness, the degree of virtue to be expected from people will vary with the circumstances. The "constitutional" politics of inclusiveness, and even an aristocratic community, require only a degree of virtue, as close to the monarchical end of the scale as the differentiated unity of the city can withstand. The fact that "constitutional" virtue does not measure up to the monarchical standard—the fact that citizens for example, may be able only to understand prudent judgments, while not being able to make them for themselves—does not rob it of its relative worth in Aristotle's eyes. But such worth as it has derives from its ranking in comparison with that higher standard. Thus, although Aristotle is tolerant of the looser approximations of virtue achieved by most political communities, he cannot embrace the notion that there is no higher order of virtue in principle than that of which every human being is capable. He does not regard prudence, for example, as the faculty of man *qua* man, but only of the rarest statesmen. Aristotle's endorsement of political community cannot be severed from his concern with superlative virtue, because superlative virtue is the absolute standard from which the relative worth of political community is derived.

More fundamentally, Beiner's and Gadamer's vision of political community is incompatible in principle with Aristotelian political philosophy because they conceive of the naturalness of political life on entirely different grounds. As we have observed, for Aristotle both the political community and monarchical rule are sanctioned by nature. That is, both shared participation in ruling and the exclusive rule of one are natural. The reasoning behind this understanding of the nature of political life is supplied by Aristotle's *Physics*, where nature is understood both in terms of spontaneous self-movement and as being analogous to the rational precision with which an artisan produces things. In other words, natural phenomena are a mixture of the spontaneous and the rationally constructed. Nature is characterized not only by self-movement, but by *technē* and *poiēsis*.[22] Extending this understanding of nature to political

22. Aristotle rejects the pre-Socratic understanding of nature as pure spontaneity or becoming because it cannot account for the forms and purposes of visible beings (*Ph.* 193a5–b20). But Aristotle also resists the opposite extreme of making nature synonymous with the rationally constructed—a point that is perhaps less obvious due to the influence of Aristotelians like Thomas Aquinas who mistakenly propounded this view in Aristotle's name (see, for example, *Commentary on Aristotle's* Physics, trans. R. J. Blackwell and R. J. Spath [New Haven, 1963], 124). While Aristotle likens nature to art in some respects in order to refute the pre-Socratic view (*Ph.* 199a10–20), his analogy for nature in all respects is that of a "doctor who heals himself" (199b27–35)—an irreducible mixture of generational substratum (the patient's sick body) and art (the doctor's medical expertise).

life, the natural realm of politics is, accordingly, a mixture of the self-government of political communities and the skills of monarchical statecraft by which prudent rulers "make people better." I have suggested how Aristotle, in contrast with Plato, resists the assimilation of political community to monarchical rule. But although Aristotle's argument cannot be driven to a purely monarchical outcome, it cannot be driven to a purely communitarian outcome either, because Aristotle's conception of the naturalness of politics requires a mixture of the spontaneous and the technical dimensions.

Liberal political philosophers such as Hobbes upset this Aristotelian balance by reducing the understanding of nature to spontaneous self-movement alone and by asserting man's capacity to turn against nature so conceived and reconstruct this purposeless flux. Rousseau reacted against this purely technical mode of statecraft by evoking the spontaneous freedom and wholeness of the natural life, and the wholeness immanent in societies relatively close to nature, in contrast with the artificiality and alienation brought about by the modern bourgeois state. Beiner and Gadamer echo the Rousseauan conviction that were man to be released from the bonds of the state and the technical reasoning that upholds it, his happiness would be free to flower. The point, however, is that not only the Hobbesian emphasis on technique cut adrift from its natural mooring but the Rousseauan emphasis on spontaneity bereft of rational construction is a distortion of what Aristotle meant by the naturalness of political life.

In Aristotle's view, although man inclines naturally toward virtue and cooperation, he does not do so automatically or merely through the removal of external constraint. On the contrary, laws and punishments are required to force recalcitrant people away from the powerful inclination toward vice. Virtuous statecraft is therefore a kind of "making" or construction that fulfills human nature by enabling it to resist its lower impulses and pursue its higher end. For Aristotle, then, although politics cannot be assimilated to production and art, neither are the latter simply alienating and restrictive. Politics are "natural" in the Aristotelian sense because they are always moving, in response to circumstances prudently assessed, between the freedom of self-government and the authority of statesmanship.

EIGHT

On Aristotle's Critique
of Athenian Democracy

Barry S. Strauss

In this paper I propose to examine two paradoxes. The first is the contrast between the extraordinary value of Aristotle's general thinking on democracy and the problematic nature of his specific evaluation of Athenian democracy. The second is the ironic nature of scientific progress, through which today's fool can correct the errors of yesterday's genius.

Aristotle's writings on politics and on democracy in particular are of the highest relevance. He left one of the most eloquent and profound statements ever made on behalf of the rule of law. His political sociology influenced Marx and remains fundamental, perhaps unsurpassed. His strictures on the dangers of indiscriminate egalitarianism are still worth heeding. Other writers in this volume discuss these topics; I propose to focus on the narrower subject of Aristotle's analysis of classical Athenian democracy.

The historian of ancient Greece learns quickly to value Aristotle's discussion of this topic, for Aristotle is certainly one of the most important analysts of and sources of evidence for Athenian political history, especially of the fourth century B.C. Two works in particular stand out, the *Politics* and the *Constitution of Athens*. In the *Politics*, Aristotle provides numerous details and critiques of the evolution and workings of fourth-century Greek democracy in general and, to a lesser extent, of fourth-century Athenian democracy in particular. In the *Constitution of Athens*, he (or at least a member of his school) both analyzes the evolution of Athenian democracy from the seventh century B.C. to the 320s B.C. and provides a detailed account of how the Athenian government worked in

Translations of Aristotle's *Constitution of Athens* are drawn from J. M. Moore, *Aristotle and Xenophon on Democracy and Oligarchy* (Berkeley and Los Angeles, 1975), with occasional modifications. All other translations are my own.

the 330s and 320s B.C. For all this, the historian of Athenian democracy is greatly in Aristotle's debt.[1]

Upon closer inspection, however, that debt turns out to be a complicated one. Aristotle's account of democracy, in or out of Athens, is neither straightforward nor unbiased. Aristotle was an avowed critic of democracy. Perhaps he would not have called democracy, as Alcibiades did, "an acknowledged folly" (Thuc. 6.89.6), nor was he incapable of praising democracy's good points. But he considered the kind of democracy that existed in most of the Greek *poleis* of his day—what he calls in the *Politics* the most recent (*neōtatē*), last (*hystatē*), final (*teleutaia*) or extreme (*eschatē*) democracy—to be undisciplined, lawless, despotic, vulgar, hostile to the upper classes, and likely to be unstable.[2] This terminology is hardly neutral and carries the implication that fourth-century democracy was bad simply because it was extreme. We may go further and say that because of his moral assessment of democracy, Aristotle's account of democracy is for historical purposes as problematic as it is essential and brilliant. The historian of fourth-century Athens, therefore, does not merely study Aristotle, he wrestles with him.

In the following pages I would like to focus on one central question, Was fourth-century Athens, as Aristotle says, an extreme democracy, or was it, within the limits of its day, that is, taking into consideration the acceptance of slavery and the subordination of women, a just and moderate regime? This question presupposes several other questions, to wit, What does Aristotle mean by extreme democracy? Does he intend his

1. On the date, authorship, and plan of the *Constitution of Athens* (*Athēnaiōn Politeia*), see P. J. Rhodes, *A Commentary on the Aristotelian* Athenaion Politeia (Oxford, 1981), 7, 51, 63. Martin Ostwald offers the following persuasive reply to Rhodes's scepticism about the Aristotelian authorship of the *Athēnaiōn Politeia*:

> Though its origin in Aristotle's school is beyond doubt, it is fashionable these days to deny Aristotle himself the authorship, largely for reasons of comparison and style. . . . Since, however, none of the other 157 "constitutions" with which Aristotle's school is credited is available for stylistic comparison, I regard these arguments as inconclusive and prefer to ascribe the work to the author to whom tradition assigns it. (*From Popular Sovereignty to the Rule of Law: Law, Society and Politics in Fifth-Century Athens* [Berkeley, 1986], xx n.1)

On the *Politics*, see C. Lord, "The Character and Composition of Aristotle's *Politics*," *Political Theory* 9 (1981); id., *The Politics of Aristotle* (Chicago, 1984), 8–24.

2. See, for example, the term *neōtatē* at *Pol.* 1305a29, *hystatē* at *Pol.* 1310b4, *teleutaia* at *Pol.* 1298a31, and *eschatē* at *Pol.* 1312b36. For these examples and discussion, see M. H. Hansen, *The Sovereignty of the People's Court in Athens in the Fifth Century B.C. and the Public Action Against Unconstitutional Proposals* (Odense, 1974), 60. For the characterization of that form of democracy as undisciplined, see, for example, *Pol.* 1319b31–32; as lawless, *Pol.* 1292a32; as despotic, *Pol.* 1292a18–19; as vulgar, *Pol.* 1319a26; as hostile to upper classes, *Pol.* 1320b19; as unstable, *Pol.* 1319b1–4. Aristotle praises democracy's good points in, among other places, *Ath. Pol.* 41.2; *Pol.* 1281a39–b21 and 1286a26–35.

generalizations in the *Politics* about extreme democracy in Greece to apply to Athens in particular? If his analysis does not appear to be solidly grounded in the facts as we know them from other sources, literary and epigraphic, what accounts for his errors? Have today's historians done an injustice to Aristotle?

I shall argue that Aristotle's account of Athenian democracy is indeed exaggerated in its criticism and, at points, inaccurate. The matter, however, does not end there. Before completing an analysis of Aristotle's account of Athens, we must consider the nature of his text and both its rhetorical and philosophical purposes. We must also pay attention to Aristotle's political position in fourth-century Athens and the wider Greek world. When we have done so, the nature of his account of Athens will, I believe, become both more complex and more interesting.

My purpose is neither to debunk Aristotle nor to relegate him to some museum of learning ("brilliant but outdated"). Rather, I wish to confront squarely the paradox of a thinker who constructs an immensely valuable theoretical framework and then seems to misapply it. The specific case, I shall argue, does not invalidate the general theory. I hope furthermore that this inquiry will also offer a salutary reminder of the limits of any generation's thought. If Aristotle nods, then surely the rest of us sleep. The truest lesson of this paper is, I trust, not Aristotle's fallibility but our own.

Aristotle discusses final or extreme democracy in several passages in the *Politics*, notably in his account in Book 4 of actual constitutions. He writes that extreme democracy is one of the four (*Pol.* 1292b25–1293a12; cf. 1318b6–1319b32) or five (1291b30–1292a38) varieties of democracy, chronologically the last to develop. As the term *teleutaia* ("final") suggests, the philosopher is employing, as elsewhere, a teleological outlook. This teleology is perhaps clearer in the *Constitution of Athens* (although, paradoxically, the terms *teleutaia dēmokratia, eschatē dēmokratia,* etc., are not employed there), but it is also traceable in the *Politics*.

J. J. Keaney demonstrates that in the *Constitution of Athens* Aristotle depicts the steady growth of democracy (with only occasional regressions) from modest beginnings to a culmination in the late fifth and the fourth centuries—for Aristotle, I might add, it is a lamentable progression from good rulers to demagogues.[3] Similarly, in the *Politics*, Aristotle describes a chronological progression from a farmers' democracy to extreme democracy (1293a1–2, 1318a1–2). He states that a farmers' de-

3. J. J. Keaney, "The Structure of Aristotle's *Athenaion Politeia*," *Harvard Studies in Classical Philology* 67 (1963): 115–46; id., "A Narrative Pattern in Aristotle's *Athenaion Politeia*," in *Studies in Honor of Sterling Dow*, Greek, Roman and Byzantine Monographs 10 (1984): 161–64; Rhodes, *Commentary on* Athenaion Politeia, 9, 11, 14.

mocracy, the first kind of democracy, is the best kind of democracy, while the final, extreme form of democracy is the worst, hardly a constitution at all (1292a32; 1318a1–2; 1319a4, b1–2). In democracy, therefore, a progression from a tolerably good, if still imperfect, regime—for Aristotle, all democracy was deviant (1279b6)—to an unendurable regime seems to be all but inevitable. By its very nature, democracy is directed to the interests of the common man (1279b8–9). Its underlying logic makes everyone equal, regardless of merit or worth, and therefore necessitates the sovereignty of the ordinary working people over the wealthy (1317b3–5). The paradox of a good democracy is that to construct it, one must fight against this fundamental principle of non-discriminating egalitarianism and prohibit the common people from holding public office (although they still can elect and audit public officials; see *Pol.* 1318b21–22, 1318b27–1319a3).

Let us turn now to the details of extreme democracy. Its prerequisites are a large increase in population and the accruing of a considerable revenue. These insure a mass of ordinary working people (*to tōn aporōn plēthos* 1293a10) who, thanks to state pay (for attending the Assembly, for example; see 1300a1–4, 1320b17–19), are able to take control of the constitution (*kyrion tēs politeias* 1293a10). Extreme democracy is defined by the fact that men, rather than laws, are sovereign, and particularly ordinary working men. When it comes to the business of government, every man of citizen status can share in office. In terms of its sociology, the state in extreme democracy is dominated by mechanics, shopkeepers, and day laborers, common people whose way of life is vulgar and whose work is all without excellence (*aretē* 1319a26–30). Usually, in such regimes, citizenship is given to the illegitimate as well as to the lawfully born, and to those with only one citizen parent, whether father or mother.

Thus, when the prerequisites are met, extreme democracy is defined by a combination of legal, institutional, and sociological terms. The common people (*plēthos*), and not the law (*nomos*), are sovereign; this comes about because decrees (*psēphismata*) are sovereign, rather than the law (*nomos* 1292a1–7).[4]

4. Such a distinction between law and decree accords well with the mainstream of classical Greek thought, both philosophic and popular, which draws a line between a law, which is meant to be general, fundamental, and permanent, and a decree, which is meant to deal with individual or temporary matters. Most classical writers and orators, likewise, praise the rule of law and agree that it is superior to the rule of men. See M. H. Hansen, "Did the Athenian *Ecclesia* Legislate After 403/2 B.C.?" *Greek, Roman and Byzantine Studies* 20 (1979): 27–28 (id., *The Athenian* Ecclesia [Copenhagen, 1983], 179–80); M. Ostwald, Nomos *and the Beginnings of the Athenian Democracy* (Oxford, 1969), 2; id., *From Popular Sovereignty to the Sovereignty of Law*, 523; J. de Romilly, *La loi dans la pensée grecque* (Paris, 1979), 208–12; R. Sealey, *The Athenian Republic: Democracy or Rule of Law?* (Univ. Park, Pa., 1987), 32–35.

Aristotle goes on to explain that the rule of decrees is brought about
by demagogues, popular leaders who flatter the common people and
turn them on the upper classes (who end up footing the bill for state pay,
often through judicial confiscations; 1320a17–21). By referring all
matters to the immediate judgment of the people (*dēmos*), the demagogues make decrees, rather than laws, sovereign. The people become
master of all (*ton men dēmon pantōn einai kyrion*), and the demagogues
master of the people. Furthermore, by censuring or indicting the magistrates, the demagogues destroy their offices and transfer their powers to
the people. In an extreme democracy, all meet to deliberate on all issues;
the magistrates can give only preliminary, and no final, judgments. In
short, an extreme democracy is all but a tyranny of the common people
over their betters. Indeed, a state in which everything is run by decrees
(*en hēi psēphismasi panta dioikeitai*) can hardly be called a constitution at all,
for "where the laws do not rule, there is no constitution" (1292a32). This
is an inversion of the order that Aristotle believes should obtain. The law
should be sovereign; the magistrates and citizen body should decide
about details only (1292a2–38, 1298a28–33).

Does Aristotle consider the Athens of his day to be an extreme democracy? If so, we must infer it, since Aristotle never calls Athens an extreme
democracy. On the other hand, he never calls any regime an extreme
democracy outright. This reticence is striking and is surely not accidental. If Aristotle had wanted to specify which regimes were extreme democracies, he could have done so. Three possible explanations for his
silence come to mind.

First, perhaps Aristotle simply did not consider Athens to be an extreme democracy. Second, perhaps he did not consider *any* regime to be
an extreme democracy in the pure sense; the details of individual cases
made them each deviate from the ideal. Third, perhaps Aristotle had a
prudent desire not to cause unnecessary offense by attaching so unflat-
tering a label to any specific *polis*. Keenly aware of Socrates' fate as he
was, Aristotle knew the importance of being politic.

The second explanation will not go very far, since Aristotle makes it
clear that extreme democracy really does exist. For example, he states
that one of the useful ways to establish an extreme democracy is to adopt
measures like those that Cleisthenes introduced at Athens (1319b1, 21).
Elsewhere, he states that "the democracy which is most considered to
[really] be a democracy nowadays" (*dēmokratiai* [*te*] *tēi malist' einai dokousēi
dēmokratia nyn*) is one in which the *dēmos* is master (*kyrios*) over the laws—
namely, an extreme democracy (1298b13–15; cf. 1292a5).

We must give Aristotle credit for distinguishing between his general
theory and the idiosyncrasies of specific cases, but that is not why he does
not label Athens as an extreme democracy. Rather, I would argue, the

reason is prudence; for Aristotle implies very strongly that the Athenian regime of his day ("the current democracy" [*hē nyn dēmokratia* 1274a6, 10]) was, in all important ways, an extreme democracy. This is clear in both the *Politics* and the *Constitution of Athens*. His description in the *Politics* of Athenian democracy refers to precisely those features that are characteristic of extreme democracy: the ascendancy of worthless demagogues who flatter the people like a tyrant, a throng of ordinary working people (in the case of Athens, specifically rowers) in power, state pay for jury service, and the people's court master (*kyrios*) of the Council and magistrates (1273b35–1274a21, 1291b23–24, 1292a1–37, 1293a1–10, 1304b22–24). Add to this the reference, noted above, to the efficacy of Cleisthenes' reforms for the establishment of extreme democracy.

The *Constitution of Athens* tells a similar story. Again, there is much emphasis on the demagogues who have led the state continually downhill since the death of Pericles (*Ath.Pol.* 28.1, 4). There is a clear statement of the sovereignty of the common people in section 41.2, which refers to the constitution established by the returned democrats in 403/402:

> It has lasted to the present day with ever-increasing power being assumed by the common people [*plēthos*]. The people [*dēmos*] have made themselves sovereign [*kyrios*] in all fields; they run everything by decrees [of the *ekklēsia*] and by decisions of the courts [*dikastēria*] in which the people [*dēmos*] are supreme.

Again, Aristotle does not use the term extreme democracy, but he characterizes this eleventh and last change of constitution in Athens as a regime in which the common people have gained ever more power. Moreover, he implies here what he states elsewhere to be the central feature of extreme democracy: the decrees of the popular assembly, rather than the laws, are sovereign (*Pol.* 1292a5–6, 23–25).

We can conclude, therefore, that Aristotle considered the Athenian constitution of his day to be an extreme democracy.[5] He only implies this, however; he never states it directly. In a careful writer like Aristotle, such an omission is not likely to have been an accident. Rather, it is, I believe, an indication of his prudence.

How well does Aristotle's analysis of extreme democracy fit fourth-century Athens? We should not expect it to fit in every last detail, for

5. See Rhodes, *Commentary on* Athenaion Politeia, 11. Hansen (*Sovereignty of the People's Court,* 13) argues that Aristotle recognizes at *Athenaion Politeia* 41.2 the separation of powers between the Assembly and the courts in Athens, and hence that Athens was not an extreme democracy. The phrase in question, however, *dikastēriois en hois ho dēmos estin ho kratōn,* "by the courts in which the people are supreme," does not indicate the separation of powers, but rather merely emphasizes the predominance of the *dēmos* in the courts (id., "Initiative and Decision: The Separation of Powers in Fourth-Century Athens," *Greek, Roman and Byzantine Studies* 22 [1981]: 351–52).

Aristotle does not tailor his general description of extreme democracy to the Athenian variety. For instance, although he says that in extreme democracy citizenship is usually given to those with only one citizen parent (*Pol.* 1319b10), he certainly knew that in Athens citizenship belonged only to people with two citizen parents (*Ath.Pol.* 42.1). One would expect, therefore, that in certain particulars, Athenian democracy would differ from the model of extreme democracy in the *Politics.* In all important ways, however, for Aristotle, Athens would fit the general pattern.[6]

Indeed, in some ways Aristotle's analysis of fourth-century democracy fits Athens quite well. The Athenian people, the *dēmos*, had made themselves sovereign—though, as we shall see, there were important restrictions on that sovereignty. The people did meet to deliberate on all issues, and the magistrates could only enforce the people's decisions or give preliminary judgments, except in a few special matters (those involving very small sums of money or confessed criminals). The vast majority of public decisions were made by decrees and not laws—though, as we shall see, this was more a matter of practicality than of disrespect for the law. The introduction in the 390s of payment for attending the Assembly (*Ath.Pol.* 41.3) made it all the easier for the common man to attend; it appears that the numbers at Assembly meetings were greater in the fourth than in the fifth century, in spite of a decline in population. There were demagogues, at least in the literal sense of the term, that is, "popular leaders." The prerequisites of extreme democracy, a large increase in revenue and population, certainly do not fit the weakened, post-Peloponnesian War Athens of 403/402, but they do fit imperial, Periclean Athens of the mid-fifth century, when, according to Aristotle (*Pol.* 1274a, 1303b), extreme democracy in Athens began, and they also fit, though to a lesser extent, the 350s under Eubulus and the late 330s and 320s under Lycurgus, when Athens enjoyed a measure of peace and prosperity.[7]

---

6. On Aristotle's ability to generalize, see Hansen, *Sovereignty of the People's Court,* 14.

7. As regards decrees and laws, around 700 decrees from fourth-century Athens have survived, but only seven laws—or, to use another measure, twenty-four men are known to have proposed laws. See M. H. Hansen, "*Demos, Ecclesia,* and *Dicasterion* in Classical Athens," *Greek, Roman and Byzantine Studies* 19 (1978): 146 n. 44 (= *Athenian* Ecclesia, 158 n. 44); id., "*Nomos* and *Psephisma* in Fourth-Century Athens," *Greek, Roman and Byzantine Studies* 19 (1978): 317–18 (= *Athenian* Ecclesia, 163–64); id., *Athenian* Ecclesia, 177; id., "The Athenian *Nomothesia,*" *Greek, Roman and Byzantine Studies* 26 (1985): 345–71. On Assembly attendance, see Hansen, "How Many Athenians Attended the Assembly?" *Greek, Roman and Byzantine Studies* 17 (1976): 121–34 (= *Athenian* Ecclesia, 7–20). On Periclean Athens, see Thuc. 1.80.3; cf. B. Strauss, *Athens After the Peloponnesian War: Class, Faction and Policy, 403–386 B.C.* (Ithaca, N.Y., and London, 1987), 73. On Eubulus, see G. M. Cawkwell, "Eubulus," *Journal of Hellenic Studies* 83 (1963): 47–67. On Lycurgus, C. Mossé, *Athens in Decline, 404–88 B.C.,* trans. J. Stewart (London, 1973), 81–86.

The major points of Aristotle's description of extreme democracy, however, do not fit fourth-century Athens. The people did indeed rule in Athens, as he says, but they evinced a much greater respect for the rule of law and were far more willing to blend the interests of the many and the few than he allows. The following pages will reevaluate Aristotle's analysis of the Athenian democracy of his own day under two different categories: (1) institutional, governmental, and constitutional, and (2) sociological. After discussing the problems in that analysis, many of which have been made clearer by important research in the last decade, we shall turn to the reasons for Aristotle's errors about the Athenian regime. These errors can be explained in part by the rhetorical purposes of Aristotle's text and by Aristotle's position in the international politics of his day.

Institutions, Government, and Constitution.   To begin with, there were important restrictions on that sovereignty of the people to which Aristotle refers, restrictions that demonstrate respect for law and constitutional procedure. "The people (*dēmos*) have made themselves sovereign in all fields," Aristotle writes (*Ath.Pol.* 41.2; cf. *Pol.* 1292a5, 26; 1293a10). The Athenian people expressed their sovereignty through the major organs of government: the Assembly, the courts, the Council, and the magistrates. The Assembly, however, held a special status in the Athenian mind as the people's voice; only the Assembly is referred to in the sources as the *dēmos*, "the People" (cf. the British custom of referring to the popular house of the legislature as "the Commons"). The Greek word *dēmos* possesses a fruitful, if confusing, semantic ambiguity. *Inter alia*, it can denote the whole people, the common people (as opposed to the upper classes), a township, or the Athenian assembly.[8]

The Athenian people (*dēmos*) had voluntarily put restrictions on the immediate efficacy of their voice, the Assembly (*dēmos*). For one thing, the agenda of the Assembly was set by the Council, which also, along with the magistrates, carried out the Assembly's will. Furthermore, with the restoration of democracy in 403/402, the Assembly's heretofore-unfettered right to pass general, permanent, and fundamental laws (*nomoi*) as well as decrees (*psēphismata*) was restricted. Thereafter, the Assembly had the power to vote from time to time that the laws (*nomoi*) should be changed, but the specific changes and final ratification depended upon a group of legislators (*nomothetai*) chosen either from

8. Technically, both the members of the Council of Five Hundred and the magistrates were considered *archai*. See Hansen, "*Nomothesia*," 352–53. On the Assembly as *dēmos*, see Hansen, "*Demos, Ecclesia* and *Dicasterion*," 127–46 (= *Athenian* Ecclesia, 139–60); on the ambiguity of *dēmos*, D. Whitehead, *The Demes of Attica, 508/7–ca. 250 B.C.* (Princeton, 1986), 364–68. See also Hansen, "Initiative and Decision," 347–51.

among the year's jurors or from the citizenry (just which is a matter of debate). To turn to judicial matters, most were in the hands of the popular courts. Indeed, the courts even had the power to declare laws and decrees invalid.[9]

These restrictions on the popular assembly (*dēmos*) placed some restrictions on direct, popular sovereignty, but in the long run, they protected democracy. The complicated system of making permanent laws (*nomothesia*) protected the *dēmos* from revolutionary change. No longer could oligarchs, as in 411 or 404, change the fundamental constitution of the state by a simple majority vote of one meeting of the Council and one meeting of the Assembly. These restrictions on the Assembly, therefore, protected democracy, but an orderly and constitutional democracy, not an undisciplined one. Aristotle says little about these restrictions (of *nomothesia* he says nothing at all) and of the ways in which they counteract the impression one might have that fourth-century democracy was unreflective and completely without checks or balances.[10]

Other developments in fourth-century democracy did restrict the direct and immediate power of the people. As P. J. Rhodes argues, Athens took a number of steps in the direction of governmental efficiency and specialization, sometimes at the expense of democracy. The most important changes were in finance. In the fifth century, Athens had a central treasury closely controlled by the Assembly, which authorized expenditures, either singly or as regular payments. By contrast, in the first quarter of the fourth century, a new financial system emerged, in which

9. For the debate on the precise workings of *nomothesia*, see H. J. Wolff, "*Normenkontrolle" und Gesetzbegriffe in der attischen Demokratie* (Heidelberg, 1970); F. Quass, *Nomos und* Psephisma: *Untersuchungen zum griechischen Staatsrecht* (Munich, 1971); D. M. MacDowell, "Law-Making at Athens in the Fourth Century B.C.," *Journal of Hellenic Studies* 95 (1975): 62–74; id., *The Law in Classical Athens* (Ithaca, N.Y., 1978), 48–49; M. H. Hansen, "Athenian *Nomothesia* in the Fourth Century B.C. and Demosthenes' Speech Against Leptines," *Classica et mediaevalia* 32 (1971–80): 87–104; P. J. Rhodes, "*Nomothesia* in Fourth-Century Athens," *Classical Quarterly* 35 (1984): 55–60; R. Sealey, "On the Athenian Concept of Law," *Classical Journal* 77 (1981–82): 289–302; id., *Athenian Republic*, 41–45, 159 n. 20.

10. Hansen has shown (*Sovereignty of the People's Court*, 19–21, and "*Demos, Ecclesia* and *Dicasterion*," 127–46 [= *Athenian* Ecclesia, 139–60]) that the word *dēmos* was rarely applied to the courts, but usually to the Assembly. This important semantic distinction does not, however, imply a political distinction; since the courts were held to represent the *dēmos* (Din. 3.16), their power implies no diminution of popular sovereignty. On changes in the constitution, see MacDowell, *Law in Athens*, 48. On Aristotle's omission of *nomothesia* and other details of fourth-century Athenian government, see Rhodes, *Commentary on* Athenaion Politeia, 35–36; Hansen, "Did *Ecclesia* Legislate?" 51–52 (= *Athenian* Ecclesia, 203–4); Sealey, *Athenian Republic*, 34 and 157 n. 3. On the spirit of fourth-century Athenian democracy and the power of the people therein, see now J. Ober, *Mass and Elite in Democratic Athens: Rhetoric, Ideology, and the Power of the People* (Princeton, 1989), which appeared after this essay was written.

funds were allocated on a prearranged plan to the various governmental departments. Furthermore, both in the 350s under Eubulus and in the late 330s and 320s under Lycurgus, the Athenians entrusted finances to the supervision of one man. In public works, the annual accounts of the supervisors of public building projects were no longer published, as they had been in the fifth century. The state now employed permanent, salaried architects, who submitted their plans not to the Assembly but to the Council or the law courts. In sum, the government became more efficient by loosening the reins of the Assembly.[11]

In military affairs, beginning in the years after the King's Peace of 387/386, there was an increasing divorce between generals and politicians. Instead of being commanded by a man who spoke to them in the Assembly, Athenian soldiers—when the troops were not mercenaries, that is—served under a strictly military man.[12]

Another restriction on popular power appeared in the third quarter of the fourth century with the revival of the Council of the Areopagus. Isocrates had prepared the ideological way with his praise of this elitist council in his *Areopagiticus* in the 350s. In the following decades, the Areopagus increased both its legal and moral power and had a growing influence on the Assembly. An important example is Demosthenes' Areopagus Decree of 343, which empowers the Areopagus to investigate alleged pro-Macedonian traitors and report its findings to the Assembly; the decree grounds the Areopagus' mandate in the "ancestral laws," that frequent rallying cry of the few.[13]

Finally, in the judicial sphere, it is worth noting that whether by design or by neglect, jury service had been made less attractive to the common man. Although state pay did in general keep up with inflation during the fourth century, jury stipends remained at three obols, a point they had reached in the 420s.[14]

Whether all of these diverse governmental trends add up to a major decrease in the power of the common man is unclear. What is certain, though, is that they were far from the "ever-increasing power . . . assumed by the common people (*plēthos*)" of which Aristotle speaks (*Ath.Pol.* 41.2).[15]

11. On finance and public building, see P. J. Rhodes, "Athenian Democracy After 403 B.C." *Classical Journal* (1980): 309–14.

12. Rhodes, "Athenian Democracy," 314–15; A. H. M. Jones, *Athenian Democracy* (Oxford, 1957), 128; J. K. Davies, *Wealth and the Power of Wealth in Classical Athens* (New York, 1981), 125–26; Strauss, *Athens After the Peloponnesian War*, 14, 37 n. 12.

13. Isoc. *Areop.* 37–56; Din. 1.62; Rhodes, "Athenian Democracy," 319–20; R. Wallace, "Undemocratic Ideology in Athenian Politics, 355–336 B.C.: Demosthenes' Areopagos-Decree" (Paper read at the Annual Meeting of the American Philological Association, December, 1986).

14. Rhodes, "Athenian Democracy," 317.

15. Rhodes, "Athenian Democracy," 322; id., *Commentary on* Athenaion Politeia, 488.

Furthermore, Aristotle goes too far when he denies that Athenian democracy was a regime of the rule of law. The opposite—that fourth-
century democracy did respect the rule of law—has been cogently argued in recent research, particularly that of M. H. Hansen. Hansen lays
great emphasis on the careful Athenian distinction between *nomos* and
psēphisma, demonstrating that the Assembly was careful not to pass general and permanent rules (*nomoi*), but to reserve them for the separate
process of *nomothesia*. Hansen also stresses the importance of the *graphē
paranomōn*, the public indictment for proposing in the Assembly an il-
legal law or decree, and the prosecution *nomon mē epitēdeion theinai*, for
"making an unsuitable law." Hansen concludes, therefore, that fourth-
century Athens was indeed ruled by law.[16]

I would agree, though with certain qualifications. For one thing, the
vast majority of the decisions of the Athenian assembly, as of any legislative body, were of a temporary and specific kind, and hence made by
decree. Aristotle, therefore, is only exaggerating somewhat when he says
that the *dēmos* runs *everything* by decrees (*Ath.Pol.* 41.2). Second, the Assembly was not entirely without say in the matter of new *nomoi;* it passed
judgment on proposals, which it then submitted to an *ad hoc* body for
final validation. Third, in practice, the *graphē paranomōn* was more a political than a legal or constitutional tool: it was largely a means of attacking prominent politicians. To sum up, the Assembly was restrained from
enacting its own whims without due regard to the fundamental laws of
the land; on the other hand, the Assembly tempered its respect for law
with a passion for politics and an insistence that the people's voice be
heard. The Assembly respected the law, but not without qualification.[17]

There is, therefore, a grain of truth in what Aristotle says; respect for
law was not the lodestar of Athenian politics. The overall thrust of his
argument, however, is seriously off base. Aristotle says that the Athenian
people run everything by decrees of the Assembly and by decisions of
the court, and indeed these two bodies accounted for most of the decisions of the state. He seriously underestimates, however, Athenian re-

16. On the rule of law, see Sealey, "On Athenian Law," 292, 301–2; id., *Athenian Republic*, 97, 146; Ostwald, *From Popular Sovereignty to Rule of Law*, xx, 522, 524. On *nomoi*,
psēphismata, and *nomothesia*, see Hansen, "*Nomos* and *Psephisma* in Athens," 127–46 (= *Athenian* Ecclesia, 139–60); id., "Did *Ecclesia* Legislate?" 27–53 (= *Athenian* Ecclesia, 179–206).
On the *graphē paranomōn*, and the *nomon mē epitēdeion theinai*, Hansen, *Sovereignty of the
People's Court*, 28, 44–54; MacDowell, *Law in Athens*, 50–52; Wolff, *"Normenkontrolle" und
Gesetzbegriffe*.

17. On the use of decrees for most decisions, see MacDowell, *Law in Athens*, 49; Hansen,
"Did *Ecclesia* Legislate?" 49 (= *Athenian* Ecclesia, 201). On the *ecclesia* and *nomothesia*, see
note 9 above. On the *graphē paranomōn* as a political tool, Hansen, *Sovereignty of the People's
Court*, 62–65. Our surviving sample of information is too small to lead to any conclusions
about the use of the *nomon mē epitēdeion theinai* procedure.

spect for the sovereignty of law, and he says nothing of *nomothesia*. Although the *graphē paranomōn* was of less practical import than it might have been, its very existence does bespeak a respect for law. Aristotle was right to say that the *dēmos* was sovereign, but wrong not to recognize that it was restrained by respect for the fundamental laws.

Sociology.   If Aristotle's account of Athenian institutions has proved to be imperfect, so too has his description of the people who ran them. According to Aristotle, the institutions of extreme democracy were dominated by the working people who lived in the city: mechanics, shopkeepers, hired laborers, and, especially in the case of Athens, rowers (*Pol.* 1291b23–24, 1319a27–28). Farmers and shepherds were more admirable than these people because they were more robust, harderworking, and less acquisitive. Moreover, because they had too little leisure and lived too far from the city to participate in politics, they would not interfere with the rule of their betters (1318b9–16, 1319a4–24). The urban *dēmos* was able to participate in politics because it received state pay. Wealthy men, on the other hand, were often too busy with their private occupations to spare time for the Assembly or the courts; and, in addition, they were not attracted by the relatively small amount of pay that the state offered. The result, therefore, was that the regime was dominated by the "mass of ordinary working people" (*to tōn aporōn plēthos* 1293a9–10) and not by the laws (1293a1–10).

Before proceeding, it is important to clarify what Aristotle means by the mass of ordinary working people (*to tōn aporōn plēthos*). Aristotle frequently divides society into two parts, (1) the *euporoi* or *plousioi* and (2) the *aporoi* or *penētes*. These are usually translated into English as the "rich" and the "poor," but that, particularly the word "poor," is not exactly what Aristotle means. What he is driving at is, rather, a distinction between (1) those few individuals who have sufficient wealth so that they do not have to work for a living and (2) the vast majority of people, some of them far from poor, who are not permitted a life of leisure but must work for a living. Rather than rich and poor, therefore, I shall speak of the rich and the ordinary working people.[18]

When Aristotle says that in extreme democracy the mass of ordinary working people are master of the regime, he presumably means, at a minimum, that the regime is run in their interests. He also means, of course, that they ran it themselves. To begin with the first point, although Athens did look after the interests of the common man in many

18. J. Hemelrijk, "Penia en Ploutos" (Diss., Utrecht, 1925), 52–54, German summary, 140–142; Davies, *Wealth in Athens*, 10–11; M. I. Finley, *The Ancient Economy* (Berkeley, 1973), 41.

ways, it also displayed the greatest respect for property. An archon began his year in office by publicly proclaiming the security of private property (*Ath.Pol.* 56.2). What many rich men suffered in other fourth-century *poleis*, the redistribution of land and the cancellation of debt, was never raised as a possibility in fourth-century Athens. For every wealthy Athenian who complained about the high cost of liturgies, there was another who gladly paid for warships and choruses as a prudent investment in the goodwill of the people. Contrary to what Aristotle suggests, therefore, Athenian democracy did not neglect the interests of the *plousioi*.[19]

Nor would it be true to say that the common people manned the government, while the wealthy were shut out. We do not know the precise social composition of the Athenian assembly. Still, our sources indicate that many of the participants at an average assembly in the fourth century were working people, and they may have been in the majority. Beginning in the 390s, Athens compensated its assemblymen, or at least a generous quota of them, for their attendance. The original stipend of one obol was rapidly raised to three obols and had reached six obols (one drachma) by Aristotle's day, and even nine obols for the ten standing meetings with heavy agendas. Since, however, an unskilled laborer in the late fourth century could make nine obols a day, this stipend was no great inducement to working people, even if the expeditious could still hurry back after a meeting for a half-day's work. Nor were farmers excluded. The Attic plain was full of farms in antiquity, most of them a short walk to the assembly place on the Pnyx. Farmers are busy people, but even they have slow seasons, when they would have time to go into town. Even Xenophon's Socrates, who had doubts about democracy, says that the Assembly was made up of farmers, as well as of artisans and merchants (Xen. *Mem.* 3.7.6).[20]

Hence, many, maybe a majority, of the assembly-goers were ordinary

19. On the rich in and out of Athens, see G. E. M. de Ste. Croix, *The Class Struggle in the Ancient Greek World from the Archaic Age to the Arab Conquests* (Ithaca, N.Y., 1981), 295–300, 608 n. 55. On liturgies, J. K. Davies, *Athenian Propertied Families, 600–300 B.C.* (Oxford, 1971), xviii–xxiv.

20. On the composition of the Assembly, see M. I. Finley, "Athenian Demagogues," in *Studies in Ancient Society*, ed. M. I. Finley (London, 1974), 11–15; E. Kluwe, "Die soziale Zusammensetzung der athenischen Ekklesia und ihr Einfluss auf politische Entscheidungen," *Klio* 58 (1976): 298–314; id., "Nochmals zum Problem: Die soziale Zusammensetzung der athenischen Ekklesia und ihr Einfluss auf politische Entscheidungen," *Klio* 59 (1977): 45–81. On ecclesiastic pay, *Ath. Pol.* 41.3; Rhodes, *Commentary on* Athenaion Politeia ad loc. On the unskilled laborer, see Rhodes, *The Athenian Boule* (Oxford, 1972), 5 n. 4; on a half-day's work, Hansen, "The Duration of a Meeting of the Athenian *Ecclesia*," *Classical Philology* 74 (1979): 48–49 (= *Athenian* Ecclesia, 136–37); on farmers, Strauss, *Athens After the Peloponnesian War*, 59.

working people, but there is no reason to think that the poor or destitute predominated. Some farmers were present, and so, for that matter, were many wealthy men. As for the courts, jury pay had not kept up with Assembly pay and was still three obols in the late fourth century, as it had been since the 420s.[21] It was therefore less attractive than Assembly pay. I doubt that many ordinary working people found time for jury duty, except perhaps the elderly and the destitute, and I doubt that either of these two groups was numerous enough to dominate the proceedings.

To turn to another part of the government, the magistracies and probably the Council were officially closed to the lowest property class, the thetes. The law, however, was apparently simply not enforced, and in any case, many members of the next highest census class, the zeugites, were still relatively poor. It has often been argued that there was a bias toward the wealthy on the Council and in the magistracies, because service required a financial sacrifice. This argument is valid to a degree; nevertheless, given the small size of the citizen population, the restriction of service to men aged thirty or over, and the prohibition against serving more than twice, at least some ordinary men who could ill afford it indeed had to serve.[22]

If we turn to the orators and generals who led fourth-century Athens, however, the *aporoi* are even less in evidence. Almost down to a man, these leaders were all wealthy. Contrary to what Aristotle says, they were not kept out of the Assembly by their private affairs. It is true that most of these leaders no longer belonged to the grand old families that, down to the death of Pericles, had always run Athens—a fact that Aristotle notes (*Ath.Pol.* 28.1). This change of status, however, was not a change in wealth—an important fact that is sometimes obscured by the polemical nature of the sources. For instance, although Aristotle calls Cleophon a *lyropoios* (*Ath.Pol.* 28.3), we should understand that he was a wealthy man whose numerous slaves made lyres, and not himself a humble artisan.[23]

To sum up, there were many ordinary working Athenians in the Assembly, perhaps a majority. There were some, though fewer, in the

21. On jury pay, see *Ath. Pol.* 62.2; Rhodes "Athenian Democracy," 317.

22. On the exclusion of thetes, though only in theory, see *Ath. Pol.* 7.4; Rhodes, *Commentary on* Athenaion Politeia ad loc. On the bias toward the wealthy, see Jones, *Athenian Democracy*, 106; Rhodes, *Boule*, 5; on thirty as the minimum age for service, ibid., 1 n. 7; on the restriction of service, *Ath. Pol.* 62.3.

23. On the wealth of Athenian leaders, see S. Perlman, "The Politicians in the Athenian Democracy of the Fourth Century B.C.," *Athenaeum* n. s. 41 (1963): 332–36; id., "Political Leadership in Athens in the Fourth Century B.C.," *La parola del passato* 22 (1967): 162; Strauss, *Athens After the Peloponnesian War*, 4. On the change in status, see Rhodes, *Commentary on* Athenaion Politeia, 344–45; W. R. Connor, *The New Politicians of Fifth-Century Athens* (Princeton, 1971), 151–62.

courts. Perhaps representing a smaller proportion, some of the magistrates and councillors were ordinary working people. On the other hand, virtually all of the orators and generals were wealthy men. Aristotle's statement, therefore, that in an extreme democracy the mass of the ordinary working people controlled the regime needs to be qualified in the case of Athens. In fact, the Athenian regime demonstrated in many ways a blending of the many and the few.

Aristotle makes much of the demagogues, popular leaders who mislead the people into subverting the rule of law and into tyrannizing the "best citizens," those men of wealth and status whom Aristotle would prefer to have rule (*Pol.* 1292a7–30). In some classical sources, *dēmagōgos* is a neutral term for orator or politician, but in Aristotle it is usually pejorative. Aristotle faults the Athenian demagogues, the leaders ever since Pericles' death in 429, both for not coming from the old aristocracy and for corrupting the people, whether with state pay or with violent, abusive, or even obscene behavior. He singles out the late fifth-century leaders Cleon and Cleophon and then dismisses all of fourth-century Athens' leaders "collectively and anonymously," as Rhodes puts it.[24] "After Cleophon," Aristotle writes, "there was an unbroken series of demagogues whose main aim was to be outrageous and please the people with no thought for anything but the present" (*Ath.Pol.* 28.4).

This blanket dismissal consigns Demosthenes and Aeschines, Lycurgus and Hyperides, and even Thrasybulus, the man who saved Athens from the Thirty in 403, to the same uncritical scorn. Aristotle accuses Athens' leaders of being unable to think of the future, but many of the surviving political speeches discuss the long-term consequences of current actions. He accuses the demagogues of flattering the people, although Cleon and Demosthenes, for example, castigate their audiences for weakness, apathy, and cowardice. One man's demagogue is another man's hero; alas, Aristotle does an injustice to the methods and achievements of some of the ancient city-state's greatest leaders.[25]

Aristotle's account of Athenian democracy, therefore, is supported by an examination of neither its participants nor its leaders. The surviving population statistics of fourth-century Athens similarly argue against the picture of a regime dominated by the mass of ordinary working people. Recent research has focused on the demographic consequences of the

24. Rhodes, *Commentary on* Athenaion Politeia, 357. On Aristotle's terminology, ibid., 323–24; more generally, see Finley, "Athenian Demagogues," in *Ancient Society*, ed. Finley, 1–25.

25. On the long-term consequences of actions, see, for example, Thuc. 3.40.7, 3.44.3, 3.47.1–5; Dem. 3.8, 4.15, 4.50; Aeschin. 1.192, 2.183. On the leaders' castigation of their audiences, see, for instance, Thuc. 3.37.1–2, 3.38.4–39.1; Dem. 3.21; 4.2, 11, 17, 20, 40–2; 9.5.

Peloponnesian War, which had a significant effect on fourth-century Athenian democracy, especially in the immediate postwar period (404–386 B.C.). As great as were the casualties incurred by hoplites, those of the thetes were even greater. By 405, a good part of the political power of the thetic class was at the bottom of the Aegean. These losses in population have much to do with the comparative quiescence of the postwar *dēmos*, which treated former oligarchs moderately and generously.[26]

As recent work by Hansen, Rhodes, Ruschenbusch, and myself demonstrates, informed, if rough, estimates of Athenian population are worth attempting. Such estimates can be drawn from a detailed reexamination of ancient accounts of battle and plague losses. I, for example, argue that although there were approximately as many hoplites as thetes (counting only men of draft age who were fit for military service) in 431 (about 20,000 each), thetes suffered over twice as many casualties in the Peloponnesian War (more than 12,000 compared with more than 5,000). Moreover, hoplites suffered nearly all of their casualties before 412; thetes very few before 415 and nearly half after 413. While hoplites, therefore, suffered little during the primarily naval battles of the Ionian War, thetes were devastated. By the beginning of the fourth century, out of a total of 14,000–16,000 Athenian citizens, there were on the order of 9,000 hoplites and 5,000–7,000 thetes. Hoplites therefore outnumbered thetes by at least 20 percent.[27]

Some eighty years later, by 322, the citizen population had risen considerably, by one third or more, to 21,000. We know that in the oligarchy established in that year, 12,000 poorer citizens were disenfranchised, 9,000 wealthier citizens left with full rights. It is interesting that while the poorer classes replenished their numbers during the fourth century, a solid core of the population prospered. A country in which 40 percent of the citizenry are prosperous enough to hold the franchise in an oligarchy

26. Strauss, *Athens After the Peloponnesian War*, 70–86, 173, 179–82.
27. Ibid.; M. H. Hansen, "Demographic Reflections on the Number of Athenian Citizens, 451–309 B.C.," *American Journal of Ancient History* 7 (1982): 172–84; id., *Demography and Democracy; The Number of Athenian Citizens in the Fourth Century B. C.* (Herning, Denmark, 1986); Rhodes, "Ephebi, Bouleutae and the Population of Athens," *Zeitschrift für Papyrologie und Epigraphik* 38 (1980): 191–201; id., "More Members Serving Twice in the Athenian Boule," *ZPE* 41 (1981): 101–2; id., "Members Serving in the Athenian Boule and the Population of Athens Again," *ZPE* 57 (1984): 200–202; E. Ruschenbusch, *Athenische Innenpolitik im 5. Jahrhundert v. Chr.* (Bamberg, 1979); id., "Die soziale Herkunft der Epheben um 330," *ZPE* 35 (1979): 173–76; id., "Die soziale Zusammensetzung des Rates der 500 in Athen im 5. Jh.," *ZPE* 35 (1979): 173–80; id., "Epheben, Buleuten, und die Bürgerzahl von Athen um 330 v. Chr.," *ZPE* 44 (1981): 103–5; id., "Noch Einmal die Bürgerzahl Athens um 330 v. Chr.," *ZPE* 44 (1981): 110–12; id., "Zum letzten Mal: Die Bürgerzahl Athens im 4. Jh. v. Chr.," *ZPE* 54 (1984): 253–69. On the difficulties of equating army figures and population figures, see Hansen, *Demography and Democracy*, 16–21.

is not a country that would be run solely in the interest of the mass of ordinary working people.[28]

A broad selection of evidence, therefore, from constitutional, institutional, political, social, and demographic history all points in the same direction: contrary to Aristotle, fourth-century Athens was not an extreme democracy, by Aristotle's own definition. Its leaders were not mindless demagogues. Although a significant percentage of the members of the Assembly and the courts were ordinary working people, it is by no means clear that they were in the majority, especially not in the courts. Many councillors and magistrates were ordinary working people, but the wealthy were overrepresented. Virtually all of the prominent orators and generals were wealthy men. Nor is it true that the power of ordinary working people in the government increased throughout the fourth century. On the contrary, for the sake of efficiency, the administration of finance, military matters, and public building became less democratic over the course of the century. The elitist council of the Areopagus, dormant since the 460s, acquired considerable influence in the late fourth century. Aristotle, unfortunately, omits these developments in his analysis.

Aristotle is correct when he writes that most of the business of government was done by decree rather than by law, but he needs to put this into perspective. Contemporary Athenian orators expressed considerable respect for the rule of law. The Athenian constitution recognized the distinction between law and decree, and it contained a separate procedure for *nomothesia*. That this procedure does not seem to have been commonly used, that most public business was done by decree, is beside the point. Rather, it is in the nature of politics that most decisions involve temporary matters, not fundamental principles. Indeed, Athens' historical experience had demonstrated that it was better to leave the fundamental law of the land untouched than to change it frequently. Despite the rule of so-called demagogues, fourth-century Athens enjoyed a stable democratic constitution for eighty years—no small achievement in the turbulent political atmosphere of classical Greece—until an oligarchy was imposed by the Macedonian conqueror in 321.

28. On the oligarchy, see Plut. *Phoc.* 28; *contra* Diod. Sic. 18.18.5, who says 22,000 citizens lost their rights. Ruschenbusch makes the case for Plutarch (see articles in *ZPE* listed in the previous note) convincingly, if perhaps with unwarranted certainty (see J. M. Williams, "Solon's Class System, the Manning of Athens's Fleet, and the Number of Athenian Thetes in the Late Fourth Century," *Zeitschrift für Papyrologie und Epigraphik* 52 [1983]: 241–45). Even if Diodorus is right, however, fourth-century Athens still seems to have had a substantial propertied class, with 29 percent of the citizens qualifying for an oligarchy. For the case for Diodorus' figures, see most recently Hansen, *Demography and Democracy*, 28–36.

In short, Aristotle exaggerates the power of the ordinary, uneducated, self-interested working people in the Athens in which he lived. He is right to say that the people rule in Athens, but he underestimates their respect for law and the willingness of the ordinary working people to share power with the wealthy. It has been argued that fourth-century Athens should be called a moderate, rather than an extreme, democracy. This is a step in the right direction, but it would be better still to dispense with this terminology altogether. To label the fourth-century Athenian regime properly, it would be necessary to rethink Athenian history as a whole, an enterprise beyond the scope of this essay. In the meantime, though, we can assign the much-criticized fourth-century democracy a provisional title that it richly deserves: constitutional democracy.[29]

The question still remains of why Aristotle's analysis of Athenian democracy is off base. There are, I believe, three main reasons; to understand them, it is necessary first to consider important biographical data. To begin with, Aristotle's own experience of thirty-one years in Athens contained bad as well as good. He may have felt respect and admiration for the city that had more than justified Pericles' claim that it was the "school of Hellas," and that was certainly the Greek world's center of philosophy, the city in which Aristotle had studied in the Academy and established his own school of the Lyceum. Athens, however, was also the city that had executed Socrates, to which Aristotle is said to have alluded as follows upon his flight to Chalcis in 323: "I will not let the Athenians offend twice against philosophy" (Diog. Laert. 5.9). For all his years in Athens, Aristotle was not a citizen—indeed, it was extraordinarily difficult for anyone to become an Athenian citizen—he was a metic. He is quoted as saying that it was "perilous [for an alien] to live in Athens."[30]

Moreover, far from being removed from the political events of the day, the bulk of the evidence suggests that Aristotle was sympathetic to Macedon's rise to power in the Greek world, which made him an opponent of the dominant tendency in Athenian foreign policy from 348 on. The most important facts are as follows. Aristotle was born in Stagira, in the Chalcidice. The major regional power, the Chalcidian League, was an oligarchy. His father, Nicomachus, was physician and adviser to the Macedonian king Amyntas III and died a wealthy man. In the 340s Aris-

29. Hansen, *Sovereignty of the People's Court*, 59–61. Cf. Sealey, *Athenian Republic*, 146, who calls Athens a republic; B. Strauss, "Athenian Democracy: Neither Radical, Extreme, Nor Moderate," *Ancient History Bulletin* 1.6 (1987), 127–29.

30. Sources for the quotation: *Vita Marciana* 421, *Vita Vulgata* 20, *Vita Latina* 44; for biographical details, see J. Lynch, *Aristotle's School* (Princeton, 1971), 93–94.

totle was employed for six years as tutor to King Philip's son Alexander. A decade later, Alexander took two of Aristotle's nephews, Callisthenes and Nicanor, on his expedition against Persia; they served respectively as an official historian and a general. Meanwhile, Aristotle had become a close friend of the man whom Alexander left behind to govern Macedonia and keep watch on Greece—the formidable Antipater, who would be the executor of Aristotle's last will and testament. Aristotle left behind correspondence with Philip, Alexander, and Antipater, although little of it survives today.[31]

Aristotle also had close ties to the tyrant of Atarneus in the Troad, one Hermias, in whose kingdom he lived for three years following his departure from Athens in 348. Aristotle advised Hermias in statecraft, married his adopted daughter, and after Hermias' death at the hands of the Persians memorialized him in a lyric poem and in an inscription for Hermias' cenotaph at Delphi.[32]

Aristotle first came to Athens to study in 367 and did not leave until 348; he did not return until 335, and stayed until his exile in 323. It has usually been thought that Aristotle left Athens in 348 following the death of Plato and Aristotle's failure to be chosen his successor as head of the Academy. It has been plausibly argued, however, that Aristotle was constrained to leave before Plato's death (redated to early 347) because of the anti-Macedonian sentiment following Philip's destruction of Olynthus. It is certainly striking that Aristotle did not return to Athens until 335, when Alexander had just put down an anti-Macedonian rebellion in the Greek city-states, and that he left Athens again precisely in 323, when the news of Alexander's death occasioned a second anti-Macedonian revolt (the Lamian War). He was under attack by the "demagogues" Demophilus and Himeraeus, both perhaps the well-known anti-Macedonian politicians of those names. In addition to alluding in 323 to Socrates' fate, Aristotle also complained of the difficulty of being a metic in Athens and of the dangers posed by the sycophants (professional informers).[33]

31. On interpreting the biographical details, see A.-H. Chroust, "Aristotle's Flight from Athens in the Year 323 B.C.," *Historia* 15 (1966): 185–92; id., "Aristotle and Athens: Some Comments on Aristotle's Sojourn in Athens," *Laval théologique et philosophique* 22 (1966): 186–96; id., "Aristotle Returns to Athens in the Year 335 B.C.," *Laval Théologique et Philosophique* 23 (1967): 244–54; id., "Aristotle Leaves the Academy," *Greece and Rome* 14 (1967): 39–43; id., *Aristotle: New Light on His Life and on Some of His Lost Works* (London, 1973), 83–176. Cf. Lord's sceptical view of Aristotle's position as tutor to Alexander in *The Politics of Aristotle*, 4–5. On Chalcidice, see M. Zahrnt, *Olynth und die Chalkidier* (Munich, 1971), 94, 242.

32. E. Barker, *The Politics of Aristotle*, (New York, 1972), xv–xvii.

33. For these details of Aristotle's life, see the works of Chroust listed in note 31 above. For Demophilus and Himeraeus, see Davies, *Athenian Propertied Families*, nos. 3455, 13346.

The picture that emerges, therefore, is of a wealthy man who came from a *polis* nearly 1,000 miles away from Athens. He had inherited a connection to the Macedonian royal court, which he energetically pursued, thus placing himself in opposition to the political tendency that dominated Athens for most of his adult life. On the other hand, Aristotle may have felt considerable affection for the city in which he spent thirty-one of his sixty-one years, the mother city of philosophy. It has been suggested that he pleaded Athens' case to Alexander after his former pupil had put down that city's revolt in 335. Aristotle had, therefore, a singular record of proximity to and distance from Athens; he was insider and outsider, friend and enemy. All of this leads us back to Aristotle's analysis of Athenian democracy and to his exaggerated emphasis on its extremism.[34]

We must remember first that Aristotle had both rhetorical and philosophical reasons to paint the defects of Athenian democracy in broad strokes. The Athenian citizens whom he met at the Academy and Lyceum tended to be men who were thoroughly disillusioned with democracy. To reach them, it made sense for Aristotle to speak their language, a language critical of the Athenian regime.[35]

This seems all the more compelling when one remembers Aristotle's interest in leading his students away from democracy. Aristotle's boyhood years were spent in a region dominated by oligarchy and monarchy, his student years in the anti-democratic atmosphere of Plato's Academy, and some of his years outside of Athens as the servant and friend of king, prince, tyrant, and aristocrat. The *Politics* makes it clear that Aristotle's ideal state was one of leisured, well-educated gentlemen; his second-best state was a "polity,"—a democracy in some respects, but one run by men of moderate landed wealth, the hoplites, and not by the common man. Aristotle had, therefore, little reason to go out of his way to highlight the saving graces of what he considered to be an essentially bad regime—Athenian democracy.[36]

34. On Aristotle's pleading Athens' case, see Chroust, "Aristotle Returns to Athens," 248–49. On the other hand, Alexander had solid reasons of realpolitik to be lenient to Athens: his desires for a quiet home front and for the support of the Athenian fleet during his invasion of the Persian empire (not to mention the difficulty of besieging Athens). See R. L. Fox, *Alexander the Great* (London, 1973), 89.

35. On the philosophic schools and democracy, see J. K. Davies, *Democracy and Classical Greece* (Glasgow, 1978), 198.

36. On the gentlemen, see C. Lord, *Education and Culture in the Political Thought of Aristotle* (Ithaca, N.Y., and London, 1982), 32, 200; on "polity", *Pol.* 1279b1–3, 1293b22–1294b41, 1295b1–1296b3, 1296b34–1297a13, 1302a13–15; and Barker, Politics *of Aristotle,* 151 n. GG. To be sure, in writing the *Athēnaiōn Politeia* Aristotle consulted an admirable variety of sources (Rhodes, *Commentary on* Athenaion Politeia, 15–37), but his interpretation of those sources demonstrates a critical appraisal of contemporary Athenian institutions.

The third reason stems from Aristotle's twenty-five-year opposition to Athenian policy toward Macedon and the consequent precariousness of his position in Athens. It is not surprising that he held Athens' leaders in low regard. It is not surprising that he considered Athens an extreme democracy, governed by low birth, low income, and vulgarity (*ageneia, penia, banausia Pol.* 1318b40–41, bracketed by some editors). It is not surprising that he would have preferred to empower an elite of educated gentlemen, who would have neither squandered Athens' resources on a war with Macedon nor persecuted philosophy. Moreover, he was not alone in this position. In the 350s and 340s, Isocrates had advocated a more elitist government for Athens under the title of Areopagite or ancestral constitution. Like Aristotle, he too courted the Macedonian king Philip, and so, for that matter, did the head of the Academy, Speusippus. Many, if not most, of Athens' leading intellectuals had broken with democracy and were in favor of Macedonian hegemony.[37]

Bad regimes sometimes carry out good policies. From Aristotle's point of view, however, this was not the case with Athenian democracy in the third quarter of the fourth century B.C. Not only was Athens an inherently imperfect regime, but it was pursuing a disastrous foreign policy and, worst of all, persecuting at home its greatest glory—philosophy. Consequently, Aristotle constructed a description of the Athenian regime that emphasized and exaggerated its worst features and did little justice to its best.

Why did Aristotle not describe an Athens that, as I have argued here, historical research indicates was a better, stabler, and more law-abiding regime than he says? One could accuse Aristotle of wearing ideological blinders, but I think it is both more charitable and more appropriate to his genius to emphasize the rhetorical nature of his work. Aristotle wished to teach others what he already knew, that Athenian democracy was inherently bad and bound to pursue mistaken policies. There was no need to tarry over this or that island of good government in a vast sea of corruption.

Let me close by returning to two of my earliest points. First, the ancient Greek historian does not go to Aristotle for a comprehensive discussion of Athenian democracy. Other points of view and other texts must also be taken into account. By the same token, however—and this is the second point—neither does the historian dismiss Aristotle as a mere polemicist. It is typical of Aristotle's honesty and genius that he himself provides the categories that allow us to analyze both Athenian democracy and his own work.

37. On Aristotle and Macedon, see the works of Chroust listed in note 31 above. On Athenian intellectuals and Macedon, see M. M. Markle III, "Support of Athenian Intellectuals for Philip," *Journal of Hellenic Studies* 96 (1976): 80–99.

Aristotle provides the student of democracy with, among other things, (1) an analysis of the stages of democracy, (2) a specific history of the development of the Athenian democracy, (3) an account of the workings of the Athenian regime in his day, (4) a typology of different democratic regimes, (5) a carefully constructed dichotomy between the rule of law and the rule of men, (6) a sociology of the opposition between the rich and the ordinary working people, and (7) an analysis of the basic principles of democracy and their inherent virtues and vices. Aristotle's analysis of Athenian democracy is, according to his own categories, skewed. Aristotle was not writing in a vacuum, however. To understand why his strictures against Athenian democracy are exaggerated, one must understand both his rhetorical purpose and his position in the political history of the Athens of his day.

The student of democracy today must read Aristotle, and not for mere antiquarian interest nor to sneer at his errors about Athens, but to appreciate the power of his analysis and to respond to his critique. Aristotle's critique of Athens is a challenge to reevaluate the meaning of our democratic heritage.

NINE

Law and the Regime in Aristotle

Richard Bodéüs

Toward the end of a recent study devoted to the relationship between ethics and politics in Aristotle, I called attention to the statements opening the last book of the *Politics,* according to which the legislator must supervise the education of the young or jeopardize the city's regime.[1] Situated on the threshold of a discussion that seems as if it ought to be the culmination of Aristotle's investigation of political matters, these statements underline the extent to which the viability of a regime and hence the permanence of the only institutional frameworks within which man as political animal can attain happiness require a condition of well-ordered law (*eunomia*).[2]

One may even wonder whether, after all, the concern to ensure the maintenance of existing regimes should not in Aristotle's view take clear precedence over the preoccupation with establishing a perfect constitution. In any case, it was the refusal to yield to the temptations of idealism that led the philosopher himself to take into consideration the historical experience of certain cities held in high repute in his own day. Aristotle saw clearly that the experience of these cities shed light on the causes of the destruction of the different regimes and thus could be used to identify the means that might make it possible to avoid such destruction. This is the purpose of the fifth book of the *Politics.* The work of Raymond Weil has shown to what extent this part of the *Politics* derives from the investigations undertaken by Aristotle of the constitutions of the Greek cities.[3] I have pointed out elsewhere that the four types of regimes ana-

Translations from the Greek, in quotations, are mine.

1. *Pol.* 1337a11–13. See R. Bodéüs, *Le philosophe et la cité: Recherches sur les rapports entre morale et politique dans la pensée d'Aristote* (Paris, 1982), 221.
2. On the notion of *eunomia*, see *Pol.* 1294a4.
3. R. Weil, *Aristote et l'histoire: Essai sur la "Politique"* (Paris, 1960).

lyzed in *Politics* 5 correspond exactly to the four groups of constitutions surveyed in Aristotle's historical investigations, according to the ancient catalogues of his works.[4]

Since Werner Jaeger, the tendency has been to see the importance of mere historical data in that part of the *Politics* as the mark as it were of the positivist spirit of Aristotle's later years, when he was interested in what is and not what ought to be.[5] But it would be a mistake to think that Aristotle had abandoned all normative argumentation when he took in hand this part of the *Politics*. The very idea that it is necessary to "preserve" constitutions—which is behind the whole investigation[6]—should suffice as a caution against such a hasty conclusion. It is true that *Politics* 5 presents itself in the final analysis as a technical manual for the use of any and all governments. In this respect, it resembles (something I think has not been sufficiently noticed) the technical treatises on rhetoric, which teach the means of persuasion while remaining largely indifferent to the moral quality of the theses that are to be defended. In analogous fashion, Aristotle forces himself in *Politics* 5 to indicate the means suitable for preserving a tyranny or democracy, an oligarchy or aristocracy. This is not to say that he holds these regimes as equivalent with respect to goodness. It is simply that what we might call the moral point of view is ignored. It is the rule of the genre. In India, for example, there exists a very rich literature in which moral and religious preoccupations are totally absent, and the sole aim is to ensure effectiveness in all practical areas of life, particularly in politics. One finds entire books of maxims of a pragmatic realism that is worthy of Machiavelli and Hobbes; but their authors abstain from pronouncing on the obligations prescribed by religious duty not out of philosophic immorality or amorality, but because they simply opted to suspend all moral judgment from the moment they engaged themselves in inquiries from another point of view. Something similar appears to have happened when Aristotle composed the fifth book of the *Politics*.

Nevertheless, some will not be able to resist objecting that Aristotle would certainly not have gone to so much trouble to survey the means that permit any sort of regime to last if he had not judged that every form of regime is worth preserving up to a certain point. The objection is not without merit; for, in Aristotle's view, every form of constitution

4. R. Bodéüs, "La recherche politique d'après le 'programme' de *L'Éthique à Nicomaque* d'Aristote," *Études classiques* 51 (1983): 23–33.

5. W. Jaeger, *Aristotle: Fundamentals of the History of His Development*, trans. R. Robinson, 2d ed. (Oxford, 1948), 263–65.

6. The study of the causes of revolution in the first part of *Politics* 5 is conducted in a way that determines the discussion in the second part of the means enabling one to avoid revolutions.

has some value; and even if one has less than another, its preservation almost always appears to him as a good (or a lesser evil) in relation to the harm occasioned by a radical change in regime and the disruption this brings in customs, which are the source of obedience to the laws.

This question, which involves the entire issue of Aristotelian realism, I have dealt with elsewhere.[7] Having insisted there on the duration of political regimes as a condition of morality, I would like now to emphasize the extent to which morality in turn—or better, education—is for Aristotle a condition of the duration of regimes. Above all, I am concerned to show that the indifference to the city's perfection displayed by Aristotle in his discussion of the varieties of regimes is the reverse side of his scrupulous attention to the legislative arrangements in every area that accompany (or do not accompany) each regime. To do this, I appeal in the first place to the criticisms directed by Aristotle, in *Politics* 2, at his predecessors and at famous legislators. On the basis of these remarks relating to failed legislation (failed in the sense that it contributes to the deterioration or even the overthrow of the political regime it ought to serve), I hope to bring to light the requirements of rationality imposed by Aristotle on the legislator and, at the same time, the priority that he attributes to measures bearing on moral education. The reader should then see that the principle of the constitutionality of the laws that Aristotle in effect invokes in *Politics* 5, when he recommends education in the spirit of the regime as a means of preserving the regime, is also presupposed in the analysis of *Politics* 2.[8] This is, it may be added, one of the most remarkable continuities in the *Politics*.

Nowhere in the course of the *Politics* is Aristotle's discussion really intended to recommend in absolute terms one particular form of constitution among those known to the Greek tradition. Aristotle is more inclined to favor a type of regime that—like the one instituted by Solon at Athens[9]—combines in judicious fashion the characteristics of different regimes. The perfection of a constitution, in his view, is a measure of the number of distinct characteristics of which it is composed.[10]

Aristotle's idea in recommending such a "mixture" of features proper

7. R. Bodéüs, "La durée des régimes politiques comme condition de la morale selon Aristote," in *Justifications de l'éthique*, Actes du XIXe Congrès de l'Association des sociétés de philosophies de langue française (Brussels and Louvain-la-Neuve, 1984), 103–8.

8. The principle of the constitutionality of laws as formulated in *Pol.* 1282b10–11; cf. 1289a13–15; for Aristotle's recommendation of education in the spirit of the regime as a means of preserving the regime, see *Pol.* 1310a12ff., cf. 1308b20–24, 1337a11–17.

9. Ibid. 1273b35–41.

10. "The more numerous the elements, the better the constitution" (*Pol.* 1266a4–5). Cf. G. J. D. Aalders, *La "Politique" d'Aristote* (Vandoeuvres-Genève, 1965), 201–37.

to different political regimes is to ensure as far as possible the preservation of the city in its constitutional integrity. Each political tendency being satisfied in its aspirations, the regime ensures its own safety, Aristotle says, in that "no part of the city would wish for another regime."[11] The harmonious equilibrium of what one may call the mixed regime is then evidently not, for Aristotle, an end in itself. It is the condition most apt to guarantee the duration of fundamental political institutions. What the philosopher demands above all of a city with regard to its constitution is that it be stable and lasting, sheltered as far as possible from changes that would bring its dissolution in the process of transforming it. I mentioned just above that the requirement of duration responds to the concern to guarantee in this way the condition without which man as political animal could not develop the habits necessary for the acquisition of virtue. In this connection, the form (aristocratic, oligarchic, or democratic) of a constitution matters less to Aristotle than the factors ensuring its stability. The "mixture" of features proper to different regimes is precisely a factor of this sort, among others that are available to the legislator. Aristotle is particularly sensitive to the responsibilities and mission of the legislator relative to protecting the regime. This is the thrust of numerous and readily identifiable remarks in Book 2 of the *Politics*.

Before beginning a critical examination of the constitutions of Sparta, Crete, and Carthage, Aristotle indicates the double intention that is ordinarily involved in the investigation of virtually all constitutions: the one, he says, "whether some aspect of the legislation is fine or not with respect to the best arrangement; the other, whether it is opposed to the presupposition and the mode of the regime they actually have."[12] It is important to pay attention to the distinction between the points of view sketched here by Aristotle. It implies, in effect, that for Aristotle the quality of a political regime can be understood in two ways, which are not necessarily linked. On the one hand, a particular regime is judged to be in conformity or not with the best arrangements that are possible in regulating the social existence of the citizens. On the other hand, it is a question of the adequacy of the institutions in place relative to the end

11. *Pol.* 1294b38–40. What is at issue above all in this passage is the equilibrium between the two principle political tendencies confronting one another in the fourth century, the democratic and the oligarchic tendency.

12. *Pol.* 1269a31–34. The Greek word *hypothesis* (translated here "presupposition") refers in this context to the ensemble of principles on which the legislator has chosen to base the constitution and which, from that time, determines its orientation. The same word elsewhere (*Pol.* 1325b35–36) designates the conditions required for the establishment of a perfect city (size of the territory, number of citizens, etc.). See P. N. M. Thiel, "Die Bedeutung des Wortes *Hypothesis* bei Aristoteles" (Diss., Freiburg, Fulda, 1919).

that the regime pursues and that serves as its fundamental principle or distinctive characteristic. Ideally, the best city in absolute terms should fulfill this double condition.[13] Failing this, one is entitled to regard as relatively good both the regime that aims at the best end that exists, even if it does not possess the institutions that would permit it to attain this end, and the regime all of whose institutions are in accord with the principle of its constitution, even if this principle does not coincide with the best that can be conceived. Of these two regimes, however, the first exists only in theory (for in reality it will pursue the end at which its institutions aim, as we shall see), while the second offers all the necessary guarantees for enduring once it is established. Leaving aside, then, the constitution that is perfect in every respect, the existence of which is a function of so many requirements that it is practically impossible for the legislator to create it, the latter is the one that will occupy Aristotle's attention.

Interpreters have tended to ignore this fact in explicating *Politics* 2, and more serious still, to misunderstand Aristotle's concerns regarding both the project of a perfect constitution and that of a constitution that is relatively good, in the sense that it succeeds in adjusting its legal arrangements to the principle of the regime.[14] To imagine that in *Politics* 2 Aristotle undertakes a study with the aim of determining the imperfections of existing regimes relative to an ideal constitution that he has in mind to elaborate is to impute to him an intention that, in any event, goes beyond the immediate intention. As we have seen, Aristotle aims rather at detailing the relative qualities of different political regimes, by either confronting their respective presuppositions with the best presuppositions or confronting these same presuppositions with their own institutions and laws. What is more, the second of these confrontations seems to have decided priority over the first, as one can see in the discussion of the constitution of Sparta. Aristotle notes clearly what it is that disqualifies the "hypothesis" on which the Spartan regime rests (its tendency to cultivate only military virtue), but he does so only incidentally and in the track of Plato.[15] Almost his entire critique (from 1269a34 to 1271b19), if one ex-

13. Let us recall that, for Aristotle, such a city is one that defines the excellence of the citizen in such a way that it coincides strictly with the excellence of the good man (*Pol.* 1277aff.). It is no doubt his thought of establishing this coincidence that leads to Aristotle's proposal, in *Politics* 7–8, of a program of education for a city that corresponds to "what one would pray for" (*kat'euchēn*). See Bodéüs, *Le philosophe et la cité*, 89ff.

14. Cf. J. Aubonnet, *Aristote: Politique, livres I et II* (Paris, 1968), 157 n. 4: "In this chapter Aristotle discusses the constitutions existing in states that are called well governed and pursues the same critical method [as in the preceding treatment of Plato]: he wants above all to point out the faults to be avoided *when what is at issue, as in his own case, is the construction of an ideal state*" (emphasis added).

15. *Pol.* 1270b41–1271b1: "Moreover, one may criticize the presupposition of the legislator, in the way Plato criticizes it in the *Laws*." (See, for instance, *Laws* 625e, 660a, 688a, 705d; cf. *Pol.* 1324b8–9).

cepts the incidental remark we have just cited, has to do with an im-
pressive set of institutions, sanctioned in most cases by law, the disagreement, contradiction, or inconsistency of which (in terms of the principles
that properly define the Lacedaemonian constitution) he goes to considerable lengths to emphasize. Unless I am mistaken, we have proof here
that our philosopher, when called on to judge the qualities of a political
regime, tended to place the accent, first and foremost, on the conformity
of its laws with the orientation of its constitution. Such a requirement,
which Aristotle underlines here over several pages, corresponds to one
he elsewhere expressly asserts as follows: "Laws should be enacted—and
all are in fact enacted—with a view to the regimes, and not regimes with
a view to the laws." [16] And, behind the requirement that one may call the
constitutionality of the laws, there undoubtedly lies concealed the principal practical request addressed by Aristotle to the politicians of his time.

Everyone is aware of the "reformist" color of Aristotle's thought, to
which the entire *Politics* is testimony. [17] Everyone remembers in particular
his opposition to Plato's dream of the establishment of a radical commu-
nism involving women, children, and property; Aristotle argues that the
prevailing mode of property ownership is better, "if provided with the
adornment of character and an arrangement of correct laws." [18] Who
knows whether the realism of Aristotle's objection to Plato's *Republic* did
not figure to some degree in the considerations that moved Plato to write
the *Laws*, thus not only giving more flexibility to his political project but
also, and above all, placing it under the sign of legislation of the most
comprehensive sort? [19] However this may be, Aristotle was probably inclined to judge that the good most accessible to existing cities that desire
improvement is to be found in the conformity of their laws to the principles of their respective constitutions. He must therefore also have
thought that the most urgent task for legislators interested in the betterment of their own cities was to strive for such conformity.

This is, it seems to me, the great lesson one learns from a reading of
Book 2 of the *Politics*. Aristotle there denounces the faults of famous
cities as so many aberrations, capable, at the extreme, of bringing ruin
on the regimes that they seem to support so successfully. But such critiques contain the implicit invitation to remedy the faults and, in so

16. *Pol.* 1289a13–15.

17. Cf. G. D. Contogiorgis, *La théorie des révolutions chez Aristote* (Paris, 1978), 250.

18. *Pol.* 1263a22–24. Aristotle's reformism, as one sees it in this passage, aims at an
enhancement of morality by means of the laws. If the establishment of a moral order necessarily requires a reform of legislation (cf. *Eth. Nic.* 10.10), one can understand why for
Aristotle the teaching of morality is a concern in the first instance of legislators in positions
of power (cf. Bodéüs, *Le philosophe et la cité*, 95ff.).

19. See on this question *Pol.* 1263b36–40, with my article "Pourquoi Platon a-t-il com-
posé les *Lois*?" *Études classiques* 53 (1985): 367ff.

doing, to aim at a more durable success, one guaranteed in turn by legislation. It is thus the case that Aristotle held legislation to be the principal
instrument for the betterment of cities, with the understanding that legislation coincides with the activation of means designed to ensure a
longer duration for the regime of which they are characteristic.

If one takes a closer look, one sees that Aristotle's criticism has as its
target two distinct things. On the one hand, it deals with actually existing
laws that, in his view, undermine constitutional principles. On the other,
it focuses on what is left out of the legislation, which risks damaging the
integrity of the constitution. In the latter case, what is involved are omissions to remedy; in the former, mistakes to correct. Both, in the final
analysis, carry the same potential danger: the eventual deterioration of
the political regime, with all the misfortunes that would bring to the city
as a whole.

What follows is a sampling of the most significant objections that Aristotle formulates on the subject of the legislative arrangements existing in
certain cities that seem to him more or less incompatible with the foundations of the constitutional order of those cities.

In Sparta's case, Aristotle takes exception to the laxity of the laws dealing with private property, which had allowed the concentration of estates in the hands of a few. "This too was poorly arranged in the laws,"
he says.[20] Wealth being above all a function of landed property, Aristotle
saw that the situation created by such laws tended to increase dangerously the number of poor persons in the city. He also understood that
other laws, designed to encourage births, had reinforced this same tendency,[21] since the demographic growth was not accompanied by a redistribution of estates. Now the tendency in question consists in augment-
ing the weight of the popular or democratic element in a city that,
constitutionally, is neither popular nor democratic. Further, the law concerning admission to the ephorate, declaring everyone eligible for this
magistracy, had also contributed to entrusting the sovereign function at
Sparta to the poorer citizens. The result was harmful to the constitution.
"From an aristocracy," Aristotle remarks, "it has become a democracy."[22]

Regarding Carthage, Aristotle observes that a good number of the
laws contravene the aristocratic and republican principles on which the
regime is based. "Some features," he says, "incline toward the people,
others toward oligarchy."[23] The latter—which require that wealth as well

20. *Pol.* 1270a18–19; cf. 1333b23.
21. Ibid. 1269b39ff.
22. Ibid. 1270b16–17. On the other hand, Sparta seems, in inconsistent fashion, to
have encouraged a plutocratic tendency as well, and its laws regarding public finance are
denounced by Aristotle as having "created a city lacking in funds, and individuals greedy
for them" (1271b16–17).
23. *Pol.* 1273a5–6.

as merit be taken into account in filling the offices, particularly the highest ones—seem to Aristotle the most important. Such a deviation counts, in Aristotle's eyes, as an "error of the legislator." And the responsibility for this denaturing of aristocracy in fact belongs to law, for the law regarding offices "makes wealth something more honored than virtue." [24]

The criticisms we have just reviewed focus on two cities, both of which appear to have broken, though in different ways, with the principle of the same regime, aristocracy, which professes to honor virtue above all else and accordingly possesses an undoubted claim to perfection. [25] But one feels that Aristotle's disappointment with the decay in the Spartan and Carthaginian regimes does not derive from the fact that these regimes are perfect in principle; in his view they are not. What he deplores instead is the inconsistency in legislation, which gives rise to a transformation of the political regime that the laws are designed to serve or produces effects opposite to those intended. In short, what Aristotle objects to are the contradictions inherent in a system of laws.

The irrationality of the system or the incoherence of the legislator can take different forms. This is clear in the case of Sparta. The Lacedaemonian constitution in its essence exhibited the advantages of a mixed regime—that is, it contained certain democratic traits in spite of the dominance of aristocratic ones. An arrangement decidedly democratic in spirit that existed in the laws of Sparta from their very origin was that regulating the common meals. Aristotle considers it an aberration, not because of the intentions of the legislator (on the contrary), but because, being poorly conceived, it ended by producing results that were entirely opposed to democracy. "The support for this should have come primarily from the common treasury, as in Crete," Aristotle writes, "but among the Spartans everyone must contribute, even though they are very poor and unable to afford the expense. Hence the result is the opposite of the legislator's intention." [26] Aristotle complains of the laws under which the Spartan senate is organized, that they established in effect a life tenure, sheltered from financial oversight and accessible only to the ambitious. The mode of eligibility, he explains, is in conformity with the spirit of a regime that encourages the appetite for honors. But it is incompatible with the appointment for life to a function without oversight, for this demands a virtue that Spartan education does not supply. [27] The contradiction that is inherent in the institution of the senate is then that it joins characteristics that are practically at odds, some resting on

24. Ibid. 1273a25–38.
25. On aristocracy's profession to honor virtue, see *Pol.* 1273a41–b1.
26. *Pol.* 1271a28–32.
27. Ibid. 1270b35ff. An analogous complaint is made with regard to the institution of the "orderers" in Crete (1272a35).

one principle of government and the others on an opposing principle.
Such a contradiction exposes the city to the danger of arbitrary power—
ruinous for a regime founded on law. As for the legislation concerning
common meals, it reveals a split between the intention of the legislator
and the situation he creates in reality. In this regard, it exposes the city to
a dangerous disequilibrium by suppressing its democratic element. As
for the different laws we spoke of earlier, they are so many arrangements at odds with the principle of the constitution itself. They thus contribute to undermining the basis of the regime. The traces of irrationality a system of laws contains are then always, for Aristotle, potential
sources of instability for the political regime, the symptoms of diseases
that attack the regime's health.

   Aristotle's efforts to ascertain the coherence of legislation in all its aspects, as a matter that is critical for the viability of the regime, make
themselves felt also in his criticism of the Platonic project. Between the
(praiseworthy) intentions behind the project and the (disastrous) effects
that the Platonic legislation would risk producing if it were actually put
into practice, Aristotle sees a radical split. Raising the issue of the law
that for Plato should regulate the community of women and children,
Aristotle asserts that "there must necessarily result from a law of this sort
the very opposite of what correctly enacted laws ought properly to
cause."[28] Conceding to his master a "philanthropic" intention, he judges
nevertheless that the legislative arrangements he had conceived would
contribute to reinforcing men's immorality rather than diminishing it.[29]
It is not the impossibility of actually establishing such a regime that motivates his basic criticism,[30] but the irrationality of the means that are mobi-
lized to serve a certain end. As he puts it, "even if one were able to do
this, one ought not do it, as it would destroy the city."[31]

28. *Pol.* 1262b3–5.
29. For Aristotle's concession to Plato, see *Pol.* 1263b15–16; for his judgment concerning the consequences of such legislative arrangements, see, in particular, 1262b29–35.
30. This impossibility is in any case noted at *Pol.* 1261a13 and 1265a17–18 as a feature
that distinguishes Plato's projected regime from the one Aristotle himself sketches in Book 7
(1335b38–39).
31. *Pol.* 1261a21. It might seem surprising to speak here of irrationality in connection
with Plato. In saying this, what I have in mind is not the lack of internal coherence of his
political project, but the absence of the necessary relationship between this project and the
ends it is designed to serve (or what amounts to the same thing, the reasons that purport to
justify it). On this point Aristotle observes that "the reason Socrates gives as to why there
should be legislation of this sort evidently does not result from his arguments"
(1261a11–12). He explains later on (1261b16ff.) the paralogism committed by Plato concerning the meaning of the term "mine," which destroys the validity of the fundamental
principle (*hypothesis*) of his supposed demonstration (1263b29–31). But it is probable that
Aristotle considers the illogicality of his master to be not the result of a failure in logic but
the result of an excessive confidence in logic abstracted from reality.

The case of Plato is exceptional in that it presents a constitutional project of which the principle is no doubt fine, but the most significant laws—of which those concerning women and children are the most remarkable, while those concerning property have to do with an area considered essential[32]—are apt to lead, according to Aristotle, to situations exactly the reverse of what was being pursued. We have here the limiting case of a regime that is ideal in its principle but that is made so fragile by the legislation accompanying, and in part constituting, it that it would self-destruct at once on account of the irrationality approved by the legislator. The necessity, always and everywhere, to relate a system of laws to the principle of the constitution has forcefully impressed itself on Aristotle as the condition without which no regime is viable. The example of Plato should then reinforce his commitment to the idea that the end assigned a constitution (its fundamental hypothesis) is often less important than the manner in which a system of laws comports with this end— the first point of merit of a political regime being its existence, which is to say, its duration.

This conclusion might surprise someone who, beginning from the same point of departure, imagined that Aristotle was ready to entrust the responsibility for maintaining such a regime in good condition to means other than the law. But this is certainly not the case. One has only to look, for example, at Aristotle's assessment of the legal procedure by which, in Crete, the defects of the regime were from time to time remedied, that is, a conspiracy to expel certain of the "orderers" (magistrates similar to the Spartan ephors) or temporarily suppress the office through a sort of coup d'état. "The cure they have found," Aristotle remarks, "is an odd one, characteristic not of political but of dynastic rule."[33] There is in this judgment an implicit condemnation of force and violence, which are held incompatible with the very existence of a political regime. The guarantee of the law, Aristotle believes, remains preferable to that which can be supplied by the (good) will of men. It is preferable above all to the situation that leaves to chance circumstance the responsibility of ensuring the survival of the political regime. The Cretan regime, for example, owes its duration to the geographic isolation of the island. But this isolation ceases with a sudden invasion of hostile foreigners, such as one that occurred recently, Aristotle says; and war then demonstrates "the weakness of the laws there," which are inadequate for maintaining the integ-

32. Cf. *Pol.* 1266a34ff., 1274b9–11, for the laws concerning women and children; these laws, according to these passages, are an innovation of Plato himself. For the laws regarding property, see 1266a36–39; they are considered essential because revolutions tend to revolve around questions of property.

33. *Pol.* 1272b2–3. As Aristotle makes clear elsewhere 1292b5–10, 1293a31–32), "dynastic" rule is that characteristic of a small oligarchy that relies on violence rather than law.

rity of the regime.[34] One recalls that at Sparta the laws on the ephorate appeared defective because they placed those high magistracies within the reach of people who were poor and vulnerable to corruption. Aristotle recognizes nonetheless that this situation contributes, in another sense, to maintaining the regime, for "the people keep quiet because they share in the highest office."[35] But this happy consequence, he also notes, might well not have been one intended by the legislator, but a result of simple chance. The same is true of the remedy for the dangers that threaten the Carthaginian regime, the periodic dispatch of a part of the popular element to the cities of the Punic empire. Aristotle observes, "But this is really the work of chance, whereas they ought to be free of factional conflict through the legislator."[36] The requirement formulated in this last remark says much about Aristotle's desire to see regulated by law all those problems of such a character as to place in peril the survival of a political regime. This leads us to consider Aristotle's criticisms relative to the absence of legislation in this or that area.

This type of omission, where it occurs, means that the legislator implicitly hopes that nature (or goodwill) and chance can regulate men in society. But none of this offers a serious guarantee from the point of view of Aristotle, who insists strongly on the extreme danger posed to the city by omissions in its legislation.

In the project of Plato as sketched in the *Republic*, for example, Aristotle calls attention to some fairly serious areas of neglect: the nature of the regime that would integrate the majority of the citizens (farmers and artisans) in the best city by the side of the guardians was not spelled out and no thought was given to the kinds of education that should be made available to the farming class, nor, more generally, to the laws that apply to this class.[37] The first omission seems to Aristotle apt to create, in effect, two mutually hostile cities under the appearance of a single one; and the second, to foster immorality and injustice.[38]

Among the arrangements discussed in the *Laws*, which involve the redistribution of landed property into equal and indivisible allotments, Aristotle regrets not finding ones that correspondingly limit births and thus avoid the pernicious consequences of an excessive population of impoverished persons. As he sums it up, "to leave it alone, as in most cities, must necessarily cause poverty among the citizens, and poverty produces

---

34. *Pol.* 1272b20–22.   35. Ibid. 1270b18–19.   36. Ibid. 1273b21–22.

37. Ibid. 1264a11ff. It has been argued that this passage does not do justice to *Republic* 417a and 419, which explain that the rules governing property do not apply outside the caste of guardians. But is Aristotle not justified in complaining that the regime of the other classes has thus been left undetermined? Aristotle formulates a similar objection to the *Laws* (*Pol.* 1264b34ff.).

38. *Pol.* 1264a24–26ff.

factional conflict and crime."[39] A little later on, when Plato is no longer specifically at issue, Aristotle even envisages the necessity of abrogating the law regulating estates at a time when the birthrate is dangerously on the increase. But he adds that "abrogation aside, it is a bad thing to have many of the wealthy become poor, for such persons are apt to become subversives."[40] It is invariably the same—virtually obsessive—concern that underlies Aristotle's efforts to remedy these omissions, the concern to guard against the risks of change in the political regime occurring in the more or less foreseeable future.

In examining the schemes of Phaleas of Chalcedon, Aristotle observes that he neglects to give certain explanations concerning the nature of education, which he nevertheless judges indispensable, that he totally neglects to take into account the requirements of organizing the city according to its international position, and that in his legislation on wealth he neglects to take into consideration property other than landed property.[41] All of these omissions, like those he complains of in the case of Plato, seem to Aristotle to undermine the viability of the regime that Phaleas dreams of instituting.

At Sparta, Aristotle cites the capital error of the legislator in neglecting the role of women. In a striking formulation, he remarks, "One must consider that legislation is lacking for half of the city." The political effects of this are not mysterious; as Aristotle argues, "their laxness concerning women is harmful with a view both to the intention of the regime and the happiness of the city."[42] Elsewhere, though in this case without explicitly indicting the negligence of the legislator, Aristotle stigmatizes the lax behavior of the ephors, which, he says, "does not agree with the inclination of the city."[43] There is no doubt that, for him, one must also see this as a failure of the laws, which is to be added to the one we have just discussed relating to women and which, like the other, is responsible for the deterioration of the Lacedaemonian regime.

All these omissions, the implications of which are often considerable, can be considered as so many disguised appeals for vigilance on the part of legislators. It is to them that Aristotle addresses himself, through his readers or listeners. It is to them that he entrusts the task of preserving constitutions, because, in his view, one cannot depend on anything other than the laws for maintaining over time a political regime.

39. Ibid. 1265b10–12. Plato (*Laws* 540d–e), who foresaw the rapid development of an excess of poor persons, thought to resolve the problem by sending them out to found colonies. Aristotle does not object to this solution; what he faults is to have let the problem arise in the first place through negligence or indifference.

40. *Pol.* 1266b12–14. Regarding abrogation, Aristotle seems to have in mind the historical case of Leucas (1266b21–22).

41. *Pol.* 1266a33ff.   42. Ibid. 1269b12–22.   43. Ibid. 1270b31–32.

Contrary to what one might imagine at first, Aristotle's appeal to the vigilance of legislators is not an incitement to legislate on everything and in detail. It is rather an invitation not to lose sight, in the course of legislating (or of abstaining from legislating), of the maintenance of the regime the laws are designed to serve.

In this connection, one observes that Aristotle's criticisms of the failure of the laws focus on the consequences that such omissions entail for education. And this is a sign of education's importance. One of the sharpest complaints Aristotle lodges against Plato is that he has lost sight of the education that is necessary for the city as a whole.[44] The looseness of Spartan women, which stands in contrast to the harshness that the Lacedaemonian regime claims to instill, leads him to say that one half of the city must be considered as lacking legislation; and he blames the education (or better, the lack of education) of the senators, who are not even relied on by the legislator himself as being good men.[45] To Phaleas of Chalcedon he objects, "Yet even if one were to arrange a moderate level of property for all, it would not help. For one ought to level desires sooner than property; but this is impossible for those not adequately educated by the laws."[46]

The overriding aim that the legislator should set for himself according to Aristotle emerges here in full clarity. Phaleas himself should not only have drawn attention to the importance of education, but also stressed that it should be the same for all.[47] What Aristotle faults him for then is to have failed to specify the nature of the education required, in the absence of which it is impossible in Aristotle's view to avoid fostering the seeds of rebellion among the intemperate.

The remark seems to hold generally for all political regimes that are threatened permanently by whoever has not contracted the habit of reining in his passions under the pressure of the laws. It holds particularly, I think, for democracy, to the extent that this regime is founded on freedom—which is understood by many as the license afforded everyone to act as they please.[48]

Plato had already emphasized the paradox of the democratic regime in this respect. A political constitution whose very principle is to nourish, in the name of freedom, what one would today call a moral "pluralism," democracy ends by resembling what he calls a marketplace of constitutions.[49] This regime grants, in effect, a license to ways of life that are at odds with it and conspire to destroy it.

44. Cf. *Pol.* 1264a12, b32–34.   45. Ibid. 1271a1–2.
46. Ibid. 1266b28–31.   47. Ibid. 1266b34–35.
48. Cf. *Pol.* 1290b1ff., 1291b34ff., 1310a28ff., 1317a40ff.
49. *Rep.* 557bff.

Aristotle judges this democratic freedom severely, in direct proportion as it encourages in its citizens a refusal to be governed by anyone.[50] A regime of laws is therefore more important there than anywhere else, on account of the dangers that this regime brings on itself. "To live with a view to the regime should not be supposed to be slavery, but preservation," Aristotle protests.[51]

In conclusion, we may add some remarks on the importance of all this for understanding the fundamental intention that guides all the investigations undertaken by Aristotle in the *Politics*. I have attempted elsewhere to show that the entirety of Aristotle's reflections on human things (the study of ethical matters and of matters relating to the organization of cities) is addressed to legislators, whom he regards as responsible for education and thus as artisans of human happiness.[52] From this point of view, the problems dealt with in the *Politics* appear in a new light. In particular, one can no longer consider them as disparate pieces of a scheme focused on providing a model constitution or ideal forms of legislation. They are simply so many reflections made available to legislators, who, in their wisdom, are charged with providing their fellow citizens with the conditions without which man cannot live or cannot live well. Succeeding the (idealistic) effort of Plato, who substituted himself for the legislators in defining in the abstract the principles of a constitution and system of laws conforming with the good, is a (realistic) project, which consists in enlightening the legislator with regard to the different questions that it falls to him to resolve—before he himself puts forward, in the situation in which he finds himself, the constitutional or legal rules that are the least removed from the good as is possible in that situation. What I have said above helps us to understand that Aristotle regarded the task of the legislator in this connection as being essentially a matter of supplementing or correcting the rules and usages currently existing, so as to confer on existing regimes the maximum possible in terms of goodness and duration (itself a function of goodness), without depending on force or fortune—truly the art of the possible.

What does one do, then, with the pages that Aristotle devotes to the best constitution, which appear at the end of the *Politics* (Books 7–8) and appear to be its conclusion? Are they a remnant of the investigations of Aristotle's "idealist" period that the philosopher could not bring himself to discard? Hardly. The conditions that are necessary for the establishment of a perfect constitution (7.1–12) and the characteristics of this constitution as such (7.13–8.7) remain a rightful concern of every legis-

50. *Pol.* 1317b14–15.
51. Ibid. 1310a34–36.
52. See R. Bodéüs, *Le philosophe et la cité*, 118ff.

lator. It is necessary for the legislator to understand—contrary to any
idealistic temptation—that the conditions in question do not depend on
him; as Aristotle expresses it, "speaking about them is a work of prayer,
having them come about, a work of chance." [53] But he must also realize
that in spite of this the excellence of the citizens remains in his power,
for "the city's being excellent is no longer the work of fortune, but of
knowledge and intentional choice." Certainly, nature—another name
for fortune—must provide men, rather than animals, as the raw matter
of the city, but what remains is "the work of education." [54] This is why
Aristotle could not fail, at the end of the *Politics,* to present a perfect constitution to legislators in the form of a model education. In doing so, he
remains faithful to the priority of the requirements that, as we have
seen, derive from the criticisms he addresses in Book 2 to the cities
highly reputed in his time.

53. *Pol.* 1331b21–22.
54. Ibid. 1332a31–b10.

CONTRIBUTORS

Richard Bodéüs is Associate Professor of Philosophy at the University of Montreal, where he teaches Greek philosophy, ethics, and politics. He is the author of *Le philosophe et la cité: Recherches sur les rapports entre morale et politique dans la pensée d'Aristote* (1982).

Carnes Lord, a political scientist specializing in political theory and international relations, is the author of *Education and Culture in the Political Thought of Aristotle* (1982), as well as of a translation of Aristotle's *Politics* (1984). He is currently Assistant to the Vice President for National Security Affairs.

Waller R. Newell is Associate Professor of Political Science at Carleton University, Ottawa, working in the areas of ancient, Renaissance, and contemporary political philosophy. His articles have appeared in the *American Political Science Review, Political Theory,* and elsewhere. He has a book in progress entitled "Ruling Passion: Studies in the Meaning of Tyranny and Princely Virtue."

Josiah Ober is Professor of Classics at Princeton University. He is the author of *Fortress Attica* (1985), *Mass and Elite in Democratic Athens* (1989), and articles on Greek history and archaeology. He is currently working on "Athenian Critics of Popular Rule," a book-length study of the relationship between ideological hegemony and discursive resistance.

David K. O'Connor is Associate Professor of Philosophy at the University of Notre Dame, working primarily in ethics and ancient philosophy. He has published articles on ancient conceptions of friendship and on interpersonal virtues. Among the most recent are "The Invulnerable Pleasures of Epicurean Friendship" (1989) and "Two Ideals of Friendship" (1990).

Stephen G. Salkever teaches political philosophy at Bryn Mawr College. He writes on the uses of Greek philosophy as a guide to explaining modern political practice, most recently in *Finding the Mean: Theory and Practice in Aristotelian Political Philosophy* (1990) and in "'Lopp'd and Bound': How Liberal Theory Obscures the Goods of Liberal Practices," in *Liberalism and the Good,* edited by R. Bruce Douglass, Gerald Mara, and Henry Richardson (1990).

Abram N. Shulsky is a Senior Fellow at the National Strategy Information Center in Washington, D.C., where he is writing an introductory text on intelligence and national security. His essay "The Concept of Private Property in the History of Political Economy" appears in *From Political Economy to Economics . . . and Back?* (forthcoming).

Barry S. Strauss is Associate Professor of History at Cornell University. He is the author of *Athens after the Peloponnesian War: Class, Faction and Policy 403–386 B.C.* (1986), coauthor of *The Anatomy of Error: Ancient Military Disasters and Their Lessons for Modern Strategists* (1990), and co-editor of *Hegemonic Rivalry from Thucydides to the Nuclear Age* (1990).

INDEX

Acquisition: and Carthage, 99–101; and the city, 85, 102–4; money economy gives rise to unnatural, 83–85; natural distinguished from unnatural, 80, 106; natural limit to, defined by good life, 82–83, 86–87, 196–97; in primitive society, 63, 80–81

Aggrandizement. *See* Graspingness

Allan, D., 140n12

Ambler, W., 27n66, 174n37

Anthropology. *See* Origins of political life

Arendt, H., 25, 167–69, 172–73, 182n72, 188, 196

Aristocracy: identity of good man and good citizen in, 198; status more important than class in, 125–26; virtue as criterion of rule in, 125, 203, 206

Athens. *See* Democracy, Athenian

Beiner, R., 191–92

Best regime: class, order, and status in analysis of, 126–29; good man and good citizen in, 147, 198, 238n13; and Hellenistic political conditions, 133–35; slavery in, 97–99, 103, 128; tension between kingship and aristocracy in, 208–9; and tension between virtue and stability, 237–38, 243, 247–48

Biology, Aristotelian: does not determine human praxis, 26–30, 33, 57; and natural acquisition, 80–81, 87, 102, 106; and political science, 19, 23–30, 53–56, 87–89, 172–73; teleological

orientation of, 15, 174; theoretical rather than practical, 46; and women, 174–75, 182

Business expertise (*chrēmatistikē*). *See* Acquisition

Callicles, 179

Carthage: commercial orientation of, 99–101; as mixed regime, 100n53, 240–41

Citizenship: criteria of, 34–35; in extreme democracy, 215; and gender, 166; relation of good man and good citizen, 147, 198, 238n13

City (*polis*): defining features of, 13, 34–35, 122; as male realm, 167; naturalness of, 27, 51–52, 60, 79, 102–4; teleological orientation of, 32, 35–36, 56, 126, 140, 175–76

Class: in aristocracy, 126; Aristotle's use of, 123–26; in democracy and oligarchy, 119–22, 223–28; Marxist and Weberian interpretations of, 113–17; and origins of political life, 70–71; and status, 123–26

Constitution. *See* Regime

Conventionalism, 52, 66, 79, 92–93, 109–10

Courage. *See* Virility

Crete, 67, 95n44, 243–44

Decree (*psēphisma*): in Athenian democracy, 219–20, 222; in extreme democracy, 215–16

Compositor: G&S Typesetters, Inc.
Text: 10x12 Baskerville
Display: Baskerville
Printer: Braun Brumfield, Inc.
Binder: Braun Brumfield, Inc.